COMMUNICATING
IN YOUR PERSONAL, PROFESSIONAL & PUBLIC LIVES

Kendall Hunt
publishing company

SARA CHUDNOVSKY WEINTRAUB - Regis College
CANDICE THOMAS-MADDOX - Ohio University Lancaster
KERRY BYRNES-LOINETTE - Collin College

Book Team

Chairman and Chief Executive Officer   Mark C. Falb
President and Chief Operating Officer   Chad M. Chandlee
Vice President, Higher Education   David L. Tart
Director of Publishing Partnerships   Paul B. Carty
Senior Developmental Coordinator   Angela Willenbring
Vice President, Operations   Timothy J. Beitzel
Senior Production Editor   Sheri Hosek
Permissions Editor   Tammy Hunt
Cover Designer   Jeni Fensterman
Web Project Editor Tracy Wiley

Cover image © Shutterstock.com

www.kendallhunt.com
Send all inquiries to:
4050 Westmark Drive
Dubuque, IA 52004-1840

Printed in the United States of America

BRIEF CONTENTS

CONTENTS

PREFACE

When we began to think about writing a basic course text, we knew we wanted to emphasize the fact that communication takes place in and influences every aspect of our lives. Thus, communication in our personal, professional and public lives became the framework for this textbook. As you read the book, you will notice that we begin each chapter with three scenarios. Each of these reflects examples of personal, professional and public situations related to the topic of the chapter. Our goal was to select real-life examples that will facilitate the discussion of how the content in each chapter influences communication in every part of your life.

While many students may perceive communication as "common-sense" and wonder why they are required to take a course that teaches them "how to talk," you'll gain a sense of the importance of studying communication as you work through each chapter in this book. Chapter 1 provides a foundation for the study of communication. In this chapter, we include an explanation of the communication process, an overview of key principles of communication, a description of the various types of communication, an analysis of the impact communication has on our lives, and a discussion of the benefits we derive from good communication.

Chapter 2 focuses on perception and its role in our interactions with others. In this chapter, we define perception, explain the perception process, and discuss factors that influence our perceptions. We talk about the way in which perception shapes how we communicate with others and how they communicate with us. An important part of our discussion is the impact of our self-concept and how it influences our communication.

The focus of Chapter 3 is on verbal communication. Various functions that verbal communication fulfills are discussed, and problems associated with verbal communication are identified. An important element of the chapter is that we identify ways to improve verbal communication that can be immediately incorporated into your daily life.

Nonverbal communication and the importance of recognizing and understanding various nonverbal behaviors is the focus of Chapter 4. We define nonverbal communication, describe the functions and types of nonverbal communication, and discuss strategies we can use to enhance both our own and others' perceptions of nonverbal communication.

One of the most overlooked aspects of communication is the importance of listening. Chapter 5 focuses on listening in our personal, professional and public lives. We describe the listening process, explain various types of listening, and identify different contexts in which listening occurs. We highlight reasons why we don't listen well at times, identify listening misbehaviors, and discuss strategies to listen more effectively.

Communication is a key element in forming and maintaining our relationships with others. In Chapters 6 and 7, we explore the concept of interpersonal communication and how our interactions influence our personal, professional, and public relationships. This chapter explains the stages of relationship development, discusses the role of self-disclosure and the impact of dialectical tensions, and addresses the role of expectations in relationships. In addition, we focus on the impact of factors such as deception, jealousy and conflict on our relationships.

Given that most of us will spend a considerable amount of time communicating in groups, Chapter 8 and 9 address how communication can help or hinder our interactions in the group context. We identify various types of groups, explain factors that affect a group, and identify strategies to enhance decision-making, team-building, and problem-solving in groups. We also focus on the area of leadership, discussing the types of leaders as well as the common theoretical approaches to leadership.

Chapters 10 through 12 focus on public speaking. We begin with a discussion of potential challenges you may face in public speaking situations, describe common types of public speeches, and examine the public speaking process. To assist students with preparing a speech, we discuss the various steps that are essential to creating an effective speech. These include researching, organizing, outlining and preparing presentational aids. Finally, we provide a step-by-step approach to the practice and delivery of public speeches as well as the reflection on them.

Given the diverse society in which we live, it is essential that we focus on communication with those who are different from us. Thus, we have devoted an entire chapter to "Communicating with Diverse Others." In Chapter 13, we discuss characteristics of culture and examine the impact that our cultural beliefs, needs, attitudes and values have on our communication with diverse others as well as on their communication with us.

Because technology has become such an integral part of how we communicate with others, Chapter 14 highlights the importance and impact of mediated communication in every area of our lives. We define mediated communication, distinguish mass media from social media, discuss the impact that media may have on our relationships and identify strategies we can use to improve our mediated communication.

Regardless of whether you are majoring in communication studies or simply taking this class as a general education elective, understanding how to promote and explain the skills you gain from this course is important. Chapter 15 provides both majors and non-majors with information about how communication is applied in our daily lives. Various contexts of communication such as physician-patient interactions, workplace communication, and family relationships are addressed. We conclude the chapter with potential career options for communication studies graduates.

In using our textbook, your instructor has access to supplemental materials. These materials include video clips relevant to content, class activities, and discussion questions. Our hope is that you will find these study aids to be helpful in identifying the many ways in which communication influences your own personal, professional and public interactions as you embark on this exploration of human communication. Look for the web icon in the text margins to direct you to online information.

Throughout this text, we combine theory, research, and practical application, and we provide strategies to improve the various aspects of communication in each chapter. Examples that are both relevant and timely underscore the importance of each topic that you study as you progress through the book. Our goal is to help you identify ways to enhance your own communication to ensure successful and effective communication in your personal, professional, and public lives.

NOTE FOR INSTRUCTORS

Our goal in writing this text was to address key issues that we identified in our 50-plus years of combined teaching experiences in a variety of educational contexts ranging from community colleges to public and private universities. We hope that the examples and question prompts included in this text speak to both **traditional** and **nontraditional** students. Some key features we included in this text to assist students in applying the content to their own life experiences include:

- **Opening scenarios** – included at the beginning of each chapter to prompt students to consider how the content applies to the personal, professional, and public contexts of their lives.
- **Chapter objectives** – appear at the beginning of each chapter to provide students with a preview of the learning outcomes.
- **Research highlights** – designed to introduce students to applied communication scholarship in various contexts.
- **Key words** – concepts and definitions provided at the end of each chapter to assist students in studying content.

To assist you in teaching this course, Dr. Brittany Beckner, Graceland University, has prepared a comprehensive Instructor's Manual that includes the following ancillary materials for each chapter:

- **In-Class Activities**
- **Discussion Questions**
- **Chapter Outlines**
- **PowerPoint™ Slides**
- **Test Bank**

In order to assist students in applying content to their everyday lives, Steve Granelli, SUNY Oswego, has prepared additional media supplements for you to incorporate into your face-to-face or online classes. The Media Supplement Guide includes the following for each chapter:

- **Links** to video clips from popular television shows and movies.
- A list of **key concepts** that can be applied to the analysis of each video clip.
- **Discussion question prompts** that can be used to facilitate in-class discussions, or posted online for students to reflect and respond.

Our hope is that these materials will assist you in creating an engaging learning experience for your students!

Sara, Candice & Kerry

ACKNOWLEDGMENTS

To complete a project of this magnitude, there are certainly many people to thank. First, Candice and Kerry, thank you so much for joining me on this project. We share a common love for teaching and I have learned so much from you both throughout this process. I am also grateful to Paul Carty for his never-ending support and Angela Willenbring for her infinite patience and responsiveness. I am also incredibly grateful to the late Dr. Kenneth L. Brown, my undergraduate advisor, who taught me so much about teaching and always served as a mentor and role model. Finally, to my husband Ross and our two children, Alissa and Justin, thank you for supporting me always and for being my biggest and best cheerleaders—you mean everything to me. –SCW

There are countless people who have contributed to this book in a variety of ways. First and foremost, I am so grateful to have worked with Sara and Kerry on this project. Your passion for teaching and your dedication to this book are unparalleled – I am so blessed to have you as my colleagues and friends. To my COMS 1010 students at Ohio University – your comments and questions have inspired many of the examples included throughout this book. Thank you for your feedback throughout the years! Jill Ross – we are incredibly grateful for your impeccable proofreading skills on this project. To Paul & Angela – words cannot express my gratitude for your patience and support as we embarked on this journey. I am so proud to be a part of the Kendall Hunt family of authors! -CTM

Thank you to my coauthors for this opportunity and experience, to mom and dad for being the first people to tell me I could be anything I wanted, and to Jason for constant, unwavering support. –KBL

We gratefully acknowledge the constructive comments of the colleagues who provided content reviews for the book. They include:

Krista Appelquist
> *Moraine Valley Community College*

Denise Besson-Silvia
> *Gavilan College*

Trudy Hanson
> *West Texas A&M University*

Kristina Horn Sheeler
> *Indiana University-Purdue University Indianapolis*

Alec Hosterman
> *Indiana University – South Bend*

Gayle Houser
> *Eastern Arizona College*

Neil Katz
> *Nova Southeastern University*

Meghann Oglesby
> *Rust College*

Tami Olds
> *Northern Virginia Community College*

John Nash
> *Moraine Valley Community College*

Maria Parnell
> *Brevard Community College-Melbourne*

David Scott
> *Utah Valley University*

Abdul Sinno
> *Clarke University*

Charles Veenstra
> *Dordt College*

Margaret Willis
> *Fairfield University*

ABOUT THE AUTHORS

Sara Chudnovsky Weintraub, Ph.D. (Boston College) is an Associate Professor in the Communication Department at Regis College in Weston, Massachusetts. She has taught the introductory course in communication for many years, the public speaking course, as well as a wide range of communication courses on the undergraduate and graduate levels. She was the president of the Eastern Communication Association in 2009 and served as a member of the National Communication Association's (NCA) Educational Policies Board from 2010-2013. In addition, Sara serves on the editorial boards for *Communication Quarterly* and *Communication Research Reports*. She has published in the *Communication Teacher* and  also served as a guest editor for a special issue on service-learning and communication. She is currently a member of NCA's Legislative Assembly and one of six team leaders on NCA's Learning Outcomes in Communication Project. Finally, she is the 2014 recipient of the Eastern Communication Association's Donald H. Ecroyd and Carolyn Drummond Ecroyd Award for Teaching Excellence.

Candice Thomas-Maddox, Ed.D. (West Virginia University) is Professor of Communication Studies at Ohio University Lancaster. She has taught the Intro to Human Communication class for the past 16 years, in addition to teaching classes at the undergraduate and graduate levels in organizational, interpersonal, intercultural, and family communication. Candice has received a variety of teaching awards including the ECA Ecroyd Teaching Award, ECA Teaching Fellows honor, OUL Professor of the Year, and Ohio University's RHE Outstanding Professor Award. She served as President for the Eastern Communication Association in 2010 and for the Ohio Communication Association from 2006-2008, and she also served as Executive Director for  both organizations. Previous co-authored textbooks that Candice has published with Kendall Hunt include *Interpersonal Communication: Building Rewarding Relationships* and *Family Communication: Relationship Foundations*. She is also the co-author of *Quantitative Research Methods for Communication: A Hands-On Approach*.

Kerry Byrnes-Loinette, Ph.D. (West Virginia University, 2010) is a professor at Collin College, a community college in North Texas that serves over 50,000 students annually. She teaches several courses including public speaking, introduction to human communication, and interpersonal communication. Her research interests include the teacher-student relationship, classroom assessment practices, and families and health issues. Her work has been published in *Communication Teacher*, *Communication Research Reports*, and *Communication Studies*. Kerry is active in the Eastern Communication Association and the  National Communication Association and recently participated in the Learning Outcomes in Communication grant project with NCA.

CHAPTER 1

Communication in Our Lives: It's More Than Just Talking

Chapter Objectives

After reading this chapter, you should be able to:

- Define communication and describe the communication process
- Describe the principles of communication
- Understand the different types of communication
- Understand variables that impact communication
- Identify the benefits of good communication

PERSONAL: You and your romantic partner are deciding what to do on a Friday night. You both want to go out for dinner, but neither of you wants to make a decision. In an attempt to be productive, you decide to offer three suggestions and allow your partner to pick. Of the options, you are most interested in the new restaurant that has just opened in your neighborhood. When presenting your options, your voice becomes louder and more animated as you describe the new restaurant. Your partner fails, however, to notice your excitement and selects one of the other options. You secretly think to yourself, "How could my partner not see how much I wanted to go to the new restaurant?"

PROFESSIONAL: You receive an email from your boss. In the email, the boss writes that she would like to meet with you regarding a recently completed project. You instantly become nervous and anxious when reading the email. You begin to wonder what your boss could want to discuss: your role in the project, how the team functioned, ideas that were discarded, or what decision-making process was utilized all seem like possible topics for discussion. You meet with your boss the following day. She then tells you she heard from others on your team that your input was vital to the successful completion of the task, and the team could not have completed their work without you. Given the positive remarks, why were you so anxious when you first read her email?

PUBLIC: You are preparing for an oral presentation. During your presentation, you plan to explain a proposal that will reduce tuition and fees for students attending a local university. You want your audience to know you are a credible source on the topic. Your careful research and expertise in this area become evident throughout your presentation, and you feel great. Your posture is strong and confident, and you remember all the details of the speech you wanted to address. After the presentation, you are approached by several audience members and praised for a job well done. You think to yourself that your preparation efforts paid off and your message was memorable, but how can you continue this for future presentations?

CHAPTER OVERVIEW

In your life, you fulfill a variety of roles. You could be a student, a wife or husband, a son or daughter, a boyfriend or girlfriend, an aunt or uncle, a coworker, a best friend, and a peer to your classmates. In each of these roles, you change your verbal and nonverbal communication to match the expectations that the other person has for the relationship. Imagine a hat rack filled with ball caps with various team logos

© BlueSkyImage/Shutterstock.com

Communication contains verbal and nonverbal elements such as gestures, facial expressions, and vocal tones.

imprinted on them. Essentially, you have a hat rack in your life. Rather than team logos on the ball caps, your hats have labels with the roles you play. You change hats depending on the role that you play and the situation in which you find yourself. Each hat has its own set of communication expectations. Suppose you're wearing a hat that says "son" or "daughter." When you put that hat on, you adjust your verbal and nonverbal behaviors to fit that role. You may be respectful and loving and avoid using profanity when speaking with your parents. Now let's imagine you're wearing your best friend hat. You adjust your behaviors again to match this role. This time, though, your verbal behaviors become more direct; you and your best friend don't "pull any punches" with each other; you are honest and open with one another. Your ability to adjust behaviors is something that can always be improved. Throughout this text, you will learn ways to adjust your behaviors and learn how communication scholars have come to understand verbal and nonverbal communicative exchanges.

COMMUNICATION DEFINED

One of the most frustrating phrases that communication students and scholars hear is "communication is just talking, everyone can do that."

Communication is so much more than just the words that we speak. It also contains nonverbal elements such as gestures, eye contact, and vocal tone. We focus more in-depth on specific aspects of verbal and nonverbal communication in Chapters 3 and 4. For now, take a moment to think about your own communicative exchanges as you reflect on the following questions:

- Have you ever experienced a conflict with someone?
- Have you ever said something you later regretted?
- Have you ever been surprised by how someone spoke to you?
- Have you ever left an interaction and thought that the other person did not understand what you were trying to say?
- Have you ever read a text message or email and felt confused by what the other person meant in the message?

If you answered "yes" to any of these questions, you have experienced communication misunderstanding. Everything you do sends a message. From a conflict resulting from a misunderstanding to wearing your favorite t-shirt, to having pierced ears or a tattoo, to your accent, to where you sit in class—all of these behaviors send messages. Communication is something we do with other individuals. *Communication* is defined as the process of sending and receiving verbal and nonverbal messages to achieve shared meaning. Once you communicate you cannot undo the message. You can apologize for something you said or how you said it, but an apology does not reverse the meanings assigned to the message. As communicators, we want to strive for effective and efficient communication. Communication scholars label individuals who can engage in effective and efficient communication as competent communicators. This concept is discussed later in this chapter.

Communication
Process of sending and receiving verbal and nonverbal messages to achieve shared meaning.

COMMUNICATION PROCESS

As the definition above indicates, communication is a process. This process is actually quite nuanced and has many facets to consider. One basic model to help us understand what the communication process looks like is the sender–message–channel–receiver (SMCR) model. Created by Lasswell (1948), it simplifies the communication process to a few basic components. Figure 1.1 provides you with an updated visual representation of this model that includes channel, context, feedback and noise.

The model illustrates the key elements that enable us to exchange messages and share meaning. The source or *sender* of the message is the individual who initiates the message. This person is responsible for encoding. During *encoding*, the message sender translates thoughts, feelings, experiences, or ideas into verbal and/ or nonverbal communication. Words may be accompanied by facial expressions, vocal tones, and eye contact to convey specific meanings. For example, if while telling a story about going skydiving for the first time you want your listener to know you were excited about the experience, you would likely smile and speak faster than usual. These encoded ideas are then to be decoded by the receiver of or interpreting the message. The *receiver* is the person who is responsible for making sense of the message. This process is called *decoding*, which involves making sense or interpreting the encoded message by assigning meanings. Consider the skydiving example. The recipient of the message listens to the story and tries to understand and interpret the speaker's experience. The *message* refers to the ideas or feelings that are said or sent. For example, if you are having a conversation with your friend about the latest episode of *The Big Bang Theory*, your message is focused on the

Sender
Individual creating the message.

Encoding
Process of translating thoughts, feelings, experiences, or ideas into words and/or gestures.

Receiver
Individual receiving the message.

Decoding
Process where individuals attempt to make sense or interpret the encoded message.

Message
Ideas or feelings that are said or sent.

FIGURE 1.1

The sender–message–channel–receiver communication model.

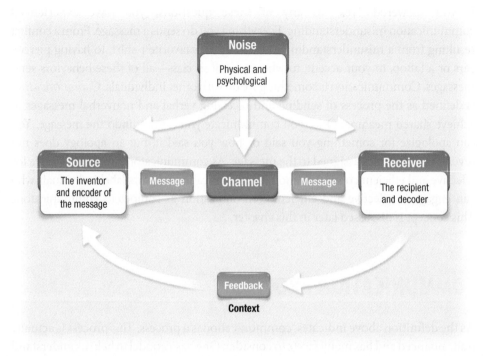

content of the television show. The content of a message is typically communicated in our verbal messages while the relational and emotional elements of a message are indicated in our nonverbal behaviors. Messages are sent via *channels*. You send messages through each of your five senses. For example, you may provide information that others can interpret through your use of eye contact, hearing, sight, touch, and even taste. Face-to-face communication, emails, phone calls, or text messages are also channels used for sending a message. For example, if you arrived late for a meeting, wearing unprofessional clothing, and smelling like you have just come from the gym, you are sending messages that can be interpreted through sight and smell.

Channel
Medium through which message is sent.

As Figure 1.1 shows, additional elements have been added to the original SMCR model to account for other factors that impact our ability to achieve shared meaning when sending and receiving messages. These elements include feedback and context. *Feedback* refers to verbal and nonverbal responses or reactions to the sender's message and may include follow-up questions, head nods, or statements that confirm that they're listening, such as "uh huh." *Context* refers to the situation or setting where the communication occurs. For example, if you are in the library studying with your friend, the context is the library. It is important to note that as the context changes, we may alter our communication behaviors. For example, while studying in the library, certain nonverbal behaviors are unacceptable. You

Feedback
Cues that the receiver provides while listening to the sender.

Context
Situation or where the communication occurs.

would not shout to your friend who you see walking by; rather, you would likely walk to your friend and speak in a hushed tone to suit the library's quiet context.

Noise is another element of the process and often very much present in our communication. Anything that interferes, detracts, or diminishes our ability to interact or listen to others is referred to as *noise*. While in your classes, have you ever sat next to a person who clicked a pen? The constant clicking can serve as a distraction and your mind may begin to wander as you ask yourself, "When will that person stop clicking the pen?" This noise may affect our ability to address and interpret the message. Two types of noise are experienced during communication. *Physical noise* consists of any type of interference that is present in the environment. Examples of physical noise include an overly loud air conditioner, a too hot room, or, as mentioned above, the person next to you clicking a pen. *Psychological noise* refers to the internal interference that impedes our accurate reception of a message. Examples of psychological noise include not listening to your professor because you're reflecting on the test you have next period, not paying attention to your supervisor's directions because you're thinking about the fight you had with your significant other before work that morning, or not recognizing positive feedback from your audience when giving a speech because you've convinced yourself that your speech is horrible. Collectively, noise is a common occurrence in our lives and is something that impacts the communication process. There are techniques, however, that can be used to overcome this type of noise and these are addressed in Chapter 5.

> **Noise**
> Anything that interferes with our ability to interact or listen to others.

> **Physical noise**
> Any type of audible interference in the communication environment that impedes our accurate reception of a message.

> **Psychological noise**
> Internal interference that impedes our accurate reception of a message.

When we consider all these elements we have a better understanding of how each influences our ability to engage in effective and efficient communication. Doing so ensures that we are aware of both situational demands and receiver characteristics and we enhance our ability to become effective communicators.

COMMUNICATION PRINCIPLES

By now you have a better understanding of the nuanced nature of communication; that is, communication is a difficult task that requires careful attention to a variety of factors. Caution should be used when engaging in verbal and nonverbal behavior because communication is a powerful tool with both benefits and potential repercussions. In fact, you have likely experienced some positive and negative outcomes because of something someone said. The principles in Figure 1.2 outline the importance of communication and serve as the foundation for understanding the process of sending and receiving messages.

FIGURE 1.2

Communication
principles.

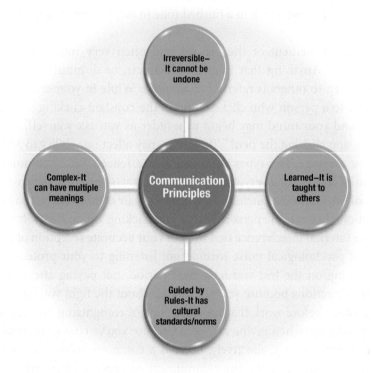

Communication Is Irreversible

Have you ever thought to yourself, "I wish I could take that last comment back?" It could have been during a conflict with a loved one in which you said something you later regretted, or perhaps it was a failed joke that you shared at a company party. Suppose you communicate disappointment in your son's performance on a school assignment. He may be devastated because he worked hard on the project. Later, it is discovered that the teacher made an error in grading. Your son actually did well, and now you communicate how proud you are of his performance and work. What are the repercussions of these messages? Does your son replace the first message you communicated (disappointment) with the second one (pride)? Once you communicate a message, it is difficult to change the meaning that the receiver has assigned. After the message is sent, we have stimulated a meaning in the mind of the receiver. In order to accomplish successful communication, which is the result of communication that is accurately sent and received, we achieve *shared meaning*. In order to achieve shared meaning, everything the speaker or sender of the message was thinking and feeling was effectively encoded in the communication, and the receiver correctly interpreted or decoded the message as intended. Keep in mind that it is sometimes difficult to achieve shared meaning. In some instances,

Shared meaning
Result of communication
that is accurately sent and
received.

we feel like we haven't made ourselves understood and may begin communicating more in an attempt to clarify our unsuccessful communication. Having difficulty in achieving shared meaning could be a result of verbal or nonverbal communication. For example, you could use a word that your receiver is unfamiliar with or a hug could be interpreted as having a deeper meaning than you intended.

Communication Is Learned

If you have ever been around a parent of small children, you have likely witnessed the process of teaching a child about appropriate behavior. The feedback we receive from others serves as a method for learning expectations of interaction. Our daily interactions teach us what is appropriate or inappropriate in any situation. This learning process begins early in life. Children are taught by their parents to look someone in the eye and shake their hand when greeting them for the first time or what language to use when at school. This could be considered explicit learning. *Explicit learning* of communication patterns and behaviors occurs when we are told what to do and when it should be done. Travelers may search for information on the Internet to help them engage in appropriate communication when visiting another country. In some instances, we learn what is considered appropriate by simply observing others. In the workplace, we learn what clothing is considered appropriate on "casual Friday" by observing our coworkers' attire during the first few weeks on the job. This observational learning of communication is described as *implicit learning*. We gather information about appropriate behaviors by watching others. We continue to learn lessons about communication rules and expectations throughout our lives as we encounter new situations and people. Each job interview, each first date, and public presentation that we encounter provides us with valuable information about what is considered appropriate and inappropriate behavior.

Explicit learning
Occurs when we are told what to do and when it should be done.

Implicit learning
Observational learning of communication behaviors.

© Goodluz/Shutterstock.com

There are rules for both verbal and nonverbal behavior that are adapted to the individual and the situation, such as a job interview.

Communication Is Guided by Rules

Closely related to the notion that our behaviors are learned is the understanding that our communication is guided by rules for what is considered appropriate and inappropriate behavior. For example, hugging the person who interviews you for a job would likely result in a negative reaction. After all, that is not the typical protocol for professional job interviews.

There are rules for both verbal and nonverbal behavior that are adapted to the individual and the situation. For example, on a first date it would be rude to ask how much money your date makes or how his or her last relationship ended. It may be acceptable to discuss these topics with someone you've known for a while, but not in an initial interaction. Rules that guide interaction can be useful because they can help us determine how to communicate in a given context. These rules can be particularly important given the complex nature of communication.

Communication Is Complex

One of the most confusing parts about communication is the multiple meanings that may be associated with a single communicative event. Consider the potential messages that are exchanged during a first date. You may have enjoyed being with the person, but are not interested in pursuing the relationship any further. At the end of the date, you give your date a hug to communicate appreciation for the enjoyable evening. However, you have to consider how long the hug should last and how much contact your bodies should have. Should you give a front hug with both arms or a side hug with a pat on the back? These are important considerations as they can be used to indicate whether you perceive the relationship as being platonic or romantic. Even when you offer a friendly hug, your date may still perceive that you are interested in pursuing a romantic relationship. Verbal behavior works in the same way. For example, imagine grocery shopping with someone for the first time. They ask you to get a "buggy" before entering the store. You may feel confused by their language. A "buggy" is another word for a cart. Oftentimes, individuals have different definitions for words that others may not understand. In this way, both nonverbal and verbal communication are nuanced and complex with multiple meanings.

Not only do we need to consider nonverbal expectations and language differences, but the entire communicative process is complex. Think about all the elements needed to communicate. Refer to the earlier model that discussed noise. A myriad of factors will interfere with your communicative process. In addition to these elements, it is important to note that while communicating, you are acting as the sender and the receiver simultaneously. While you are creating and sending messages, you are also making sense of the other person's message. For example, if you are sharing bad news with a friend and you are not sure what her reaction will be, you are monitoring her nonverbal behaviors and making any necessary adjustments. Communication is an ongoing, back-and-forth process whereby both people are acting as a sender and a receiver of a message. This highlights the concept that communication is transactional in nature.

Communication Contains Both Content and Relational Information

Words that we say (verbal communication) and how we say them (nonverbal communication) are used to provide information to the receiver. Each message that we send contains two types of information: content and relational. *Content information* refers to the verbal communication, the actual words being said and their corresponding meanings. *Relational information* refers to information that helps us understand the type of relationship between the interactants (e.g., personal, professional, or public) and the emotions and feelings of a message. This can be reflected in our nonverbal messages that accompany the spoken words. This relational information provides insight into how the content or the verbal message should be interpreted. Consider the following example:

> A romantic couple living together discuss their evening plans. One partner wants to go out with friends, while the other partner wants to stay home. The partner who wants to go out for the evening is excited and quickly describes the friends' plans. "Everyone is going out. Friends are home for the holidays and this will be the only chance everyone has to hang out together." The other partner asks in a quiet voice while not making eye contact, "Will your former partner, Terri, be there?"

The plans for the evening and the question of who will be attending is the content of the message. The relational content being communicated is that one partner is excited about sharing time together, while the other is feeling insecure about their relationship. Relational content is indicated through nonverbal elements such as the excited tone of voice, quick vocal rate, quiet tone, or lack of eye contact.

In sum, both the process and the principles of understanding and using communication provide a foundation through which we can more effectively interact with others. Recall the hat rack example from the beginning of the chapter. You play different roles in your life, and these roles each have different verbal and nonverbal communicative behaviors. Our communication decisions are guided and influenced by the roles we play in addition to the many communication characteristics outlined in the previous sections. In the next section, you will learn about the different types of communication you experience in your personal, professional, and public lives.

Content information
Verbal communication or the actual words being said.

Relational information
Information that helps us understand the type of relationship between the interactants and the emotions and feelings of a message.

© leungchopan/Shutterstock.com

TYPES OF COMMUNICATION

Consider all the people with whom you interact on a daily basis—romantic partners,
coworkers, friends, and family. You may even find that you have conversations with
yourself or talk to the television or radio. Many types of communication have been
identified and studied by communication scholars to help us better understand our
interactions (see Figure 1.3).

Intrapersonal

⮞ Intrapersonal communication
Most basic type of communication; communication with ourselves.

Have you ever rehearsed a phone conversation in your mind before you even
picked up the phone to dial the number? If so, you have engaged in *intrapersonal
communication*. Intrapersonal communication occurs when we envision or have
a conversation with ourselves. Because it involves only you, this is the most basic
type of communication. You may have been faced with making a decision about
something and had an internal dialogue weighing the pros and cons of your
options. Or perhaps you have given yourself a pep talk before an interview or oral
presentation. Each of these situations is an instance of intrapersonal communication
in which we first talked to ourselves before adding others to our interaction.

FIGURE 1.3

Types of
communication.

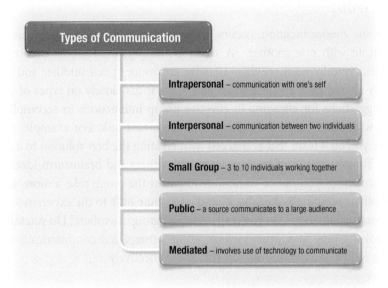

> **Interpersonal communication** Interactions that take place between two people who simultaneously take on the roles of both sender and receiver.

> Small group communication occurs when a collection of at least three people communicate and collaborate with one another.

Interpersonal

When we engage others in message exchange, a different type of communication is experience. *Interpersonal communication* is defined as interactions that take place between two people who simultaneously take on the roles of both source and receiver. Both people in the interaction allow the other's actions to impact their subsequent behavior. As a source, you send a message but are also receiving feedback cues from the recipient of your message. In communication, the receiver of the message listens to the message and adjusts his or her behavior to correspond with the source's message. For example, during a meeting with your boss, you may monitor his or her actions or behaviors while you speak. In this way, you are monitoring nonverbal communication while you are also providing verbal and nonverbal communication. You are simultaneously the source of the message and the receiver of the message. Communication between two people is similar to a tennis match in that both individuals send tennis balls (messages) back and forth, each adjusting to and responding to the other's messages.

© Golden Pixels LLC/Shutterstock.com

Small Group

Small group communication occurs when a collection of at least three people communicate with one another. A well-functioning small group is comprised of individuals, typically no more than 10, who are aware of one another and achieve a commonly shared goal. In Chapters 8 and 9, we focus closely on types of groups as well as suggestions for engaging in effective group interactions to accomplish goals. Working with others can be a difficult and important task. For example, your boss may place you on a team that is charged with creating the best solution to a company problem. To solve the problem, you meet with others and brainstorm ideas. During the brainstorming, you notice some individuals in the group take a more active role whereas others seemingly "kick back" and contribute little to the experience. How do you address this situation? Do you confront these group members? Do you talk to your boss? Knowing how to address various group settings and communication styles is important to help the group work together more effectively.

© Halfpoint/Shutterstock.com

Public communication typically occurs when a source communicates information to a relatively large audience.

Public

Public communication typically occurs when a source communicates information to a relatively large audience. The audience serves as the receiver of the message. During a public communicative event, the audience's attention is focused on the source, with feedback restricted to primarily nonverbal cues. For example, feedback will likely be limited to smiles or head nods during a presentation. However, once the presentation is over, a question-and-answer period may allow for some interaction between the speaker and the audience. The goal of your presentation can range from entertaining, to persuading, to informing an audience. These ideas are discussed in Chapters 10, 11, and 12. Public communication is a valued skill in which you will likely participate in your personal, professional, and public lives. For example, you may be asked to give the best man or maid of honor speech at a friend's wedding or voice opinions to the local school board. For now, know that public communication is a skill and you can become more proficient in it.

Mediated

Mediated communication involves the use of technology as a channel of delivery for a message. This channel is used to compensate for being separated by physical distance. Each time you use a phone or a computer to communicate, you are engaging in mediated interaction. Mediated communication encompasses *mass media communication* and *social media communication*. Mass media communication is large-scale communication that includes a large audience and a channel other than face-to-face to communicate. When you watch television and listen to commercials, you are a receiver of mass media communication. You are not near the product's advertisers yet the commercial is a form of interaction. The audience is large, hence the term "mass," and the channel for communicating is the television, hence it's mediated. Social media communication is technology based and works to build communities of people. Social media communication includes websites such as Facebook or Instagram. These websites work to build communities of people and are thus considered social media.

> **Mass media communication**
> Large-scale communication that includes a large audience and a channel other than face-to-face.

> **Social media communication**
> Mediated communication that works to build communities of people.

COMMUNICATION APPREHENSION

As you can see, our personal, professional, and public lives utilize a number of different types of communication. Perhaps while reading about the various types of communication you may have thought to yourself that you were more comfortable with one type of communication over another. For example, you may be quite relaxed when interacting with your friends and family members, but the notion of presenting an oral presentation in a classroom or at work makes you extremely nervous. Maybe you've received an email or phone call from your boss stating that he or she needs to meet with you. Upon receiving the message, you imagine what he or she could possibly say to you. In imagining the interaction, you begin to feel anxious, your hands start to sweat, or your pulse quickens. This experience is called communication apprehension. *Communication apprehension* is the fear or anxiety we experience when faced with real or imagined communication interactions. Noteworthy in the definition is the inclusion of real and imagined interactions. Have you ever become nervous or anxious just thinking about a situation where you might be expected to communicate? For example, perhaps you experienced a conflict with a friend or family member that needs to be addressed. While preparing for the discussion, you think about the things you want to say. You notice that your hands become sweaty and your pulse quickens. Simply thinking about certain types of communication can make individuals nervous. The Personal Report of Communication Apprehension (PRCA) Scale was developed by communication scholar James C. McCroskey (1982) in an attempt to understand different situations that may cause us to experience communication apprehension. Complete the scale in Figure 1.4 and indicate the extent to which you agree or disagree that each statement applies to your communication behaviors.

> **Communication apprehension**
> Fear, nervousness, or anxiety we experience when faced with real or imagined communication interactions.

Strongly Disagree = 1; Disagree = 2; Neutral = 3; Agree = 4; Strongly Agree = 5

_____ 1. I dislike participating in group discussions.

_____ 2. Generally, I am comfortable while participating in group discussions.

_____ 3. I am tense and nervous while participating in group discussions.

_____ 4. I like to get involved in group discussions.

_____ 5. Engaging in a group discussion with new people makes me tense and nervous.

_____ 6. I am calm and relaxed while participating in group discussions.

_____ 7. Generally, I am nervous when I have to participate in a meeting.

_____ 8. Usually, I am comfortable when I have to participate in a meeting.

_____ 9. I am very calm and relaxed when I am called upon to express an opinion at a meeting.

_____10. I am afraid to express myself at meetings.

_____11. Communicating at meetings usually makes me uncomfortable.

_____12. I am very relaxed when answering questions at a meeting.

_____13. While participating in a conversation with a new acquaintance, I feel very nervous.

_____14. I have no fear of speaking up in conversations.

_____15. Ordinarily I am very tense and nervous in conversations.

_____16. Ordinarily I am very calm and relaxed in conversations.

_____17. While conversing with a new acquaintance, I feel very relaxed.

_____18. I'm afraid to speak up in conversations.

_____19. I have no fear of giving a speech.

_____20. Certain parts of my body feel very tense and rigid while giving a speech.

_____21. I feel relaxed while giving a speech.

_____22. My thoughts become confused and jumbled when I am giving a speech.

_____23. I face the prospect of giving a speech with confidence.

_____24. While giving a speech, I get so nervous I forget facts I really know.

To obtain your score, use the following directions. You will add your scores for items together.

- Group discussion: 18 — (scores for items 2, 4, and 6) + (scores for items 1, 3, and 5) Score: _____
- Meetings: 18 — (scores for items 8, 9, and 12) + (scores for items 7, 10, and 11) Score:_____
- Interpersonal: 18 — (scores for items 14, 16, and 17) + (scores for items 13, 15, and 18) Score: _____
- Public speaking: 18 — (scores for items 19, 21, and 23) + (scores for items 20, 22, and 24) Score: _____
- To obtain your total score for the PRCA, simply add your subscores together. Total:_____
- Your scores can range from 24 to 120. A score below 51 represents people who have very low communication apprehension; between 51 and 80, average communication apprehension; and above 80, high communication apprehension.

FIGURE 1.4

McCroskey's (1982) Personal Report of Communication Apprehension Scale.
Source: Courtesy of Dr. James C. McCroskey, Department of Communications Studies, University of Alabama-Birmingham.

Your total score indicates exactly how much anxiety you experience in a variety of communication contexts. As you probably noticed, your scores will vary based on two dimensions: the source and the context. You may be nervous communicating with some sources and not others. For example, you may be comfortable speaking with a friend or coworker, but you become very nervous when speaking with those in an authoritative role. The situation or context also affects your anxiety. You may be calm when speaking in a small group of coworkers, yet you become extremely nervous when delivering a presentation at a professional convention in front of people you do not know.

Thus far, we have defined communication and discussed the communication process, the guiding principles of communication, and the various types of communication we use in our public, personal, and professional lives. You have also gained an understanding of communication apprehension or the anxiety one can feel when thinking about or engaging in interaction. As a communicator, it is important to consider who is receiving your message, the context in which you find yourself, and the content of your message. When we consider these elements and allow them to guide our verbal and nonverbal communication, we are striving to become more communicatively competent.

COMMUNICATION COMPETENCE

Have you ever interacted with someone and thought the person's behavior was inappropriate? Perhaps you found yourself pondering why the person said or did something or why their behaviors did not match the situation. Using effective communication and having successful interactions with others is an outcome we can achieve. Communication is something we can control. Your goal should be to strive for appropriate behaviors in all contexts and with all content. Successful navigation of the communication process is essential to becoming a competent communicator. Competence involves the capacity to alter verbal and nonverbal behaviors in creating appropriate and effective messages—messages that "fit" the situational demands of the interaction in addition to helping us reach shared meaning with the receiver of our message.

> **Communication competence**
> Ability to produce messages that are perceived as appropriate and effective.

Communication Competence Defined

Communication competence is defined as an individual's ability to produce messages that are perceived as appropriate and effective. It is based on the understanding that communicators should possess three key elements in order to achieve competence: knowledge, skill, and motivation (Spitzberg & Cupach, 1984). *Knowledge* refers

> **Knowledge**
> Understanding of the appropriate messages or behaviors used in a given situation or with a particular person.

to our understanding of the appropriate messages or behaviors that should be used in a given situation or with a particular person. For example, in the United States, it is common to shake hands during an initial interaction. While we may have knowledge of what's appropriate or effective, it's also important to possess the ability to actually engage in those actions. *Skill* refers to the ability to produce or utilize the appropriate behaviors. For example, you may know that an effective oral presentation has an introduction, a body, and a conclusion, but you may lack the skills required to deliver a quality presentation. Finally, *motivation* refers to a desire to obtain results or accomplish a goal. We have to want to be competent communicators. Collectively, communication competence requires knowledge of what constitutes effective communication, the skills or ability to engage in those behaviors that are appropriate to the situation and effective in creating shared meaning, and a desire or motivation to be perceived as competent.

Achieving Competence

A first step in becoming an effective communicator is to measure your current level of communication competence. To establish your baseline communication competence, complete the Communication Competence Scale (Wiemann, 1977) included in Figure 1.5. As you answer the questions, reflect on your general communication patterns and behaviors.

There are no right or wrong answers to the questions included on this survey—only opportunities for growth. In some instances, you may have found your response to be, "It depends." Competence involves considering the situation and the topic *in addition to* the person with whom you are communicating. Assessing situational elements is a key component to achieving competence. Chances are you have encountered situations that required you to complete a situational analysis without even realizing it. Have you ever adjusted your message based on the situation or the person with whom you were speaking? Have you ever told your parents about how you spent your evening but provided different details about the same evening to a friend? We collect information that guides our decisions regarding how to best proceed with conversations. Consider how you would ask your boss for a raise. You would likely address the situation by customizing your verbal and nonverbal behaviors to that specific situation. You might schedule a meeting with your boss and arrive early and dressed in a suit. The verbal message would be organized so that you first demonstrate how committed you are to the organization and then address why you believe you deserve a raise. How you communicate in this situation would likely be different from the verbal and nonverbal behaviors you would use while terminating a romantic relationship. Competence requires us to evaluate several different elements in determining what is acceptable in a given communication situation.

> **Skill**
> Ability to produce or utilize the appropriate behaviors.

> **Motivation**
> Desire to obtain results or accomplish a goal. We have to want to be competent communicators.

Strongly Disagree = 1; Disagree = 2; Neutral = 3; Agree = 4; Strongly Agree = 5

_____ 1. I find it easy to get along with others.
_____ 2. I can adapt to changing situations.
_____ 3. I treat people as individuals.
_____ 4. I interrupt others too much.
_____ 5. I am rewarding to talk to.
_____ 6. I can deal with others effectively.
_____ 7. I am a good listener.
_____ 8. My personal relations are cold and distant.
_____ 9. I am easy to talk to.
_____10. I won't argue with someone just to prove I am right.
_____11. My conversational behavior is not "smooth."
_____12. I ignore other people's feelings.
_____13. I generally know how others feel.
_____14. I let others know I understand them.
_____15. I understand other people.
_____16. I am relaxed and comfortable when speaking.
_____17. I listen to what people say to me.
_____18. I like to be close and personal with people.
_____19. I generally know what type of behavior is appropriate in any given situation.
_____20. I usually do not make unusual demands of my friends.
_____21. I am an effective conversationalist.
_____22. I am supportive of others.
_____23. I do not mind meeting strangers.
_____24. I can easily put myself in another person's shoes.
_____25. I pay attention to the conversation.
_____26. I am generally relaxed when conversing with a new acquaintance.
_____27. I am interested in what others have to say.
_____28. I don't follow conversations very well.
_____29. I enjoy social gatherings where I can meet new people.
_____30. I am a likeable person.
_____31. I am flexible.
_____32. I am not afraid to speak with people in authority.
_____33. People can come to me with their problems.
_____34. I generally say the right thing at the right time.
_____35. I like to use my voice and body expressively.
_____36. I am sensitive to others' needs of the moment.

To determine your score, reverse-code your answers for 4, 8, 11, 12, and 28. That is, if you answered 5, your answer would become a 1, if you answered 4, your answer would become a 2. Now sum your scores. Higher scores indicate higher levels of communication competence.

FIGURE 1.5

Wiemann's (1977) Communication Competence Scale. Source: From *Human Communication Research, Volume 3, Issue 3, March 1977* by John M. Wiemann. Copyright © 1977 John Wiley and Sons. Reprinted by permission.

COMMUNICATION ETHICS

➤ **Ethics**
Standards, values, beliefs, and principles we use to help us determine what is right or wrong.

Our communication is often guided by personal standards of what we consider to be right or wrong, good or bad, and correct or incorrect. These guidelines serve as our personal ethics. *Ethics* are the standards, values, beliefs, and principles we use to help us determine what is acceptable or unacceptable behavior. It is important to note that there is no universal ethical standard. We each create and abide by our own ethical code of conduct. Some individuals view ethical behaviors as defined by laws or the legal system. If it is illegal, a behavior would be deemed unethical. Others evaluate ethical behaviors using a religious doctrine. If a religion believes it, then the behavior is acceptable or ethical.

Ethics and communication work together. When we think about the relationship between ethics and communication, we should take into consideration what behaviors will help us achieve our intended outcomes. As communicators, we do not want to mislead or manipulate our listeners. For example, suppose your friend begins to tell a personal story and asks you to keep the information secret, to not share the information. An ethical communicator would respect the friend's request and keep the information private rather than violating the friend's wishes. Considering the ethical implications of our decisions when communicating with others and a commitment to achieving communication competence are things that

1. Seek to have the best possible interactions.
2. Listen.
3. Speak nonjudgmentally.
4. Speak from your own experience.
5. Seek to understand others.
6. Avoid speaking for others.
7. Share what you are comfortable sharing.
8. Respect boundaries.
9. Avoid interrupting.
10. Give everyone time to speak.

Source: Northern Virginia Ethical Society. (2007).

FIGURE 1.6

Ten guidelines for ethical communication.

we control. They are behaviors that we should use and strive to incorporate in all aspects of our lives. Figure 1.6 highlights some key considerations when applying ethical considerations to your communication with others.

BENEFITS OF COMMUNICATION

By now, we hope that you realize just how important communication is in all aspects of your life—personal, professional, and public. Communication is a skill that, when used appropriately, can benefit you in each of these areas. Consider the ways in which you currently adjust your communication when interacting with others. For example, you shake your boss's hand while greeting her, but you hug your romantic partner in greeting. A more formal communication style is used when speaking with your grandparents, while your interactions with friends include the use of slang and is more relaxed. Our communicative behaviors change depending on with whom we are interacting and the situation or setting in which we are communicating.

In Our Personal Lives

Personal relationships can be some of the most rewarding as well as the most challenging connections in our lives. When we use effective communication,

Your communication behaviors change depending on who you are with and where you are.

© Halfpoint/Shutterstock.com

we can experience a host of benefits, including *relational satisfaction*, which is feeling positive and content in our relationships, and *emotional closeness*, which is a perception or feeling of trust or solidarity with another individual. Improving your communication in personal relationships can contribute to these positive outcomes. Techniques you should consider using to enhance your communication:

1. *Understand yourself.* The more you understand your thoughts, the better you can communicate them to others. Knowing your own communication style and preferences can lead to more effective interactions. For example, you might prefer to address challenging conversations by sending text messages as opposed to confronting them face-to-face.

2. *Use honesty.* Being open and truthful with others can help create meaningful relationships.

3. *Take time to listen.* Active listening is a choice. By staying motivated and engaged in the conversation, you can enhance connections with others.

4. *Engage in meaningful conversations.* Even discussing topics we do not necessarily enjoy talking about, engaging in tough talk can help us learn about others' personal perspectives and their perceptions of a situation.

Successful relationships are the by-product of effective communication. Our personal lives are not the only area that will benefit from enhanced communication. Interactions in our professional lives can prosper as well if effective communication is used.

In Our Professional Lives

Fortune 500 executives indicate that the most sought-after skills when hiring new employees include effective oral and written communication (Hansen & Hansen, n.d.). By working to enhance communication in your professional life, you can experience a variety of positive outcomes including monetary gains, enhanced professional status, and more satisfying workplace relationships. Some suggestions for enhancing your communication in a professional setting include the following:

1. *Ask questions.* When you're unclear of a task or how to complete an assigned task, ask questions so you understand the other person or get clarification on a point.

2. *Include others.* Be sure to include others in dialogue, reach out to those you may not know.

3. *Offer your ideas.* When you have an idea about how to complete a project, offer it to others.

4. *Be direct.* Assign tasks in a direct manner.

5. *Use inclusive language.* Use language such as "we" and "us" to create team cohesion.

It is safe to say that we all want to be successful in our chosen careers. Effective communication can contribute to that success in terms of promotions and opportunities. Our public lives can also benefit from being able to successfully share our ideas with others.

In Our Public Lives

Communication can seem even more important when you are delivering a message to a large audience such as during an oral presentation. When our public speaking skills are strong and we deliver the message in a way that meets our audience's needs, we can experience increased perceptions of competence and credibility. Toastmasters, an organization dedicated to enhancing public speaking skills, provides the following suggestions for enhancing your public presentation skills:

1. *Know your material.* The topic matters.
2. *Practice.* Rehearse and revise as necessary.
3. *Know the audience.* Greet audience members and ask them questions.
4. *Recognize that people want you to succeed.* Audiences are rooting for you.
5. *Don't apologize for nervousness.* Audiences rarely notice a speaker's nervousness.
6. *Concentrate on the message.* Focus on content.

Our public lives not only include effectively presenting our ideas in a public context, but also our civic engagement and the images we portray to the public, such as posts to social media profiles such as Twitter, Instagram, or Facebook. Consider steps that you should take to carefully manage your public persona so as to avoid creating a negative perception.

A FOUNDATION FOR STUDYING COMMUNICATION IN OUR LIVES

While reading this chapter, you may have found that you have additional questions about communication, specifically questions that centered on your personal, professional, and public lives. Perhaps those questions pertained to the different ways that we communicate. Have you ever heard the saying, "It's not what you say, but how you say it?" In Chapter 3, we focus on the role of language and words in creating verbal messages, and Chapter 4 introduces various types of nonverbal communication and explores the relationship between nonverbal and verbal communication. The tone of your voice, rate of speech, eye contact, facial expressions, posture, and gestures offer a variety of ways to communicate different meanings. Not only do our words and nonverbals play an important role in our interactions with others, but also our ability to listen effectively ensures effective communication (Chapter 5).

As you read this chapter, you may have contemplated how communication impacts your relationships with others. In Chapters 6 and 7, we examine the role that communication plays in our personal, professional, and public relationships. We build connections with others by exchanging verbal and nonverbal messages. Consider the fact that we use communication to share details about ourselves, to learn about others' experiences, and to create mutual understanding. We also continue or maintain our relationships by building on previous interactions. Throughout your academic and professional careers, you may find that you spend a considerable amount of time working in groups. Chapters 8 and 9 provide valuable information for enhancing group dynamics to ensure that goals are accomplished.

In addition to working effectively in groups, being able to present your ideas and share information with others in public contexts will be essential to your professional success. In Chapters 10, 11, and 12 we describe the public speaking process and share strategies to enhance your speeches.

Perhaps you contemplated how technology has changed or influenced your interactions and connections with others in your personal, professional, and public lives. In Chapter 14 we focus on how technology impacts our ability to communicate effectively in our relationships with others. Finally, in Chapter 15, we focus on applying communication to our lives across a variety of contexts.

CHAPTER SUMMARY

Communication is important, and the messages that we exchange with others are both memorable and long-lasting. As much as we would sometimes like, our communication cannot be undone. Once performed, the communicative act cannot be taken back. It is important to remember that our communicative behaviors are a dynamic process; they are not static elements. Rather, our communication changes based on who we are interacting with, where we find ourselves, and the type of message being discussed. We can work to improve our communication and, when we do, we will experience positive outcomes such as better relationships, monetary gain, and enhanced credibility.

Channel Medium through which message is sent.

Communication Process of sending and receiving verbal and nonverbal messages to achieve shared meaning.

Communication apprehension Fear, nervousness, or anxiety we experience when faced with real or imagined communication interactions.

Communication competence Ability to produce messages that are perceived as appropriate and effective.

Content information Verbal communication or the actual words being said.

Context Situation or setting where the communication occurs.

Decoding Process where individuals attempt to make sense or interpret the encoded message.

Emotional closeness Perception or feeling of trust or solidarity with another individual.

Encoding Process of translating thoughts, feelings, experiences, or ideas into verbal and/or nonverbal communication.

Ethics Standards, values, beliefs, and principles we use to help us determine what is right or wrong.

Explicit learning Occurs when we are told what to do and when it should be done.

Feedback Verbal or nonverbal response or reaction to the message.

Implicit learning Observational learning of communication behaviors.

Interpersonal communication Interactions that take place between at least two people who simultaneously take on the roles of both sender and receiver.

Intrapersonal communication Most basic type of communication; occurs when we envision or have a conversation with ourselves.

Knowledge Understanding of the appropriate messages or behaviors used in a given situation or with a particular person.

Mass media communication Large-scale communication that includes a large audience and a channel other than face-to-face.

Mediated communication Communication that involves the use of technology as the channel of delivery.

Message Ideas or feelings being communicated.

Motivation Desire to obtain results or accomplish a goal. We have to want to be competent communicators.

Noise Anything that interferes with our ability to interact or listen to others.

Physical noise Any type of audible interference in the communication environment that impedes our accurate reception of a message.

Psychological noise Internal interference that impedes our accurate reception of a message.

Public communication Occurs when a source communicates information to a relatively large audience.

Receiver Individual receiving the message.

Relational information Information that helps aid understanding of a relationship, emotions, and feelings in a message.

Relational satisfaction Feeling positive and content in our relationships.

Source Individual creating the message.

Shared meaning Result of communication that is accurately sent and received.

Skill Ability to produce or utilize the appropriate behaviors.

Small group communication Communication that occurs between at least three individuals.

Social media communication Technology based communication that works to build communities of people.

REFERENCES

Hansen, R. S., & Hansen, K. (n.d.). *Quintessential careers: What do employers really want? Top skills and values employers seek from job-seekers.* Retrieved from http://www.quintcareers.com/job_skills_values.html

Lasswell, H. D. (1948). The structure and function of communication society. In L. Bryson (Ed.), *The communication of ideas* (pp. 37–51). New York: Harper & Bros.

McCroskey, J. C. (1982). *An introduction to rhetorical communication* (4th ed). Englewood Cliffs, NJ: Prentice-Hall.

Northern Virginia Ethical Society. (2007). *Ten basics of ethical communication.* Retrieved from http://www.esnv.org/web/ten-basics-ethical-commun.

Spitzberg, B. H., & Cupach, W. R. (1984). *Interpersonal communication competence.* Beverly Hills, CA: Sage.

Toastmasters. (n.d.). *10 tips for public speaking.* Retrieved August 10, 2010, from http://www.toastmasters.org/MainMenuCategories/FreeResources/Need HelpGivingaSpeech/TipsTechniques/10TipsforPublicSpeaking.aspx.

Wiemann, J. M. (1977). Explication and test of a model of communicative competence. *Human Communication Research, 3,* 195–213.

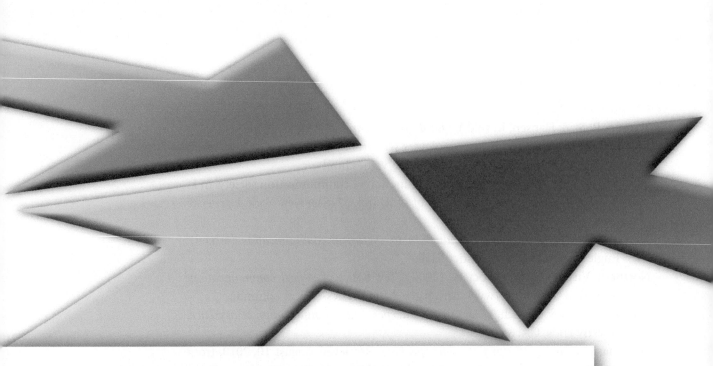

CHAPTER 2

Perception and Communication:
A Matter of Perspective

Chapter Objectives

After reading this chapter, you should be able to:

- Define perception
- Explain the perception process
- Identify the various influences on perception
- Define self-concept and explain how it develops as well as the impact it has on your communication
- Define self-esteem and explain the impact it has on your communication
- Identify the impact our perceptions of others have on our communication with them

PERSONAL: New neighbors move next door and you go over to meet them. You introduce yourself. The husband is very friendly and begins to talk about the move and living in a new area. He seems very outgoing and likeable. His wife, on the other hand, says very little and only smiles occasionally. When you leave, your impression of him is very positive, but you don't have a great impression of his wife. Time goes by and you sometimes see the neighbors working outside or shopping at the local supermarket. Each time, you are struck by how pleasant he is but how aloof his wife seems to be. Little by little, you get to know her, and now you realize your first impression of her was inaccurate. She isn't cold, snobby, or any of those things you previously thought. She is, however, very shy and introverted, and it takes her a while to get comfortable with new people. How could you have been so wrong?

PROFESSIONAL: Your organization has been acquired by a larger corporation, and you are nervous that the new CEO will restructure your department and may lay off some employees, perhaps even you. The CEO has spent weeks meeting with you and coworkers in your department and has asked to examine many documents from the previous years. Although the CEO has said nothing about restructuring or downsizing, you assume that is the possible reason for all of the analysis that is occurring. At the end of the month, the CEO calls the entire department together to congratulate them on their past performance and to indicate what the CEO calls a "better than bright" future. Although you perceived the CEO to be going through this process in order to determine who would stay and who would go, the CEO was simply spending time learning about the company. You are happy for the mix-up and are glad nobody will be let go. You say to yourself, "I was nervous for no reason. How could I have completely misread the situation?"

PUBLIC: You have decided to attend the town meeting because there is an important issue on the agenda. The town needs to vote on the school budget for the upcoming year. Your children are still in the school system, so you are in favor of the expanded budget. You naturally assume that everyone will be in favor of it because a good school system usually increases property values. When you arrive at the meeting, you are stunned to hear that most of the people in the room are opposed to the proposed budget. While you realize it will raise your taxes somewhat, one of the primary reasons you moved to this town was because of the school system, and now you don't want the quality of your children's education to be affected by this. How can anyone be against the budget even if it means higher taxes? Why don't these people see what you see?

CHAPTER OVERVIEW

In our personal, professional, and public lives, there will always be occasions when we see things differently from others. These variations can be caused by a difference in perception. Can one person interpret something one way while another person sees or hears the exact same thing and interprets it in a totally different way? The answer is absolutely "yes." In this chapter, you will learn why we see and interpret things differently and how it influences our communication with others. In addition, you will learn how your own perceptions influence who you are and how you communicate.

PERCEPTION DEFINED

➤ Perception
Process by which we select, organize, and interpret stimuli to make sense of our world.

Perception is a process consisting of three parts that we use to make sense of messages we encounter. We select, organize, and interpret stimuli so that they make sense to us. This happens constantly in our personal, professional, and public lives. For example, a friend asks you if you would like to go to a concert together. You eagerly confirm that you would like to go, as long as the tickets are not too expensive. Your friend buys the tickets and sends you a text message informing you how much you owe. When you learn the price of the ticket, you are shocked because your perception of "not too expensive" is clearly much different than your friend's perception. Differences in perception may cause minor misunderstandings or even major communication breakdowns.

When two fans watch the same football game, they may have very different perspectives about a controversial play.

Since perception is a cognitive process that helps us to understand our experiences, how we receive, filter, and interpret behaviors and conversations may not be the same as how someone else will complete the process. In essence, perception is the key to how we assign meaning in our interactions with others and thus, it has a significant impact on how we communicate and how we understand the communication of others. Understanding the perception process will enable you to consider the potential misunderstandings that may occur and help you communicate more effectively.

© Diego Cervo/Shutterstock.com

THE PERCEPTION PROCESS

Selection

The *perception process* has three phases: selection, organization, and interpretation (see Figure 2.1). The first phase is *selection*. Needless to say, at any given moment in our lives, there are many stimuli in our environment that may compete for our attention. We simply cannot focus on everything, so we select those stimuli that we feel are significant. That is why two people may see the same thing but "see" things differently. For example, when two fans watch the same football game, they may have very different perspectives about a controversial play. One fan may have focused on watching one player while the other fan focused on a different player. Because the two fans selected different things to attend to in the game, they may have a difference of opinion about the outcome of the play. Although they have seen the same play per se, they each focused on something different. As a result, the selection portion of the perception process will affect how each of them moves through the next phases of the process. As we discuss later in the chapter, what you select may be influenced by who you are, your relationship with another person, your culture, your expectations or prior experiences, or even your mood at any given time.

Organization

Organization is the second phase of the perception process. Once we select or focus our attention on some particular aspect or characteristic of the stimuli we selected, we need to organize it in a way that makes sense to us. We may relate what we receive to something we have already experienced. For example, when you hear someone with a great laugh, you may be interested in getting to know that person because his or her laugh reminds you of one of your friends who also has a great laugh. In our quest to organize what we receive, we use a categorization process. We may categorize people based on the roles we view them as fulfilling or by our assumptions about their personalities. Is this person a student, a teacher, or a parent? Is this person funny, serious, or responsible? Using this organizational process to make sense of others is natural in our interactions; however, we need to

Perception process
A three-step process that includes selection, where we focus our attention on something and ignore other elements in the environment; organization, where we form what we have received into meaningful patterns; and interpretation, where we attach meaning to what we have selected and organized.

Selection
The first part of the perception process where we focus our attention on something within our environment.

FIGURE 2.1

The perception process.

Organization
The second phase of the perception process, which involves categorizing what we have received.

be careful of our assumptions and conclusions, and be cautious of overgeneralizing others. Doing so may prevent us from being accurate in our overall perceptions. In addition, as your experiences change throughout your life, you may alter the way in which you categorize stimuli. Thus, the way you once categorized romantic relationships in middle school is probably very different from the way in which you currently look at romantic relationships. Once we have organized what we have received, we move to the interpretation phase.

Interpretation

⇒ Interpretation
The third phase of the perception process where we attach meaning to what we have selected and organized.

The final step of the perception process is *interpretation*. This is where we attach meaning to what we have selected and organized. We may interpret what one person says to us differently than if someone else said it based on our relationship with the other individual. For example, if a friend says, "You are crazy!" you would likely assume the friend is joking; whereas, if someone you don't know or barely know said the same thing, you might interpret the same message as an insult. In addition, your personal experiences may also influence how you interpret a message. For example, you had a great relationship with your previous supervisor. It was very relaxed and you would even play jokes on each other. When your new supervisor was hired, you assumed you could approach tasks and the relationship in general in the same lighthearted and humorous way. The new supervisor, however, did not share the same view and told you to "take your work more seriously." The relationship you have with another person, the experiences you have had in your life, as well as other factors may cause you to interpret what you have received and organized in different ways.

Overall, the process of selecting something from the many stimuli received through our senses, and organizing and interpreting them in a way that makes sense, is the cognitive process known as perception. In the next section, we focus on the factors that influence how we go through the perception process.

THE INFLUENCES ON PERCEPTION

There are many factors that affect our perceptions, as you can see in Figure 2.2. These may include characteristics such as our age, gender, physical characteristics, cultural background, past experiences, and even our present mood. Your awareness of these factors will help you understand the perception process more clearly.

FIGURE 2.2

Potential factors that influence our perception.

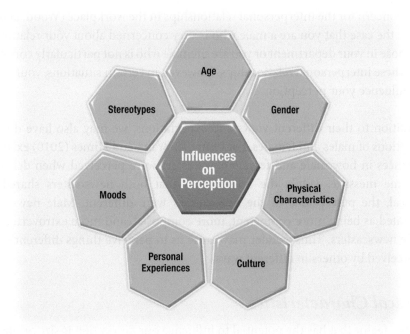

Age

Your age may influence how you perceive something. When you were younger, you may have thought the stories your grandparents told you were repetitive and boring. As you grew older, you realized the importance of these stories and their significance for your family. Things that don't seem important to us when we are one age could become very important at another age. The reverse may also be true. Perhaps when you were younger, you couldn't imagine ever being able to sleep without your favorite stuffed animal. Now, you remember your stuffed animal fondly, but you can sleep well without it. Consider the fact that when you were younger you may have felt uneasy discussing your romantic interests with your parents, but as an adult, you may be much more comfortable sharing information and even asking them for their perspective on your romantic relationships.

Gender

Gender may also influence our perceptions. How we view things may be related to whether we are male or female. While this isn't always the case, males and females may perceive the same thing differently. For example, both males and females in the workplace want to achieve their goals; however, it has been said that females may be more interested in nurturing and enhancing their relationships, while males, on the other hand, may be more interested in simply getting the task completed without as much concern for the interpersonal relationships in the workplace (Wood, 2003). It may be the case that you are a male who is very concerned about your relationship with those in your department or you are a female who is not particularly concerned about these interpersonal relationships. However, in certain situations, your gender may influence your perception.

In addition to their different views and expectations, we may also have different perceptions of males and females. For example, Brann and Himes (2010) examined differences in how male and female newscasters were perceived when delivering the same message. While the information that both newscasters shared was identical, the perceptions of the newscasters were different. Male newscasters were rated as being more competent, more composed, and more extroverted than female newscasters. Thus, gender may cause us to perceive things differently or to be perceived by others in different ways.

Physical Characteristics

Another factor that has the potential to influence our perception is size or physical ability. For example, one of your authors had a pink stuffed bear as a child. She remembered the bear as being life-sized! Many years later when she found the bear in her parents' attic, she asked her mother if she had washed the bear and put it in the dryer, thus shrinking it. Her mother indicated she had not done that. Clearly, when she was very small, the bear appeared to be much larger than it actually was. While she had grown over the years, her perception of one of her favorite childhood toys had remained unchanged. When we are small, things seem much bigger to us. Imagine what it is like for a child to walk in a crowded store holding a parent's hand. The much larger parent probably doesn't realize that the world looks much different from the small child's vantage point. The same thing might be true for those of you who exercise on a regular basis. Weights that may be considered "light" for someone who has lifted for some time may seem extremely "heavy" for someone new to strength training. As you reflect on these examples, imagine the miscommunication that might occur when your interpretation of something is different from someone else's interpretation.

Culture

Our culture also influences how we perceive the behaviors and messages of others. If you have ever traveled to another country, you have probably experienced firsthand how different things may be. Not only may the language be new to you, but also the types of food, styles of dress, and even smells may be unique. As a result, you probably perceived things differently from someone who was a native of that country.

Culture influences how we perceive the behaviors and messages of others.

If you are from a culture that values direct eye contact, you would most likely perceive someone looking directly at you as being respectful. If, however, the other person is from a culture where it is disrespectful to look someone in the eyes when talking, you may perceive their lack of eye contact as being rude and misinterpret the situation if you don't understand the differences in cultural expectations. Suppose you are from a culture that values punctuality, and you are meeting a business client from a culture that views time as being flexible. She arrives to your scheduled meeting 25 minutes late, and you misinterpret her late arrival as being unprofessional even though it is acceptable to show up 25–30 minutes after a scheduled starting time in her culture. Examples like these occur more often than we realize and can cause individuals to misread a communication situation.

Personal Experiences

As we alluded to earlier, your own personal experiences may affect your perceptions. For example, suppose you hire a contractor to do some work in your home. Upon her arrival, the contractor thanks you multiple times and expresses her appreciation for the work. She explains that the recent economy has resulted in fewer jobs and more competition from other contractors. Her personal experience in struggling to find work has caused her to perceive the opportunity to work on your home differently than she would have if job options were readily available. Her personal experience of the shift in availability of work opportunities has changed the perceptions she had about her livelihood and the customers who pay for her services.

Moods

Our moods also influence our perceptions. Something that you would not usually find upsetting may bother or annoy you because of your present mood. Suppose you typically enjoy having a coworker or neighbor drop by your office unexpectedly to chat. On one particular day, however, you are trying to complete a project by a deadline and don't have time to talk. Due to your stress level, you may perceive that person to be bothersome or annoying on this particular day, whereas on other days, you would welcome the casual conversation. You may try to cut off the conversation, simply stop listening, or say something you might regret later.

If our mood is positive, it may also influence our perception of a situation. Suppose you have just received an "A" on a paper or a promotion at work. If you are in a great mood, something that might bother you on any other day simply does not seem to alter your positive outlook. Thus, whether your mood is positive or negative may influence your communication with others or their communication with you.

Stereotypes

➤ Stereotypes
Generalizations we hold about a group or a category of people.

The *stereotypes* or generalizations we hold about a group or a category of people may also affect our perceptions. When we stereotype someone, we apply our general perceptions of a particular group to an individual. This helps us simplify the process of perception and form a quick impression of the person. Reflect on some of your own perceptions of groups of people based on their economic status, cultural background, religious beliefs, education level, or other factors. Perhaps you perceive wealthy people as being self-absorbed and selfish, while someone else may perceive them as being generous and hard-working. Being aware of our stereotypes is important to ensuring effective communication. When we only use our own stereotypes to guide our communication with others, we increase our risk of miscommunication. After all, our stereotypes are not always entirely accurate.

As you can see, there are many factors that potentially alter how you perceive something. Understanding that you may perceive something in a totally different way from others is key to becoming a more effective communicator. Unfortunately, many of us incorrectly believe that the way in which we perceive something is exactly how others perceive it. It is important to realize that others may not share your perception of the same thing and learn to engage in the practice of checking your perceptions.

PERCEPTION CHECKING

How do we make sure that our perceptions are accurate? While you may have heard the advice "Go with your instinct!" checking our perceptions for accuracy is an important step to ensure effective communication. *Perception checking* is the process whereby we validate the accuracy of our perceptions. There are several different strategies you can use to check your perceptions. The following suggestions, which also appear in Figure 2.3, are often used to help us ensure our perceptions are correct.

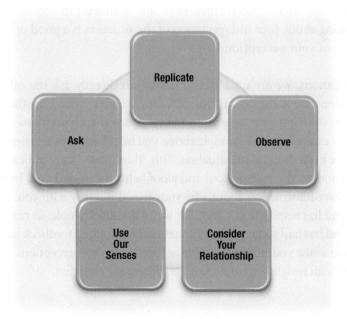

➤ **Perception checking**
The process whereby we validate the accuracy of our perceptions.

Use Our Senses

Your senses include what you see, hear, touch, taste, and/or smell. We often rely on our senses to help us determine the accuracy of what we perceive and how we process that information. For example, if you open the refrigerator and notice that the expiration date on a container of milk has passed, you probably assume the milk has spoiled. If you're brave enough, you might check your perception that the milk is sour by opening the container and smelling the milk. If it smells strange, our perceptions are confirmed. Perhaps you decide to further check your perceptions by pouring the milk into a glass. If you notice that it is curdled, your perceptions are confirmed again. You may even decide to go one step further and taste the milk

FIGURE 2.3

Strategies for checking perceptions.

to determine if your perception is correct. In this example, you used a variety of your senses (i.e., sight, smell, and taste) to ensure that you perceived something accurately. While it is easy to judge whether or not our perception of spoiled milk is accurate, it is not always quite as easy to check to confirm that our perceptions in communication situations are accurate. Our ability to check the accuracy of our perceptions to ensure we are on the "same page" as others is vital in our personal, professional, and public lives.

Ask

One way to determine if your perception of something is accurate is to simply ask the other person if your interpretation of the situation is correct. Suppose you are at a party and one of your friends has barely spoken to you all evening. In addition, the last few times you've seen one another, the friend has seemed quiet and standoffish. If you perceive that your friend is angry with you, perceptions might be checked by asking, "I feel like you are upset with me, is that true?" While your friend may respond, "No, I'm okay...," your friend's verbal response may not reveal her true feelings. Thus, it is important to listen to *how* the response is said to help you determine whether your perceptions are correct. Depending on the tone of voice or the facial expressions that accompany the response of "I'm okay..." a variety of meanings could be perceived. It could be that your friend has been preoccupied with a project or a personal issue. If, on the other hand, your friend's response isn't convincing, your perception of the situation may be accurate and you may need to discuss this further. Even if it is difficult to address the situation directly, asking about your interpretation of the situation is a good option to check the accuracy of your perception.

In some situations, we are unable or unwilling to directly ask the other person if our perceptions are accurate. In these situations, consider asking others who have observed the situation or people you trust to give you an honest assessment of the situation. For example, in the example above, you might ask another friend to confirm or reject your perception of the situation. This "third party" may indicate to you that he also has noticed the friend's cool and aloof behavior toward you. In fact, he may be able to share information about why your friend is angry with you, may indicate that the friend has responded in a similar way with other people, or may inform you that the friend has had some personal issues lately. Soliciting feedback from someone you trust can assist you in checking the accuracy of your perceptions, and perhaps provide you with insight regarding how to address the situation.

Replicate

When scientists want to test a finding to confirm their conclusions, they repeat the study. Each time they receive the same results, it helps them know their results were not simply due to chance. In much the same way, you may be able to confirm your perceptions by repeating the behavior. Suppose a supervisor asks an employee to take an additional shift on several occasions, and each time the worker replies "No." The supervisor may perceive the worker as someone who is unmotivated and not a team player. Each time the worker refuses to take on additional responsibility, a negative perception of this worker is reinforced. Furthermore, each time the supervisor asks and receives a negative response, it confirms the supervisor's perception. Of course, there could be other reasons why the worker is unable to accept additional responsibilities. In this example, to further check his perceptions, the supervisor could also implement the strategy mentioned in the previous section and directly ask the employee why he never accepts an additional shift.

Observe

In order to clarify our perception of a situation, we may need to simply observe. As you will learn in Chapter 4, while words may provide us with information about how others are feeling or thinking, nonverbal communication (i.e., tone of voice, facial expressions, gestures, eye contact, etc.) provides valuable cues to assist in perception checking. In the public arena, we may not ever have the opportunity to speak firsthand to a candidate who is running for political office. Instead, we check our initial perceptions of the candidate by observing them. Do they seem genuinely concerned about the issues with which we are concerned? What does the candidate's nonverbal communication say about his or her beliefs? Our observations help confirm or disconfirm our perceptions. It is important to remember that our own actions sometimes speak louder than words. Just as we use our observations to confirm our perceptions of others, they do the same when checking their perceptions of us.

Consider Your Relationship

Your relationship with someone can also help you to check your perceptions. If you have a close relationship, you might understand a behavior more readily than if this person was simply an acquaintance or someone you just met. For example, if you have worked closely with someone in your organization for several years and that person exhibits uncharacteristic behavior, your relationship with the person and knowledge of their typical behavior will assist you in checking your perception of their current behavior.

Overall, there are several strategies that can be used to check our perceptions and to enhance our ability to avoid misunderstandings. It is important to remember that there may be several interpretations of the same behavior, so checking your perceptions will help you interpret a situation more accurately. Think about being in a restaurant and receiving what you consider to be "poor service" from a server. Is your immediate conclusion that the server is terrible? Could it be that the person is just having a bad day? Is this person new at the job? Could the server be stressed because the restaurant has had a sudden influx of customers? Could the kitchen be to blame for not getting all of the orders from one party out at the same time? Might this person be stressed about an issue not related to waiting on tables at the restaurant? Checking your perceptions of a situation will help you correctly interpret a situation and will help you respond appropriately.

Our perceptions of others are only one part of the interaction equation. Another key element is our self-perceptions. Understanding how we see ourselves and the image that we want to portray to others is essential to ensuring effective communication.

PERCEIVING THE SELF

In the previous section, we discussed what perception is, what factors influence our perceptions, and some strategies we may use to check our perceptions. In the next section, we turn our attention to the way in which we perceive our "self" and how this influences the way in which we communicate with others and how they perceive and communicate with us.

Self-Concept

> **Self-concept**
> A set of perceptions we have about ourselves.

Our *self-concept* consists of the perceptions and beliefs we have about ourselves. It is relatively stable yet it can change and evolve as we grow and gain new life experiences. Self-concept is multidimensional and thus we describe ourselves in a variety of ways. Stop for a moment and consider how you would define yourself. Our gender, race, and ethnicity are some of the more common ways by which we define ourselves. We may also define ourselves by our occupation, roles, education, physical attributes, or personality traits. Each description of yourself contributes to your self-concept. Elements of your self-concept may change over time. For example, at one point in your life, you may define yourself through roles such as sibling, son or daughter, or student. Although some of these roles would not change, you may add new roles throughout your life such as spouse or partner, parent, aunt or uncle, employee, or supervisor to your list.

Some aspects of our self-concept are based on objective facts while other dimensions may be more subjective. For example, the color of your eyes and your height in inches are facts about you. You may say that you are "tall;" however, that is subjective because what may be perceived as being "tall" to one person may not seem very tall to another. Thus, if you are the tallest of your friends and family at 5 feet 7 inches, you may consider yourself tall until you become friends with someone who is 6 feet. If, on the other hand, you say, "I am 5 feet 7 inches," then you are communicating what is factual.

You may perceive yourself as a strong student, a great athlete, or a talented artist. Since we don't always judge ourselves exactly as others see us, others may not see us in this same way. For example, some contestants on *American Idol* auditions explain to the judges that they perceive themselves to be excellent singers. When they actually audition for the show, the judges may disagree with these perceptions.

The Development of the Self-Concept

From the time we are born, our self-concept begins to develop. Our experiences and interactions play an important role in the development of our self-concept. Sullivan (1953) noted that our view of self is created and shaped by how we think others view us. It is our perception of how we imagine others see us. This is known as *reflected appraisal*. Through our interactions with others, our self-perception may be confirmed or changed.

Significant others in our lives play an important role in the development of our self-concept. For most of us, our parents or primary caregivers provide the first messages that create our self-concept. When babies cry and their needs are met, a sense of security and love is communicated. As children grow older, they may receive positive or negative messages about behaviors ranging from manners, to athletic ability, to academic performance and these shape their sense of self. Your self-concept continues to evolve as you encounter new relationships and experiences. If we receive positive affirmation, we are more likely to embrace the feedback and enjoy something, thus adding to our self-concept regarding that element of our lives. Generally speaking, if we are told we are good at something, we are more likely to continue to do it and, as a result, often become better at it. For example, when you are learning to dance, if you receive positive feedback, you are much more likely to continue to practice. Because you continue to practice, you become better at dancing. In this sense, we may engage in what is known as the *self-fulfilling prophecy*. In other words, when we believe something is true, we respond in ways to ensure that the prediction is fulfilled. Naturally, there are many things that don't respond to the "think method." It is important to note that just

⮞ Reflected appraisal Development of our sense of self based on how we believe others view or see us.

⮞ Self-fulfilling prophecy The idea that when we believe something is true, it may become true. In other words, when we expect a particular outcome, either positive or negative, it is more likely that outcome will occur.

Teachers, coaches, friends, and supervisors also play a crucial role in shaping our self-concept.

© Monkey Business Images/Shutterstock.com

because we "think" something is true, it will become a reality. Recall our earlier example of the *American Idol* candidates. Just because they believe they have talent and perhaps their friends or family members even tell them they sing beautifully, it does not necessarily make it true. We don't become a great singer just because others say we're good and we believe them.

Needless to say, the reverse is also true. If you believe you are not good at something, you may fear or avoid it and then the self-fulfilling prophecy is fulfilled. For example, perhaps you had a bad experience when you were asked to present the results of a team project to another department. From that time on, you avoided speaking in public because you believed you were not good at it. Naturally, avoiding all public speaking situations will perpetuate your belief in your inability to speak in public and hence, this becomes a self-fulfilling prophecy.

As we enter school, our teachers and our peers influence our self-concept as well. For example, if your teacher told you that you were good in science or if you received good grades on your assignments when you were in elementary school, this becomes part of your self-concept. If you receive positive feedback on your science homework and tests, it reinforces this element of your self-concept. In addition, you will most likely feel positive about doing your science homework, which, in turn, will help you maintain this portion of your self-concept. Unfortunately, teachers may also have a negative influence on the self-concept of their students by saying something negative about their work instead of offering constructive criticism. Hopefully, you have not had this experience but there is a vast difference between someone telling you that you did very poorly versus pointing out the areas that were not strong and indicating how you could have improved upon the assignment.

Likewise, our peers influence the development of our self-concept. Think back to elementary school again. If you were the one that other children invited for play dates in elementary school, you probably viewed yourself as friendly and likeable. Similarly, if you did something funny and your peers laughed, you most likely began to believe you are funny. On the other hand, if you did something you thought was funny and nobody laughed, you also received a clear message from your peers.

In your professional life, your self-concept may also evolve. For example, suppose you are sitting in a meeting with senior management and you make a suggestion that your boss confirms as being valuable and worthwhile. At the next meeting, another suggestion you offer is received with enthusiasm. With each instance, you begin to view yourself as someone who could pursue a higher management position in the organization. When you receive this type of feedback and are praised for certain traits, they are more likely to become part of your self-concept.

Overall, early in our lives, parents and caregivers, teachers and peers send messages that influence our self-concept. As we go through life, our friends, family, supervisors, and colleagues continue to influence our self-concept. In turn, this influences how we communicate with others. In the next section, we discuss some of the barriers that prevent us from having an accurate self-concept.

Barriers Preventing an Accurate Self-Concept

There are several issues that may prevent us from forming a clear and accurate self-concept. As previously mentioned, your self-concept is created and developed through your interactions with others. You tend to construct a sense of who you are based on how others see you and communicate with you. Unfortunately, their perceptions of you may be inaccurate and this can cause you to see yourself inaccurately. For example, what if you are told you are the *best* artist or the *smartest* child by your parents, but when you begin school, you do not receive the same messages? On the other hand, what if you are told you are *worthless* or that you were a *mistake*? Consider the impact these types of messages would have on a person's self-concept. For better or worse, the messages we receive from significant others have an impact on our self-concepts; but these messages may or may not be accurate, and this may cause inaccuracy in our self-concepts.

As we previously indicated, the self-concept consists of perceptions we have about ourselves that are relatively stable. Unfortunately, these relatively enduring perceptions may pose a barrier that prevents us from developing an accurate self-concept since they cause us to be resistant to information that could alter our perceptions. Certainly, having a strong sense of self is a good thing, but if it prevents us from accepting valid messages about who we truly are, it can be problematic. Suppose you have always considered yourself to be poor at expressing yourself when writing. Perhaps you earned good grades in your English courses, but struggled to complete essays and received very little positive feedback from your teachers about your writing. When you entered college, you took the writing course required for all first-year students and was placed in a course with a teacher who inspired a passion for writing. When your first paper was returned with a grade of "A," you thought it was a mistake or a fluke. When you received the next paper back with the same grade, you thought, "This can't be right." On the third paper, your teacher wrote that you had a strong talent for writing and that she hoped you would continue taking writing courses in the future. Despite the positive feedback, it was difficult for you to change your belief that you were only an average writer. The challenge is, once we have a relatively stable sense of self, we find it difficult to change our perceptions. This may prevent us from having an accurate self-concept at times.

Another type of inaccurate perception we have of ourselves is that we may judge ourselves more critically in some instances than others may. For example, a recent college graduate may perceive herself as unmarketable because her final grade point average was lower than many others in her major. She doubts she will get the job she wants due to this. During her interview, the interviewer is impressed with her enthusiasm and sense of responsibility and offers her the job. In this example, she judged herself more harshly than the interviewer judged her.

As mentioned earlier in the chapter, the self-fulfilling prophecy may also prevent us from possessing an accurate self-concept. What if you majored in accounting and took a job at a large public accounting firm that required all employees to pass the CPA examination within the first year of employment? If you believe you will do poorly on the exam because you simply "don't do well on standardized tests of any kind," you may wind up behaving in ways that ensure the fulfillment of your prophecy. For example, you may talk yourself out of going to the review course you signed up to take, preparing for the class, or studying on your own. You rationalize to yourself, "Why bother if I won't do well on this type of test anyway?" If you employ any of these tactics, you are on the path to confirming your own prophecy of poor performance. Having this type of perception can create a barrier to developing an accurate self-concept.

A final barrier is the *self-serving bias*. This involves a tendency for taking personal credit for the positive outcomes for our actions, and directing the blame toward others

> **Self-serving bias**
> The tendency for us to interpret the things we do in the most positive way or deny personal responsibility for the negative things that happen to us.

for the negative outcomes. Thus, if you do well on an exam, it is because you studied. If you do poorly on the test, however, you may attribute the negative outcome to the difficulty of the test, to the instructor's poor teaching style, or to the teacher's unfair grading. In a 1982 study of job-seekers in Britain, Furnham found that individuals tend to take credit for their own abilities and skills when they are successful in securing a job, while they blame their lack of success in securing a job on factors that are beyond their control. This self-serving bias, or our tendency to judge ourselves less harshly than we judge others, may again cause us to have an inaccurate self-concept.

Overall, there are several barriers that may prevent us from having an accurate self-concept. Additionally, there may even be elements of our self-concept about which even we aren't aware at a given point in time. Many years ago, one of the authors had a student whose young child was killed by a drunk driver. She became a tireless advocate for stronger laws to help prevent drunk driving. In her work with Mothers Against Drunk Driving, she did a great deal of public speaking. On one occasion she said to the class, "If anyone had ever told me I would be speaking in public and involved with trying to change public policy, I would never have believed it. I have always viewed myself as just a mom." Keeping this information in mind is important as we discuss self-esteem and its influence on perception and communication.

Self-Esteem

Closely related to self-concept is *self-esteem*, the subjective evaluation of our worth. How we feel about ourselves, or the value we place on our abilities and behaviors, is our self-esteem. Whereas self-concept deals with our identity or a description of ourselves, our self-esteem gauges the value or extent to which we are happy or unhappy with the various dimensions of our self-concept. For example, when you feel really good about your ability as an actor, you have high self-esteem about acting. As you audition for various roles, you do so with confidence. When you communicate about your ability to act, you do so in a positive manner. On the other hand, if you have low self-esteem regarding your acting ability, you may shy away from auditions and communicate in a negative manner about your acting ability.

Self-esteem The subjective evaluation of our worth; how we feel about ourselves or the value we place on our abilities and behaviors.

Just as your self-concept is not always objective, neither is your self-esteem. For example, you may have low self-esteem because you do not have accurate information or feedback from others. You may be doing fine in your new job, but you may not be listening accurately to the feedback you receive from your supervisor or colleagues. Your misinterpretation of their messages may lead you to believe you are not good at what you do. On the other hand, even when some people aren't doing particularly well at something, they may ignore negative feedback they receive, and their self-esteem will remain intact despite the contradictory information. When a manager conducts an annual evaluation, an employee may perceive that he has been doing an outstanding job. If you were to ask the manager, she may view the employee as "unmotivated" because he is simply doing what is required based on his job description and "clocking out" at the end of the day. The employee will likely maintain the perception that he is great at what he does because he is completing the tasks that are required without taking into account the quality of his work performance. Overall, the set of perceptions we have about ourselves, our self-concept, and our self-esteem (i.e., the value we place on our abilities and behaviors) influence how we communicate with others. This, in turn, impacts the perceptions that others form of us. How we present ourselves and how we perceive others is the focus of the next section.

Self-Presentation

Have you ever behaved in a particular way to impress someone? Do you communicate differently with friends than you would with someone you are just meeting for the first time? If so, you are like most people. We tend to present ourselves differently based on the situation. *Self-presentation* influences how we want others to perceive us. Goffman (1959) spoke of the "face," which is the view you want others to have of you. We present ourselves differently as a situation changes, and we change our communication depending on our relationship with the other person. For example, you may present yourself one way as a student speaking with your professor and in another way as a student speaking with a classmate. In the first scenario, you may

Self-presentation
Presenting yourself to another as you would like to be perceived.

A manager and an employee could have an entirely different perception of job performance.

©Adam Gregor/Shutterstock.com

be polite and positive about the course, commenting to the professor on the relevance of a recent lecture to your future career goals. When speaking with a friend about the course, you may use slang and indicate you are taking the course simply because it fulfills a requirement for your major.

While we willingly present one view of our "self" to the world, we simultaneously hide aspects of our private self by masking certain behaviors (Goffman, 1959). For example, have you ever put on a brave face when you are actually nervous about something? Have you ever been upset about a breakup but smiled and minimized the hurt you felt inside? If so, you have worn a mask to conceal how you truly feel about that part of your "self."

© StockLite/Shutterstock.com

Self-presentation may influence how we present ourselves in personal situations versus professional ones. According to Guadagno, Okdie, and Kruse (2012), "People tend to present and sometimes exaggerate or fabricate their characteristics in an attempt to create their desired impression" (p. 642). In today's world, the notion of self-presentation naturally brings up how individuals present themselves online. If you have ever "met" anyone online, you may have presented yourself in a particular way. In a survey of 80 individuals who had submitted online profiles to a variety of online dating websites, Toma, Hancock, and Ellison (2007) found 81% of those surveyed lied about one or more of their physical attributes including their height, weight, or age. Similarly, individuals who are shy may be more confident when communicating online and present themselves in a much more self-assured manner because the interaction is not face-to-face. In fact, some of our students reported feeling more confident communicating online because they felt they were not being judged on how they look, dress, or sound. Presenting yourself online may not reveal your true self to another and others may wonder if the self you have revealed is accurate.

Shy individuals may be more confident and self-assured when communicating online.

Is it possible to improve our sense of "self?" Absolutely! Becoming aware of who we are and who we would like to become may help us enhance our self-concept and self-esteem. Through careful reflection, we may be able to focus on the areas of our "self" that we would like to strengthen. Since our sense of self evolves and is always "in process," we have the ability to find ways in which we may improve. This can be accomplished a number of ways: through the courses we take, the relationships we nurture, or the help we seek from professionals.

Thus far, we have focused on perceiving the self. In the next section, we discuss how we perceive others. Our perceptions of others have an impact on how we interpret their communication and how we communicate with them.

PERCEIVING OTHERS

How We Perceive Others

At the beginning of the chapter, we talked about some of the factors that influence our perceptions such as gender, culture, age, and our past experiences. It is important to keep these in mind as we discuss how we perceive others.

Not only do the words that others say cause you to form impressions, but a person's nonverbal communication may also cause you to perceive that individual in a particular way. Seiter, Weger, Kinzer, and Jensen (2009) studied "whether a debater's background nonverbal behavior affected audience perceptions of her and her opponent's likeability" (p. 1). Four versions of a televised debate were created with the nonspeaking opponent shown on a sub-screen while listening to the speaker shown on the main screen. In one version, the nonspeaking opponent had a "neutral expression." In another, the nonspeaking opponent showed "occasional disagreement." In the third version, the nonspeaking opponent showed almost "constant disagreement" while in the fourth version, both "agreement and disagreement" were displayed by the nonspeaking opponent.

After viewing the debates, the participants rated the debaters' likeability. Analysis indicated that the "background behavior had no effect on perceptions of the speaking debater's likeability ratings. This suggests that, when judging a candidate's likeability, audiences rely on the candidate's own behavior, perhaps not trusting the opinion of the nonspeaking opponent, who may be seen as biased. On the other hand, such behavior was associated with lower likeability ratings for the debater who was communicating nonverbally" (Seiter et al., 2009, pp. 7–8).

Our perception shapes the impressions, or mental images, we form of others. Have you ever met a person for the first time and after only a few minutes of speaking with that individual thought to yourself, "What a friendly person?" You may also have met someone for the first time and not been impressed at all. Perhaps you've heard the phrase, "You never get a second chance to make a first impression." If so, you begin to realize the importance of first impressions. While first impressions are powerful, we need to keep an open mind and build on our initial perceptions in order to develop an accurate perception of that person.

When we perceive someone to be similar to us, we may decide to develop and maintain a relationship with that person (Wright, 2004). In Chapter 6 we explore the importance of similarity when initiating and developing relationships with others. If you start a new job and meet a colleague at employee orientation who attended the same college and shares a passion for the same professional baseball team, your apparent similarity with this person may cause you to perceive that you both view things in the same way.

Earlier in the chapter we discussed the impact of stereotyping. At times, we form impressions of others based on the stereotypes we hold. Our stereotypes may be positive or negative; however, we always need to be mindful of the fact that just because someone belongs to a certain group, it does not mean that person possesses all of the qualities you have come to expect about that group or that your stereotypes are accurate. Unfortunately, many of us hold on to our first impressions even when we receive information that contradicts those impressions. If you believe someone is insincere, you may maintain that impression even in the face of contrary evidence. Certainly, we need to keep an open mind about others and allow ourselves to move beyond first impressions when we receive new information that helps us obtain more accurate perceptions of others.

Another problem with our perceptions of others is that we may focus on the negative as opposed to the positive. Clearly, if the negative aspects overshadow the positive ones, we have a right to take that into consideration. However, if the individual has several positive qualities and we focus exclusively on one negative aspect, this distorts our perception of that person and influences our relationship.

Finally, when we are forming our impressions of others, we need to keep in mind that not everyone acts or thinks like us. Often, we assume that others hold similar beliefs, values, and attitudes. Have you ever pulled a prank on someone that you thought was funny, but the person became upset by your actions? While you may view your prank as humorous, the person pranked may consider it childish. The differing perceptions of your behavior may negatively impact your interaction with one another.

Improving How We Perceive Others

People may not always form accurate perceptions of others. How can we avoid the potential pitfalls of impression formation and improve our perceptions of others?

First, we need to keep an open mind. Although we may form first impressions, we need to make sure we continue to gather more information and be willing to modify our impressions. Being open to receiving new information about the other person, even if it goes against our first impression, is important.

Empathy
The ability to understand how someone else is feeling or thinking.

Another way to improve how we perceive others is through empathy. *Empathy* is the ability to understand how someone else is feeling or thinking. Seeing something from another person's perspective can help us understand what that individual is experiencing and how it may impact their communication. For example, if a parent and a teenager have a disagreement about a curfew, if they each stop for a minute and consider the perspective of the other, they may better understand one another's concerns and this may help to reduce the potential for conflict. Perhaps the parent could ask herself, "How would I feel if I were a 16-year-old?" in an attempt to see things from the teen's point of view. The teenager could reflect, "I guess if I was the parent, I would probably be nervous that something bad was going to happen to my child." The process of perspective-taking enhances our ability to see things from the other person's point of view and enables us to communicate more effectively.

Finally, as we mentioned earlier in the chapter, it is wise to check your perceptions. This will help ensure that the way in which you have interpreted something is actually how the other person intended to convey it. The same strategies you use to make sure your perceptions of situations are correct can be used to gain more accurate perceptions of others. Overall, increasing the accuracy of our perceptions helps reduce the potential for miscommunication. This approach can help us gain clarification, withhold judgment, and limit defensiveness.

CHAPTER SUMMARY

In this chapter, we have defined perception and examined its process. As indicated in the chapter, there are various elements including our age, gender, culture, and mood that influence our perceptions. Naturally, the process we go through as we select, organize, and interpret what our senses take in and the various elements that influence our perceptions have a strong impact on how we communicate with others and they communicate with us.

We also defined self-concept as the perceptions we have of ourselves and discussed how the self-concept develops through our communication with significant others including parents or caregivers, teachers, peers, colleagues, and supervisors. We also outlined some of the barriers that prevent us from having an accurate sense of self. Furthermore, we defined self-esteem and explained the impact this also has on communication. Finally, we highlighted the relevance of our perceptions of others in the communication process. Overall, the perceptions we have of ourselves and others and their perceptions of us influence our communication with one another. Understanding the important role of perception in the communication process will enable us communicate more effectively.

KEY WORDS

Empathy The ability to understand how someone else is feeling or thinking.

Interpretation The third phase of the perception process where we attach meaning to what we have selected and organized.

Organization The second phase of the perception process, which involves categorizing what we have received.

Perception Process by which we select, organize, and interpret stimuli to make sense of our world.

Perception checking The process whereby we validate the accuracy of our perceptions.

Perception process A three-step process that includes selection, where we focus our attention on something and ignore other elements in the environment; organization, where we form what we have received into meaningful patterns; and interpretation, where we attach meaning to what we have selected and organized.

Reflected appraisal Development of our sense of self based on how we believe others view or see us.

Selection The first part of the perception process where we focus our attention on something within our environment.

Self-concept A set of perceptions we have about ourselves.

Self-esteem The subjective evaluation of our worth; how we feel about ourselves or the value we place on our abilities and behaviors.

Self-fulfilling prophecy The idea that when we believe something is true, it may become true. In other words, when we expect a particular outcome, either positive or negative, it is more likely that outcome will occur.

Self-presentation Presenting yourself to another as you would like to be perceived.

Self-serving bias The tendency for us to interpret the things we do in the most positive way or deny personal responsibility for the negative things that happen to us.

Stereotypes Generalizations we hold about a group or a category of people.

REFERENCES

Brann, M., & Himes, K. L. (2010). Perceived credibility of male versus female television newscasters. *Communication Research Reports, 27*(3), 243–252.

Furnham, A. (1982). Explanations for unemployment in Britain. *Journal of European Social Psychology, 12,* 335–352.

Goffman, E. (1959). *The presentation of self in everyday life.* Garden City, NY: Doubleday/Anchor Books.

Guadagno, R. E., Okdie, B. M., & Kruse, S. A. (2012). Dating deception: Gender, online dating, and exaggerated self-presentation. *Computers in Human Behavior, 28,* 642–647.

Seiter, J. S., Weger, Jr., H., Kinzer, H. J., & Jensen, A. S. (2009). Impression management in televised debates: The effect of background nonverbal behavior on audience perceptions of debaters' likeability. *Communication Research Reports, 26*(1), 1–10.

Sullivan, H. S. (1953). *The interpersonal theory of psychiatry.* New York: Norton.

Toma, C., Hancock, J., & Ellison, N. (2007). *Separating fact from fiction: An examination of deceptive self-presentation in online dating profiles.* Paper presented at the annual meeting of the International Communication Association.

Wood, J. T. (2007). *Gendered lives: Communication, gender, and culture* (7th ed.). Belmont, CA: Thomson Wadsworth.

Wright, K. B. (2004). On-line relational maintenance strategies and perceptions of partners within exclusively Internet-based and primarily Internet-based relationships. *Communication Studies, 55,* 418–432.

CHAPTER 3

Understanding Verbal Communication: Choosing Your Words Wisely

Chapter Objectives

After reading this chapter, you should be able to:
- Define verbal communication
- Describe the functions of verbal communication
- Explain the problems with verbal communication
- Identify ways to improve your verbal communication
- Understand the importance of message formation

PERSONAL: You have been dating the same person for about six months. You decide that you are in love with your partner and want to share your feelings. You plan a special night, complete with all your date's favorite activities and foods. At the end of the date, you decide the moment is right and confess your feelings. During a quiet moment, you look at your partner and, in a hushed tone, you say, "I love you." Your partner looks at you and smiles. Instead of saying "I love you too!" your partner pauses. Did I say the wrong thing?

PROFESSIONAL: You have been assigned to work with a group at your company to create a new solution for an ongoing problem. You and your coworkers, a team of seven people, begin brainstorming. Following the principles of effective brainstorming, the group writes everything on a dry-erase board; all ideas are considered and nothing is ruled out. As you're brainstorming, you and your team hit a mental roadblock and decide to take a short break. During the break, you are ruminating on a possible idea. Finally, after the break, the team comes up with a new idea that seems innovative and appropriate to solve the problem. As the group becomes increasingly excited about the new idea, your boss walks in, sees the solution on the whiteboard, and considers the idea. Finally, your boss says, "This is a unique approach, team." What did your boss' comment *really* mean?

PUBLIC: It is election season, and you decide to attend a local debate in your community. You are an undecided voter and intend to gather as much information as possible from the candidates and their speeches. You sit near the front of the room and take notes while listening so you can refer back to them later. As you're listening to the candidates, you hear one of them describe a college education as "increasingly less important. Instead, what our young people need is real-world experiences. A classroom just does not benefit them." As a college graduate, you begin to wonder if the candidate even considered that there might be college students in the audience listening to his message. How risky is the candidate's speech?

CHAPTER OVERVIEW

What images or perceptions come to mind when you hear or read the following words: *Republican/Democrat, Buddhist, pro-choice, gay, freak, lawyer, teacher, mother*? While reading this list, you probably associated a variety of meanings with these terms, both positive and negative. Perhaps you identify with one of the above words and would use it as a personal description. Perhaps you have used one of the above words to describe someone or something in your life. Our language system is a powerful tool. When we communicate orally, we call it *verbal communication*. Any time we interact—be it face-to-face, via email or text message, or by phone—we are engaging in verbal communication. Toomey (1999) described words as powerful, with the ability to inform and comfort, to stimulate and inspire. They can also do harm; words can hurt our spirit, harm our self-esteem, and damage our confidence.

VERBAL COMMUNICATION DEFINED

➤ **Verbal communication**
The meaning that is created with words, also referred to as language.

In order to understand *verbal communication*—the meaning that is created with the use of words—we have to consider not only the words we use and individual assessments or perceptions we have of others, but we also need to consider with whom we are interacting. What you say and to whom you say it are important factors in determining how to compose a message. It is safe to say that you have experienced situations in which you did not know what to say, but you also may not have wanted to interact with the person. Perhaps you have even experienced a situation in which you did not know what to say due to the setting of the communication. Sometimes, it is simply easier to communicate with some people than it is with others. For example, you may have an easier time communicating ideas to a friend as opposed to sharing ideas in a small group setting. The Willingness to Communicate Scale (WTC; McCroskey, 1992; McCroskey & Richmond, 1987) was developed to assess personal orientations toward communication. It evaluates how likely you are to initiate conversations and interact across a variety of situations. This can be particularly difficult because when we initiate conversations, especially those with individuals with whom we have never met or interacted, we can only guess at how others might respond to our decision to start a conversation. To calculate your own "willingness to communicate," complete the assessment found in Figure 3.1.

Your answers to the Willingness to Communicate Scale reflect your preferences for communicating with different types of receivers in a variety of communication contexts. Some of us prefer or are more willing to communicate with those close to us in an interpersonal relationship, whereas others of us are more comfortable interacting with strangers. As you reflect on your own preferences for verbal communication, consider how your individual willingness to communicate, your language preferences, and contextual or situational differences work together to inform your choices. As we discussed in Chapter 1, effective verbal communication is a choice. It is something that can be improved upon when we consider all of the factors involved in becoming an effective and engaged communicator.

When answering the questions, presume you have free choice in the matter and indicate the percentage of times you would choose to communicate in each type of situation. Indicate in the space to the left of each item what percent of the time you would choose to communicate (0 = Never to 100 = Always).

_____ 1. Talk with a service station attendant.
_____ 2. Talk with a physician.
_____ 3. Present a talk to a group of strangers.
_____ 4. Talk with an acquaintance while standing in line.
_____ 5. Talk with a salesperson in a store.
_____ 6. Talk in a large meeting of friends.
_____ 7. Talk with a police officer.
_____ 8. Talk in a small group of strangers.
_____ 9. Talk with a friend while standing in line.
_____ 10. Talk with a waiter/waitress in a restaurant.

_____ 11. Talk in a large meeting of acquaintances.
_____ 12. Talk with a stranger while standing in line.
_____ 13. Talk with a secretary.
_____ 14. Present a talk to a group of friends.
_____ 15. Talk in a small group of acquaintances.
_____ 16. Talk with a garbage collector.
_____ 17. Talk in a large meeting of strangers.
_____ 18. Talk with a spouse (or girl/boyfriend).
_____ 19. Talk in a small group of friends.
_____ 20. Present a talk to a group of acquaintances.

To determine your score, use the following scoring formulas.

Scoring:
Context subscores
Group Discussion: Add scores for items 8, 15, and 19; then divide by 3.
Meetings: Add scores for items 6, 11, and 17; then divide by 3.
Interpersonal: Add scores for items 4, 9, and 12; then divide by 3.
Public Speaking: Add scores for items 3, 14, and 20; then divide by 3.

Receiver-type subscores
Stranger: Add scores for items 3, 8, 12, and 17; then divide by 4.
Acquaintance: Add scores for items 4, 11, 15, and 20; then divide by 4.
Friend: Add scores for items 6, 9, 14, and 19; then divide by 4.
To determine your total WTC score, add the subscores for stranger, acquaintance, and friend. Then divide by 3. All scores, total scores and subscores, will fall in the range of 0 to 100.

Norms for WTC scores:
Group Discussion >89 High WTC, <57 Low WTC
Meetings >80 High WTC, <39 Low WTC
Interpersonal Conversations >94 High WTC, <64 Low WTC
Public Speaking >78 High WTC, <33 Low WTC
Stranger >63 High WTC, <18 Low WTC
Acquaintance >92 High WTC, <57 Low WTC
Friend >99 High WTC, <71 Low WTC
Total WTC >82 High Overall WTC, <52 Low Overall WTC

FIGURE 3.1

McCroskey's (1992) and McCroskey & Richmond (1987) Willingness to Communicate Scale. Source: Reliability and Validity of the Willingness to Communicate Scale by James C. McCroskey, from *Communication Quarterly, Volume 40, Issue No 1, Winter 1992.* Copyright © 1992 Routledge. Reprinted by permission of Taylor & Francis Ltd, http://www.tandfonline.com.

THE NATURE OF LANGUAGE

Cher's 1989 hit song "If I Could Turn Back Time" describes an all-too-common situation. In the song, Cher sings about her desire to take back what she has said. However, as we learned in Chapter 1, communication cannot be undone. Once words are spoken, they are open to interpretation by both the intended receiver and anyone who happens to observe the interaction. Cher's song uses the analogy of comparing words to weapons, and she points to the power of words and their potential to hurt others and as something that can't easily be forgiven. It is important to note that words themselves and the symbols that create words have little value. People and context give words meaning. Stated another way, meaning is in people, not in words. When Cher describes language as being hurtful, it is because she selected words that had significant meaning for the receiver, and the words were perceived to be harmful or hurtful. Recall the list of words at the beginning of the chapter. Given your individual assessment of each of the words, some of them may have seemed negative, others seemed positive, and you may have evaluated others as having little to no value. As we discuss the process of attaching meaning to words based on indivduals' perception and the setting or context in which an interaction takes place, it is important to consider several key principles about the nature of language.

Language Is a Symbol System

> **Symbols**
> Abstract ideas or concepts that represent something and can be both verbal and nonverbal.

Symbols are defined as abstract words, ideas, or concepts that represent conceptual ideas; they represent something and can be both verbal and nonverbal. Language is made of symbols that have unique meaning. Symbols refer to agreed-upon reference points. For example, the word *cat* has been assigned as a reference to a four-legged animal that has whiskers and makes meowing and purring sounds. Any time we hear someone say the word *cat*, however, each individual has a unique mental image that is referenced. You may think of Garfield, the cartoon cat that you watched on television, the cat you had as a small child, or you may recall your cousin's cat that scratched you when you attempted to pet it.

Language Is Culturally Determined

> **Culture**
> Learned system—that is, something that you acquire from others—of beliefs, values, and knowledge.

Meaning is culturally bound. The meaning of a symbol is not universal; rather, the referent associated with the meaning of a symbol is connected to one's culture. *Culture* is a learned system of knowing; it is acquired from others. An example of the meaning in our language system being culturally bound is the word *toboggan*. Someone from Kentucky or Ohio might use the word *toboggan* to refer to a knit hat worn in the winter months. To someone else, *toboggan* refers to a long sled. You could feel confused about what the receiver means in his or her message. If you traveled to England, for example, and someone said you needed a "dummy" to soothe your baby, you may be unclear about what the person means. The word *dummy* in British English refers to the United States' concept of a pacifier for a baby. The meaning you assign to this word is based on your cultural understanding of the word's referent.

Language Has Both Denotative and Connotative Meaning

Denotative meaning refers to the dictionary definition or the literal meaning of the word. It is the meaning that is widely agreed upon by members of a society. Conversely, *connotative meaning* is much more individualized and reflects the unique personal views of speaker or source. For example, the denotative meaning of the word *home* is "a house, apartment, or other shelter that is the usual residence of a person, family or household" (*www.dictionary.com*). However, the connotative meaning an individual might associate with the word *home* could be negative. For example, if you are fighting with your roommates or family members, hearing the phrase "home" could trigger feelings of anger or sadness; thus, when using the word *home* you actually consider it to be an establishment that makes you feel unhappy.

➤ **Denotative meaning**
Dictionary definition of a word or the literal meaning of a word.

➤ **Connotative meaning**
Individualized meaning that reflects unique personal views of the user of the language.

Language Constantly Evolves

It is important to note that our language changes in response to stimuli in our world. As we introduce the new concepts through methods such as technological innovations, medical breakthroughs, passage of laws, or other developments in our society, we add new words to our vocabulary. We are constantly adding new symbols to our vocabulary because the world around us changes. According to 2012 article in the *Wisconsin Gazette*, the Global Language Monitor revealed the most commonly used phrases in English-speaking countries for that year ("Top Words"). To qualify for the list, at least 25,000 citations must be cited in print or Web sources. The list included:

1. Gangnam style
2. Global warming/climate change
3. Fiscal cliff
4. The deficit
5. God particle
6. Rogue nukes
7. Near-Earth asteroid
8. Binders full of women
9. Arab Spring
10. Solar max

Our language system and verbal communication are dynamic. The words we use change in response to stimuli in our world. Popular language changes with each decade, technology innovation, and social movement. The language we use is directly connected to the times in which we live.

THE FUNCTIONS OF LANGUAGE

Simply stated, verbal communication has a purpose in our lives; it works for us, and it performs a role in our daily interactions. It enables us to express our own thoughts, feelings, attitudes, and beliefs, and it also helps us learn more about others as we gather information about a host of topics. There are several general functions of our language system: the cognitive function, group identity function, and social reality function (Figure 3.2). Each of these has a place in your personal, professional, and public lives. The *cognitive function* describes using language to gather information, to reason, and to make sense of the world. You experience countless examples of the cognitive function in your daily interactions with others. Examples of this include, on a first date, you and your partner exchange stories about childhood; during a performance review with your boss, you ask a question about the future of the company; or while giving an oral presentation, you provide statistics relevant to your topic.

Cognitive function
Using language to gather information, to reason, and to make sense of the world.

The *group identity function* focuses on the use of language as a signal of membership or solidarity in a group. Often, individuals outside the group do not understand the unique meanings associated with the words used. Perhaps your family refers to you by a nickname that your friends don't know. As you begin your career, you may discover that there is a unique language spoken in your chosen field of work. For example, while attending a school board meeting, you may discover that attendees use language such as QEP (quality enhancement plan) that those who are new to the meeting may not fully understand.

Group identity function
Using language as a signal of membership in a group or a sign of solidarity with a collection of individuals. Often, individuals outside the group do not understand the meaning in the verbal communication.

Finally, the *social reality function* focuses on how language is used to reflect the reality of the world around us. Language changes and responds to the world in which we live. For example, you could assign a nickname to a romantic couple (e.g., "Brangelina" describes Brad Pitt and Angelina Jolie); during a meeting at work, you learn of budget cuts and begin to call the person making the budget cuts the "Grim Reaper;" or while describing the most up-to-date technology, you call the device by the name given to it by its creators.

Social reality function
Using language to create our reality of the world around us. Language changes and responds to the world in which we live.

FIGURE 3.2

The functions of
language.

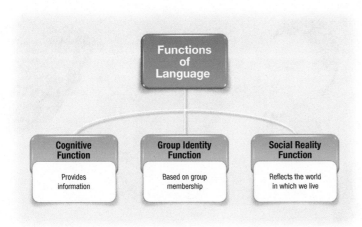

As you can see from these examples, our language system provide us with information or knowledge, showcases our memberships and alliances with groups of people, and responds to the unique world in which we live. These three basic functions, and there are likely many more you could name, provide important information for our lives.

THE IMPORTANCE OF LANGUAGE

Not only does language serve a variety of functions, but it also has unique benefits for our personal, professional, and public lives. In the following sections, we discuss the importance of language in these interactions.

In Our Personal Lives

One of the most important qualities of our language is its unique ability to help build relationships. We can use verbal communication to learn more about a person and then use that acquired information as a guide to help us determine if we want to build a relationship with that individual. For example, while on a first date you and your partner begin discussing your respective families. Your date indicates that while growing up, if anyone in the family broke a rule, the family would gather and have "family talks." These talks included everybody discussing their feelings and establishing rules for future interactions. Upon hearing this story, you immediately become excited because your family used a similar discipline technique, and you begin to share your story. This story-sharing is called *self-disclosure* and refers to the sharing of personal information with others in an attempt to build or maintain a relationship. During the self-disclosure process, individuals typically share

Self-disclosure
The sharing of personal information with others in an attempt to build or maintain a relationship.

How much information about yourself do you disclose to someone you've recently met?

© AntonioDiaz/Shutterstock.com

meaningful information verbally (Derlega & Chaikin, 1977). We assign value, whether positive or negative, to self-disclosures. When we engage in self-disclosure, we experience positive outcomes such as increased physical health (Greenberg & Stone, 1992) and self-esteem (Afifi & Caughlin, 2006), as well as gaining insight about information (Kelly, Klusas, von Weiss, & Kenny, 2001). Based on our assessment of the self-disclosure, we then make decisions regarding relational development. These assessments are highly individualized. What one person regards as an "awkward disclosure," another person may deem as important information. Self disclosure is discussed in further detail in Chapter 6.

In Our Professional Lives

Not only do we experience benefits to build and sustain our interpersonal relationships, but we also experience benefits in our professional lives. Johnson (n.d.) has outlined several benefits verbal communication has in professional communication, including promoting diversity, building teams, and increasing morale. Previously, we discussed the idea of communication being bound to a culture. If we use language effectively and understand the unique cultural distinctions in our language system, we create an open, inviting atmosphere where all voices are welcomed and incorporated. Another benefit of verbal communication is its ability to help us build better teams. Verbal communication can be used to create bonds among individuals. It works to strengthen relationships as well as to clarify tasks and gather information.

Another benefit of verbal communication is its potential to increase employee morale. Have you ever received a positive message from a boss? Perhaps while giving an oral presentation you received positive verbal feedback as a result of something you said? These rewards have a positive impact. They make you feel good and, as a result of this good feeling, you're probably going to feel like a valuable source of information.

In Our Public Lives

Considering our language in our public lives is especially important. Oftentimes when we engage in public communication, our audience has little knowledge of who we are as people. They do not know us, the real us, and what we hold to be important. Consider giving an oral presentation to a group of people who had limited information about you. Before you begin speaking, you are introduced by name and job title. The audience only receives information about your professional credentials. They do not, however, know other, more personal aspects of your life. If while giving your presentation you make a verbal misstep and alienate your audience, they may be less forgiving of your mistake than if you had presented your message to an audience of people who know you and understand who you are as a person.

If your audience knows you as a person, they will be more forgiving if you make a mistake when giving a presentation.

© Yuriy Rudyy/Shutterstock.com

As you can see, language is an important component of any interaction. Knapp, Stohl, and Reardon (1981) identified a key reason to focus on verbal communication. They argued, "Some interpersonal messages are reported to be remembered for a long time and to have a profound influence on a person's life" (p. 27). In thinking about your own life, you can probably recall several messages that had a profound influence on you. Perhaps you can recall the first time someone said, "I'm proud of you," "I love you," or "You're not attractive." Positive or negative, our choice of words matters and can leave a lasting impression. Not only are you likely able to recall influential messages, but you are probably also able to recall hardships, miscommunications, or conflicts you've experienced as a result of verbal communication.

THE CHALLENGES OF LANGUAGE

Our language system presents a number of challenges and considerations that we need to examine when creating the verbal message; that is, language is not a flawless set of symbols. In fact, a number of words or phrases we commonly use can create problems when used in certain contexts, talking with particular individuals, or addressing a given topic. More specifically, our language system is abstract, can communicate power and bias toward others, can be used to control the type of environment that develops while with others, and is affected by context and technology. As you read the next sections, consider how you may have experienced a situation with one of the challenges associated with our language.

Bias

> **Bias**
> Language that conveys stereotypes, insensitivity, or negativity toward a group of people or about a topic.

Our language system shapes our view of the world and influences our perceptions. Biased language comes in many forms. When we describe language as having *bias*, we refer to the potential for language to convey stereotypes, insensitivity, or negativity toward a group of people or about a topic. Table 3.1 contains descriptions of the different biases our language may convey, a verbal example of the bias, and an alternate verbal message that can convey the same meaning without showing bias.

The examples of bias in language in Table 3.1 are just four of the main ways in which our words can communicate intolerance or negativity about a group of people or ideas. This language, while not offensive to all, has become, in general, negatively valued in our culture. The words can potentially elicit a negative evaluation, conflict situation, or even relationship termination. However, by reframing our language—into what is frequently referred to as "politically correct" language—we can communicate more neutrally and potentially avoid miscommunications with individuals.

TABLE 3.1

Types of Bias in Language.

Type of Bias	Example	Corrected Verbal Communication
Stereotyping language – assumes an overgeneralization about a group of people.	"Even though she's a female, Mary exhibited outstanding leadership skills during the meeting."	"Mary exhibited outstanding leadership skills during the meeting."
Sexist language – does not account for both male and female experiences and instead communicates about ideas as inherently male or female	Fireman, policeman, mailman	Fire fighter, police officer, mail carrier
Ability language – focuses on the shortcomings of a person rather than emphasizing the person as a human.	Disabled man, handicapped woman, wheelchair-bound man	Person with a disability
Racist language – insensitive and derogatory language about a group of people.	Guido, Indian giver, Bible banger	Italian, person who takes back a gift, a religious person

Ethical versus Unethical Use of Language

Words are used in the creation of messages that have the potential to be ethical or unethical. Remember in Chapter 1 that we discussed ethical communication and that *ethical communication* stems from your ability to be honest and uses a set of standards to guide appropriate or positive behaviors. What one person perceives as being ethical may be perceived as unethical by another. Some use the law as a standard of ethical behavior; that is, if it is legal, then it is considered ethical. If it is illegal, then it is unethical. Others use religion to determine ethical and unethical behavior. When considering our verbal communication and ethics, there are several guidelines you can use as you form your messages (Figure 3.3).

One of our primary goals as communicators should be to share information that is truthful, honest, and representative of what we are currently experiencing. When constructing our verbal messages, we want to present information that is truthful. Additionally, we should always be forthcoming. That is, we should be prepared with answers and have the ability to provide an answer when needed. Next, we need to be consistent. We should use the same standards to guide our language choices across contexts and topics. Finally, we need to be clear. We need to select language that has a clear meaning to the receiver.

> **Stereotyping language**
> Language that assumes an overgeneralization about a group of people.

> **Sexist language**
> Language that does not account for both male and female experiences and instead communicates about ideas as inherently male or female.

> **Ability language**
> Language that focuses on the shortcomings of a person rather than emphasizing the person as a human.

> **Racist language**
> Insensitive and derogatory language about a group of people.

> **Ethical communication**
> Individual's ability to be honest and use a set of standards to guide appropriate or positive behaviors.

FIGURE 3.3

Guidelines for ethical communication.

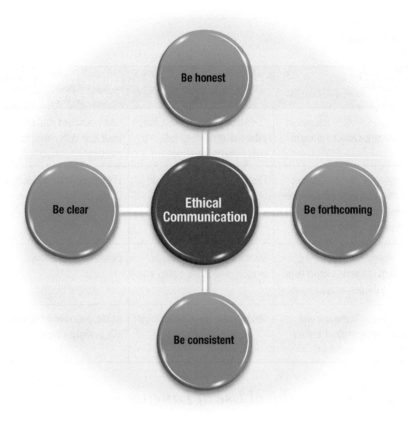

When we decide not to use the above behaviors, we could potentially create an environment where individuals feel mistrust, that we are not individuals with whom they can share thoughts. In response to those feelings, an individual may use a defensive style of message production as a result. Defensive communication (Gibb, 1961) can be a result of perceived differences in standards; that is, you and the individual you are interacting with perceive different expectations of appropriate behavior and communication. A *defensive message* is produced in response to some kind of threat (Gibb, 1961). The threat does not necessarily need to be explicit (e.g., "I am going to kick you out of the apartment if you don't tell me the truth"); rather, a threat may be more implicit in the message (e.g., "I need to know what is happening right now!"). When engaging in unethical verbal communication, you could prompt this reaction in an individual. An additional plausible reaction is *supportive communication*. This type of communication occurs when an individual feels as though he or she has little reason to have anxiety or concern about the communication being received. Supportive and defensive reactions come in many forms. For example, supportive communication can be an empathetic message. This would be a message that

Defensive message
Message that is produced in response to some kind of threat.

Supportive communication
Type of communication that occurs when an individual feels as though he or she has little reason to have anxiety or concern about the communication being received.

takes care of others' emotions or experiences. It can be conveyed in phrases such as "I understand your perspective" or "That situation would really upset me too." In these types of responses, the message is offering solidarity within the experience, communicating that he or she is sharing the experience. However, a defensive response could come in the form of a certainty message. *Certainty messages* do not account for others' perspectives or views; that is, they discount the others' stance on a topic. A certainty message would sound like "What you're saying is not correct" or "Your opinion doesn't even make sense." When these messages are produced, it seems as if the originator of the message only believes in his or her perspective. As you can see, the way in which we present information and how much information we present can create a number of reactions, both positive and negative. Using ethical guidelines for speaking can help get positive reactions and supportive communication from others.

> **Certainty messages**
> Certainty messages do not account for others' perspectives or views; they discount the others' stance on a topic.

Context

A second ethical consideration involves our word choices based on the communication context or setting. You need to consider "where" you are interacting with others in determining "what" to say. For example, where would you want to have a conversation when you're ending a romantic relationship? In a crowded restaurant? Via a text message? In a private setting such as a home? The setting in which you find yourself—be it at work, at home, or in front of an audience—provides useful information that should be considered when creating the verbal message.

Some strategies to potentially enhance the use of verbal communication in your personal life include the following:

- Creating verbal messages with the goal of building or strengthening relationships. Solicit disclosures from others, ask them questions, and share your own stories.
- Focusing on the dynamics of other people's relationships so you can incorporate that information into your verbal communication.
- Sending thoughtfully constructed messages when using mediated forms of interaction, such as a text message. The recipient cannot experience our nonverbal communication so messages sent electronically need extra care.
- Willingness to address sensitive topics. In comfortable, intimate locations, people tend to feel more relaxed and open to communicating about potentially sensitive issues.

In your professional life, your verbal communication style should include a clear, context-appropriate expression of what you think, how you feel, and what you would like from the communicative interaction. Remember, our workplace communication style is likely quite different than our interpersonal communication style. It is imperative that you not be demanding during these instances; rather, you should be sure to communicate that both people matter in the interaction. According to the Department of Education, Employment and Workplace Relations (n.d.), your communication should include:

- Expressing your own thoughts, feelings, and needs.
- Making reasonable requests of other people (while accepting their right to say "no").
- Standing up for your own rights.
- Saying "no" to requests from others at times, without feeling guilty.

Finally, when communicating during an oral presentation in a public setting, there are some key considerations to incorporate in the creation of your messages. In Chapters 11 and 12, you will learn additional details about crafting a message. Keep in mind:

- Determine if the topic is appropriate for discussion in a public setting.
- Take your audience into account. Try to gather as much information as possible about who is getting the information.
- Consider the size of the space in which you are presenting. Adjust your delivery to account for large or small spaces.

Technology

An 2012 article in *Entertainment Weekly* paid tribute to celebrities who passed away during the year. Each of the brief memorial statements was written by another celebrity. In one particularly interesting statement paying tribute to Dick Clark, Grammy award winning musical artist, Prince communicated how much Clark meant to him in the following statement:

> Dick Clark was always very generous and kind 2 us whatever the circumstance. He would call U personally and always speak with grace and candor that is rare in an industry that is rife with gamesmanship. That kinda class is sorely missed. Not sure why but Mr. Clark seemed 2 genuinely like me, and Eye liked him also. (2012, p. 43)

What is your reaction to the statement? You probably notice some abbreviations that you use in your own text messages, such as *U*, *2*, and *kinda*. However, in this format, an in memoriam statement written to convey meaning and emotional impact, the style is likely inappropriate.

Consider the following real-life example of a face-to-face interaction between two roommates:

Roommate 1: Hey, what are you up to?

How can the method of delivery change the perception of the message?

© rangizzz/Shutterstock.com

Roommate 2: Not much, you?

Roommate 1: Nothing. Want to get out of the house and see that movie?

Roommate 2: Totes! That will make Kelly (roommate 3) so jelly!

Roommate 1: (*pauses*) Um, sure?

Roommate 2: It totes will! Kelly has been asking me to see it with her so the two of us going without her will make her mad.

Roommate 1: Ohhhhhh, yes, she will be jealous.

Perhaps you have experienced a similar situation in which your verbal communication style used when interacting with others via technology, such as abbreviations when texting, carries over to your offline or face-to-face interactions. What if the above example had occurred via text or email? In Chapter 14, we discuss the impact of using mediated channels to exchange messages. The example of the conversation between two roommates seems appropriate in an online format but feels out of place in the face-to-face context. That is, some messages or phrasing are more appropriate or suited to mediated formats. In addition, you should consider the appropriateness of using mediated channels instead of an in-person conversation when discussing specific topics. Consider the following verbal messages and determine if they should be said via a mediated channel such as text messaging or if face-to-face communication is more effective.

- "We need to talk."
- "I love you."

- "Let's have pizza for dinner."
- "I'd like to offer you a promotion."
- "How about we go to the late movie tonight?"

As you can see from the above examples, sending some messages via text or email are appropriate. However, due to our limited access to tone of voice, rate of speech, or facial expressions, it is often easy to misinterpret the meaning sent via a text or email message.

Regional Differences

As we travel through the United States and internationally, we notice differences in language usage. When you go to the grocery store and need something to hold your groceries, do you use a cart or a buggy? Do you drink a pop, a soda, or a Coke? These examples represent regional differences in language usage. They also represent differences in *dialect*. Regardless of what you choose to put your groceries in (cart or buggy) and whatever you decide to drink (pop, soda, or Coke), you are using language that is specific to a region.

Have you ever thought that someone "talked funny" when you traveled to a new place or watched a movie that was set in a particular region? Maybe you have identified distinctions in how someone from Massachusetts, Georgia, or Minnesota speaks and thought they did not sound like you. This is due to our individual accents. In fact, we all have an accent. An *accent* refers to how we pronounce words. Accents differ by region and country and can impact how we perceive someone. In fact, you might hold perceptions about certain accents. For example, individuals with a Southern accent might be perceived as friendly. Individuals with an East Coast accent, such as a New Yorker, may be perceived as rude because of a more abrupt communication style. Collectively, accents are a common occurrence and inform our perceptions of others, be it positively or negatively. Verbal communication clearly has a large role in our lives and is something to which we need to give attention. With its potentially different uses, spending time carefully creating messages is an important component in developing competent communication.

MESSAGE FORMATION AND DESIGN

One idea to consider when thinking about your verbal communication is how the message is put together. Scholars call this idea *message formation*. When we focus on how things are said, that is, how the verbal component should be created, we can produce effective messages. One of the first ways we can work to produce effective

> **Dialect**
> Distinctive vocabulary or pronunciation typically associated with geographical regions.

> **Accent**
> Way in which we pronounce words.

> **Message formation**
> Way in which a message is put together.

If you have something important to discuss with your partner, you should select a comfortable location where you both feel relaxed.

© zstock/Shutterstock.com

messages is by considering the content (what the message is about), the context (the situation), and the relationship (the connection between the sender and receiver). What kinds of verbal communication would you create if you experienced the following examples?

- You need to break up with your romantic partner of six years. You feel as though the situation has gone from good, to poor, to bad. You constantly fight about money and the division of labor in the house. Your partner, while someone who does not enjoy fighting, does seem fairly happy in the relationship and does not want to break up. You, however, feel it is best to end things for your own personal sanity. One possible solution to this scenario is to select an effective context or location to talk with your partner. You would want to pick a comfortable location where you and your partner feel relaxed, such as the living room. When communicating, it is best to use "I feel" messages. For example, you may say, "I feel stressed when I have to do most of the chores." By doing this, you avoid blaming the partner. Saying "You do not help with the house," while true, could put a partner on the defensive and use language that justifies actions.

- Your boss has assigned you to lead a group of people on a special project. The company has lost money in the past on special projects but your boss thinks the current project is a revenue-making endeavor and believes in your ability to lead. You know, however, that if the project fails, you will experience serious consequences, such as a pay cut, demotion, or even termination. You would prefer not to lead the project and want to tell your boss your wishes but are nervous to approach the topic. A possible solution to this problem is to first arrange a meeting with your boss. This could be done by email or face-to-face, but you should communicate a desire to talk about the project and serve as the leader. You may even suggest that you and your boss get a coffee or lunch while talking. This makes the context seem more informal and could make you feel more comfortable approaching the topic. At the start of the meeting, you should use messages that showcase your appreciation for being asked to serve as the leader and your boss' perceptions of your ability. For example, you could say, "Thank you for the opportunity to serve as the leader of such an important project. Having a boss that believes in my abilities is very important." After that, you could address your fears by using "I feel" statements.

- You have been asked to act as the master of ceremonies during a "roast" that honors your father. Attending the roast are your father's professional contacts as well as a majority of your family members. You want to write jokes about your father but because of the different types of people in the audience you are unsure about which topics to address.

    You could start by gathering information from those who will be attending the event. You could ask for the anecdotes or special stories or information they would like to hear while attending the event. If possible, you could visit the venue in which you will be speaking. By knowing what others will want to listen to and feeling comfortable in the venue, you will likely feel more at ease with the assigned task.

Another technique used to understand how messages should be created is verbal modeling. Listening to how others speak, and then consciously using the same words or phrases they use, is called *verbal modeling*. By doing this modeling behavior, you are building rapport with that person and cultivating a positive relationship. One theory communication scholars utilize to understand changes in verbal communication is the ***Communication Accommodation Theory*** (Giles, Coupland, & Coupland, 1991; Giles & Ogay, 2007; Giles & Smith, 1979). In general, the theory argues that we change our verbal communication during the course of an interaction. This idea is labeled *accommodation* and is a result of perceptions you have of the people with whom you're interacting. Below are the theory's basic principles (Giles & Ogay, 2007).

- Communication is influenced by several factors, including the immediate situation, the individual's orientations toward the situation, and past sociohistorical contexts; that is, events that have occurred in the past directly impact current situations.

> **Verbal modeling**
> Listening to how others speak, and then consciously using the same words or phrases they use.

> **Communication Accommodation Theory** Theory that argues we change our verbal communication during the course of an interaction based on our perceptions of the interaction and with whom we are speaking.

- Communication is also a way to share thoughts, feelings, emotions, and group memberships. For example, when one of this book's authors started working at her college, she noticed her coworkers had a special language of sorts. Everything was abbreviated. Each of the college campuses had an abbreviation (e.g., SCC, PRC, and CPC) and committees each had abbreviations too (e.g., COAT, CAB, and GEO). When she visited her family for the holidays, having worked at her college for only 3 months, she used the abbreviations as a signal of accommodation to speaking like her coworkers and showing her membership as part of the college's faculty.
- People have expectations for accommodation. These expectations are based on social and societal norms and range from nonaccommodation to overaccommodation.
- Individuals use two types of accommodation: convergence and divergence. To *converge* means that individuals become more similar in their verbal choices and to *diverge* means that individuals become increasingly different in their verbal choices.

Converge
When individuals become more similar in their verbal choices.

Diverge
When individuals become increasingly different in their verbal choices.

Ultimately, message formation is a skill. Creating messages is something that we can improve upon over time. Similar to ideas presented in Chapter 1 that dealt with achieving communication competence, creating appropriate verbal communication is a skill that can be strengthened if you are motivated to assess each situation and consciously work to improve it. While a number of strategies and solutions are possible, the website *www.littlethingsmatter.com*, designed to improve different areas of your life, lists the following behaviors as ways to improve verbal communication (Smith, 2010).

1. *Be friendly.* We keep company with individuals who are pleasant and communicate in positive ways. Individuals who use a warm tone, smile, and positive words are people we want to be around.

2. *Think before you speak.* Have you ever interacted with someone who made you think, "He/she should really think before speaking!" Perhaps you have even thought to yourself, "I really should not have said that; if only I'd have thought about what I was going to say *before* saying it." Sometimes we find ourselves saying whatever comes to our minds without first thinking about how best to communicate. This can end in negative conversational outcomes and poor personal perceptions.

3. *Be clear.* In the chapter, we discussed the multiple meanings, content and relational, communication holds. Because our communication has so much value, it is important to think about what we are going to say as well as to spend time carefully assessing the most efficient means to communicate. Efficient communication has a clear meaning. The receiver

is able to decode what is being sent and does not have to ask him- or herself what is being said.

➤ Conversational narcissism
Extreme self-focus in a conversation in which an individual does not allow the other person in the interaction an opportunity to speak.

4. *Don't talk too much.* Have you ever interacted with someone who talked the entire time and barely let you speak? This can be very frustrating. Communication scholars have labeled this behavior *conversational narcissism* (Vangelisti, Knapp, & Daly, 1990), or extreme self-focus in a conversation.

5. *Be authentic.* Not only do we like surrounding ourselves with pleasant people, but we also enjoy sharing our time with individuals who are genuine in their communication behaviors. To be genuine means that we can be real and communicate in a way that is from the heart.

6. *Practice humility.* To have humility means that you have a modest view of your own importance. Have you ever interacted with someone who made him- or herself sound overly important or made you think that he or she was acting "too big for their britches?" We like sharing our time with someone who respects others and presents him- or herself in a genuine matter.

7. *Speak with confidence.* You needn't sacrifice self-confidence to practice humility. To be confident means you are self-assured, comfortable, and appreciate your own abilities. You can speak confidently by choosing and adjusting the words, vocal tones, body language, and eye contact you use.

8. *Focus on your body language.* Not only do our words matter, but our body language also serves as an indicator of how the other person should interpret those words. In paying attention to our body language, we are helping clarify the meaning and tone of our messages and making the receiver's job easier.

9. *Be concise.* Have you ever interacted with someone who just cannot get to the point? Perhaps you have felt frustrated while listening to someone ramble? We want to avoid these behaviors. When planning your words, ask yourself, "How can I say what needs to be said using the fewest number of words possible while still being courteous and respectful?"

10. *Listen first.* By listening before speaking, we can be sure to incorporate language the other person is using, ask follow-up questions, and avoid interrupting the other person.

11. *Check yourself.* While communicating with others, perform a brief, mental check-in concerning your behaviors. Ask yourself, "Am I using language that others would find offensive? Am I asking the other person questions? Am I contributing positively to the conversation?"

CHAPTER SUMMARY

Overall, your verbal communication should be something that you consider when crafting your message and preparing for an interaction. Our verbal communication is not only something that is important because of the information it provides for us, but also for the possible outcomes associated with our language, such as relationship development, professional gain, or the creation of a memorable message. Our verbal communication is ultimately in our control and can be something that is improved upon over time. That is, we can create effective and efficient messages if we first consider to what our message pertains, to whom are we sending the message, and in what context the message is being sent.

KEY WORDS

Ability language Language that focuses on the shortcomings of a person rather than emphasizing the person as a human.

Accent Way in which we pronounce words.

Bias Language that conveys stereotypes, insensitivity, or negativity toward a group of people or about a topic.

Cognitive function Using language to gather information, to reason, and to make sense of the world.

Communication Accommodation Theory Theory that argues we change our verbal communication during the course of an interaction based on our perceptions of the interaction and with whom we are speaking.

Connotative meaning Individualized meaning that reflects unique personal views of the user of the language.

Converge When individuals become more similar in their verbal choices.

Conversational narcissism Extreme self-focus in a conversation in which an individual does not allow the other person in the interaction an opportunity to speak.

Culture Learned system—that is, something that you acquire from others—of beliefs, values, and knowledge.

Defensive message Message that is produced in response to some kind of threat.

Denotative meaning Dictionary definition of a word or the literal meaning of a word.

Dialect Distinctive vocabulary or pronunciation typically associated with geographical regions.

Diverge When individuals become increasingly different in their verbal choices.

Ethical communication Individual's ability to be honest and use a set of standards to guide appropriate or positive behaviors.

Group identity function Using language as a signal of membership in a group or a sign of solidarity with a collection of individuals. Often, individuals outside the group do not understand the meaning in the verbal communication.

Message formation Way in which a message is put together.

Racist language Insensitive and derogatory language about a group of people.

Self-disclosure The sharing of personal information with others in an attempt to build or maintain a relationship.

Sexist language Language that does not account for both male and female experiences and instead communicates about ideas as inherently male or female.

Social reality function Using language to create our reality of the world around us. Language changes and responds to the world in which we live.

Stereotyping language Language that assumes an overgeneralization about a group of people.

Supportive communication Type of communication that occurs when an individual feels as though he or she has little reason to have anxiety or concern about the communication being received.

Symbols Abstract ideas or concepts that represent something and can be both verbal and nonverbal.

Verbal communication The meaning that is created with words, also referred to as language.

Verbal modeling Listening to how others speak, and then consciously using the same words or phrases they use.

REFERENCES

Afifi, W. A., & Caughlin, J. P. (2006). A close look at revealing secrets and some consequences that follow. *Communication Research, 33*, 467–488.

Department of Education, Employment and Workplace Relations. (n.d.). *Workplace communication*. Retrieved from www.regionalskillstraining.com/sites/default/files/content/WC%20Book%201.pdf.

Derlega, V. J., & Chaikin, A. L. (1977). Privacy and self-disclosure in social relationships. *Journal of Social Issues, 33*, 102–115.

Driscoll, D. L., & Brizee, A. (2010). *Stereotypes and biased language*. Retrieved fromhttp://owl.english.purdue.edu/owl/resource/608/05/.

Gibb, J. (1961). Defensive communication. *Journal of Communication, 11*, 141–148.

Giles, H., Coupland, J., & Coupland, N. (1991). Accommodation theory: Communication, context, and consequence. In H. Giles, J. Coupland, & N. Coupland (Eds.), *Contexts of accommodation*, (pp. 1-68). New York, New York: Cambridge University Press.

Giles, H., & Ogay, T. (2007). Communication accommodation theory. In B. Whaley & W. Samter (Eds.), *Explaining communication: Contemporary theories and exemplars*, (pp. 293-310). Mahwah, NJ: Erlbaum.

Giles, H., & Smith, P. (1979). Accommodation theory: Optimal levels of convergence In H. Giles & R. N. St. Clair (Eds.), *Language and social psychology*, (pp.45-65). Baltimore: Basil Blackwell.

Greenberg, M. A., & Stone, A. A. (1992). Emotional disclosure about traumas and its relation to health: Effects of previous disclosure and trauma severity. *Journal of Personality and Social Psychology, 63*, 75–84.

Johnson, R. (n.d.). *What are the benefits of effective communication in the workplace?* Retrieved from http://smallbusiness.chron.com/benefits-effective-communication-workplace-20198.html.

Kelly, A. E., Klusas, J. A., von Weiss, R. T., & Kenny, C. (2001). What is it about revealing secrets that is beneficial? *Personality and Social Psychology Bulletin, 27*, 651–665.

Knapp, M. L., Stohl, C., & Reardon, K. K. (1981). "Memorable" messages. *Journal of Communication, 31*, 27–41.

McCroskey, J. C. (1992). Reliability and validity of the willingness to communicate scale. *Communication Quarterly, 40,* 16–25.

McCroskey, J. C., & Richmond, V. P. (1987). Willingness to communicate. In J. C. McCroskey & J. A. Daly (Eds.), *Personality and interpersonal communication* (pp. 119–131). Newbury Park, CA: Sage.

Prince. (2012, December 21). Dick Clark. *Entertainment Weekly, 1238,* 43.

Smith, T. (2010). *10 verbal communication skills worth mastering.* Retrieved from www.littlethingsmatter.com/blog/2010/11/30/10-verbal-communication-skills-worth-mastering/.

Toomey, M. (1999). *The power of language.* Retrieved from www.mtoomey.com/poweroflanguage.html.

Top words, phrases, names of 2012: Apocalypse, Gangnam Style, Newton. (2012, December 31). *Wisconsin Gazette.* Retrieved from www.wisconsingazette.com/breaking-news/top-words-phrases-names-of-2012-apocalypse-gangnam-style-newtown.html.

Vangelisti, A. L., Knapp, M. L. & Daly, J. A. (1990). Conversational narcissism. *Communication Monographs, 57,* 251–274.

CHAPTER 4

From Styles to Smiles: Understanding Nonverbal Communication

Chapter Objectives

After reading this chapter, you should be able to:

- Define nonverbal communication and identify its characteristics
- Explain Expectancy Violation Theory
- Identify the relationship between nonverbal and verbal communication
- Describe the types of nonverbal communication
- Explain the functions of nonverbal messages
- Discuss the role of emoticons in communicating nonverbal messages online
- Identify strategies to enhance how others perceive your nonverbal communication

PERSONAL: You send an email to your best friend to make plans for Friday night. Typically, your friend's responses are filled with smiley faces :-) and acronyms such as LOL. Emails always end with TTFN and BFF somewhere at the close of the message. This time your friend's response is short and to the point, "Sounds good." The message seems uncharacteristic of her typical responses. Confused, you wonder, did I do something to upset my friend?

PROFESSIONAL: It's been a tough month at work. Your team has put in excessive overtime to prepare for an important client presentation. The big day has finally arrived, and your team delivers a flawless and impressive sales pitch. As you depart the conference room, your boss touches your arm and says, "Your presentation was outstanding. We should celebrate!" Is there a hidden meaning behind the touch?

PUBLIC: When registering for a Economics 101 class with nearly 200 students enrolled, you immediately assume it will be boring. However, after the first couple of weeks, you discover that it has been exactly the opposite. During lectures, the professor walks around the large classroom instead of standing behind the podium, and she smiles and makes eye contact with students as she calls on them to offer examples and share stories. One day when you answer a question correctly, she touches her nose with one finger while pointing at you with the other and says, "Right on target!" as she nods her head enthusiastically. At the end of the semester you wonder how you could have found an economics class to be so interesting. What happened to help you focus your attention in this class?

CHAPTER OVERVIEW

We have all heard phrases such as "It's not what you say, but how you say it" and "Actions speak louder than words." Have you ever stopped to think about what these phrases really mean and how they relate to human communication? As you review the scenarios above, the impact of nonverbal messages becomes more apparent. In our personal lives, we encounter numerous nonverbal messages on a daily basis to which we must assign meaning. Messages range from those delivered by a roommate who rolls his eyes as you ask him to please wash his dishes, to the friend who continually glances at her cell phone while you recount the highlights of the most recent episode of *Glee*. Consider the vast number of nonverbal messages we encounter in our professional careers. Countless hours are spent making a decision about how to dress for an interview in order to create a professional image, or you may replay a recent meeting in your mind wondering if there was a "hidden meaning" behind your boss' silence and text messaging as you presented your report.

In this chapter, we explore the many facets of nonverbal communication and analyze the relationship between verbal and nonverbal messages. In addition, we discuss the types of nonverbal communication and the roles they play in our interactions with others.

NONVERBAL COMMUNICATION DEFINED

The importance of nonverbal communication in our daily lives is highlighted by the amount of time we devote to describing, understanding, and explaining the meanings associated with cues that accompany the spoken message. In 2011, the world focused its attention on the nonverbal cues exhibited during the Casey Anthony trial to add meaning to the verbal testimony delivered in the courtroom. Did her lack of eye contact indicate that she was lying? Was anxiety or nervousness being communicated as she bit her bottom lip while listening to the prosecution's witnesses? Or were these simply nonverbal behaviors that were the result of fatigue?

> ➤ Nonverbal communication
> Exchange of meaning without the use of words.

In Chapter 3, we focused on the verbal messages that we use to create shared meaning with others. *Nonverbal communication* refers to the meaning that is created without the use of words. This includes behaviors such as facial expressions, gestures, touch, and how we use time. Experts estimate that nonverbal messages account for 65–93% of the meaning in our spoken communication. Stop for a moment and consider the powerful role that these unspoken messages play. More than half of the meaning of any verbal message is likely to be attributed to the nonverbal component. If you decide to enroll in another communication class, you will notice that many textbooks devote a chapter to examining the role of nonverbal messages. In fact, many colleges have an entire course in their curriculum that focuses solely on the study of these "hidden" messages. Even when we do not say a single word, chances are that someone will assign meaning to our silence, facial expression, posture, or attire. Throughout this chapter, we will explore each of these types of nonverbal communication.

CHARACTERISTICS OF NONVERBAL COMMUNICATION

As we begin to explore the various nonverbal codes that are used to stimulate meaning in the minds of others, we first discuss the characteristics of these intriguing messages (Figure 4.1).

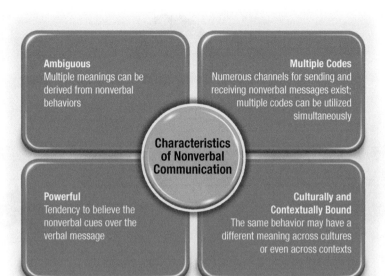

FIGURE 4.1

Characteristics of
nonverbal
communication.

Ambiguous

Nonverbal codes may be ambiguous. After all, we attach meanings to just about every nonverbal behavior. A server might touch your arm as she drops the bill on your table. Was her touch meant to indicate interest, or did it occur by accident? A 1984 experiment in which 114 restaurant patrons received some form of touch found that if a customer was briefly touched on the shoulder or on the palm of the hand as change was being returned, tipping tended to be higher (Crusco & Wetzel, 1984). An employee who notices his supervisor yawn during a meeting may think that she finds his presentation to be boring. However, her yawn may be the result of exhaustion from a late night working on a client report. Multiple meanings can be assigned to a single behavior. Unlike verbal communication, where we have established grammatical rules and dictionaries may help us specify the meanings of words, explanations for "how" we should interpret nonverbal behaviors are often unclear.

Multiple Codes

One potential explanation for "why" nonverbal communication is vague and unclear may be the result of the multiple codes that are used to exchange meaning. For example, touch, dress, facial expression, tone of voice, personal space, and use of time all offer cues in the sending and receiving of messages. What complicates the process even more is the fact that multiple nonverbal channels can be utilized simultaneously. Consider the flight attendants who smile while shaking their head and instructing passengers, "Please turn off your electronic devices during

Why does she smile and shake her head as she tells you to turn off your electronic devices?

© Chinaview/Shutterstock.com

takeoff and landing." At first, smiling while telling someone "no" may seem to be contradictory. But consider the flight attendants' goal. They want to encourage a positive flight experience for the passengers and reinforce that the request is nonthreatening. Smiling communicates a positive attitude in this instance, while shaking their head communicates that a behavior needs to be changed.

Culturally and Contextually Bound

Another characteristic of nonverbal communication is that it is culturally and contextually bound (Figure 4.2). A fascinating area of study in nonverbal communication involves the differences that exist when crossing cultural or contextual boundaries. While the "thumbs-up" gesture communicates "great job" or "agreement" in the United States, it is perceived as an obscene gesture in Iran that is equivalent to the U.S. gesture of using the middle finger. Not only do different expectations exist across cultures, but variations can also exist across contexts within a single culture. Consider the changes you make to your speaking volume when entering a library or church compared to the intensity of your voice when cheering on your favorite sports team. Understanding how meanings of nonverbal behaviors change depending on the culture or context is important to avoid misunderstandings.

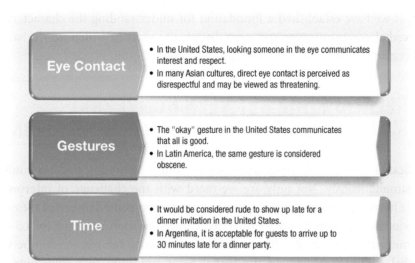

FIGURE 4.2

Cultural differences in the meanings associated with nonverbal behaviors.

Eye Contact
- In the United States, looking someone in the eye communicates interest and respect.
- In many Asian cultures, direct eye contact is perceived as disrespectful and may be viewed as threatening.

Gestures
- The "okay" gesture in the United States communicates that all is good.
- In Latin America, the same gesture is considered obscene.

Time
- It would be considered rude to show up late for a dinner invitation in the United States.
- In Argentina, it is acceptable for guests to arrive up to 30 minutes late for a dinner party.

Powerful

To say that nonverbal communication is powerful is almost an understatement. Consider the following example. You have been contemplating a drastic new haircut for months. Finally, you muster the courage to make the change. As you approach your friend after the haircut, you see a look of shock on his face. Your question of, "So, what do you think?" is answered with hesitation as he raises his eyebrows and unconvincingly says, "Well … it looks really great. You've always been a trendsetter!" Are you going to believe that your friend thinks your new hairstyle is attractive? Probably not. This reflects the value and power that we assign to nonverbal cues. Often we turn to these cues to uncover the true meaning behind a verbal message. The phrase "It's not what you say, but how you say it" highlights the importance that we place on nonverbal cues. When verbal and nonverbal messages contradict one another, we tend to believe the meaning assigned to the nonverbal cues. Why does this occur? Perhaps the answer is best explained by examining the two levels of meaning associated with messages. Recall in Chapter 1 our discussion of content and relational meanings. *Content meaning* involves understanding the information that is being shared. We rely on the words that are spoken to gain an understanding of the content that the sender wishes to communicate. Nonverbal communication is the source from which we uncover the *relational meaning*, or the emotional reactions associated with a message. Often, the relational meaning gives cues as to the relationship between the two individuals who are interacting. The words chosen by your friend in response to your haircut may have been positive, but the accompanying nonverbal cues are powerful and ultimately hurt your feelings because you trust him to be supportive.

➤ **Content meaning**
Actual information that is being exchanged in a message.

➤ **Relational meaning**
Emotional response associated with a message.

Now that we have established a foundation for understanding the characteristics of nonverbal communication, we next discuss the ways in which nonverbal and verbal communication are connected to one another.

THE RELATIONSHIP BETWEEN NONVERBAL COMMUNICATION AND VERBAL COMMUNICATION

As indicated earlier, nonverbal messages are often communicated via multiple codes simultaneously. Not only are we faced with the challenge of interpreting multiple nonverbal codes, but they are also often accompanied by verbal messages. As previously mentioned, since nonverbal communication accounts for 65–93% of the meaning in a message, it is important to examine the relationship between nonverbal communication and the verbal communication that contributes the remainder of the meaning (Figure 4.3).

Repeating or Restating

Repeating
Replicating the verbal message by following it up with a corresponding nonverbal message.

In some instances, we may use nonverbal messages to repeat or restate the words that are spoken. The function of *repeating* is defined as the use of a corresponding gesture or behavior that has a meaning similar to the verbal message in an attempt to ensure that the intended meaning was communicated. Shrugging your shoulders while saying "I have no idea" indicates your inability to answer a question. We have a tendency to repeat messages to eliminate potential confusion or misinterpretation. The decision to shrug your shoulders stems from your desire to eliminate any suspicion that you might be hiding something or trying to deceive someone.

FIGURE 4.3

The relationship between verbal and nonverbal communication.

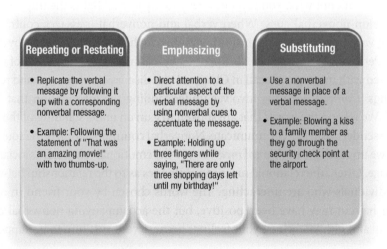

Repeating or Restating

- Replicate the verbal message by following it up with a corresponding nonverbal message.

- Example: Following the statement of "That was an amazing movie!" with two thumbs-up.

Emphasizing

- Direct attention to a particular aspect of the verbal message by using nonverbal cues to accentuate the message.

- Example: Holding up three fingers while saying, "There are only three shopping days left until my birthday!"

Substituting

- Use a nonverbal message in place of a verbal message.

- Example: Blowing a kiss to a family member as they go through the security check point at the airport.

Emphasizing

The function of *emphasizing* may be used when we want to direct attention to a particular aspect of the spoken message. In this instance, nonverbal cues may be used to accentuate or emphasize the part that we feel is important. Slapping your forehead while saying, "How could I have been *so* stupid!" is one example of how you may indicate your frustration with yourself for making an irrational decision. Recall our earlier discussion of the relational meaning that is added by a nonverbal message. By slapping your forehead you are not only communicating the content meaning of acknowledging that you made a mistake, but you are also showing the intensity of your frustration with yourself.

What message are you conveying by shrugging your shoulders?

© Warren Goldswain/Shutterstock.com

Emphasizing
Directing attention to a particular aspect of the verbal message by using nonverbal cues to accentuate the message.

Substituting

Sometimes we are unable to communicate a message using spoken words. In these instances, *substituting* nonverbal cues may be used instead of the verbal message to convey meaning. Consider the following example. Leah, Alex, and Claire are enjoying lunch together when Claire asks if they think her boyfriend might be cheating on her. Leah and Alex have proof that Claire's boyfriend has indeed been unfaithful. When Claire asks, "So what do you think? Should I be suspicious?" Leah looks across the table at Alex and raises her eyebrows and frowns. Without saying a word, Leah communicates that Claire should be suspicious. Instead of offering verbal confirmation, Leah's facial expressions speak volumes.

Substituting
Using a nonverbal message in place of a verbal message.

TYPES OF NONVERBAL COMMUNICATION

In our earlier discussion of the characteristics of nonverbal communication, we stated that there are multiple codes or channels that may be used. While there are many codes that have been addressed by communication scholars, we examine eight primary codes or channels of nonverbals in this chapter: kinesics, haptics, facial expressiveness, oculesics, vocalics, proxemics, chronemics, and dress and artifacts.

Kinesics

Kinesics
Study of the messages communicated by the use of body movements and gestures.

Kinesics, or the study of how we communicate meaning through the use of body movements and gestures, is perhaps the most widely researched and documented category of nonverbal behavior. Humans find it fascinating to study the body language of others. Ekman and Friesen (1969) identified various categories of body movements and gestures. These include adaptors, emblems, illustrators, and regulators.

Can you recall a time when you were nervous while taking an exam and discovered that you were tapping your pencil on the desk or biting your lip? If so, you used a nonverbal gesture to help you adjust to the stress of taking the exam. *Adaptors* are gestures or body movements that are performed instinctively. Often these behaviors are used to indicate one's emotional state. Weariness, boredom, impatience, anxiety, and nervousness are some of the emotions most frequently communicated via adaptors. Do you ever drum your fingers on the desktop when you become bored with a lecture? Have you ever caught yourself tapping your foot while you nervously wait to be called in for a job interview? Can you recall a time when you wearily rubbed your neck after working for several hours writing a research paper? If so, you have involuntarily communicated your emotions. As we cross cultural boundaries, these adaptors may become more apparent as we adjust to our new surroundings.

Adaptors
Nonverbal gestures that are often performed without intent; may be used to indicate the emotional state or feelings associated with the verbal message.

Sometimes you may be able to understand what someone is trying to communicate simply by watching their gestures. For example, your friend may hold out her palm to communicate that you should "Stop!" *Emblems* refer to those nonverbal gestures that have a direct verbal translation within a culture or context. It is important to keep in mind that the meanings associated with emblems are both culturally and contextually bound. Consider the "hook 'em horns" gesture performed by fans of the University of Texas at Austin. This gesture is formed by extending the index and pinkie fingers while the thumb holds the remaining two fingers against one's palm. UT fans display this gesture during the school's fight song or after a sports team earns a victory. However, in some European cultures, this same gesture is used to indicate spousal infidelity. In 2005, Norwegians were shocked to see media coverage of President George W. Bush and his daughter Jenna displaying this gesture as a greeting to fellow Texas Longhorn alumni. In Norway, the gesture is associated with a salute to Satan. To further complicate the issue, consider the meanings associated with this gesture among other co-cultures within the United States. In Columbus, Georgia, police have identified the gesture as a symbol used by members of a criminal gang, while fans of the heavy metal music culture use the same gesture as a sign of solidarity and appreciation for music.

Emblems
Nonverbal gestures that have a direct verbal translation. A common meaning for a gesture exists among members of the same culture.

Illustrators are used to add emphasis or additional meaning to the spoken message. To witness how often we use illustrators, conduct this simple experiment. Ask someone to give you directions to a location. Chances are that they will gesture to the right when explaining that you need to make a "right turn" and they will probably hold up two fingers as they instruct you to "continue through two stoplights before you turn left." These illustrators are used to provide a visual representation of our verbal directions. Unlike emblems, illustrators tend to be more universal and, thus, are less likely to result in misunderstandings or confusion.

➤ **Illustrators**
Gestures used to clarify or add emphasis to a verbal message.

The final category of gestures is known as regulators. *Regulators* refer to those gestures or body movements that are used to control the flow of communication. Suppose a parent is explaining important instructions to the babysitter as he prepares to go out for the evening. As he is talking, a child keeps trying to interrupt. By simply holding up his index finger as he continues to talk, the father has indicated that the child should wait for his turn to speak. In the classroom, students raise a hand to request a turn to speak, and professors may point toward a student to indicate that it is her turn to contribute to the conversation. During a business meeting, a colleague may nod his head toward you to designate that it is your turn to offer a suggestion. All of these gestures assist us in enhancing the flow of verbal communication.

➤ **Regulators**
Nonverbal gestures that are used to control the flow of communication.

Haptics

In a scene from the TV show *Friends*, Chandler becomes extremely uncomfortable when his male boss slaps him on his backside as he exits the conference room at the conclusion of a business meeting. While most would consider this nonverbal gesture to be inappropriate, Chandler's boss explains that it is his way of communicating "Good job!" *Haptics* is the study of the meanings associated with the use of various types of touch. Examples of touch include tickling, embracing, punching, and guiding. Consider the functions associated with the diverse forms of touch. An elementary school teacher who wants to silence

Raising a hand in class is an example of a regulator.

➤ **Haptics**
Study of how touch is used to communicate meaning.

© hxdbzxy/Shutterstock

a student who is talking during class may place a hand on the student's shoulder to indicate that she finds the talking to be disruptive. If a new colleague asks you directions to another location in your office building, you might place your hand on their elbow to guide them as you walk with them down a crowded corridor.

Our interpretations of touch vary based on the person who initiates the touch and the role that he or she plays. Four categories of touch identified by Thayer (1988) illustrate this point. *Functional-professional touch* is typically initiated by professionals in order to accomplish a task associated with their occupation. Doctors, dentists, hairdressers, and tailors are granted permission to initiate touch as part of their professions. In addition, there are other situations not linked to a specific occupation that may require you to initiate functional-professional touch. These include helping a classmate who has slipped on a wet floor in the hallway or lending a hand to a person who is descending the steps on a bus. In both of these situations, touch is being used to accomplish a task or help someone. *Social-polite touch* is used as a form of greeting or acknowledgment. Examples include initiating a handshake with a potential employee at the beginning of a job interview or patting a coworker on the back after she delivers a flawless sales presentation. *Friendship-warmth touch* is often reserved for family members and close friends. Messages of affection and caring are communicated by this type of touch. Patting your friend to congratulate them after their graduation ceremony and hugging your aunt at the annual family reunion are common examples. The final category of touch, *love-intimacy touch*, is the one that often results in the greatest misinterpretation. Intense caring, physical attraction, and strong emotions are indicated via this type of touch, and it is typically reserved for close family and romantic partners. Examples of love-intimacy touch include hand-holding, kissing, and caressing. Misunderstandings occur in instances when love-intimacy touch is incorrectly interpreted as a signal that someone is seeking a more intimate relationship.

It is important to note that love-intimacy touch, when used inappropriately, can be considered sexual harassment. Understanding the norms for each type of touch is essential to avoiding this type of situation. It is important to note that the meaning of touch differs across cultures. In some Asian cultures, it is perfectly acceptable for two females to hold hands while walking down the street. In the United States, this same behavior would conjure meanings associated with one's sexuality. Even within a culture, the reactions to touch may differ significantly. Women are more often the recipients of touch, while women tend to be more reserved than men in touching the opposite sex. Not only is it important to recognize cultural differences in touch, but it is also important to recognize that individuals differ in their desire to receive touch. *Touch apprehension* refers to the anxiety or discomfort associated with both sending and receiving messages of touch. To identify your own level of

---

Functional-professional touch Touch typically initiated by professionals in order to accomplish a task associated with their occupation.

Social-polite touch Touch used as a form of greeting or acknowledgment.

Friendship-warmth touch Touch used to communicate messages of affection and caring.

Love-intimacy touch Touch reserved for close family members and intimate partners; used to communicate intense emotions and caring.

Touch apprehension Fear or anxiety associated with touch that often results in withdrawing from or avoiding situations in which touch is used.

Directions: Below are 14 statements that people sometimes make about themselves. Please indicate whether or not you believe each statement applies to you by marking in the space before each item number whether you:

Strongly Disagree = 1; Disagree = 2; Are Neutral = 3; Agree = 4; Strongly Agree = 5

_____ 1. I don't mind if I am hugged as a sign of friendship.

_____ 2. I enjoy touching others.

_____ 3. I seldom put my arms around others.

_____ 4. When I see people hugging, it bothers me.

_____ 5. People should not be uncomfortable about being touched.

_____ 6. I really like being touched by others.

_____ 7. I wish I were free to show my emotions by touching others.

_____ 8. I do not like touching other people.

_____ 9. I do not like being touched by other people.

_____ 10. I find it enjoyable to be touched by others.

_____ 11. I dislike having to hug others.

_____ 12. Hugging and touching should be outlawed.

_____ 13. Touching others is a very important part of my personality.

_____ 14. Being touched by others makes me uncomfortable.

Scoring: To determine your score on the Touch Apprehension Scale, complete the following steps:

Step 1. Add scores for items 1, 2, 5, 6, 7, 10, and 13

Step 2. Add the scores for items 3, 4, 8, 9, 11, 12, and 14

Step 3. Complete the following formula: Score = 42 + Total from Step 1 − Total from Step 2

Score should be between 14 and 70

Scores >50 indicate a high touch orientation (Approacher). Scores <30 indicate a low touch orientation (Avoider). Scores

between 40 and 50 indicate no strong touch orientation—amount of touch will typically be that of the general culture.

FIGURE 4.4

Touch Apprehension Scale. Source: Richmond, Virginia Peck; McCroskey, James C.; Hickson, Mark L., *Nonverbal Behavior in Interpersonal Relations, 7th,* © 2012. Printed and electronically reproduced by permission of Pearson Education, Inc., New York, New York.

comfort with touch, complete the scale in Figure 4.4. If you attempt to pat someone on the back or give them a hug and they back away, this is a sign that they may be touch-avoidant. Refrain from engaging in touch with these individuals as it causes them to be uncomfortable and could be perceived negatively.

Facial Expressiveness

Have you ever had someone tell you that your face is an "open book?" Statements such as this one reflect the vast number of nonverbal cues that can be communicated via our facial expressions. Many consider the face to be the primary channel for communicating our emotions, and this is often the nonverbal area consulted for information about the relational meaning behind a message. While some people may put on a "poker face" and hide their emotions, others are not able to conceal their feelings as easily. Have you ever watched comedians on *Saturday Night Live* try to refrain from laughing? Simply seeing the corners of their mouths turn up in a suppressed grin as little wrinkles form at the corners of their eyes is enough to cause most people to laugh along with them. Consider the range of expressions you can create simply through movement in your eyebrows, lips, nose, and forehead. Ekman and Friesen (1971) conducted research across cultures and identified six emotions that appear to be universal in their nonverbal expression: sadness, anger, disgust, fear, surprise, and happiness.

Intensification
Exaggeration or overemphasis of a felt emotion via facial expressions.

Deintensification
Subduing or controlling the intensity of emotion that is expressed.

Masking
Replacing the actual emotion that is experienced with a more appropriate and socially desirable facial expression.

Neutralization
Refraining from exhibiting any type of emotion via facial expressions.

Due to our awareness of the vast array of messages communicated via our facial expressions, we often employ facial management techniques to assist us in managing how much emotion we communicate. Tactics used include intensification, deintensification, masking, and neutralization. *Intensification* is when we exaggerate or overemphasize the felt emotion. Perhaps you found out that your friends were planning a surprise birthday party for you. Rather than hurt their feelings, you decide to "go along" with the surprise. As you enter the restaurant and everyone shouts "Happy Birthday!" you act as though you are completely shocked, when in reality you knew about the party all along. *Deintensification* involves subduing or "toning down" the amount of emotion that is expressed. Perhaps you earned an "A" on a recent exam for which you and a friend studied for countless hours. As you exit the classroom, your friend says, "I can't believe it! I studied so hard and still only earned a C−. How did you do?" Rather than risk hurting your friend's feelings by grinning from ear to ear, you offer a slight smile and say, "I did alright." In instances where it is essential to replace the true emotion being felt with one that is more appropriate and socially desirable, we use the facial technique of *masking*. While getting ready to approach the podium to speak before City Council about a proposed change in an existing law, your neighbor asks, "Are you nervous?" Your stomach may be in knots, but you mask your nerves by smiling confidently and responding, "Not at all!" *Neutralization* involves withholding the expression of any emotion. Some refer to this as exhibiting one's "poker face." Suppose you are in a stressful business meeting and you hear your boss say, "We get our minds fixed up all the time when we're trying to explain ourselves to clients." While your first instinct is to smile and perhaps even giggle at her incorrect use of the word *fixed* instead of *mixed*, you neutralize your facial expressions and act as though her sentence was perfectly coherent.

Oculesics

A more concentrated focus on the study of how we use eye behavior as a part of our overall facial expressiveness is referred to as *oculesics*. Have you ever been able to accurately evaluate how your coworker or classmate was feeling just by looking at their eyes?

Oculesics
Study of how eye behavior is used to communicate meaning.

It is difficult to conceal the emotions and messages that are visible in our eyes. In many instances we are unable to control our eye behavior. Scientists have focused on pupil dilation as one area that reveals numerous clues about individuals. Our pupils contract and expand based on the amount of light in a room or in reaction to our attraction or interest in another person. It is impossible to control these reactions.

Just as there are rules for language use, there are rules for eye contact. Argyle (1975) points out the implications of staring at others, as well as the meanings attributed to gaze behavior. When examining the differences in eye behavior for males and females, researchers have discovered that women tend to maintain eye contact for longer periods of time and are more willing to initiate eye contact. However, these conclusions can be applied only to the U.S. population. As stated earlier, when examining the implications for eye contact in other cultures, it is important to keep in mind that the expectations and the norms for eye behavior may vary. In many Asian

Women tend to maintain eye contact for longer periods of time than men.

© auremar/Shutterstock.com

cultures, direct eye contact is a sign of disrespect, whereas in the United States many children are told to look their elders in the eye when they are spoken to or we assume that they are lying. Even within the U.S. borders, differences exist that may result in miscommunication. For example, African Americans are more likely to look at others when speaking than when they are listening. European Americans tend to look more when they are listening than when they are speaking. Understanding these preferences for eye contact can assist you in avoiding misunderstanding in your social and professional interactions.

Vocalics

Vocalics is the study of how we use characteristics of the voice to stimulate meaning, and includes any sounds that are produced that are not words. We may gain valuable cues as to the amount of interest or liking that one feels by listening to the vocal cues that are being sent, and we may even be able to make some guesses about the personality of others based on the sound of their voice. Our voice has been compared to our thumbprint as a means for identifying individuals. Can you recall a time when you knew who you were speaking to on the telephone even before they identified themselves by name? Think about the perceptions we associate with various vocal characteristics. One's speech rate may invoke judgments of credibility. A hesitant rate of speech may be viewed as incompetent or reluctant, while a rapid speech rate may be perceived to be insincere, deceptive, nervous, or enthusiastic. Vocal volume is also closely linked to perceptions of credibility and trustworthiness. One who speaks in an audible tone is perceived to be confident and honest, while a soft, hushed tone implies ineptitude and perhaps even deception. Credibility is often the aspect most often identified via one's vocal behavior. The use of vocal segregates or vocal fillers such as "um," "y' know," "like," and "so" conjure images of incompetence.

Silence is a unique form of nonverbal communication, and some would challenge our decision to include it in this discussion. Much like other forms of nonverbal communication, silence stimulates meaning. Consider the messages and meanings often attributed to silence. A romantic partner might use silence to indicate his or her disapproval of another's behavior in an attempt to punish, also known as the "silent treatment." We might also find ourselves using silence to conceal information from another, or you might use silence to simply indicate that you are thinking about what was being said and are developing an appropriate response. It is important to note the different interpretations of silence across cultures. In the U.S., silence may be perceived as indicating a lack of preparation or confidence, whereas it is valued in many Asian cultures and viewed as a sign of wisdom.

Based on their touching behaviors, what kind of relationship might these people have?

© mangostock/Shutterstock.com

Proxemics

Proxemics is the term used to refer to the study of how space is used to communicate messages. Edward T. Hall (1966) is among the first researchers to examine the meanings attributed to how we use space. He developed various categories to describe our preferences for personal space in the United States. Think about personal space as your own "bubble" that surrounds you. The size of the personal space bubble expands and shrinks depending on your relationship to the other person in the conversation. Hall labeled the four zones of personal space as intimate, personal, social, and public (Figure 4.5).

➤ **Proxemics**
Study of messages communicated through our use of personal space and territoriality.

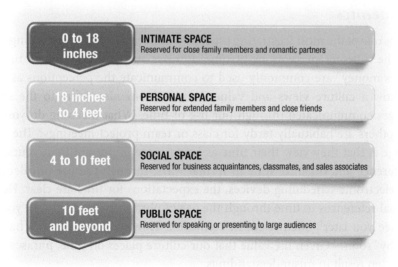

0 to 18 inches	**INTIMATE SPACE** Reserved for close family members and romantic partners
18 inches to 4 feet	**PERSONAL SPACE** Reserved for extended family members and close friends
4 to 10 feet	**SOCIAL SPACE** Reserved for business acquaintances, classmates, and sales associates
10 feet and beyond	**PUBLIC SPACE** Reserved for speaking or presenting to large audiences

FIGURE 4.5

Hall's proxemic zones.

Not only are there individual differences in our comfort zone with the use of personal space, but there are also cultural differences. In the United States, women tend to take up less space and maintain closer distances when interacting with close friends as compared to males. While U.S. Americans are most comfortable interacting at a distance of approximately 4 feet in casual conversations, Latin Americans and Middle Easterners prefer a much closer conversational distance. This may lead to perceptions of intrusion or standoffishness when they are speaking with U.S. Americans.

In addition to understanding the meanings associated with how we view and use personal space, important messages are conveyed through our approach to our territory and surrounding environment. You may choose to arrange the furniture in your home as a function of space constraints or for visual effect. Such arbitrary arrangements would not be acceptable in the Chinese culture, where *feng shui* involves studying the relationship between humans and the environment. This Eastern philosophy teaches humans the best means for maintaining harmony between human and nature, placing emphasis on the arrangement of space and furniture as well as on the use of color. Humans, by their very nature, are territorial. We take pride in staking claim to "our space" by leaving markers to indicate that we "own" an area. Have you ever walked into a classroom and placed your books on the desk and your coat on the back of the chair before leaving to grab a soda before class? Do you try to communicate your identity in your cramped office cubicle by placing photos of your family members, bumper stickers of your favorite sports teams, and mementos from recent vacations on your desk? Vanity plates are placed on automobiles to share information with other drivers who pass us on the freeway. These are examples of strategies used to claim territory and to offer clues into our identities.

Chronemics

Perhaps one of the most frustrating aspects of nonverbal misunderstandings results from the different perceptions of time. Phrases such as "don't waste time" and "time is money" are commonly used to communicate the perceptions associated with how a culture views and values time. *Chronemics* refers to the study of messages communicated through our use of time. What meaning do you assign when others are habitually tardy for class or team project meetings? The implied message is that they view their time as being more important than yours. When we reference and organize time in formal ways, through the use of calendars or other electronic scheduling devices, the expectations for time are clear. However, informal references to time through the use of phrases such as "I'll call you soon" and "See you later" often result in confusion. How long is "later?" What do we mean by "soon?" Given the value that our culture places on time, phrases such as these often result in misunderstandings.

Chronemics
Study of how meanings are assigned based on our use of time.

Like other forms of nonverbal communication, body piercings and hair color can also create impressions.

© dean bertoncelj/Shutterstock.com

It is important to understand the expectations associated with time. Tardiness is almost always perceived in a negative way, with adjectives such as *unprofessional*, *inconsiderate*, and *lazy* used to describe people who are habitually late. Messages associated with how we manage and use time differ across cultures. For example, in the United States it would be considered rude to show up more than 10 minutes after the scheduled start time for a dinner at a friend's home. In other cultures, it would be acceptable to arrive up to an hour late for dinner. Being late in one culture is not viewed the same way in another culture.

Dress and Artifacts

A final code of nonverbal communication is dress and artifacts. Mark Twain is quoted as saying, "Clothes make the man. Naked people have little or no influence on society." His quote emphasizes the perceptions that are associated with how we dress, in addition to the impact of other artifacts such as jewelry, glasses, tattoos, and body piercings. Consider the careful planning that goes into choosing just the right outfit for an interview or a date. Our clothing choices communicate messages before we engage in a conversation. As you travel on vacation, consider your reaction to a complete stranger who happens to be wearing a shirt from your university. Any other time you probably would not give them a second glance, but since you are in a distant location, you use their clothing as a topic to initiate a conversation by greeting the other person with a phrase such as, "Let's Go Bobcats!" Books such as *Dress for Success* (Molloy, 1988) provide valuable insight into the perceptions associated with our clothing choices.

NONVERBAL COMMUNICATION ONLINE: EMOTICONS AND ACRONYMS

While many are quick to criticize online communication as removing the "emotion" from messages, new methods for compensating for the lack of nonverbal cues in texts, emails, and social media posts are being created every day. In the face-to-face environment, we are able to smile or nod to indicate our agreement with something that is said. One only needs to glance at a Facebook newsfeed to identify multiple ways in which we share our emotions in our written messages.

Emoticons, acronyms, and capitalization are the most commonly used techniques for letting others know nonverbally how we feel about something they have said or posted online. Some programs actually offer users icons or artwork to insert into messages to convey emotions ranging from rage to embarrassment. Examples of some of the most commonly used emoticons and acronyms are in Figure 4.6.

Walther and D'Addario (2001) pointed out that perhaps one of the most influential distinctions between face-to-face and online communication is our ability to choose to communicate our emotions. While we are often unable to prevent "nonverbal leaks" that offer insight into our feelings during a face-to-face conversation, we voluntarily choose to share this information in the online context.

FIGURE 4.6

Examples of commonly used emoticons and acronyms.

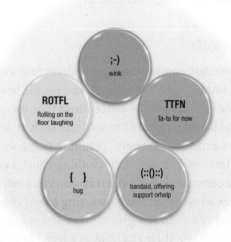

NONVERBAL IMMEDIACY

Have you ever wondered why some people just seem more drawn to and responsive to others? While some may link this connection to the verbal messages that are being exchanged, our nonverbal behaviors actually play an important role in this response. *Nonverbal immediacy* refers to the physical and psychological closeness established with another person as the result of specific nonverbal behaviors we employ. Mehrabian (1971) developed this principle to explain why we are drawn to certain people. In the 1986 movie *Ferris Bueller's Day Off*, the teacher has a monotone speaking voice and constantly looks at the podium as opposed to glancing around the classroom. It is no wonder his students fall asleep at their desks! When we engage in nonverbal immediacy, people tend to view us as approachable and warm. As a result, our messages tend to be more persuasive, and individuals have a tendency to want to engage in verbal communication with us.

Nonverbal immediacy Use of nonverbal behaviors to enhance the perceptions of physical or psychological closeness with others.

Examples of nonverbal behavior that are perceived to be immediate include positive facial expressions, increased eye contact, appropriate use of touch, decreased physical distance, and vocal variety (see also Figure 4.7). Studies that have examined the use of nonverbal immediacy across a variety of contexts (e.g., healthcare setting, classroom, business office) yield the same positive results. People who incorporate nonverbal immediacy as part of their normal communication repertoire are perceived as more influential and more likeable.

FIGURE 4.7

Nonverbal immediacy strategies.

Nonverbal Immediacy Strategies

- Smile
- Lean toward the other person
- Nod
- Decrease physical distance
- Increase eye contact

NONVERBAL SENSITIVITY

Communication competence is based not only on one's effective and appropriate use of verbal communication strategies, but also on the ability to interpret and respond to meanings associated with the nonverbal codes discussed above. *Nonverbal sensitivity* refers to one's ability to accurately decode the nonverbal cues that signal affect or emotion. If you are able to detect that your friend had a bad day when she avoids making eye contact and speaks in a sad tone, you have engaged in nonverbal sensitivity. Earlier in this chapter, we discussed the role of nonverbal communication in providing emotional or relational insight into messages. An important element of competent communication requires us to assess and evaluate nonverbal cues based on our social, cultural, and relational expectations. Awareness of these cues can enhance your ability to both display and respond to these messages in effective ways.

➤ **Nonverbal sensitivity** Ability to accurately decode the nonverbal cues that signal the mood or emotions of others.

CHAPTER SUMMARY

Throughout this chapter, we have discussed the prevalence of nonverbal behaviors and the value of understanding the meanings associated with them in our personal, professional, and public lives. The characteristics of nonverbal communication were emphasized, and the relationship between verbal and nonverbal communication was discussed. Increasing your awareness of the importance placed on nonverbal cues in the assignment of meaning is a key factor in enhancing your communication competence not only within your own culture, but also in your interactions with others from a variety of cultures and co-cultures. After all, there is credence in those common phrases of "It's not what you say, but how you say it!" and "Actions speak louder than words." By understanding the multiple codes that we use to communicate nonverbally, you will enhance your ability to display as well as interpret these "hidden" messages that are communicated in most interactions.

Adaptors Nonverbal gestures that are often performed without intent; may be used to indicate the emotional state or feelings associated with the verbal message.

Chronemics Study of how meanings are assigned based on our use of time.

Content meaning Actual information that is being exchanged in a message.

Deintensification Subduing or controlling the intensity of emotion that is expressed.

Emblems Nonverbal gestures that have a direct verbal translation. A common meaning for a gesture exists among members of the same culture.

Emphasizing Directing attention to a particular aspect of the verbal message by using nonverbal cues to accentuate the message.

Friendship-warmth touch Touch used to communicate messages of affection and caring.

Functional-professional touch Touch typically initiated by professionals in order to accomplish a task associated with their occupation.

Haptics Study of how touch is used to communicate meaning.

Illustrators Gestures used to clarify or add emphasis to a verbal message.

Intensification Exaggeration or overemphasis of a felt emotion via facial expressions.

Kinesics Study of the messages communicated by the use of body movements and gestures.

Love-intimacy touch Touch reserved for close family members and intimate partners; used to communicate intense emotions and caring.

Masking Replacing the actual emotion that is experienced with a more appropriate and socially desirable facial expression.

Neutralization Refraining from exhibiting any type of emotion via facial expressions.

Nonverbal communication Exchange of meaning without the use of words.

Nonverbal immediacy Use of nonverbal behaviors to enhance the perceptions of physical or psychological closeness with others.

Nonverbal sensitivity Ability to accurately decode the nonverbal cues that signal the mood or emotions of others.

Oculesics Study of how eye behavior is used to communicate meaning.

Proxemics Study of messages communicated through our use of personal space and territoriality.

Regulators Nonverbal gestures that are used to control the flow of communication.

Relational meaning Emotional response associated with a message.

Repeating Replicating the verbal message by following it up with a corresponding nonverbal message.

Social-polite touch Touch used as a form of greeting or acknowledgment.

Substituting Using a nonverbal message in place of a verbal message.

Touch apprehension Fear or anxiety associated with touch that often results in withdrawing from or avoiding situations in which touch is used.

Vocalics Study of meanings associated with the use of the voice and includes pitch, rate, and volume.

REFERENCES

Argyle, M. (1975). *Bodily communication*. London: Methuen.

Crusco, A. H., & Wetzel, C. G. (1984). The Midas touch: The effects of interpersonal touching on restaurant tipping. *Personality and Social Psychology Bulletin, 10,* 512–517.

Ekman, P., & Friesen, W. W. (1969). The repertoire of non-verbal behaviour: Categories, origins, usage and codings. *Semiotics 1,* 49–98.

Ekman, P., & Friesen, W. W. (1971). Constants across culture in the face and emotion. *Journal of Personality and Social Psychology, 17,* 124–129.

Hall, E. T. (1966). *The hidden dimension*. New York: Doubleday.

Mehrabian, A. (1971). *Silent messages*. Belmont, CA: Wadsworth.

Molloy, J. T. (1988). *New dress for success*. New York: Warner Books.

Richmond, V. P., & McCroskey, J. C. (2004). *Nonverbal behavior in interpersonal relations* (5th ed.). Boston: Allyn & Bacon.

Thayer, S. (1988). Close encounters. *Psychology Today, 22,* 30–36.

Walther, J. B., & D'Addario, K. P. (2001). The impacts of emoticons on message interpretation in computer-mediated communication. *Social Science Computer Review, 19,* 324–347.

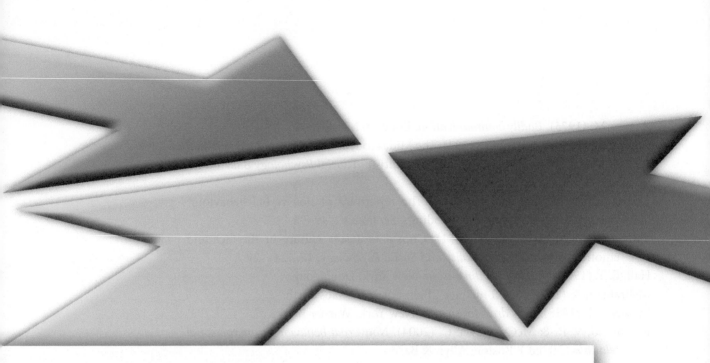

CHAPTER 5

Listening in Our Lives: I Know You "Hear" Me, But Are You Listening?

Chapter Objectives

After reading this chapter, you should be able to:
- Describe the listening process
- Describe the types of listening that we routinely do in our lives
- Identify the different contexts in which listening occurs
- Illustrate the potential barriers to listening
- Identify several listening misbehaviors
- Describe strategies for engaging in more effective listening

PERSONAL: Your friend comes to you with a problem. Although you are busy, you put everything aside and patiently listen as your friend explains the entire story. You listen attentively because you can tell your friend really needs your help. You don't interrupt while your friend is speaking, although, at various points, you paraphrase what your friend has said, and at times you ask for clarification. You put a great deal of effort into listening because you know just how important good listening is to a friendship, and your friend has done the same for you in the past. You want to show your friend that you have listened thoughtfully and fully understand. Do good listeners make good friends?

PROFESSIONAL: You are working on a project and trying to make a deadline. Your direct supervisor comes to your office and wants to go over the details for the next project you will be coordinating. You really want to listen to your supervisor; however, you are concerned that you won't finish this project in time, and so you find it difficult to pay attention to what is being said. Your supervisor asks if you have any questions about the next project and you reply "no;" however, when you try to recount what has been said you can't accurately remember the details. You know it is important to listen to your supervisor, but you realize you did not listen. When you are distracted by something, what happens to your ability to listen effectively?

PUBLIC: The election for state senate is approaching, and you aren't quite certain which candidate will get your vote. Fortunately, the two candidates are debating on television, and you feel this will give you a great opportunity to decide which person you believe will do the best job as your state senator. You settle into a comfortable chair and remove all other distractions. You listen to each candidate respond to the moderator's questions and to each other. You try to listen objectively, and you are also keenly aware of each candidate's verbal responses and their nonverbal communication. After the debate, you feel you have gained a great deal of knowledge about both candidates and you feel ready to cast your vote. How has your ability to listen effectively helped you to arrive at this important decision?

CHAPTER OVERVIEW

Have you ever experienced a situation in which you perceived that someone was not listening to you? Perhaps while speaking with a friend, you noticed your friend's eyes "glaze over" and the response to your question was a distracted "huh?" Can you recall a time when you "tuned out" during a professor's lecture? The good news about listening is that it is under our control. We make the choice whether to engage in effective listening or not.

Effective listening is an important part of our personal, professional, and public lives. Most likely, you are impressed by those who listen carefully and respect their ability to do so. Many people feel that good listeners make good friends, students, colleagues, supervisors, teachers, parents, clergy, and more. We value good listening, yet many of us are not particularly effective as listeners. Consider how much you can learn when you make an effort to listen effectively. Think about how well you can carry out your supervisor's instructions if you listen carefully. Consider the quality of the decisions you make when you listen to all of the facts. Contemplate the respect you will gain from others when you listen and give them your complete attention. We know how important listening is to the communication process and to our interpersonal relationships, yet we often assume that hearing and listening are the same. In this chapter, you will learn about the listening process, the types of listening we do, the various contexts in which listening takes place, barriers that prevent us from listening effectively, listening misbehaviors and what we can do to improve our ability to listen.

THE LISTENING PROCESS

Many of us anxiously wait for a traffic report on the radio or for a weather update; however, once these announcements air, we often discover that we can't remember anything that was said. Even though you thought you were listening, you were not. As we begin to look at the listening process, it is important to distinguish between *hearing* and *listening*. *Hearing* is simply the physiological act of attending to sounds. It is a physical process. Thus, if your hearing is not impaired, you will perceive the sounds. *Listening*, on the other hand, is psychological because it involves processing the sounds in order to understand, interpret, and respond to what you have heard. Unfortunately, many of us confuse the two and think hearing something implies that we are listening. As we go through each step of the listening process, analyze your own ability to incorporate each part of the process when you are listening.

≫ Hearing
The physiological act of taking in sounds.

≫ Listening
A psychological process where you take in the sounds and process them in order to understand, interpret, and respond to what you have heard.

FIGURE 5.1

The HURIER model.

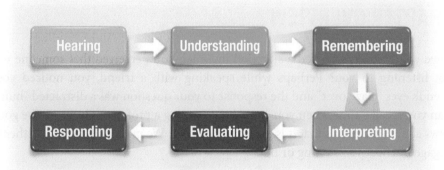

Brownell (2013) outlined the process of listening using the "HURIER model" (Figure 5.1). Each of the letters of this model represents one part of the listening process. *H* stands for hearing, *U* for understanding, *R* for remembering, *I* for interpreting, *E* for evaluating, and the final *R* for responding. Let's take a closer look at each step of the process.

Hearing

As Brownell (2013) indicated, **hearing** involves receiving and processing sounds. At any given moment, we are exposed to a number of sounds. If you stop reading right now and listen, you might hear people chatting in the hallway, the sound of construction outside of your window, a fan or air conditioner running in your room, music playing or a television on in the next room, or perhaps the sound of a cell phone ringing in the distance. In order to complete the first step of the listening process, you need to select which sound you will choose to focus your attention on and try to ignore the other sounds around you. If you are unable to focus your attention on one thing—for example, what your best friend is saying—there is little chance you will be an effective listener.

With regard to hearing, Brownell (2013) discussed *auditory discrimination*, which allows us to distinguish between sounds. In other words, it involves our ability to know what we have heard, and to focus on the vocal or paralinguistic cues of the person who is speaking. Our ability to distinguish between these sounds assists us with the next step of the process.

Auditory discrimination
The ability to distinguish sounds.

Since we can't possibly focus on all of the available sounds at any given time, Brownell (2013) pointed to factors that cause us to pay attention to certain things. These may include our interest level, the importance of what is being said, our past experiences, and even our current level of motivation. For example, if you are a football fan and someone nearby begins to speak about the newest athlete to join your favorite team, chances are you will focus your attention on that discussion rather than focusing on other sounds. Perhaps your boss is giving you instructions, and you know these guidelines are essential to the successful completion of your current project. Knowing the importance of this message will influence you to attend to the message rather than the conversation occurring in the next cubicle.

It is important that you learn to focus your attention to engage in effective listening. Doing so will ensure more accurate interpretation of the intended messages. Brownell (2013) and others recommend several strategies to help listeners focus their attention. First, it is important to eliminate any potential distractions. Those

If you perceive a message to be important or useful, you will focus on it more.

© Pressmaster/Shutterstock.com

distractions may be anything in the environment that draws away your ability to focus, such as the conversations of other people or the noise from construction going on close by. Distractions may also be internal. For example, you may be concerned about a friend or family member or nervous about an upcoming deadline at work. Whether the distractions are external or internal, they may create an inability to focus your attention. Eliminating any type of distraction will help you attend to and focus on the message, and this will help you complete the listening process more effectively.

Thought–speech differential
Difference between what human beings can understand per minute (roughly 400–500 words) and the rate at which the average person speaks (roughly 120–180 words per minute).

A second recommendation is to take advantage of what is known as the *thought–speech differential*. Although some estimates vary, we can comprehend roughly 400–500 words per minute, yet the average person speaks at a rate of only 120–180 words per minute. As a result, for every minute you spend listening to someone, you have spare time. What you do with that spare time can either help or hinder your ability to listen effectively. If you use your extra time to process the speaker's message, repeat it, and make sense of it, you will increase your chances of accurate listening. However, if you use your extra time to daydream or contemplate your plans for later, your ability to listen effectively will be impaired.

Scopic listeners
Listeners who develop an open interest in many topics.

Another tip is to establish and maintain a positive attitude toward listening. Brownell (2013) suggests becoming a "scopic listener" because *scopic listeners* develop "an interest in many topics and have not limited their exposure to preconceived notions about what is 'useful' or 'important'" (p. 84). Identify a way to become interested in what a speaker is saying or to find relevance in the message and you will most likely be a more effective listener. For example, you are taking a course to fulfill a general education requirement and at first, you don't see any connection between the course and your major. You want to do well in the course, however, so you decide to find the relevance between the course content and your intended career path. Because you have trained yourself to be a scopic listener, you are able to relate the course material to your major and your eventual career goals and hence, you become a more effective listener.

Finally, Brownell (2013) and others suggest becoming both physically and mentally prepared to listen. Consider sitting in the front row during a lecture or meeting to engage more effectively with the speaker, or make certain your environment is as comfortable as possible so that you can focus on the message. The more you do to help prepare yourself to listen, the more effective you are likely to be during this first step in the process as well as throughout the process.

Understanding

Understanding the message is the next step of the listening process. *Understanding* involves making sense of the message. As you learned in Chapter 3 when we discussed verbal communication, it is important for the listener to receive and understand the message as the speaker intended. While this appears to be a simple concept, it is often more difficult than it seems. As you have already learned both from the text and through your own personal experiences, the meaning or message a speaker sends is not always what a listener receives. In order to listen effectively, one must understand the message. It is the speaker's responsibility to use clear, descriptive, and concrete language to help a listener understand the message as it is intended. However, given our experiences, we may respond to a word in a way that is completely different from what the speaker intended. Recall previous discussions about the multiple meanings of a single word. For example, consider the word *love* and the many ways in which someone might define the word. If you have recently fallen in love, you would probably define it differently than someone who has had a bad romantic experience. Consider also the differences between enduring love, puppy love, the love between a parent and a child, and the love between spouses or partners. Simply using the word *love* leaves listeners open to a variety of ways of understanding the message.

Brownell (2013) also provided suggestions to help ensure that accurate understanding takes place. One recommendation is to ask questions. If you want to make sure you

> ➤ **Understanding**
> Making sense of the
> message you heard.

Asking questions helps you make sure you're on the right track.

have understood the speaker, simply ask questions to ensure you are on the right track. Questions can be used to gain further clarification or explanation, or they can secure confirmation that your understanding of the message was correct.

Another suggestion is to allow the other person to complete the message without interrupting, then ask questions or respond. Many of us tend to interrupt a speaker because we think we know what the speaker is going to say, because we prefer speaking to listening, or because we think we have something to offer the speaker. As Brownell (2013) stated, "The urge to interrupt is the greatest when you have strong opinions and are listening to someone who also appears certain of his viewpoint. *As soon as emotions heighten, neither individual is listening effectively*" (p. 115). As listeners, if we permit the speaker to deliver the complete message without interruption, we are more likely to understand the message.

Remembering

Remembering
The act of retaining something in your memory.

Suppose someone speaks to you, but you cannot remember anything that was said? Have you truly listened? The third component of the HURIER model involves remembering the message. *Remembering* is the act of retaining something in your memory. According to Brownell (2013), there are three types of memory systems: immediate, short term, and long term. If you attend to something, it is placed in your *immediate memory*. In other words, if something captures your attention

Immediate memory
Attending to something that is later discarded or placed in short- or long-term memory.

or if you find something to be interesting, your brain will place the information in your immediate memory and decide what to do with it. It typically involves remembering for a split second. It may be a story on the news or a comment made by a coworker. It might be a phone number you are given and then you do not remember it once you have dialed it. Essentially, our immediate memory serves as our filter for determining what is important to remember for later and what information should be immediately purged. Once you include the information in your immediate memory, you can determine whether it should be placed in either your short-term or long-term memory.

Short-term memory, as the name implies, may be stored for only a brief time. You might determine later on that it is important enough to be moved into your long-term memory or that it can be forgotten. Since we can't remember everything we hear, our short-term memory is limited in the amount that can be stored. You need short-term memory to function well in a classroom situation. When you are listening to a lecture, for example, you write a note when you feel a piece of information is important. You do this to aid your memory of the idea or fact. Later, you may decide to study this particular piece of information further or not but it is there to be retrieved. Similarly, in your interpersonal relationships, you use your short-term memory just to be able to converse with someone successfully. When speaking with a friend or a coworker, you use your short-term memory to carry on a conversation. Once the conversation is over, you may not remember every detail of what was said or you may decide to store some of what was said in your long-term memory.

> ➤ **Short-term memory**
> Memory with a limited capacity that is stored for a brief time unless it is important enough to be moved into long-term memory.

Brownell suggests some strategies to help you with your short-term memory. Two of the strategies are repetition and chunking. *Repetition* can help improve your short-term memory by repeating to yourself over and over again the information you need to remember. If you have ever gone into a grocery store without a list and wanted to remember the items you needed, you have probably used this strategy. By repeating your list of items as you drive to the store, you have improved your chances of remembering the items until you reach the check-out line. *Chunking* is another strategy that may help you maintain information in your short-term memory by remembering information in sections or pieces ("chunks"). Suppose you need to remember a phone number. Rather than trying to remember 10 different digits (the area code plus the phone number), you would most likely "chunk" the 10 digits into three parts—the first three numbers for the area code, the next three digits, and the final four numbers. Ask your friend to repeat the phone number, and this is likely the format used to repeat it back to you. Chunking works best when we group items into groups of three to five bits of information.

> ➤ **Repetition**
> A strategy to help improve your short-term memory by restating to yourself over and over again what you need to remember.

> ➤ **Chunking**
> A strategy that helps maintain information in short-term memory by remembering information in sections or pieces ("chunks").

Finally, *long-term memory* is our brain's filing system. It consists of information that you may have heard months or even years ago. It has a limitless capacity and is often compared to a filing system because it helps us store new information in the right place and retrieve previously stored information efficiently. Brownell provides several strategies designed to enhance your ability to remember information long-term. One strategy involves *association*, which is making a connection between one thing and another. For example, if you have met someone in one context but see them in another, remembering the context in which you met them could help you remember their name or other important information about them. *Categorization* is the process of classifying information and is another strategy used to enhance our long-term memory. Placing information into logical categories enables us to retrieve the information when needed. For example, you might want to remember things you need to prepare for a party. Instead of trying to remember every item required, you might categorize the list into appetizers, main course, and dessert. These categories will help you remember the specific items once you are in the grocery store. A final strategy involves the use of mnemonic devices. *Mnemonic devices* are techniques that help you retain information in a more effective way than in its original form. When the information is in a form that our brains relate to more easily, we are more likely to remember it. These actually can improve both your short-term and long-term memory. You may have used these to study for a test. In fact, the HURIER model is an acronym to help you remember the various elements of the listening process (i.e., hearing, understanding, remembering, interpreting, evaluating, and responding).

Interpreting

Interpreting is the next element of the listening process. *Interpreting* goes beyond the actual words that are said and focuses on the verbal, nonverbal and relational components of the message. Is someone being sincere or sarcastic? Are they annoyed or simply bored or distracted? As we all know, the words themselves do not necessarily reflect the speaker's intent.

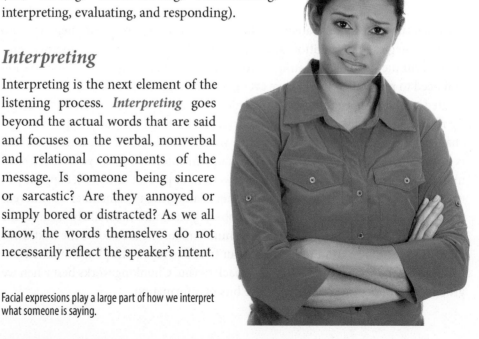

Facial expressions play a large part of how we interpret what someone is saying.

© PathDoc/Shutterstock.com

It is not only what a speaker says but also how the message is presented that can make a difference in our interpretation. In addition, sometimes we need to listen to what *isn't* being said to correctly interpret a message. What *didn't* the speaker say that may help us to interpret the intent of the message? What was reflected in the speaker's tone of voice, facial expression, and posture? Nonverbal clues combined with the speaker's verbal message may help listeners to correctly interpret the intended meaning. In addition, Brownell (2013) noted, empathy is a "key element that enables you to go beyond the literal meaning of the words you hear and begin to consider the speaker's feelings and indirect messages" (pp. 172–173). Thus, just as you have learned in Chapter 2, the ability to see something from another person's perspective and to perhaps put yourself into his or her situation (i.e., empathy) will also increase the chances of you correctly interpreting the message you receive.

Evaluating

Every day, we are bombarded with advertisements on the radio or on television; candidates tell us why they are the best person for the job over other candidates and salespeople extoll the benefits of their products. How do we go about discerning which messages are truthful and which ones stretch the truth? Evaluating messages we receive is another important step in the listening process. When we are *evaluating* messages, we are considering the message, the credibility of the speaker, and separating fact from opinion to judge the meaning of the message. As listeners, we need to make certain we distinguish between what is fact and what is opinion. Speakers may allude to something as being factual when it is actually only an opinion. As listeners, we need to evaluate the validity of the message, credibility of the source, potential errors in the speaker's logic, speaker bias, and/or the emotional appeals the speaker employs to persuade the listener. Doing all of this will help you become the type of listener who does not merely accept everything a speaker says at face value, but one who critically examines a speaker's message and effectively evaluates its meaning.

> **Evaluating**
> Considering the message and the credibility of the speaker and separating fact from opinion to judge the meaning of the message.

Responding

Responding is selecting the appropriate message to send back to the speaker and is the final element in the listening process. How you respond to a message is often determined by the nature of the situation, the speaker, and the message itself. You may respond differently to your supervisor than to a friend. Consider how your response might differ if you receive an invitation to go out to dinner with a friend versus receiving a plea for help. The way in which we respond to a message is very important in all areas of our lives. At times, we develop scripts or habitual responses we use in routine situations and expect others to respond in much the same way. One

> **Responding**
> Selecting the appropriate message to send back to the speaker.

of the most common examples is to respond by saying "fine" when someone asks us how we are feeling. These responses might be acceptable, however, what if they are not the responses we should be giving at that moment? As listeners, we need to listen carefully in order to select the appropriate response given a particular situation, speaker, and message. Knowing how to respond in each particular circumstance will help us become more effective listeners. In addition, it is important to remember that we usually give both a verbal and a nonverbal response to someone. Thus, as mentioned previously, it isn't just the words we say but also our nonverbal communication that convey the meaning of our response to the other person or persons with whom we are communicating. For example, if you tell a coworker that you will "cover her shift" but your nonverbal communication clearly indicates you are not happy to do so, your response will send the message that you do not actually want to do her this favor. As you learned in Chapter 4, when there is a discrepancy between your verbal and nonverbal message, people tend to trust the nonverbal over the verbal response. Thus, when responding, we need to be aware of both what we say and how we say it. Overall, because our listening effectiveness is often judged by our responses, it is a critical element in the process.

TYPES OF LISTENING

Now that we have analyzed the process of listening, let's focus our attention on the types of listening that we engage in throughout our personal, professional, and public lives. The various elements of the process are more or less critical based on the type of listening that we engage in at any given time. In this section, we discuss four types of listening: informational, critical, empathic, and appreciative (see Figure 5.2).

Informational listening
Listening to understand or comprehend.

Informational listening involves listening with the goal of understanding or comprehending. When you are pay attention to an instructor delivering a lecture, a supervisor offering instructions, a newscaster explaining a story, or a person giving directions, the goal should be to understand the information being provided. In essence, you are listening to learn. We may increase our ability to listen effectively by asking questions to clarify the speaker's message, or we may paraphrase what the speaker has said to ensure that what we have heard is actually what the speaker intended. As a speaker who is sharing information, it is important to speak in an organized manner, use clear and descriptive language, and provide support for our ideas to assist the listener in understanding our message.

Critical listening
Listening to make a judgment.

A second type of listening is *critical listening*. This is sometimes referred to as *discriminative listening* or *evaluative listening* because this type of listening involves judging the message. When we listen critically, our goals should be to concentrate

We need to listen critically to a candidate to assess how to vote.

© Picsfive/Shutterstock.com

on the speaker's main ideas, the support provided for these ideas, the organization of the ideas, as well as the speaker's credibility and motive(s) for speaking. Thus, we are called upon to analyze and evaluate the message from the speaker. For example, in order to select the best product within a category, consumers need to listen critically to what a salesperson says (or perhaps does not say) to determine which specific brand to purchase. Suppose a consumer plans to purchase a new flat-screen television. In addition to hearing what the salesperson has to say, the consumer may watch product reviews posted on YouTube and television commercials and critically

FIGURE 5.2

Types of listening.

Informational Listening	• Listening to understand or comprehend something • Listening to a teacher lecture, a supervisor give instructions, a person giving directions to a restaurant
Critical Listening	• Listening to evaluate or judge a message • Listening to decide which product to buy, which candidate to support or if you should or should not be persuaded to do something
Empathic Listening	• Listening to see a situation from someone else's perspective or to understand what someone else is feeling. • Listening to a person who is dealing with a health issue, listening to a friend who broke up with a romantic partner
Appreciative Listening	• Listening for enjoyment • Listening to a favorite musician, birds chirping, children laughing

Do you love the sound of waves crashing on the shore?

© Alexy Shrinkevich/Shutterstock.com

listen to analyze the qualities of the different models of televisions. Any time we need to make a judgment or a decision, we need to listen critically in order to gather the information needed to make an informed choice.

➣ Empathic listening
Listening from the other person's perspective to support or help that person.

The third type of listening is *empathic listening*. As previously indicated, being empathic involves seeing a situation from someone else's perspective or trying to understand what someone else is feeling. Empathic listening demonstrates your ability to listen to another person with sensitivity and concern. As empathic listeners, we need to listen to understand the speaker's feelings in a given situation while resisting the temptation to impose how we would necessarily feel in a similar situation. Suppose a friend receives bad news about a loved one's health or discovers they weren't offered a job promotion they were expecting. Listening with empathy is important both to that person and to your relationship. In order to demonstrate you are listening, you may nod your head to acknowledge the information, encourage the speaker to continue by saying phrases such as "go on," or paraphrase what the speaker has said. Empathic listeners demonstrate they care about us, and we value our relationships with those individuals.

➣ Appreciative listening
Listening for enjoyment.

A final type of listening is *appreciative listening*. Do you have a favorite type of music or a favorite musician or band? Do you find yourself listening to their music more often than other singers or bands? Perhaps you love listening to the sound of waves crashing on the beach or birds chirping outside your window. You may enjoy speaking to a friend for hours simply because you enjoy listening to your friend's stories. If you listen to something purely for the enjoyment of it, you are experiencing appreciative listening. This type of listening varies from person to person, but for many, listening for enjoyment provides relaxation and can reduce the stress in one's life.

You probably do most, if not all, of these types of listening every day in a variety of settings. In the next section, we focus on the contexts in which the different listening types occur.

LISTENING IN VARIOUS CONTEXTS

Listening occurs in virtually every context of our lives and thus it plays an important role in our perceived effectiveness as a communicator. In this section, we take a brief look at the various contexts in which listening occurs (see Figure 5.3).

Listening in Families

Our families provide one of the earliest and most enduring contexts in which listening takes place. Very early in our lives, it is through listening that we learn language from our family members. By listening to our parents and siblings, we learn how to speak ourselves. Our parents or siblings might help focus our attention by showing

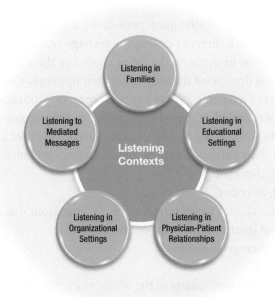

FIGURE 5.3

Listening in various contexts.

Early in our lives, we learn language from our family members.

© BlueOrange Studio/Shutterstock.com

us a ball, and then saying the word *ball*. In addition to learning language, we learn family rules and expectations by listening to our parents, siblings, and relatives. Parents may advise children to "Look both ways before you cross a street," "Don't talk to strangers," "Be polite," or "Be kind to others." Listening to these messages provides us with important lessons that we carry throughout our lives. Recall our discussion in Chapter 2 regarding the impact of messages received in the family on the development of our identity.

Perhaps one of the most challenging periods in the parent–child relationship involves listening (or lack thereof) during the teenage years. Parents may feel that teenagers do not listen to them or that they challenge their authority. Teenagers may feel that parents don't trust them or value their opinions. Coakley and Wolvin (1997b) administered a listening survey to 37 teenagers. Students were also asked to have their parents complete a similar listening questionnaire. In the study, the teens were asked to indicate what they perceived to be the most effective listening behaviors used by their parents. Some of their responses included:

"Listens without judging"
"Is caring, attentive"
"Gives me a chance to get out *all* of my feelings from inside"
"Listens but does not interrupt or give advice"
"Listens—then gives feedback"
"Lets me talk"
"Cares—really cares; listens to the whole story; tries to get a full understanding of what I'm feeling" (p. 120)

In addition, the parents were asked why they thought their teenagers did not listen effectively to them and the teenagers were asked to consider why they believed their parents did not listen to them. Some of the reasons given by both sides included preoccupation; lack of attention; jumps to conclusions; gets angry; interrupts; listens selectively; fatigue; thinks he or she has heard it all before; and gets defensive. Certainly, teenage–parent listening can be complicated, but it is an important listening relationship.

While a substantial amount of listening occurs in the parent–child relationship, listening among siblings is another important aspect of the family context. Did you have a sibling who told you how to find your classroom in the school he or she already attended? Perhaps you shared secrets or fears with one another. Later in life, you might listen as each of you offers advice on a variety of life events such as marriage, childrearing, caring for aging parents, or personal health issues.

Listening to your grandparents recount stories of their youth or their lives or listening to aunts and uncles tell stories about your parents provides other forms of listening within a family context. How we listen and how our family members listen to us can make a big difference throughout our lives. By listening to our family members, we can learn a great deal. In addition, because listening demonstrates caring, taking the time to listen to a family member can enhance our family relationships.

In the classroom, it is important for both teachers and students to listen to each other.

© Monkey Business Images/Shutterstock.com

Listening in Educational Settings

Schools and other educational settings are listening contexts in which we spend a considerable amount of time. Developing the ability to listen effectively can ensure our success in learning and retention of information. Imhof (2008) estimated that students devote approximately two-thirds of their time to listening. Unfortunately, as many scholars have pointed out (e.g., Brownell, 2013; Coakley & Wolvin, 1997a; Nichols & Stevens, 1957), speaking, reading, and writing have received more attention in educational settings than listening, despite the fact that listening is the skill used most often in educational contexts. How much time have you devoted to studying the process of listening compared to learning about reading and writing? The fact is, we rarely receive formal training in the process of listening. Instead, we are simply told it is a behavior that is important to our success. From elementary school through college, we listen to teachers offering directions and providing content. We also learn by listening to others in the classroom as they offer opinions, provide examples, and/or ask for clarification. When we are able to listen effectively, we are much more likely to understand and retain what we learn in the classroom. In turn, this may help us be more successful learners.

Just as it is important for students to be effective listeners in the classroom, it is also important for teachers to listen carefully to students. By doing so, teachers gain insights regarding what students do or do not understand, and how they perceive topics or information being discussed. As in other communication contexts, both teachers and students are responsible for successful listening.

Listening in Physician–Patient Relationships

Needless to say, listening is a crucial skill to ensure understanding in the healthcare context. Patients need to listen to their physicians carefully to understand what the diagnosis is, what treatment regimen should be followed, the prognosis for a particular illness or disease, and instructions and potential side effects for various medications. Listening to one's physician is not always easy, especially if the physician uses technical language or is not clear in the explanation of a diagnosis. Furthermore, listening in the health context may be complicated as a result of the fear or anxiety associated with medical treatment. Providing a second set of ears by bringing someone to the appointment might help a patient to listen more effectively. In addition, taking notes to retain important information and/or asking questions to gain clarification may also help the patient in the listening process.

Listening is a joint effort. Just as it is important for the patient to listen to the physician, it is equally important for the physician to listen to the patient. Imagine how dangerous it would be if a physician did not listen to a patient's medical history or to symptoms the patient is currently experiencing. Davis, Foley, Crigger, and Brannigan (2008) stated, "Research indicates that when healthcare providers listen to patients, there is more compliance with medical regimens, patient satisfaction is increased, and physicians are less vulnerable to malpractice lawsuits" (p. 168). Developing a listening relationship in this context is certainly important, and when physician and patient listen effectively to each other, they develop a level of trust that fosters an improved level of care. As Davis et al. indicated, both the patient and the physician have a "stake in how well the other listens and attends to the sharing of information" (p. 172). Overall, effective listening helps us receive and give the best healthcare possible.

Being a good listener can make a difference in the quality of healthcare you receive.

Listening in Organizational Settings

While effective listening is important in our personal relationships, it is also essential to our professional success. When you listen effectively on the job, it will help you understand and complete the responsibilities of your position and the respect your coworkers and superiors have for you will be enhanced. While effective listening in the organization will increase your chances of being successful in your job, ineffective listening can decrease your chances of obtaining a promotion or even staying in the job you have. As was true in the other contexts already discussed, listening in the organizational context is a two-way street. Not only do employees need to listen to supervisors, but it is equally important for supervisors to listen to employees. When effective listening takes place in an organization at all levels, it is more likely that trust among supervisors and employees will increase. Other potential outcomes of effective listening may be increased productivity, greater levels of job satisfaction, and higher levels of organizational commitment. In addition, effective listening with customers can make the difference between a happy customer and an unhappy one. As Flynn, Valikoski, and Grau (2008) indicated, "Focusing on improving listening skills should not only help organizations improve their outcomes but also assist employees in realizing their career aspirations" (p. 145).

Listening to Mediated Messages

The last context we discuss is listening to the various messages we receive via the media. Consider for a moment the number of messages you receive on a daily basis by listening to news highlights on your computer or cell phone or commercials for products. If you tracked the number of items you listen to through various media for one day, you would be overwhelmed by the number of messages you receive. How you listen to these may be influenced by your age, gender, political affiliation, education, religion, or any other number of factors. How many of us listen to messages from the media and take the information at face value without questioning it or trying to separate fact from opinion? Since the various news outlets choose what stories will air and how the stories will be told, the media has the potential to shape the attitudes and beliefs of the viewers. Given the various forms of media we now have, it is easy to receive and find a great deal of information. What information is important? What is reliable? Does the constant barrage of social media prevent us from effectively listening? If we are checking our email and texts while we are trying to listen to a friend speak, can we possibly be listening effectively? It is important to realize that how we listen to the media and the mediated messages we receive may have a significant impact on our lives. Knowing when to use informational, critical, empathic, appreciative, or a combination of the various types of listening will help you listen to mediated messages more effectively.

Now that we have discussed the various contexts in which listening occurs and their prevalence and importance in our lives, it is important to understand what prevents people from listening effectively.

BARRIERS TO LISTENING

There are many reasons why we don't listen effectively. These include fatigue, distractions, your physical state, environmental constraints, your motivation to listen, and speaker style. Fatigue is one barrier to effective listening. How effectively do you listen when you are tired? Many of us lose the focus we need to listen when we are exhausted. Are there specific times during the day when you know you listen better than at others? Perhaps you're not a "morning person" but rather someone who does your best listening in the afternoon. Awareness of this information could guide you to schedule meetings or classes at times when you know you will be able to best focus on listening. If you are unable to alter your meeting or class schedule, an awareness of this potential listening barrier could enable you to develop strategies to enhance your ability to listen more effectively.

Some people do not listen effectively is because their attention is focused elsewhere. For example, have you ever tried to listen to a lecture or a friend or colleague when you are worried about something else? If you have a deadline at work or a paper due for class, it is difficult to concentrate on listening. Consider how frustrating this must be for both the speaker and the listener. Some strategies you may consider when faced with these potential distractions include blocking other concerns from your mind in order to listen effectively or, if the circumstances warrant it, letting the speaker know that this is not a good time for you to listen and ask if you might schedule a better time to meet.

When you are not feeling well, you might not listen well. Unfortunately, this could occur in the doctor's office when it is important *to* listen well. In this circumstance, you might find that taking notes, asking questions, and getting clarification from the physician might help you stay focused on what is being communicated.

At times our listening is inhibited simply because the environment we are in prohibits us from doing so. If you have ever been to a concert or a club playing loud music, you probably have experienced frustration at not being able to hear what your friend was saying. In this instance, the environment itself became a barrier to your ability to listen. If you are trying to focus on what someone else is saying and there are competing noises such as conversations at the next table, background noise from the television, or a bad cell phone connection when talking on your cell phone, it makes it difficult to engage in effective listening behaviors. Other environmental factors may impede the listening process as well. Consider your own ability to listen effectively when you're in a room that is too crowded or too hot, or if the speaker does not have a microphone when speaking in a large auditorium. These environmental distractions can cause us to lose focus. Again, becoming aware of these factors and developing ways to refocus our attention will help us listen more effectively.

Some people do not listen well is because they are not interested in what is being said. When this occurs, some individuals tend to "tune out" or disengage from listening. They might think about their upcoming vacation or what they need to accomplish for the rest of the day. Once listeners lose focus on what is being communicated, it is difficult to recapture their attention. Again, if you can develop strategies to conquer this, it will help you in your ability to listen effectively. As mentioned earlier in this chapter, some listeners find the motivation to listen to things that aren't particularly interesting by finding a reason to listen. They become scopic listeners and thus might say to themselves, "This will be helpful when I am interviewing for my next job," or "This will help me do well on the upcoming test." Others may conquer their distractions by promising themselves some type of reward if they listen well.

Finally, some people have a difficult time listening due to the presentational style of the speaker. Some speakers do not make it easy for listeners to pay attention. If the speaker is disorganized or uses language that is not easily understood by the audience, it is difficult to fully engage in active listening. Consider the speaker who reads his speech and never establishes eye contact, doesn't give examples with which the listener can identify, or uses a monotone voice, few facial expressions, or has little enthusiasm for his or her topic. Similarly, consider the speaker who merely places all of his or her information on PowerPoint™ slides and then simply reads everything that is on each slide. Likewise, consider the speaker who turns off the lights and turns on the screen so that you only hear the speaker. If you have experienced any of these examples, you know how difficult it can be to maintain your attention. The point here is that it is the responsibility of both the speaker and the listener to take steps to help make the listening process as effective as possible.

LISTENING MISBEHAVIORS

As you learned in the previous section, there are many reasons why people don't listen. You could probably relate to some of these reasons. In this section of the chapter, we take a look at some specific listening misbehaviors that interfere with effective listening (see Figure 5.4).

Pseudo-listening
Pretending to listen to others while thinking about something else.

The first type of listening misbehavior is *pseudo-listening*. These listeners merely pretend to listen. You probably know individuals who are very good at doing this. They may nod while you are speaking to indicate agreement, smile or laugh at the appropriate times, or make statements such as "uh-huh" or "hmmm" to indicate they understand what you are saying. However, they are not truly listening. While you may realize this is occurring, you may not always recognize when a pseudo-listener is not listening to you. Unfortunately, with this type of listening misbehavior, pseudo-listeners may miss critical information they need to continue a conversation, or they may insult or hurt the person to whom they should be listening. Consider how good it feels to know that someone is really listening to you, and make a commitment to being an engaged listener in your personal, professional, and public lives.

Selective listening
Listening to only portions of an entire message.

Another type of misbehavior is *selective listening*. With selective listening we only listen to part of what the speaker is saying. For example, when you listen to the evening news, you may miss some news stories but listen more closely to information that interests you. Perhaps you only listen to the sports highlights when you are anxious to know if your favorite team won their game. While this might not hurt the newscasters, if you apply selective listening to a more personal

FIGURE 5.4

Types of listening misbehaviors.

Types of Listening Misbehaviors

Pseudo-listening	Selective listening	Stage hogging	Defensive listening	Insensitive listening
Listeners who may look like they are listening but are only pretending to listen.	Listeners who select and listen to only portions of what the speaker is saying.	Listeners who often interrupt the speaker or turn the conversation toward themselves.	Listeners who believe others are attacking them and that affects what they receive.	Listeners who do not go beyond the actual words that are used; they listen solely to the verbal component and do not pick up on the speaker's nonverbal communication.

listening situation (i.e., a conversation between spouses or partners, parent/child, or even friends), you can see how only focusing on the parts of the conversation that interest you will affect your relationship with that person.

Do you know anyone who prefers to speak rather than listen? Or, have you ever told a friend that you were not feeling well only to have that friend launch into a discussion of how he is feeling? If so, you have experienced the listening misbehavior of *stage hogging*. Listeners who stage-hog often interrupt the speaker or redirect the conversation to focus on themselves. This type of misbehavior may cause the speaker to feel that the listener is insensitive or doesn't care about his experiences.

Defensive listening causes listeners to believe others are attacking them, and they often become defensive or take information personally. A simple question such as a supervisor who asks an employee when she anticipates taking her lunch break might be taken personally by a defensive listener. If you are listening defensively, you would probably assume that the supervisor was displeased with the timing of your lunch break or dissatisfied with your work.

Insensitive listening is another listening misbehavior. To be effective listeners, we need to pay attention to what is being said, the words the speaker uses, how something is said, the speaker's facial expressions, and perhaps even to what is *not*

Stage hogging
Turning the conversation toward oneself rather than listening fully to the other person.

Defensive listening
When a listener perceives what is said as a personal attack.

Insensitive listening
When listeners pay attention only to a speaker's words but fail to interpret other nonverbal cues that would enhance understanding of the speaker's intent.

being said. It is important to "listen between the lines." Unfortunately, insensitive listeners do not go beyond the actual words that are used; they listen solely to the verbal component of the message. They fail to incorporate the other features of the message to truly understand what the speaker is trying to convey.

There are other listening misbehaviors that you will likely encounter. An awareness of the ones mentioned above will assist you in identifying listening behaviors to avoid as you listen in your personal, professional, and public lives. In fact, there are many things listeners can do to improve their ability to listen more effectively.

IMPROVING YOUR LISTENING

Throughout this chapter, we have provided several ways to improve the various elements of the listening process and have offered strategies for improving your listening effectiveness. As this chapter closes, we provide several suggestions that apply to all areas of listening that will help you improve your ability to listen well.

Find a Reason to Listen

One way to improve your listening is to find a reason to listen. If you can find value in listening to something or someone, it will help you attend to the message. Tell yourself that listening will help you in school, in your professional aspirations, or in your personal life. As a result, you may be more motivated to engage in effective listening. If you can identify an interest in or the relevance of a message, there is a greater chance you will listen to it. This isn't always easy, but reassuring yourself of the value or importance enhances your likelihood of effective listening.

Stay Focused

Another suggestion is to find ways to stay focused. For some people, this involves asking questions for clarification; others find taking notes helps them to listen carefully. In addition, some listeners try to listen for the speaker's main ideas to help them maintain their listening effectiveness. Others try to paraphrase what the speaker has said as a way of understanding the message but also as a way to help them stay focused.

Listen Fully and Fairly

A third suggestion is to offer the speaker your complete, uninterrupted attention. It is important not to prejudge the speaker or the message but to listen to it fully and fairly before making any type of judgment. Some listeners immediately tune out a

FIGURE 5.5

Ways to improve
listening.

Ways to Improve Listening

- Find a reason to listen
- Stay focused
- Listen fully and fairly
- Examine the speaker's evidence and credibility
- Prepare to listen

speaker if they don't share the same opinions on an issue. For example, in a political speech, a Republican might immediately tune out a Democrat because they are committed to different parties.

Examine the Speaker's Evidence and Credibility

Another suggestion is to examine each message carefully so that you understand what the speaker is actually saying. Is the speaker using valid and reliable support? Does he or she rely on the use of emotion to persuade you to believe or do something? Is the speaker a credible source? What is the meaning or intent behind the message? Do you trust this speaker? What is the speaker not saying? All of these factors need to be considered in order to listen effectively.

Prepare to Listen

Finally, make sure you are prepared to listen. This might require you to create an environment that is suitable for listening. Thus, if you are listening to a friend, you might need to move away from your computer and reposition your chair so you are facing your friend. Arrive at your classroom early so you can sit toward the front where you can see the speaker. If you know there is a time of day when you don't tend to listen well, if possible, try to schedule meetings when you know it is easier for you to listen.

These are just a few suggestions for the ways in which you can help yourself listen more effectively. As you work toward becoming a more competent communicator, it is important to analyze how you listen, what prevents you from listening, and how you can improve your own listening effectiveness.

CHAPTER SUMMARY

In this chapter, we defined the listening process, discussed the types of listening that occur, examined the various contexts in which listening occurs, and discussed why many of us don't listen well. In addition, we covered some of the listening misbehaviors some people possess and have made some suggestions regarding the ways in which you may become a more effective listener. As stated at the beginning of this chapter, if you listen effectively, you will demonstrate to others that you value them. You will be a better friend, parent, employee, supervisor, student, and more if you learn to listen well. Since listening is such a large part of our personal, professional, and public lives, it is important to understand the process of listening and how we can become better at it.

KEY WORDS

Appreciative listening Listening for enjoyment.

Association Making a connection between one thing and another; a strategy used to aid memory.

Auditory discrimination The ability to distinguish sounds.

Categorization The process of classifying information or placing information into logical categories; a strategy used to enhance memory.

Chunking A strategy that helps maintain information in short-term memory by remembering information in sections or pieces ("chunks").

Critical listening Listening to make a judgment.

Defensive listening When a listener perceives what is said as a personal attack.

Empathic listening Listening from the other person's perspective to support or help that person.

Evaluating Considering the message and the credibility of the speaker and separating fact from opinion to judge the meaning of the message.

Hearing The physiological act of taking in sounds.

Immediate memory Attending to something that is later discarded or placed in short- or long-term memory.

Informational listening Listening to understand or comprehend.

Insensitive listening When listeners pay attention only to a speaker's words but fail to interpret other nonverbal cues that would enhance understanding of the speaker's intent.

Interpreting Going beyond just the actual words that are said; focusing on the verbal, nonverbal, and relational components of the message.

Listening A psychological process where you take in the sounds and process them in order to understand, interpret, and respond to what you have heard.

Long-term memory The brain's filing system, which has a limitless capacity to store information that you may have heard months or even years ago.

Mnemonic devices Techniques that help you retain information in a more effective way than in its original form (i.e., lists, acronyms).

Pseudo-listening Pretending to listen to others while thinking about something else.

Remembering The act of retaining something in your memory.

Repetition A strategy to help improve your short-term memory by restating to yourself over and over again what you need to remember.

Responding Selecting the appropriate message to send back to the speaker.

Scopic listeners Listeners who develop an open interest in many topics.

Selective listening Listening to only portions of an entire message.

Short-term memory Memory with a limited capacity that is stored for a brief time unless it is important enough to be moved into long-term memory.

Stage hogging Turning the conversation toward oneself rather than listening fully to the other person.

Thought–speech differential Difference between what human beings can understand per minute (roughly 400–500 words) and the rate at which the average person speaks (roughly 120–180 words per minute).

Understanding Making sense of the message you heard.

REFERENCES

Brownell, J. (2013). *Listening: Attitudes, principles, and skills* (5th ed.). Boston: Allyn & Bacon.

Coakley, C. G., & Wolvin, A. D. (1997a). Listening in the educational environment. In M. Purdy & D. Borisoff (Eds.), *Listening in everyday life: a personal and professional approach* (pp. 179–212). Lanham, MD: University Press of America.

Coakley, C. G., & Wolvin, A. D. (1997b). Listening in the parent–teen relationship. *International Journal of Listening, 11*(1), 88–126.

Davis, J., Foley, A., Crigger, N. & Brannigan, M.C. (2008). Healthcare and listening: A relationship for caring. *International Journal of Listening, 22*, 168–175.

Flynn, J., Valikoski, T., & Grau, J. (2008). Listening in the business context: Reviewing the state of research. *International Journal of Listening, 22*, 141–151.

Imhof, M. (2008). What have you listened to in school today? *International Journal of Listening, 22*, 1–12.

Nichols, R. G., & Stevens, L. A. (1957). *Are you listening?* New York: McGraw-Hill.

CHAPTER 6

Understanding Interpersonal Relationships: Starting Off on the Right Foot

Chapter Objectives

After reading this chapter, you should be able to:

- Define interpersonal communication
- Identify the various types of interpersonal relationships
- Describe the various stages of relationship development
- Explain theories of relationship initiation
- Understand the role of disclosure and reciprocal disclosure on relationships
- Discuss the strategies used to manage dialectical tensions to maintain relationships

Personal: Since meeting in an 8:00 A.M. biological science class at Midwest University, you and Kyla have become best friends. Each of you approached the first class meeting with tremendous apprehension. After all, navigating the first week of classes as first-year college students was bad enough. As you began reviewing the course syllabus, Kyla asked you if you had purchased the textbook yet. You replied that you had found a used copy from an online vendor, and that led to a discussion of how much you both had paid for your textbooks. Over the next few weeks, the two of you sat next to one another in class and decided to study together for your midterm examination. You were both surprised to find how much you had in common with one another. Will a casual conversation that began as a random interaction in a college class evolve into a lifelong friendship?

Professional: You were both excited and nervous about your new position with a major telecommunications firm. This was the job you had dreamed about for the past year! You knew how important it was to make a great first impression, so you searched the company website and Googled your new boss and some of your new coworkers to get a sense of what they were like before your first day on the job. As you scanned the pages of the company website, you were pleasantly surprised to discover that your new boss was an alumni of your university. This would be valuable information to assist you in "breaking the ice" during your first few days on the job. You also located one of your coworker's Facebook pages, where you discovered that you both are fans of the same Major League Baseball team. You hoped to use this information to start a conversation in the company cafeteria. The more information you found on the Internet, the more confident you became about approaching your first week at the company. How will you fit in and what types of relationships will you have with your new boss and coworkers?

Public: You have always enjoyed politics and eagerly anticipated the upcoming presidential election. In the weeks leading up to the event, your political science professor contacted you and asked if you would be willing to host a Twitter page to inform students about the election issues. Following each presidential debate, you posted comments about the topics that were discussed. Soon you found that some of your Twitter followers were re-tweeting your comments on their pages. Eventually, some of these followers sent you a friend request on Facebook since they perceived from your posts that they shared similar viewpoints about the candidates and issues. How do common interests influence an interpersonal relationship?

CHAPTER OVERVIEW

If you were asked the question, "Are you currently involved in a relationship?" how would you respond? When we've presented this question to our own classes, more than half of the students are typically reluctant to raise their hand. However, after some encouragement we are able to persuade all students to raise their hand. A narrow perception of what constitutes a "relationship" causes them to refrain from responding. Usually students indicate that they perceive a relationship to be romantic in nature. The reality is that you are involved in a variety of relationships. In this chapter we examine how we use communication to initiate relationships and explore the progression of relationships from that first "hello." We also analyze the challenges of maintaining relationships over time and the strategies used to manage tensions we experience in relationships and provide suggestions for creating a satisfying communication climate.

INTERPERSONAL COMMUNICATION DEFINED

Interpersonal communication Communication between two people in which one person stimulates meaning in the mind of the other.

In Chapter 1, we identified various communication contexts. *Interpersonal communication* is defined as communication between two people in which one person stimulates meaning in the mind of the other. Recall the three scenarios at the beginning of the chapter. Whether you engage in conversation to reduce ambiguity about a biology class or share your experiences as first-year college students, searched the Internet for information about your new colleagues to help build effective relationships or engaged in conversations with others who shared similar attitudes and beliefs as you about the candidates in the upcoming election, you have used communication to accomplish your goals. Chances are that you have engaged in interpersonal communication with a variety of individuals. When we engage in interpersonal communication with others, relationships may be formed.

TYPES OF INTERPERSONAL RELATIONSHIPS

When we asked you to indicate if you were currently involved in a relationship, your initial reaction may have been one of hesitation. As mentioned earlier, our initial perception of what constitutes a relationship typically focuses on romantic ties. By expanding our definition to include the wide variety of relationships we form, the impact of interpersonal communication on relationship formation is obvious. Relationships are created and defined by the mutual exchange of information and feelings over time. Within the various contexts of our lives, we form countless relationships with others as we exchange messages and communicate.

Our family interactions may include many different relatives.

© Monkey Business Images/Shutterstock.com

Some examples of relationships that have been examined by communication scholars include friendships, workplace relationships, physician–patient relationships, family relationships, educational relationships, and, of course, romantic relationships. Within each context, several relationships may exist simultaneously. For example, workplace relationships may include a variety of connections, including those between coworkers, supervisors, and subordinates as well as organizational members and their customers or clients. Similarly, our family interactions may consist of parent–child relationships, sibling relationships, and other connections with relatives. Researchers have also devoted attention to the study of educational relationships that are formed between teachers and students, or among students themselves. Each of these relationship contexts is unique, and we are strategic in our approaches to communication in each of them. After all, our relationships with our parents are managed much differently than those with our boss or coworkers. For example, while you may feel comfortable openly disagreeing with your sibling or parent, restraint may be in order if you don't see eye to eye with your boss.

Have you ever stopped to think about "why" or "how" each of your relationships began? In some instances, relationship formation is involuntary. We are born into our family and have no choice in selecting our parents, siblings, grandparents, and other family relationships. Similarly, it's rare that we get to pick and choose who we want to work with when hired for a new job. Other relationships are voluntary. Romantic partners choose one another based on looks or compatibility, patients have a choice of doctors to see when seeking medical treatment, and friendships may be formed for a variety of reasons. Regardless of whether our relationships are voluntary or involuntary, communication is the foundation for initiating, maintaining, and strengthening our connections with others. Likewise, poor communication may cause an interpersonal relationship to break down and even terminate.

RELATIONSHIP STAGES

Can you recall how you first met your best friend? What did you say to one another? Berger and Calabrese (1975) examined communication that takes place when we first initiate a relationship. Through their research they identified three primary stages of interaction that are experienced when speaking with someone for the first time: entry, personal, and exit (Figure 6.1).

>== **Entry stage** First stage of relationship development that relies on expectations for behavioral norms to guide communication. Characterized by small talk and exchange of demographic information.

The *entry stage* of relationship development relies heavily on cultural or societal expectations for behavioral norms. During this stage, individuals engage in "small talk," which is characterized by the sharing of basic demographic information. Conversations are filled with back-and-forth questions such as "Where are you originally from?" or "What's your major?" Questions that are asked during this stage often follow societal norms for the initial stages of a relationship. Consider how you would respond to the question, "How are you?" Social norms would predict that you would say, "Fine! How are you?" During this stage it would be considered inappropriate to ask questions of a more personal nature or provide a

FIGURE 6.1

Interactions during relationship stages.

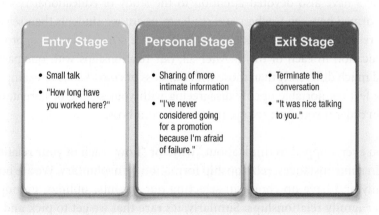

Have you ever had a special connection with a friend almost from the moment you met?

© bikeriderlondon/Shutterstock.com

detailed in-depth response about your day. Typically our communication focuses on demographic or superficial information.

Once the decision has been made to continue the relationship past the initial stage, we progress to the second stage of relationship development. The *personal stage* is characterized by the exchange of more personal or emotional information such as one's attitudes, beliefs, and values. There is no specified timeline for progressing from the entry stage to the personal stage. As you reflect on your initial conversations with your close friends, you may have discovered that you had an immediate connection and began to disclose personal issues fairly soon. Others may find that they need to spend more time in the "getting to know you" phase before moving on to share more personal information. While you may be willing to tell someone what your major is when asked, revealing the reasons for choosing your major or sharing why you're passionate about your field of study is often reserved for the personal stage.

The *exit stage* of relationship development involves making the decision to terminate or end the pursuit of a relationship. During this phase we decide if there is sufficient liking or similarity to continue our relationship. Can you recall a time when you met someone, but your communication focused solely on demographic questions and eventually you determined that you had nothing in common? It's important to

> **Personal stage** Second stage of relationship development that is characterized by the exchange of more personal or emotional information such as one's attitudes, beliefs, and values.

> **Exit stage** Final stage of relationship development that involves making the decision to terminate or end the pursuit of the relationship; characterized by sufficient liking or similarity.

note that we do not necessarily progress through all three of these stages. After all, you're probably able to recall a time when you met someone, exchanged some basic information about yourself, and quickly came to the conclusion that you didn't have enough in common to continue the conversation. Both verbal and nonverbal messages are used to indicate a lack of interest in pursuing a relationship. Avoiding eye contact or crossing one's arms and taking a step backward may signal disinterest, or a polite and vague statement such as "See you around sometime!" may signal that the relationship will not continue.

While it's important to understand "how" we use communication to start or initiate new relationships, we also need to explore the primary reasons why we decide to interact with others in the first place.

ATTRACTION THEORY

What else besides physical attraction draws you into a romantic relationship?

© StockLite/Shutterstock.com

Byrne (1997) proposed that we are initially drawn to others on the basis of attraction. The reasons why we are attracted to others vary depending on our needs or goals. Suppose you were to create three lists that address the following questions:

- What are the characteristics that you consider physically attractive about another person?
- What are the characteristics that you look for when deciding with whom you would enjoy "hanging out" or spending free time together?
- What characteristics are important to you when deciding who you want to collaborate with on a group project?

If you were to compare the things included on each of the three lists, chances are that they would be different. McCroskey and McCain (1974) identified three different types of attraction that come into play when deciding to initiate a relationship (Figure 6.2). When we hear the word *attractive*, our initial instinct is to identify physical characteristics. *Physical attraction* refers to those aspects that cause us to be physically drawn toward another. Perhaps you've heard the phrase "Beauty is in the eye of the beholder." This reinforces the notion that each person has a unique perspective regarding what they view to be physically attractive. Some may be drawn to a particular hair or eye color, and others may focus on muscular physique or height. Earlier in this chapter we identified different types of relationships that we form. Romantic relationships are most often initiated as a result of physical attraction between two people. While physical attraction plays an influential role in our initial decisions to communicate and attempt to form relationships with others, it is only one type of attraction. As we talk to one another and exchange personal information, we may discover that not only are we physically attracted to the person, but there are social aspects that we are drawn to as well.

> **Physical attraction** One of three types of attraction; refers to characteristics that cause us to be physically drawn toward another.

A second set of characteristics that influence decisions to form relationships is *social attraction*. While physical attraction focuses on physical characteristics, social attraction is defined as those characteristics that we seek in forming relationships with those whom we enjoy spending time and socializing. What qualities would you use to describe your best friend? Instead of focusing on their eye color or physique, chances are that you would use descriptors such as "honest," "spontaneous," or "funny" to explain why you enjoy spending time together. Friendships are the type of relationships that are most often described by referencing one's social attractiveness. However, it is not unusual for romantic partners to also explain their relationship by emphasizing the social qualities that make a partner special. This is because self-disclosure, or sharing private and intimate information

> **Social attraction** Characteristics that we seek in forming relationships with those whom we enjoy spending time with and socializing.

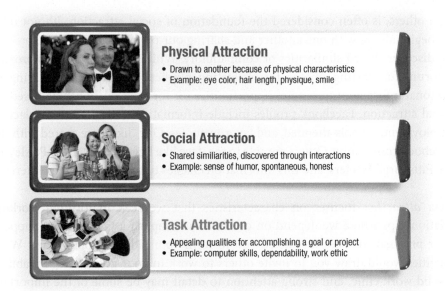

Physical Attraction
- Drawn to another because of physical characteristics
- Example: eye color, hair length, physique, smile

Social Attraction
- Shared similarities, discovered through interactions
- Example: sense of humor, spontaneous, honest

Task Attraction
- Appealing qualities for accomplishing a goal or project
- Example: computer skills, dependability, work ethic

FIGURE 6.2

Types of relational attraction.

with others, is often considered the foundation of social attraction. It's not until we begin talking with one another and sharing our preferences and attitudes that we discover shared similarities or compatibility. While social media sites provide a forum for posting photos for evaluating physical attractiveness, sharing of personal information promotes opportunities for forming relationships based on social attraction. Facebook profiles include information such as current place of employment, schools attended, and favorite quotes. Our "likes" are shared with the Facebook community. Others are able to see if we like Reese's Cups, Brad Paisley, or the Pittsburgh Steelers, and this information enables us to identify shared interests.

Task attraction focuses on characteristics that we seek in forming working relationships where we depend on others to accomplish a task or goal. Suppose your professor or boss instructed you to form your "ideal" project team. What qualities would draw you to invite others to work in your group? Dependability, a solid work ethic, and strong attention to detail may be some of the important

> **Task attraction**
> Characteristics that are identified as being important when forming working relationships where we depend on others to accomplish a task or goal.

aspects you would seek in your team. After all, their dazzling smile, dimples, shared interest in the *Twilight* book series, or sense of humor may make the time spent together more enjoyable, but these factors may not necessarily facilitate your progress toward your work goal. Instead, skills, attitudes, and work ethics are the primary qualities that we focus on in evaluating another as one with whom we would like to work on a project.

Depending on our needs or goals, we use one of the three types of attraction as the basis for initiating and forming relationships. Once we've identified our goal and evaluated someone as being attractive, the next step involves sharing information so we know what to expect.

UNCERTAINTY REDUCTION THEORY

How would you feel if your professor distributed a course syllabus that included the following list of assignments that would be used to assign your grade:
- Tests
- Term paper
- Discussion/participation

Suppose that no additional information is provided. How would you respond? Chances are that you would ask questions in order to clarify the expectations for the class. Some questions that may immediately come to mind may include:
- How many tests?
- What is the format for the exams: multiple choice, short answer, or essay?
- How many points is each exam worth?
- What chapters will be covered on each test?
- When will the tests be given?

Humans are generally uncomfortable with uncertainty. Just as there would be questions that need to be answered to reduce ambiguity about a class syllabus, there is also a need for information to decrease our uncertainty when forming relationships. Communication is the tool that we use to reduce our uncertainty, and question-asking is the most common strategy to reduce our initial discomfort or ambiguity.

COLLEGE STUDENTS AND DATING: WHAT'S YOUR GOAL?

Mongeau, Serewicz, and Therrien (2004) surveyed college students and asked them to identify their primary reason or "goal" for going on their most recent first date. Three "first-date goals" were identified:

1. **Reduce uncertainty** – the first date provides an opportunity to gain more information about the other person's attitudes, interests, and goals to determine if a relationship could be pursued
2. **Enjoyment** – views the date as an opportunity to simply have fun
3. **Relational escalation** – attempts to explore the potential for the relationship to progress into "something more" and leads to additional dates; explores romantic feelings

Uncertainty Reduction Theory
Explains how we engage in conversations during the initial stages of a relationship to decrease our uncertainty about others.

In 1975, Berger and Calabrese established *Uncertainty Reduction Theory* to explain how we use communication in the initial stages of a relationship to decrease our uncertainty about the other person. This theory describes how we use verbal and nonverbal communication in order to decrease our level of ambiguity. It proposes that in situations where we are uncertain, we increase our communication to help us understand others and better predict how they may respond. While we may be physically attracted to someone, it is difficult to determine if we want to pursue a relationship until we actually talk with them. Eye contact and smiling are nonverbal cues that may indicate that the person is open to initiating a conversation and then verbal communication takes over. Job interviews are one way that potential employers and candidates reduce their uncertainty about one another. Even after a new employee is hired, the uncertainty reduction continues. Employee orientation programs provide valuable information about benefits and expectations, and during casual conversations in the break room or at lunch you may discover that your new boss is not a "morning person" and thus you should avoid approaching her with questions until after she's had her third cup of coffee.

Active strategies
A method of reducing uncertainty that involves directly soliciting information about another person.

Passive strategies
Method of reducing uncertainty that involves indirect or unintended methods of gathering information when initiating a relationship.

Most people use one of three tactics to reduce uncertainty: active, passive, and interactive strategies (Figure 6.3). *Active strategies* involve soliciting information by asking third parties about another person. For example, if you are attracted to your friend's sibling, you may casually ask your friend if he or she is currently seeing anyone. At times, more discreet or indirect strategies are preferred to decrease our ambiguity. *Passive strategies* are implicit or unintended means to gather information during the initial stages of a relationship. Scanning someone's Facebook page, glancing at their hand to see if they're wearing a wedding ring, or

FIGURE 6.3

Active	Passive	Interactive
• Solicit information about others via a third party	• Indirect observation to reduce uncertainty about another	• Direct communication with another to decrease ambiguity
• Example: Asking your sibling if your mother has plans for the holidays.	• Example: Looking at your daughter's Facebook page for clues about her recent mood.	• Example: Calling a coworker and asking if they are interested in joining you for happy hour after work.

Uncertainty reduction strategies.

observing them as they interact with others in the campus cafeteria are all passive strategies to reduce uncertainty. *Interactive strategies*, or direct communication, are an additional tactic for uncovering information about others. Directly asking a coworker what he thinks about a new reality show on television, seeking clarification from your instructor about concepts that will be included on an exam, or posting a question to a political candidate's blog to solicit additional information on an economics project are all interactive strategies to reduce ambiguity.

> **Interactive strategies** Using direct communication to reduce uncertainty in the initial stages of a relationship.

A job interview helps reduce uncertainty between potential employers and employees.

© racom/Shutterstock.com

SELF-DISCLOSURE

Answering questions and exchanging information is an important part of the uncertainty reduction process. Recall our discussion of self-disclosure in Chapter 1. *Self-disclosure* refers to the sharing of personal information with others in an attempt to build or maintain a relationship. Our decision about what types of information to reveal and how much to share is often determined by the status of our relationship.

Breadth refers to the variety of topics we are willing to discuss with others. In the initial stages of a relationship, we tend to "play it safe" and discuss a wide array of demographic or superficial information as we attempt to reduce our level of uncertainty and get to know someone. During this time, we may focus on sharing only a little bit of information about a wide variety of topics. Speed dating offers a glimpse into just how quickly a variety of topics can be discussed. In this process, couples are given approximately 10 minutes to find out if they are potentially compatible. The goal is to meet several different people at a dating event rather than spending 2–3 hours on a date only to discover later that they had nothing in common with one another. A rapid exchange of information occurs, and the speed-daters quickly share information on topics ranging from occupation, life goals, hobbies, favorite foods, musical interests, and more. Given the time constraints, the opportunity to engage in an in-depth discussion about topics isn't possible.

The level of intimacy or details that you share about a given topic is referred to as the *depth* dimension of disclosure. Cultural and social norms often dictate what information is appropriate to share depending on the length of the relationship

> **Self-disclosure**
> Sharing of personal information with others in an attempt to build or maintain a relationship

> **Breadth** Variety of topics that we are willing to disclose about ourselves in discussions with others.

> **Depth**
> Level of intimacy or amount of detail that is disclosed about a particular topic.

WHO'S MORE APPREHENSIVE ABOUT EXPRESSIONS OF COMMITMENT?

While men are often stereotyped as being more apprehensive to express their commitment in a relationship, a 2013 article published in the United Kingdom's *Daily Mail* newspaper actually reports the opposite. On average men say those three little words (AKA: "I love you") 88 days after engaging in a serious relationship, compared to the 134 days that women wait before saying them. Men are also more likely to disclose their intimate feelings during the first month of dating, with 39% of men saying "I love you" compared with 23% of women.

Source: When WILL he say "I love you"? (n.d.).

and the context or setting. During an interview, a candidate may answer questions about a variety of topics. At that time, there isn't an opportunity to discuss long-term goals for professional development or specific attitudes about a work team's compatibility. Sharing of personal attitudes and opinions is often reserved until after you've been employed with the organization for a while and are asked to share your thoughts during an annual employee review. Similarly, would it be appropriate to say "I love you" on a first date? Probably not. Disclosures of this depth would be reserved until partners have spent some time getting to know one another.

While the majority of research on self-disclosure has focused on face-to-face interactions, scholars are now exploring the ways in which information exchange has evolved on social media sites. Consider the types of information that are shared on sites such as eHarmony, Match.com, Facebook, LinkedIn, Twitter, and Instagram. Before social media, several conversations or dates may have been needed before reaching a point where we comfortably share personal information that is publicly displayed in online profiles and status updates. Now we openly reveal information that was previously reserved for possibly a third or fourth conversation with another person. By the time we meet one another face-to-face, our conversations focus on more intimate or personal sharing about topics already identified by scanning a Facebook page or online dating profile. In the professional context, interviewers may

FACEBOOK DISCLOSURES: WHAT ARE WE SHARING?

A 2010 study by Nosko, Wood, and Molema identified three types of information that Facebook users disclose on their profiles:

- Standard/identifying information – demographic information that enables others to locate you online (e.g., gender, email address, profile photo, city/state of residence)
- Sensitive/personal information – detailed information that could be used to locate a person (e.g., current status, tagged photos, employer, and relationship status)
- Potentially stigmatizing information – information that could be viewed as socially stigmatizing by others (e.g., sexual orientation, birth year, religious or political views)

Who is more likely to "play it safe" when posting information to their Facebook page? The study found that as we get older, we refrain from disclosing as much personal information on social media sites. How does relationship status impact the type of information that we publicly disclose to others? Those who are single and interested in pursuing a romantic relationship tend to disclose more information than those who are already involved in a committed relationship.

Don't disclose anything online that you wouldn't want your parents or employer to read.

© Andrey_Popov/Shutterstock.com

find they no longer need to ask a potential employee to disclose the reasons for leaving a previous job if the information was posted on a LinkedIn profile or Facebook page. Even university presidents and elected officials have turned to social media to disclose their attitudes and thoughts with public audiences. At Butler County Community College, President Nicholas Neupauer, Ed.D., created a President's Blog to share his attitudes about a variety of topics, ranging from "Superbowl XVII: 10 Reasons Not to Watch" to revealing details about his own experiences as a student (*www.bc3.edu/ president*). Social media outlets provide celebrities with the opportunity to connect with their fans through personal disclosures. From Hillary Duff's sharing of her baby's first photos on Instagram to Mariah Carey's tweet to disclose the title of her next album, celebrities use these channels to create relationships with their fans and to enhance perceptions of closeness.

The option of sharing information openly and freely online comes with some cautions and responsibilities. Keep in mind that anything that is disclosed on Internet sites has the potential to be viewed by the public. As a rule of thumb, if you wouldn't be comfortable having your parents or employers read the information you share, think twice before disclosing it. Fortunately, sites provide users with the opportunity to manage who they allow to see the breadth and depth of their disclosures through the use of privacy settings. While you may share a breadth of information—ranging from your anticipation for the upcoming weekend, frustration with a midterm exam, or exhaustion from a long shift at work—privacy settings enable you to limit who is able to read the depth of your disclosures. You can create a closed Facebook group with your friends to discuss a professor's class assignments in more detail, or private messages can be sent to coworkers to vent about a slacker on a recent project that you completed at the office.

Disclosure and liking often go hand-in-hand. Kowalski (1999) found that the more we like someone, the more likely we are to share personal information. As we exchange more disclosures with one another, our liking for one another tends to increase. The challenge lies in determining what information is "safe" to share and at what point in our relationship should we disclose it. Recall our earlier discussion of Uncertainty Reduction Theory. Employers attempt to reduce their level of ambiguity about potential employees by asking them to disclose or share personal information about themselves that is directly relevant to the job. However, due to the fact that you may have only briefly met the interviewer, you may be uncomfortable disclosing your answers to questions such as "What is your biggest weakness?" or "What are your salary expectations?" The awkwardness experienced may be explained by the lack of reciprocal disclosures that are exchanged in an interview setting. Interviewees are expected to share a lot of information, whereas interviewers reveal very little about themselves. *Reciprocal self-disclosure* refers to the notion that individuals will engage in a similar exchange in terms of the types of information shared and the amount of information disclosed when communicating with one another. Consider how awkward it would be for an instructor to ask students to disclose their most embarrassing moments during an icebreaker activity on the first day of class. Even though everyone would be expected to share a similar story, the disclosures would be perceived as inappropriate given the fact that individuals have just met one another. The following exchange illustrates our expectations for reciprocal disclosures in our interpersonal relationships.

> **Reciprocal self-disclosure** Similar exchange of the type of information shared and the amount of information disclosed when communicating with others.

KYLA: Wow! I'm overwhelmed! There has been so much information shared during today's new employee orientation that my head is spinning!

ANDRE: I know what you mean, but don't worry. We're in this together. My cousin got me this job, and he said that the first few days are overwhelming. By the way, my name is Andre.

KYLA: I'm so sorry for venting! I'm Kyla. It's nice to meet you.

ANDRE: No worries! To be honest, I'm feeling overwhelmed, too! I don't think I took as many notes in my entire college career as I've taken today. Where did you work before joining Avicon?

KYLA: Actually, this is my first job. I just graduated from West Virginia University in May.

ANDRE: No way! I'm a WVU alum, too! Communication studies major from the Class of 2010. What was your major?

KYLA: Corporate communication! Did you ever have Dr. Simpson for COMS 2040?

ANDRE: She was the best! I learned so much from her final case study project. What a small world! By the way, I'm meeting my cousin for coffee in the cafeteria after orientation. He's going to try to give me some "inside scoop" on what to expect on my first day on the job here. Would you like to join us?

KYLA: That's so nice of you to invite me. I'd love to!

Both new employees engage in reciprocal disclosures by sharing their mutual feelings of being overwhelmed, and as a result of their conversation they discover that they both attended the same school and studied with the same professors. As one person shares new and significant information that is revealed because of his or her increased trust and comfort with the other, the other discloses as well.

As you consider what information to share and when to share it, consider the following guidelines to ensure that you practice effective and appropriate self-disclosure:

- How well do I know the other person? Can I trust him or her with the information I'm about to share?
- If I share this information, do I risk embarrassing myself or the other person?
- Is our relationship at a point where sharing this information is appropriate? Will I seem pushy or do I feel pressured to disclose?
- How relevant is the information that I'm sharing?

Asking yourself these four simple questions may be the key to ensuring that your disclosures are appropriate and effective in reducing uncertainty and initiating relationships with others. As the level of intimacy and the nature of our relationships change, so do our disclosures.

SOCIAL PENETRATION THEORY

Social Penetration Theory Explains how individuals share more information with one another as the relationship progresses.

Altman and Taylor (1973) created *Social Penetration Theory* to explain how individuals share information with one another as relationships develop and move from one stage to another. Essentially, social penetration theory focuses on building and maintaining relational closeness. More specifically, the theory illustrates how we transition from discussing superficial topics in the beginning stages of a relationship to exchanging more private and personal information as the relationship becomes more intimate. Altman and Taylor used the analogy of an onion to describe the layers of information that are revealed as relationships become more intimate. Fans of the movie *Shrek* may recall how Shrek uses the onion analogy to disclose his feelings and emotions to Donkey:

SHREK: For your information, there's a lot more to ogres than people think.
DONKEY: Example?
SHREK: (*holds up an onion, which Donkey sniffs*) Example . . . uh . . . ogres are like onions!
DONKEY: They stink?
SHREK: Yes... No!
DONKEY: Oh, they make you cry?
SHREK: No!
DONKEY: Oh, you leave 'em out in the sun, they get all brown, start sproutin' little white hairs . . .
SHREK: (*peels an onion*) *No!* Layers. Onions have layers. Ogres have layers. Onions have layers. You get it? We both have layers. (*walks off*)
DONKEY: Oh, you both have *layers*. Oh. You know, not everybody likes onions. What about cake? Everybody loves cake!

The onion analogy helps illustrate the various levels of information that we reveal as our relationships progress from initiation to more intimate stages. Altman and Taylor identified four levels of information that we're willing to disclose depending on the nature of our relationships. These include superficial, personal, intimate and private information. The layers of information are illustrated in Figure 6.4.

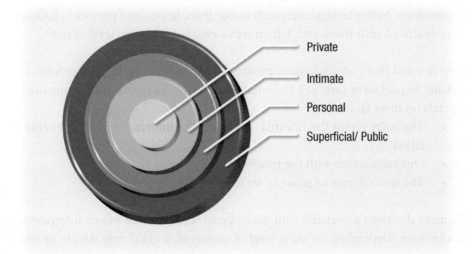

FIGURE 6.4

Social penetration "onion" model.

What topics do you talk about when you first meet someone?

© Maridav/Shutterstock.com

During our initial meeting with others, we tend to focus on more *superficial* or demographic information. Topics such as your college major and hometown are considered "safe" topics to disclose when we first meet someone. As our relationship progresses, we tend to reveal more *personal information* such as our favorite foods, hobbies, and pet peeves. Once we feel comfortable with the other person and have established a level of trust in our relationship, more *intimate information* is shared. Our experiences, occupational goals, and values are examples of topics that are disclosed at this level. *Private information* is often reserved for only our closest relationships. At this level, secrets such as our fears, hopes, and personal challenges are only shared with those with whom we've established a high level of trust.

Keep in mind that our disclosures progress from being superficial to private. Our decision to peel away layers of the onion and reveal the next layer of information depends on three factors:

- The costs versus the rewards of sharing the information (e.g., benefits vs. risks)
- Our satisfaction with the relationship
- The level of trust or security we feel with the other

We make decisions associated with social penetration in each of our interpersonal relationships. Depending on their level of closeness, a child may decide to reveal more intimate details with one parent as opposed to the other. For example, Janelle may find that she feels more comfortable sharing her fears about the upcoming birth of her baby with her mother rather than her stepfather. Employees share different information with coworkers and supervisors depending on the level of trust. Alaina may disclose to her coworkers that she has been calling in sick so that she can take care of her elderly mother who has been having health issues. She is not willing to share the same information with her supervisor because she's afraid that he will perceive her as being distracted by her mother's health concerns and not capable of leading her team of coworkers. She perceives the risks of telling her boss about the health issues as outweighing the benefits, so she keeps that information hidden from him.

FROM INITIATION TO INTIMACY: THE RELATIONSHIP DEVELOPMENT MODEL AND COMING TOGETHER

Now that we've examined the role that communication plays in our relationships, let's explore the ways in which our relationships progress from the beginning stages to the most intimate levels. Knapp (1978; Knapp & Vangelisti, 2003) expanded the model initially proposed by Berger and Calabrese (1975) and created the relationship development model to explain how individuals engage in initial conversations and build on their communication as they progress from one stage to the next in relationships. We discuss the first five steps of Knapp's model here, and in Chapter 7 the remaining five stages that describe how relationships may deteriorate and end are presented. Figure 6.5 provides a preview of each of the stages of coming together.

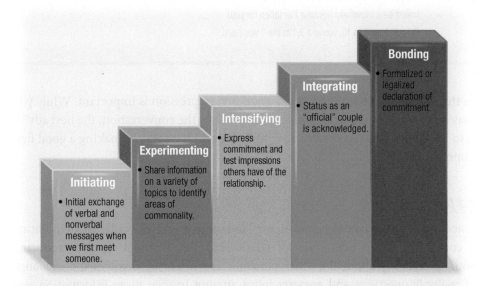

FIGURE 6.5

Knapp and Vangelisti's (2003) stages of coming together in a relationship.

Initiating

Initiating
First stage of coming together in the relationship development model. Focuses on the initial communication that occurs when we first meet someone.

Have you ever struggled with finding the "right" words to say when you meet someone for the first time? *Initiating* a relationship focuses on the initial communication that occurs when we first meet someone. Communication during this stage typically focuses on demographic information that is superficial and descriptive. Often the most challenging part of this stage is figuring out how to "break the ice" and start the conversation. Polite questions such as "Is this seat taken?" or "Hi, how are you?" are considered "safe" conversation-starters to determine if the other person is interested in continuing the conversation. Earlier in this chapter we discussed the role that attractiveness plays in our decisions to form relationships. Physical attractiveness is often one of the most influential factors when we're deciding to initiate a conversation. Nervous anticipation and anxiety are typical during this stage, and we feel pressure to find the perfect opening line. Unfortunately, this nervousness may cause some to resort to the use of "cheesy" pickup lines that are uncharacteristic of their normal behavior. Figure 6.6 includes examples of ineffective conversation-starters.

FIGURE 6.6

Examples of ineffective pickup lines.

SAMPLE PICKUP LINES

- Are you an interior decorator? Because when I saw you, the room became beautiful!
- If I was a stoplight, I'd turn red every time you passed by just so I could stare at you a little bit longer.
- Are you from Tennessee? Because you're the only 10 I see!
- I must be a snowflake because I've fallen for you!
- On a scale of 1 to 10, you're a 9. I'm the 1 you need.

In the initiation phase, portraying a good first impression is important. While you may be tempted to use a witty pickup line to start the conversation, the best advice is to just be yourself. Sincerity and confidence go a long way in making a good first impression.

Experimenting

Experimenting
Second stage of relationship development that involves the exchange of multiple questions and answers as we attempt to gain more information about the other person and to identify areas of commonality.

Once you have survived the challenging (and sometimes awkward) task of initiating a conversation, the next stage of relationship development involves reducing your uncertainty about the other person. *Experimenting* involves the exchange of multiple questions and answers in an attempt to gain more information and

RELATIONSHIP INITIATION IN ACTION: *THE BIG BANG THEORY*

On the television sitcom The Big Bang Theory, the character Sheldon exhibits a clear lack of social skills that is showcased in his attempts to build and maintain interpersonal relationships. In the season 3 "The Maternal Congruence" episode, Sheldon's struggle is evidenced in his efforts to start a conversation with his roommate Leonard:

> SHELDON: I made tea.
> LEONARD: I don't want tea.
> SHELDON: I didn't make tea for you. This is my tea.
> LEONARD: Then why are you telling me?
> SHELDON: It's a conversation-starter.
> LEONARD: That's a lousy conversation-starter.
> SHELDON: Oh, is it? We're conversing. Checkmate.

identify areas of commonality. The focus of disclosure in this phase is on covering a breadth of topics. Safe topics of conversation that are often discussed during this stage include one's major, hobbies, or other demographic questions. Social attraction is often uncovered during this phase as partners exchange information to identify commonalities. Recall our earlier discussion of uncertainty reduction. This is the goal during the experimenting stage, and reciprocal disclosures are expected. You'll know that you're in the experimenting stage when you experience a rapid exchange of questions and answers. Questions such as "So is this your first job since graduating from college?" may be followed with "Yes, but I interned with a similar company for my last semester so I'm familiar with this organization. Was this your first job after college?" While the majority of our relationships stop at this stage and we are satisfied with being merely acquaintances, there may be times when we decide to proceed even further. As a result of the information gathered during this phase, we may decide to continue to the next stage.

Intensifying

If we decide that our goal is to pursue a long-term relationship with another, chances are that we will proceed to the intensifying phase of the relational development model. *Intensifying* is characterized by more intimate expressions of commitment and by testing the impressions that others may have formed about the relationship.

Intensifying
Third stage relationship development that is characterized by more intimate expressions of commitment and by testing the impressions that others may have formed about the relationship.

During this stage, the depth of disclosures become more intimate as we share personal information with one another. Knapp and Vangelisti (2003) identified three verbal clues that are characteristic of intensifying. These include:

- First-person plural references ("We need to decide what we're going to do next weekend so I can submit my work schedule.")
- Direct references to the relationship and commitment to one another ("I can't wait for you to meet my family at my cousin's wedding this summer!")
- Creation of nicknames for one another ("Pumpkin," "Sweetie")

While the initiating and experimenting phases are encountered at the start of almost all types of interpersonal relationships, intensifying is typically reserved for romantic relationships and close friendships. When we're uncertain about the other person's commitment to the relationship, this stage may incorporate secret tests to reduce our uncertainty. Examples of tests may include physical separation for a period of time or making public verbal references to the other as your "boyfriend" or "girlfriend" to gauge the reaction.

Integrating

> **Integrating**
> Fourth stage of coming together in relationship development in which the lives of partners begin to merge and their status as a couple is acknowledged both personally and publicly.

During the *integrating* stage of relationship development, the lives of both partners begin to merge and their status as a couple is acknowledged both personally and

---

RELATIONSHIP INITIATION IN ACTION: *THE BIG BANG THEORY*

In "The Desperation Emancipation" episode in season 4, Sheldon's uncertainty about the status of his relationship with Amy is evidenced in the following conversation with his roommate Leonard:

> *(Sheldon yelling Leonard's name all the way down the stairs until he finds him)*
> LEONARD: Yeah, what?
> SHELDON: Amy Farrah Fowler has asked me to meet her mother.
> LEONARD: Yeah, so.
> SHELDON: What does that mean?
> LEONARD: Well, you know how you're always saying Amy is a girl who is your friend but not your girlfriend.
> SHELDON: Uh huh.
> LEONARD: Well, you can't say that anymore.

publicly. Their identities begin to merge as their social circles come together and they begin to share a network of friends who also view them as a couple. For example, signs that a romantic relationship has reached the integrating stage may include the exchange of personal items such as clothing and pictures that can be used to indicate the status of their relationship to others.

Bonding

Bonding is the final stage of coming together. Formalized or legalized declarations of commitment mark this phase as couples publicly acknowledge their dedication to one another.

Perhaps the most common indicators of personal bonding are engagements and weddings. At this stage of the relationship, couples want to declare their goal to pursue a long-term, exclusive relationship. In our professional lives, we may engage in formal bonding as we enter into formal business partnerships with other companies or organizations.

Weddings are an example of bonding.

Bonding
Final stage of coming together in the relationship development model. Formalized or legalized declarations of commitment mark this phase as couples publicly acknowledge their dedication to one another.

Movement from one stage of relationship development to the next isn't necessarily as clear and concise as it may seem. Knapp and Vangelisti (2003) proposed the following things to consider as you evaluate your own relationships and determine which stage you may be currently experiencing:

1. While we typically progress through the stages in the order presented in the model, we may need to revisit prior stages in order to strengthen the relationship before continuing on to future stages.
2. As we decide whether to proceed to the next stage, each partner engages in an analysis of the potential rewards of continuing the relationship. Questions that we may ask ourselves include "Do I feel the same way the other person does?" and "Am I ready to move to the next stage of this relationship?"
3. Each relationship is unique in terms of the amount of time spent at each phase of the relationship development process. While some relationships may go through all five stages in a matter of a few months, other couples may need a few years before reaching the point of being ready to publicly declare their commitment.

CHAPTER SUMMARY

Throughout this chapter we have answered some of the questions about how we use communication to form interpersonal relationships and described various stages that we experience as relationships progress from the beginning stages to more intimate levels. While most of the research on these stages has focused on romantic relationships, we encourage you to consider the role that communication plays in your own relationships as you transition from the initial stages of a relationship to the later stages. Each relationship that you experience is unique, from initiating a conversation with a new coworker or sharing information with a group of classmates via an online discussion board. It is important to consider the appropriateness of the information you self-disclose to others depending on the nature of the relationship. While the process of initiating relationships may be filled with anxiety, communication is the key to reducing your uncertainty and building connections that can last a lifetime.

KEY WORDS

Active strategies A method of reducing uncertainty that involves directly soliciting information about another person.

Bonding Final stage of coming together in the relationship development model. Formalized or legalized declarations of commitment mark this phase as couples publicly acknowledge their dedication to one another.

Breadth Variety of topics that we are willing to disclose about ourselves in discussions with others.

Depth Level of intimacy or amount of detail that is disclosed about a particular topic.

Entry stage First stage of relationship development that relies on expectations for behavioral norms to guide communication. Characterized by small talk and exchange of demographic information.

Exit stage Final stage of relationship development that involves making the decision to terminate or end the pursuit of the relationship; characterized by sufficient liking or similarity.

Experimenting Second stage of relationship development that involves the exchange of multiple questions and answers as we attempt to gain more information about the other person and to identify areas of commonality.

Initiating First stage of coming together in the relationship development model. Focuses on the initial communication that occurs when we first meet someone.

Integrating Fourth stage of coming together in relationship development in which the lives of partners begin to merge and their status as a couple is acknowledged both personally and publicly.

Intensifying Third stage relationship development that is characterized by more intimate expressions of commitment and by testing the impressions that others may have formed about the relationship.

Interactive strategies Using direct communication to reduce uncertainty in the initial stages of a relationship.

Interpersonal communication Communication between two people in which one person stimulates meaning in the mind of the other.

Passive strategies Method of reducing uncertainty that involves indirect or unintended methods of gathering information when initiating a relationship.

Personal stage Second stage of relationship development that is characterized by the exchange of more personal or emotional information such as one's attitudes, beliefs, and values.

Physical attraction One of three types of attraction; refers to characteristics that cause us to be physically drawn toward another.

Reciprocal self-disclosure Similar exchange of the type of information shared and the amount of information disclosed when communicating with others.

Self-disclosure Sharing of personal information with others in an attempt to build or maintain a relationship.

Social attraction Characteristics that we seek in forming relationships with those whom we enjoy spending time with and socializing.

Social Penetration Theory Explains how individuals share more information with one another as the relationship progresses.

Task attraction Characteristics that are identified as being important when forming working relationships where we depend on others to accomplish a task or goal.

Uncertainty Reduction Theory Explains how we engage in conversations during the initial stages of a relationship to decrease our uncertainty about others.

REFERENCES

Altman, I., & Taylor, D. (1973). *Social penetration: The development of interpersonal relationships.* New York, NY: Holt, Rinehart & Winston.

Are Friendships Key To Workplace Happiness? (n.d.). *Forbes.* Retrieved March 20, 2014, from http://www.forbes.com/2010/04/21/workplace-happiness-friendship-forbes-woman-well-being-relationship.html.

Berger, C. R., & Calabrese, R. J. (1975). Some exploration in initial interaction and beyond: Toward a developmental theory of communication. *Human Communication Research, 1,* 99–112.

Byrne, D. (1997). An overview (and underview) of research and theory within the attraction paradigm. *Journal of Social and Personal Relationships, 14,* 417–431.

Habelow, E. (2010, April 21). Are friendships key to workplace happiness? *Forbes. com.* Retrieved from www.forbes.com/2010/04/21/workplace-happiness-friendship-forbes-woman-well-being-relationship.html.

Knapp, M. L. (1978). *Social intercourse: From greeting to goodbye.* Boston, MA: Allyn & Bacon.

Knapp, M., & Vangelisti, A. (2003). Relationship stages: A communication perspective. In K. M. Galvin & P. J. Cooper (Eds.), *Making connections: Readings in interpersonal communication* (3rd ed., pp. 158–165). Los Angeles, CA: Roxbury.

Kowalski, R. M. (1999). Speaking the unspeakable: Self-disclosure and mental health. In B. R. Kowalski & M. R. Leary (Eds.), *The social psychology of emotional and behavioral problems* (pp. 225–248). Washington, DC: American Psychological Association.

McCroskey, J. C., & McCain, T.A. (1974). The measurement of interpersonal attraction. *Speech Monographs, 41,* 261–266.

Mongeau, P., Serewicz, M., & Therrien, L. (2004). Goals for cross-sex first dates: Identification, measurement and contextual factors. *Communication Monographs, 71,* 121–147.

Nosko, A., Wood, E., & Molema S. (2010). All about me: Disclosure in online social networking profiles. The case of Facebook. *Computers in Human Behavior, 26,* 406–418.

When WILL he say "I love you"? Men take 88 days to say those three words - but girls make their man wait a lot longer... (n.d.). *Mail Online.* Retrieved March 20, 2014, from http://www.dailymail.co.uk/femail/article-2289562/I-love-Men-88-days-say-girlfriend-women-134-days-say-boyfriend.html.

CHAPTER 7

Improving Interpersonal Communication: Relationships Don't Just "Happen"

Chapter Objectives

After reading this chapter, you should be able to:

- Explain the role of expectations in relationships
- Describe dialectical tensions that impact communication in relationships
- Recognize strategies used to maintain relationships
- Differentiate between the five stages of relationship dissolution
- Discuss the impact of deception, jealousy and conflict on relationships
- Explain four methods of conflict management

Personal: You and your best friend decided to attend the same college. During your first year, you're both partnered as a team for biology lab assignments. As the semester progresses your friend thinks that your lab team is functioning well. However, you feel like you're doing all of the work while your friend "skates by" and receives good grades based on the long hours you put into the lab assignments. You're growing tired of doing all the work and find yourself becoming irritable when your friend boasts about how "easy" the class is. You know the two of you need to talk before your relationship suffers, but how do you begin the conversation?

Professional: You enjoy your career as the director of fundraising for the local arts center. Since the center is a nonprofit agency, your job requires you to spend long hours researching and recruiting potential donors. You are very successful at this job, and many of the donors you recruit indicate that it's your sense of humor and communication style that has caused them to feel connected to the arts center and resulted in their donations. Each year you make a point to send thank-you notes and birthday cards to the donors. While you feel like you're doing a good job, you want to do more. How can you continue improving the relationship between the center and its donors?

Public: You've been dating your partner for nearly 6 months, and secretly you've been hoping that she would want to take your relationship to the next level and discuss a future together. However, recently, you have been experiencing some rough patches in the relationship, with your partner hanging out with her friends more frequently. You attribute this to the fact that your partner simply needs time alone and misses spending time with her friends. Imagine the surprise you feel when a friend calls and asks what happened between you and your partner. Confused, you ask your friend what she is talking about. Your friend tells you to check your partner's Facebook page. You notice the relationship status has changed from "in a relationship" to "single." How could she have made such a personal announcement in such a public manner on social media without telling you? How should you respond?

CHAPTER OVERVIEW

Ben Affleck alluded to the effort that goes into maintaining relationships during his acceptance speech at the 2013 Academy Awards ceremony. When acknowledging his wife, actress Jennifer Garner, Affleck stated, "I want to thank you for working on our marriage for ten Christmases. It is work, but it's the best kind of work. And there's no one I'd rather work with." This quote ignited a media frenzy of speculation regarding the status of his marriage, but Affleck later stated that he

All relationships encounter challenges or issues.

was simply pointing out that relationships require work and commitment. Realizing that we need to dedicate time and energy and focus on the vital role communication plays in sustaining our relationships is an important step in ensuring that we build and sustain satisfying connections in our personal, professional, and public lives.

In Chapter 6, we discussed the processes involved in initiating relationships. In this chapter, we will experience a "reality check" as we discuss some of the challenges and issues we face in our attempts to maintain our connections with others. We also examine the warning signs that relationships may be in trouble. Maintaining satisfying relationships takes work, and communication is the foundation for making this possible. Even if you've had a great relationship with a friend, a family member, or a coworker for several years, you're bound to encounter some issues from time to time. Recognizing the warning signs, identifying the key issues, and implementing effective communication strategies will better equip you to be able to overcome some of these potential relational challenges.

EXPECTATIONS IN RELATIONSHIPS

Have you ever stopped to consider the expectations you hold for yourself? Because you're enrolled in college, chances are you anticipate that you will earn a degree that will assist you in your career goals. What expectations do you have for your performance in classes? Do you expect to do well in your science courses? Now reflect on the expectations that you have for those with whom you have a relationship. You may anticipate that your parents will call you on your birthday, your best friend will keep a secret that you shared, or your coworkers will keep you informed of the latest "office gossip." But what happens when those expectations are not met? How do you react? If you're like most people, you probably experience feelings of disappointment, hurt, or even anger.

As humans, we all form expectations for ourselves and for others. Recall our discussion of social scripts from Chapter 6. If someone greets you with "Hi! How are you?" the expectation is that you will respond with, "Fine! And you?" Consider how you would react if the person responded with, "I've had a horrible week! I lost my student ID card, failed my history exam, and now my car won't start." Chances are you would abruptly end the conversation and wonder why they responded that way. *Relational expectations* are the explicit and implicit anticipations for ideal verbal and nonverbal responses. They consist of our forecasts or predictions for how others should behave or reply in a given situation.

Unspoken or unrealistic expectations are often cited as a problematic area in relationships. Ironically, at times we may find that we are unaware of the expectations we hold for others. It should come as no surprise that relationship problems arise when we don't clearly communicate or don't realize that we anticipate others to behave in particular ways. Consider the following example of Jayme, who was a newlywed. She anticipated that her new husband would prepare breakfast, have a fresh pot of coffee ready when she woke, and greet her by commenting on how beautiful she looked. She was frustrated and disappointed to find that her husband liked to sleep late and didn't enjoy breakfast or coffee. As Jayme complained to her mother, she was shocked when her mom responded by laughing. Her mother commented, "What did you expect, Jayme? After all, you didn't marry your father!" That's when Jayme realized that she expected her new husband to follow the same routine that her own father had practiced each morning with her mother. We all have preconceived notions about how others should behave or respond, but we may not always be aware of them ourselves.

Burgoon (1978) examined the role of communication in situations where our anticipations are not met. *Expectancy Violation Theory* examines our communication responses when our anticipations are not met. When a person does not meet our expectations, we call it a violation. While initially we may perceive violations as being negative, it's important to note that at times they may be positive. Consider our earlier example where you anticipate that your parents will acknowledge your birthday with a phone call. Imagine your surprise if a positive violation occurs when your parents arrive at your workplace at the end of your shift to take you out to dinner at your favorite restaurant where they present you with front-row tickets to your favorite band's sold-out concert. You expected a phone call but instead were pleasantly surprised by their visit, dinner, and tickets. The same scenario could also have resulted in a negative violation if you expected a phone call from your parents and they forgot your birthday. This would be upsetting because you assume that parents would always acknowledge their child's birthday. Afifi and Metts (1998) surveyed people about their expectations for friends and romantic partners and asked them to recall the last time they said or did something unexpected. Nine categories of relational expectancy violations were identified. Figure 7.1 summarizes these categories.

The nine categories include both positive and negative expectancy violations. Criticism, relationship de-escalation, transgressions, and acts of disregard tend

> ⇒ **Relational expectations**
> The explicit and implicit predictions for anticipated or ideal verbal and nonverbal responses. They consist of our forecasts for how someone should behave or reply in a given situation.

> ⇒ **Expectancy Violation Theory**
> Examines the role of communication when our anticipations are not met. Violations may be perceived as positive or negative.

to be perceived as violations that have negative implications in the relationship. Relationship escalation, acts of devotion, and gestures of inclusion are categories of violations that are typically viewed in positive ways. Uncharacteristic relational behavior and uncharacteristic social behavior may be perceived positively or negatively depending on the nature of the violation. Consider the example from Figure 7.1 in which a coworker flirts with you and then asks you on a date. If you are interested in the coworker, this could be perceived as a positive uncharacteristic relational behavior. However, if you are already involved in a romantic relationship and are not interested in the coworker, the flirting may cause you to feel uncomfortable and would be perceived negatively.

FIGURE 7.1

Afifi and Metts's (1998) categories of expectancy violations in relationships.

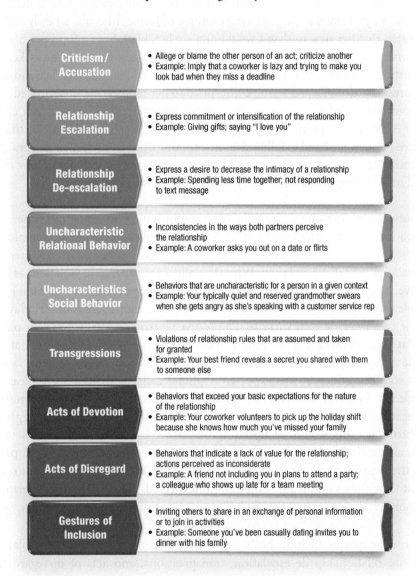

Criticism/ Accusation	• Allege or blame the other person of an act; criticize another • Example: Imply that a coworker is lazy and trying to make you look bad when they miss a deadline
Relationship Escalation	• Express commitment or intensification of the relationship • Example: Giving gifts; saying "I love you"
Relationship De-escalation	• Express a desire to decrease the intimacy of a relationship • Example: Spending less time together; not responding to text message
Uncharacteristic Relational Behavior	• Inconsistencies in the ways both partners perceive the relationship • Example: A coworker asks you out on a date or flirts
Uncharacteristics Social Behavior	• Behaviors that are uncharacteristic for a person in a given context • Example: Your typically quiet and reserved grandmother swears when she gets angry as she's speaking with a customer service rep
Transgressions	• Violations of relationship rules that are assumed and taken for granted • Example: Your best friend reveals a secret you shared with them to someone else
Acts of Devotion	• Behaviors that exceed your basic expectations for the nature of the relationship • Example: Your coworker volunteers to pick up the holiday shift because she knows how much you've missed your family
Acts of Disregard	• Behaviors that indicate a lack of value for the relationship; actions perceived as inconsiderate • Example: A friend not including you in plans to attend a party; a colleague who shows up late for a team meeting
Gestures of Inclusion	• Inviting others to share in an exchange of personal information or to join in activities • Example: Someone you've been casually dating invites you to dinner with his family

As you reflect on the list of expectations identified in Figure 7.1, consider how expectations permeate every relationship you encounter. From anticipated behavior during a job interview to perceptions of what's considered appropriate disclosures on one's Facebook page, we expect certain responses and behaviors. In order to avoid miscommunication, the best advice for healthy relationships is to clearly, explicitly communicate expectations. When others violate our expectations, pause and consider potential reasons why the violations occurred as opposed to rushing to judgment or jumping to conclusions. Doing so may help preserve the relationship. Sometimes our differing expectations for communication and behaviors in relationships may result in dialectical tensions.

DIALECTICAL TENSIONS

Can you recall a time when you were frustrated because you have an extremely close relationship with your best friend, yet you felt somewhat isolated from others? Maybe you've wondered why you've always enjoyed and looked forward to your family's annual summer vacations together at the Outer Banks, yet you yearn to go someplace different and exciting? Can you imagine the frustration you might experience if a professor didn't provide a syllabus outlining the schedule for the semester? While spontaneous class discussions and assignments may be a refreshing change from the traditional class format, the lack of structure and clarity about course grading and expectations may be frustrating. Expectations in our relationships create needs that motivate us to make choices about our communication. Sometimes we experience conflicting expectations, and there is a struggle between two opposing needs that we want to fulfill.

Dialectical tensions
Contradictory pulls between opposing goals or desires in a relationship.

Baxter (1988) described *dialectical tensions* as contradictory pulls between opposing goals or desires in a relationship. She identified three primary dialectical tensions in her initial research (Figure 7.2).

FIGURE 7.2

Primary dialectical tensions (Baxter, 1988).

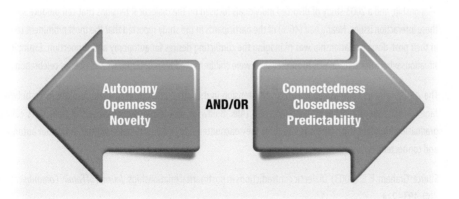

| Autonomy Openness Novelty | AND/OR | Connectedness Closedness Predictability |

Autonomy versus connectedness focuses on our desires to maintain our independence yet still be close to others. Consider the athlete who is dedicated to his team, yet also enjoys his individual time in the spotlight when he performs well during games. *Openness versus closedness* reflects our need to share information with others while keeping some aspects of our lives private. Teachers may allow students a glimpse into their personal lives by accepting friend requests from students and making some areas of their Facebook profile visible to the public, yet keeping some content private to cautiously refrain from sharing information that is too personal. *Novelty versus predictability* addresses our need to experience things that are new and different while simultaneously wanting routine and consistency. If your organization acquires a new company, you may look forward to the changes in your workplace and working with new colleagues, yet you worry about how you'll get along with one another and the impact the merger will have on your work responsibilities and routine.

How do these tensions influence our communication? In order to negotiate the tensions we experience in our relationships, we need to communicate with others. Consider the situation where you are comfortable and enjoy being part of a connected, committed relationship. However, from time to time you may experience a desire for a "night out" with your friends to maintain those relationships. Simply explaining your desire to spend time with others may help alleviate the chance of any inaccurate perceptions your partner may form. Reassurances about the relationship help confirm that you wish to remain connected while maintaining your own identity and friends.

DIALECTICAL TENSIONS AFTER DIVORCE

Couples experiencing a divorce often encounter numerous communication challenges as they terminate their relationship, and a 2003 study of divorced individuals focused on the dialectical tensions that can produce some of these interaction issues. Nearly half (46%) of the participants in the study reported that the most prominent tension in their post-divorce relationship was managing the conflicting desires for autonomy and connection. Examples of situations where this tension was most prevalent were children's weddings or birthdays and holiday celebrations.

The 2009 movie *It's Complicated* illustrates this tension in its portrayal of the post-divorce relationship between Jane (Meryl Streep) and her ex-husband, Jake (Alec Baldwin). The tensions experienced at their son's college graduation highlight the numerous struggles they encounter in their quest to balance their desires for autonomy and connectedness.

Source: Graham, E. E. (2003). Dialectic contradictions in postmarital relationships. *Journal of Family Communication, 3*(4), 193–214.

Researchers have examined dialectical tensions across a variety of relationship contexts. It should come as no surprise that in long-distance relationships the tension most frequently experienced by romantic partners is the novelty versus predictability dialectic (Sahlstein, 2006). Couples plan times when they would communicate to ensure a level of certainty in their relationship, but also realize that the time spent apart produced uncertainty. In the professional context, employees indicate that openness and closedness is a tension often experienced with coworkers who are also considered to be close friends. Conflicting desires to be open in communicating with one another compete with workplace rules and guidelines for confidentiality of information (Baxter & Bridge, 1992).

Reflect on the tensions you have experienced in your own relationships with friends, family members, coworkers, or even classmates. Chances are you'll discover that you experience these struggles in virtually every relationship. The key is to communicate about the tensions when they arise in order to work through them instead of denying their existence. Doing so will enhance your ability to maintain your relationships with others.

RELATIONSHIP MAINTENANCE

As Ben Affleck pointed out in his Academy Awards speech, relationships take work. Not surprising, Duck (1988) pointed out that we spend more time maintaining and sustaining our relationships than in the initiation or termination phases of the

relationship life cycle. Figure 7.3 summarizes the four components of relationship maintenance that have been identified as important to sustaining our connections with others (Dindia & Canary, 1993).

FIGURE 7.3

Key components in maintaining relationships (Dindia & Canary, 1973).

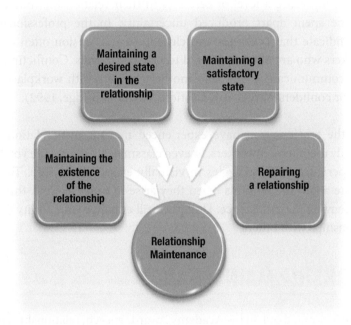

Maintaining the Existence of the Relationship

It is easier to keep in touch and maintain relationships now more than ever before. Social media sites such as Instagram and Facebook have made it easy for individuals to stay in contact with high school and college friends after graduation, and they enable families to share photos and keep up-to-date on activities from a distance. Before electronic media, family and friends often kept in touch with one another by sending cards at holidays and birthdays, or by making periodic phone calls to one another. By engaging in periodic communication with our friends, coworkers, and loved ones, we are at least able to keep the relationship alive.

Maintaining a Desired State in the Relationship

A second component of relational maintenance involves communicating to ensure that the status of the relationship "fits" with your goals and desires. Perhaps your goal is to maintain your current friendship with a coworker. This could be accomplished by extending invitations to go to lunch or out for drinks after work. However, the goal may be to maintain the current state of the relationship and keep it from escalating and becoming more intimate. Suppose a coworker who you've been friends with for

Friends who make the effort to spend time together communicate how much they value the relationship.

© YanLev/Shutterstock.com

the past couple of years asks you out on a date. The notion of a romantic relationship with a coworker makes you uncomfortable, but you don't want to jeopardize your friendship. Once you identify your level of comfort with the relationship, you communicate in a way that will help you accomplish your relational goals.

Maintaining a Satisfactory State

Ensuring that both parties perceive the relationship as thriving and satisfactory is the goal of the third component of relationship maintenance. Friends from college may plan a weekend beach getaway in order to spend time together. While the sharing of text messages and Facebook posts keeps them connected in the interim, the annual trip and time spent together communicates how much they value the relationship. It is important to note that both individuals in a relationship should experience satisfaction with the current relationship state.

Repairing a Relationship

As we stated earlier, relationships require work. Maintaining relationships is a continual task that requires time and effort. Perhaps the recent birth of a new child has kept friends from enjoying weekly dinners together, and they begin to feel disconnected. Scheduling time to meet once a month for a meal or a movie communicates the value of the relationship and restores the level of closeness previously experienced. Because relationships take work, they will likely hit "rough spots" where the relationship isn't functioning as it has in the past. When this occurs, we have to repair the relationship.

What strategies do we use to maintain our relationships with others? A study by Canary, Stafford, Hause, and Wallace (1993) examined the communication strategies that we use to sustain our connections. These strategies are summarized in Figure 7.4. As you review the list, notice that some of the tactics include negative behaviors such as avoidance and antisocial messages. Keep in mind that these may be effective in situations where we want to maintain a desired status in our relationship with another person. For example, if Xander only perceives Sierra as a friend when it becomes apparent that she is interested in pursuing a romantic relationship, he may flirt with other women in her presence to send a message that he's not interested in

FIGURE 7.4

Communication strategies used to maintain relationships (Canary et al., 1993).

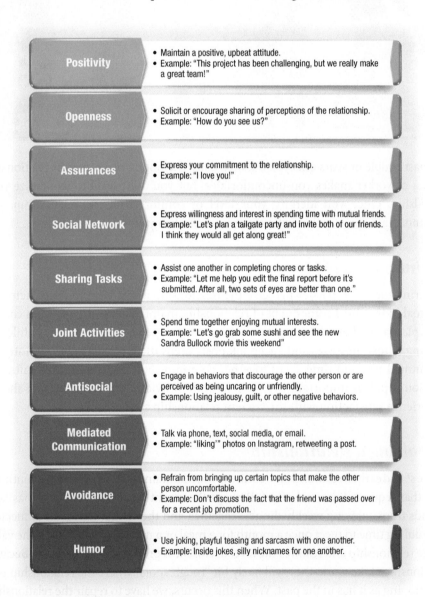

Positivity	• Maintain a positive, upbeat attitude. • Example: "This project has been challenging, but we really make a great team!"
Openness	• Solicit or encourage sharing of perceptions of the relationship. • Example: "How do you see us?"
Assurances	• Express your commitment to the relationship. • Example: "I love you!"
Social Network	• Express willingness and interest in spending time with mutual friends. • Example: "Let's plan a tailgate party and invite both of our friends. I think they would all get along great!"
Sharing Tasks	• Assist one another in completing chores or tasks. • Example: "Let me help you edit the final report before it's submitted. After all, two sets of eyes are better than one."
Joint Activities	• Spend time together enjoying mutual interests. • Example: "Let's go grab some sushi and see the new Sandra Bullock movie this weekend"
Antisocial	• Engage in behaviors that discourage the other person or are perceived as being uncaring or unfriendly. • Example: Using jealousy, guilt, or other negative behaviors.
Mediated Communication	• Talk via phone, text, social media, or email. • Example: "liking'" photos on Instagram, retweeting a post.
Avoidance	• Refrain from bringing up certain topics that make the other person uncomfortable. • Example: Don't discuss the fact that the friend was passed over for a recent job promotion.
Humor	• Use joking, playful teasing and sarcasm with one another. • Example: Inside jokes, silly nicknames for one another.

being more than friends. It's important to note that these behaviors have been studied across a variety of relationships, and researchers have found that friends, coworkers, romantic partners, and married couples report using many of the same strategies.

While we spend the vast majority of time invested in maintaining our relationships, there may come a time when it becomes apparent that the connection is beyond salvage or repair. In those instances, it may actually be healthier and ultimately more satisfactory for both partners to terminate the relationship as opposed to continue working on it.

RELATIONSHIP DISSOLUTION

In Chapter 6, three stages of the relationship life cycle were introduced: initiation (entry), maintenance (personal), and dissolution (exit). *Relationship dissolution* occurs when one or both partners perceive the relationship as being dissatisfactory and make the decision to end their connection. The five stages of coming together in relationships were discussed in Chapter 6. Knapp (1978) also identified five stages that provide clues that a relationship may be in trouble and prompt partners to consider whether it is worth saving. It's important to keep in mind that partners may not necessarily perceive that they are experiencing the same stage at the same time. In fact, one person may "skip" a stage while the other follows them in sequence. Figure 7.5 summarizes Knapp's five stages that indicate that the quality of a relationship may be deteriorating.

➤ **Relationship dissolution**
When one or both partners perceive the relationship as being dissatisfactory and the decision is made to terminate the connection.

Differentiating

In the initial stages of a relationship, partners spend considerable time communicating and getting to know one another better. In the *differentiating* stage, couples may find that they spend more time disagreeing or emphasizing their differences as opposed to focusing on the things they have in common. In fact, this stage may signal that two people involved in a relationship are heading in different directions. For example, Sasha states that she enjoys eating out; Kyla might comment that she is tired of going to restaurants and actually prefers cooking at home. Cory may talk about how much she looks forward to spending time with her friends, and Renea may comment on how annoying and obnoxious Cory's friends are. While on the surface it may appear as though this stage is solely negative, it can provide an opportunity for relational partners to reexamine their own individual identities and find ways in which to restore their independence. For example, Sasha might decide to go out to eat with friends a few times a week and Cory may go out with friends without Renea. Doing so can be beneficial when trying to manage the autonomy-versus-connectedness tensions that occur in relationships.

➤ **Differentiating**
First stage in the process of relationship dissolution in which partners focus on their differences as opposed to their commonalities.

FIGURE 7.5

Knapp's and Vange-
listi's (2003) stages
of coming apart in
relationships.

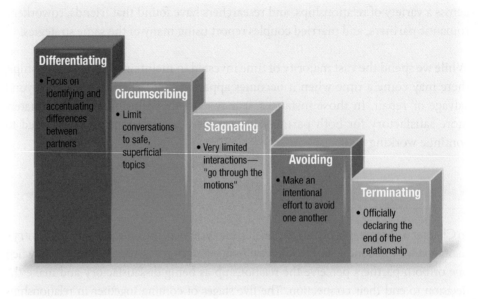

Circumscribing

Circumscribing
Second stage in the
process of relationship
dissolution in which
communication is limited
to safe, superficial topics.
Both the quality and
quantity of conversations
between partners is
limited.

The second stage of relationship dissolution, *circumscribing*, is indicated when couples begin to drift apart in the quality and quantity of their communication. Intimate conversations where thoughts, feelings, and dreams were shared are replaced with interactions that focus on safe, superficial topics. Questions such as "How was the traffic on your commute from work?" may be met with short responses such as "Lousy!" Partners find that they no longer feel comfortable engaging in discussions about intimate or personal topics.

Stagnating

Stagnating
Third stage of relationship
dissolution in which
communication between
partners is limited and
the goal is simply to
maintain a status quo.

Have you ever been near a stagnant pond? If so, you would probably describe the water as smelling "stale." It's quite appropriate that Knapp (1978) referred to his third stage of coming apart as *stagnating* since during this phase communication is at a standstill. Partners in this stage simply "go through the motions." They may attend events together, but once they return home they retreat into their own worlds with very little interaction between them. Conversations about the state of the relationship are ignored in an attempt to avoid a conflict. Preserving the relationship is no longer a priority, and it's almost as if they're playing a "waiting game." Eventually, the prospect of saving the relationship becomes difficult and partners may resort to physically avoiding one another.

Communication between partners is limited during the stages of coming apart.

© Iakov Filimonov/Shutterstock.com

Avoiding

Avoiding, the fourth stage of coming apart, is illustrated when relational partners make a conscious effort to avoid one another. Roommates may plan class schedules on opposite days to avoid being around one another, or married couples may spend time with friends or family members in an attempt to minimize the time they spend with one another. In essence, partners are exhausted at the prospect of acting like the relationship is worth saving, and they use avoidance to escape potential opportunities that might require them to discuss it.

> **Avoiding**
> Fourth stage in the relationship dissolution process in which partners make an effort to avoid being in the physical presence of one another.

Terminating

While counselors and self-help books often encourage relational partners to communicate with one another and try to "work it out," the reality is that some relationships are beyond repair. Let's face it, some relationships are toxic and are potentially damaging to one's identity, self-esteem, or physical or mental well-being. Rather than continue to live with a roommate when you dread being in your apartment, or working with colleagues who continually put you down and cause you to feel inferior, it may be in your best interest to *terminate* the relationship. As a result of the end of the relationship, partners are faced with the task of rediscovering their sense of self and reexamining their identity as individuals. It's important to note that just because a relationship experiences one or more of the stages of coming apart, it may still be repaired. A couple may decide that they want

> **Terminating**
> Final stage of relationship dissolution when one or both partners experiences a level of dissatisfaction that motivates them to end the relationship.

to try and work things out by seeing a counselor. As a result, the termination stage is avoided and the relationship is salvaged.

What communication behaviors contribute to the eventual demise of relationships? It's impossible to pinpoint specific ones. However, three factors that are frequently reported as causing issues in a variety of relationships include deception, jealousy and conflict.

BARRIERS TO EFFECTIVE INTERPERSONAL RELATIONSHIPS

Increasing awareness of some of the core communication issues that can create problems in our relationships is often a crucial element in maintaining or restoring our connections to a healthy and satisfactory state. While research has identified a variety of communication behaviors that often create relational challenges, three of the most common issues include the use of deception, the presence of jealousy, and the management of conflict. Why would we include a discussion of communication behaviors that have the potential to damage relationships in a chapter focused on improving them? An increased awareness and understanding of the messages that have the potential to destroy relationships may be the very key to repairing and maintaining them.

Deception

Can you recall a time when you have told a lie to avoid hurting someone's feelings? Perhaps you claimed that you needed to study instead of joining your parents or in-laws for dinner.

Maybe you told your boss that you already had plans for the weekend when she asked you if you were available to cover a coworker's shift. If you've ever been deceptive in your communication with others, you're not alone. Serota, Levine, and Boster (2010) found that on average people report telling approximately two lies per day (see Table 7.1). While this may seem exaggerated, consider the various ways we deceive others. A salesperson may deceive a customer who asks "How do I look in this outfit?" in order to avoid hurting the customer's feelings or losing a potential sale. Perhaps you have lied to a server in a restaurant who asks, "How is your dinner?" and you respond "Great!" even though your dinner is cold. Simple responses to avoid hurting someone's feelings or to avoid an unpleasant situation can be considered deceptive communication. It's important to consider both the short- and long-term effects of deception on our relationships.

© Photographee/Shutterstock.com

Have you ever been deceptive in your communication with your boss?

Deception has been defined as intentionally sharing a message with the goal of causing the other to adopt a false conclusion or belief. Recall our earlier discussion of relationship expectations. When a friend, coworker, or family member knowingly deceives us, we may experience hurt and disappointment. After all, our expectation is that relationships are based on honesty and trust.

Scholars have identified five types of deception that are often used in relationships: lies, concealment, equivocations, exaggerations, and minimizations. *Lies* involve fabricating or falsifying information. Suppose a coworker asks if you'd like to join her at a symphony performance on Saturday evening. If you don't enjoy classical music, you may lie and tell her that you already have other plans, even if you don't. *Concealment* involves withholding some important or relevant information. If your boss asks if you've received any updates from a vendor regarding a shipment date for software that is crucial to completing a project, you might reply, "He just sent an email this morning!" What you don't say is that the email indicated that the software would be delayed. *Equivocation* is often used in situations where we attempt to spare someone's feelings. This strategy involves using vague or ambiguous language to avoid speaking the truth. Suppose your best friend gets a new haircut. When she asks you what you think, you respond with, "Wow! It's so different!" In reality, you don't like the haircut, but you don't want to risk hurting

Lies
Form of deception that involves the fabrication or falsification of information.

Concealment
Form of deception that involves withholding important or relevant information.

Equivocation
Deception strategy in which one uses vague or ambiguous language in an attempt to avoid speaking the truth. Often used in situations where we attempt to spare someone's feelings.

Exaggeration
Form of deception that involves stretching the truth, adding details or information to enhance a story, or repeating oneself in an attempt to be convincing.

Minimizing
Form of deception when we downplay the truth.

your friend's feelings. *Exaggeration* involves stretching the truth, adding details or information to enhance a story, or repeating oneself in an attempt to be convincing. Job interviews or online dating profiles may be situations in which individuals attempt to make themselves look better by embellishing details about their lives. A final type of deception involves *minimizing* or downplaying the truth. Suppose you fall on the steps at work while carrying a pile of papers. A coworker asks if you're hurt and to avoid further embarrassment you state, "No, I'm okay" when you're really in pain.

TABLE 7.1

Statistics on the Number of Lies Told in the United States

Percentage of adults who admit to telling lies "sometimes" or "often"	12%
Percentage of women who admit to occasionally telling harmless half-truths	80%
Percentage of patients who lied about following a doctor's treatment plan	40%
Average number of lies per day told by men to their partner, boss, or colleague	6
Average number of lies per day told by women to their partner, boss, or colleague	3

Source: Database Records.com – *Newsweek*. (2012).

Truth bias
Expectation that people in close relationships will be honest with one another. Thus, deception may be ignored or overlooked due to our expectations for the truth to be told.

Behavioral familiarity
Strategy to assist in identifying deception. The level of familiarity with typical patterns of behaviors enables us to easily identify uncharacteristic behaviors that may signal deception.

Since statistics seem to indicate that 12% of people admit to telling lies "sometimes" or "often," how can you identify whether someone is telling you the truth or not? While some claim that it's as simple as looking for avoidance of eye contact, wringing hands, or fidgeting, it's not always that easy. The *truth bias* often interferes with our ability to see deception with close friends, romantic partners, or family members. Essentially, this bias involves our expectation that people with whom we are in a close relationship will be honest with us. Because we trust and expect them to be honest with us, deception may be ignored or overlooked. Perhaps you can recall a situation when your friend was deceived by his or her romantic partner. While the deception may have been blatantly evident to others, it may not have been as apparent to the person being deceived. *Behavioral familiarity* is one strategy that we can use to help identify dishonesty. Because we become so familiar with the typical behaviors of those with whom we have close relationships, we are better equipped to identify when their actions are uncharacteristic of their normal behaviors. For example, if your partner comes home from work and immediately launches into a detailed description about her day, yet she rarely shares any information about work, you may become suspicious or question why her behavior is atypical or uncharacteristic.

Park, Levine, McCornack, Morrison, and Ferrara (2002) studied 202 college students and identified three primary means through which deception is typically revealed. These include physical evidence, third-party information, and confessions. In 2009, professional golfer Tiger Woods's deception was revealed when his then wife Elin Nordegren discovered text messages to other women on his cell phone. Physical evidence can range from text messages that romantic partners discover on a cell phone to an incomplete report that an employee told his boss was finished. Third-party information involves others sharing or revealing information about the deception. A sibling who tells his parents about his sister coming home after curfew after she claimed that she was in bed by midnight serves as a third-party informant. Confessions may occur when guilt or direct confrontation occurs. A coworker may admit that she lied about not being able to cover her own shift last weekend as a result of the guilt she experiences after hearing how you had to miss your brother's birthday celebration because you were working in her place.

Deception can be detrimental to our relationship in that it has the potential to diminish our level of trust and respect for the other person. Another communication behavior that has also been found to impact our level of satisfaction in relationships is jealousy.

Jealousy

Fans of the Disney *Toy Story* series of films are familiar with the ways in which jealousy can impact relationships. The movie showcases the adventures of Woody, a toy cowboy who has always been Andy's favorite, as he becomes consumed with jealousy when he discovers that Andy prefers Buzz, a gift he received for his eighth birthday. Eventually the pair works through their mutual jealousy and discovers that their friendship is more important than vying for Andy's attention.

Jealousy is defined as a negative or destructive communicative response to a perceived threat to a relationship. Competition for the other person's time, attention, or affection may result in negative or damaging communication behaviors. One example of jealousy that can occur between siblings is often referred to as *sibling rivalry*. Competition for parents' attention may cause brothers and sisters to react in hurtful ways toward one another. Jealousy also occurs in our friendships and in our relationships with coworkers. Consider how you might feel if your boss promotes a coworker you worked with on a recent project instead of offering you the promotion. Jealousy can also be experienced in our public lives. Reviewing Facebook posts and Instagram photos from a friend's recent vacation in Hawaii can cause you to be envious.

Jealousy
Negative or potentially destructive communicative response to a perceived threat to a relationship.

Did you compete with your brothers and sisters for your parents' attention?

©Andresr/Shutterstock.com

Six types of jealousy were identified by Bevan and Samter (2004). These include family, friend, romantic, power, intimacy, and activity jealousy. The first three types (*friend*, *family*, and *romantic jealousy*) occur when we fear that our relationships with a friend, family member, or romantic partner will be altered by the presence of others. *Power jealousy* evolves in situations where other tasks or obligations are perceived as being more important than your relationship. Workplace friendships may become strained when status differentials or job responsibilities cause work to take precedence over the relationship. Status differentials, job titles, and social position can all result in power jealousy. *Intimacy jealousy* occurs in situations where partners choose to disclose intimate or private information with others outside the relationship. Suppose Mia decides to tell her friend about her recent financial strains instead of confiding with her sister. This decision to share intimate information with another person may cause a strain in the sister relationship. Finally, *activity jealousy* results from the amount of attention that a relational partner dedicates to an interest or hobby. Consider the frustration experienced if it's perceived that your friend would rather spend time playing Xbox or working as opposed to devoting time to your relationship.

Are you guilty of attempting to make a partner jealous? How do we try to invoke these negative reactions in others? Cayanus and Booth-Butterfield (2004) examined tactics that romantic partners use in an attempt to make one another jealous. (See

Figure 7.6 for a scale rating your attempts at evoking jealousy.) The results of this study found that the longer we're involved in a relationship, our use of these jealousy-evoking behaviors decreases. Perhaps this is because we become more secure in our connection with the other person and no longer feel the need to test his or her commitment or loyalty.

Jealousy is communicated in a variety of ways. Giving others the silent treatment, flirting, expressing anger, and a variety of other emotional responses all offer clues that we perceive competition in our relationship.

Conflict

Evoking jealousy and deceiving others has the potential to evolve into conflict. While some partners may paint a beautiful picture of their relationship and insist that they never disagree or fight with one another, the reality is that all relationships encounter challenges from time to time. Why deny that conflict occurs in our relationships? Perhaps it's because of the negative perception typically associated with conflict. But not all conflict is bad—in fact, some conflicts may be productive

FIGURE 7.6

Evoking Jealousy Scale (Cayanus & Booth-Butterfield, 2004). Source: Evoking Jealousy Scale from *Communication Quarterly, Volume 52, Issue 3, 2004* by Jacob L. Cayanus & Melanie Booth-Butterfield. Copyright © 2004 Routledge. Reprinted by permission of Taylor & Francis Ltd, http://www.tandfonline. com.

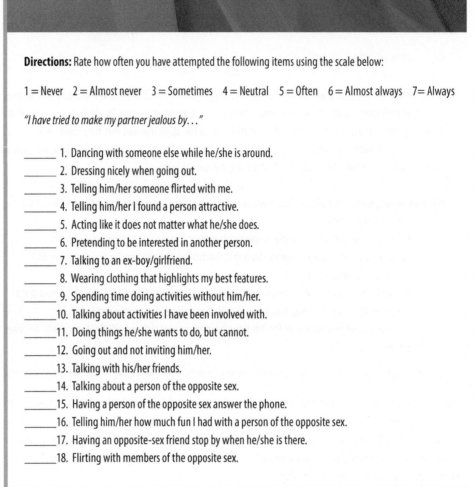

Directions: Rate how often you have attempted the following items using the scale below:

1 = Never   2 = Almost never   3 = Sometimes   4 = Neutral   5 = Often   6 = Almost always   7 = Always

"I have tried to make my partner jealous by..."

_____ 1. Dancing with someone else while he/she is around.
_____ 2. Dressing nicely when going out.
_____ 3. Telling him/her someone flirted with me.
_____ 4. Telling him/her I found a person attractive.
_____ 5. Acting like it does not matter what he/she does.
_____ 6. Pretending to be interested in another person.
_____ 7. Talking to an ex-boy/girlfriend.
_____ 8. Wearing clothing that highlights my best features.
_____ 9. Spending time doing activities without him/her.
_____10. Talking about activities I have been involved with.
_____11. Doing things he/she wants to do, but cannot.
_____12. Going out and not inviting him/her.
_____13. Talking with his/her friends.
_____14. Talking about a person of the opposite sex.
_____15. Having a person of the opposite sex answer the phone.
_____16. Telling him/her how much fun I had with a person of the opposite sex.
_____17. Having an opposite-sex friend stop by when he/she is there.
_____18. Flirting with members of the opposite sex.

Evoking Jealousy Scale from *Communication Quarterly, Volume 52, Issue 3, 2004* by Jacob L. Cayanus & Melanie Booth-Butterfield. Copyright © 2004 Routledge. Reprinted by permission of Taylor & Francis Ltd, http://www.tandfonline.com.

for the health of a relationship. Differences of opinion are expressed and negotiated, diverse perspectives are shared, and frustrations are expressed openly with the goal of resolving them.

Conflict

Expressed struggle between two or more interdependent parties who perceive incompatibility, scarce resources, and interference from others as obstacles in accomplishing their goals.

Conflict is defined as "an expressed struggle between at least two interdependent parties who perceive incompatible goals, scarce resources, and interference from the other party in achieving their goals" (Hocker & Wilmot, 1991, p. 12). This definition proposes five key components of conflict, which are highlighted in Figure 7.7. By examining each of these components more closely, we are better equipped to understand and explain possible causes that contributed to the conflict in the first place.

All relationships experience conflict at times.

© conrado/Shutterstock.com

One element that all conflicts have in common is that there is an *expressed struggle* between at least two partners. Expressed struggle emphasizes the importance of the open expression of conflict. If one partner is unaware of the problem, issues are not likely to be resolved. In order for conflict to occur, both partners in the relationship must be *interdependent*. We're more likely to experience frustration when issues arise with those to whom we feel connected. For example, you will likely experience conflict with romantic partners, family members, or coworkers but not the stranger sharing an elevator ride. *Perceived incompatible goals* contribute to the frustration experienced in conflict, and often impede the progress of accomplishing our objectives. Suppose Olivia is the leader of a team who must achieve a sales goal in order for team members to earn a bonus. She may become frustrated when she perceives Tyler as contributing very little to the team's efforts. The bonus depends on their success as a team, and Olivia perceives Tyler as being a slacker. Tyler feels that Olivia is trying to make herself look good so she can be considered for a promotion that he would also like to pursue. Olivia and Tyler are interdependent coworkers with *perceived incompatible goals*. In this example, we also see the presence of the fourth component of conflict, *perceived competition for scarce resources*. Suppose there is only one promotion planned in the company in the near future, and Tyler and Olivia both want to be the candidate selected. Another example of this can be witnessed in sibling conflict, where brothers and sisters may compete for their

➤ **Expressed struggle**
Conflict is openly expressed and each partner is made aware of the presence of issues in the relationship.

➤ **Interdependence**
Contributing factor to conflict that results because relational partners depend on each other in some way.

➤ **Perceived incompatible goals**
Relational partners are perceived as focusing on different goals.

➤ **Perceived competition for scarce resources** Individual perceived another to be competing for limited resources.

| Expressed Struggle |

| Interdependence |

| Perceived Incompatible Goals |

| Perceived Competition for Scarce Resources |

| Perceived Interference in Achieving One's Goals |

FIGURE 7.7

Key components of conflict.

➤ **Perceived interference in achieving one's goals** Component of conflict in which an individual perceives another to be interfering in their ability to accomplish a goal.

parents' time or attention. Resources that create conflict can include anything that we consider to be of value—time, money, relationships, material possessions, attention, or even status. A final component of conflict is *perceived interference in achieving one's goals*. Recall the conflict between Olivia and Tyler. Each of them perceives the other to be interfering in their ability to achieve the goal of a promotion. Conflict is likely to occur when others create barriers to our goal attainment. Learning how to use communication to effectively manage conflicts is important in our personal, professional, and public lives.

CONFLICT MANAGEMENT

Individuals choose to approach conflict in different ways. When we're faced with a conflict, there are typically two routes that we can pursue. Either we can communicate and address the conflict, or we can "bury our head in the sand" and avoid it. Understanding the implications of our selection of conflict management strategies is important in determining the best option for maintaining or preserving our relationship. Table 7.2 summarizes the four approaches to conflict management and highlights the strengths and weaknesses of each.

TABLE 7.2

Conflict Management Strategies

Conflict Management Strategy	Example	Advantage	Disadvantage
Avoidance	"Everything's fine—there's not a problem."	Protects feelings of others and gives time to reflect on the issues and analyze your perspective	Problem is not resolved
Competition	"You have no clue what you're talking about! I was selected as team leader and I know what's best for all of us."	Helps bring issues out in the open when time is of the essence and action needs to be taken.	May damage the relationship if one perceives that the other doesn't respect his or her feelings.
Accommodation	"You're right. I don't know what I was thinking" or "I don't care—you decide."	Quick resolution of the issue and preservation of the relationship.	May result in one partner often being "taken advantage of" in the relationship.
Collaboration	"I understand why you don't agree with me. Let's talk about this and see if we can find an answer together."	Preserves the relationship and both parties feel as though their voices were valued.	May take considerable time and effort.

Avoidance is probably the most frequently used strategy and it also happens to be the most ineffective approach for managing conflict. Denying the presence of a conflict means that the issue is unresolved. When this occurs, the frustration or anxiety remains and we may continue to harbor negative emotions and feelings. Taking time to "cool off" does not necessarily indicate that someone is avoiding conflict. In fact, reflecting on the issues and carefully considering the various perspectives of the situation may be beneficial to the discussion and resolution.

> **Avoidance**
> Conflict resolution strategy that involves denying the presence of a conflict.

Often when both partners have strong opinions, a *competition* approach to managing the conflict emerges. Struggles for power or control are often present with this strategy, and relationships could potentially be damaged if the competition escalates to a point where aggressive communication behaviors are exchanged. Classmates working on a group project may experience high levels of stress as the deadline looms. Two team members both want to "take charge" of the project to ensure it is completed according to their standards. The stress and struggle for leadership may cause them

> **Competition**
> Approach to conflict management in which individuals struggle or compete for power or control.

to criticize one another's contributions, with neither team member willing to give in to the other's suggestions. While competition is effective at openly discussing issues when situations must be addressed quickly, continual debate and ongoing opposition may be frustrating and further escalate the conflict.

Accommodation differs from the avoidance approach in that this strategy recognizes the presence of a conflict, but one party concedes or gives in to the other in an attempt to resolve things. While this may be a "quick-fix" solution, one person runs the risk of being viewed as a pushover or a "doormat" for others. Consider our earlier example of the classmates who are working on a project that is due soon. Rather than struggling for control of the project, one member always "goes along to get along" with the rest of the team, even when he does not agree with their ideas.

Scholars agree that the most effective approach to conflict management is *collaboration*. This strategy requires both parties to communicate their concerns while proposing solutions that would be acceptable. The ultimate goal is to determine an option that is mutually agreeable to all parties involved. It's important to note that while this is the most desirable strategy for effective conflict management, it's also the most time-consuming.

> **Accommodation**
> Conflict management strategy that recognizes the presence of a conflict, but one party concedes or gives in to the other in an attempt to resolve the issue.

> **Collaboration**
> Most effective conflict resolution strategy that requires both parties to communicate their concerns while proposing solutions that would be acceptable.

CHAPTER SUMMARY

Throughout this chapter we've explained some of the communication challenges encountered in relationships and identified opportunities for addressing these issues. Being able to recognize the warning signs of challenges or difficulties is important if the relationship is to be saved. In this chapter we have presented the final five stages of coming apart. It is important to note that simply because a relationship encounters one of these stages, it is not predestined for failure. Relationships are not always easy. We often hurt the ones we love the most because we have a vested interest in one another. Recognizing the warning signs and identifying potential communication behaviors that got us to that point in the first place are important steps in ensuring our potential to maintain healthy relationships.

Accommodation Conflict management strategy that recognizes the presence of a conflict, but one party concedes or gives in to the other in an attempt to resolve the issue.

Autonomy versus connectedness Dialectical tension that focuses on one's desire to be close to another while maintaining independence.

Avoidance Conflict resolution strategy that involves denying the presence of a conflict.

Avoiding Fourth stage in the relationship dissolution process in which partners make an effort to avoid being in the physical presence of one another.

Behavioral familiarity Strategy to assist in identifying deception. The level of familiarity with typical patterns of behaviors enables us to easily identify uncharacteristic behaviors that may signal deception.

Circumscribing Second stage in the process of relationship dissolution in which communication is limited to safe, superficial topics. Both the quality and quantity of conversations between partners is limited.

Collaboration Most effective conflict resolution strategy that requires both parties to communicate their concerns while proposing solutions that would be acceptable.

Competition Approach to conflict management in which individuals struggle or compete for power or control.

Concealment Form of deception that involves withholding important or relevant information.

Conflict Expressed struggle between two or more interdependent parties who perceive incompatibility, scarce resources, and interference from others as obstacles in accomplishing their goals.

Dialectical tensions Contradictory pulls between opposing goals or desires in a relationship.

Differentiating First stage in the process of relationship dissolution in which partners focus on their differences as opposed to their commonalities.

Equivocation Deception strategy in which one uses vague or ambiguous language in an attempt to avoid speaking the truth. Often used in situations where we attempt to spare someone's feelings.

Exaggeration Form of deception that involves stretching the truth, adding details or information to enhance a story, or repeating oneself in an attempt to be convincing.

Expectancy Violation Theory Examines the role of communication when our anticipations are not met. Violations may be perceived as positive or negative.

Expressed struggle Conflict is openly expressed and each partner is made aware of the presence of issues in the relationship.

Interdependence Contributing factor to conflict that results because relational partners depend on each other in some way.

Jealousy Negative or potentially destructive communicative response to a perceived threat to a relationship.

Lies Form of deception that involves the fabrication or falsification of information.

Minimizing Form of deception when we downplay the truth.

Novelty versus predictability Dialectical tension that addresses our need for routine and consistency and our conflicting desire to experience things that are unique.

Openness versus closedness Dialectical tension that reflects our need to share information with others while keeping some aspects private.

Perceived competition for scarce resources Individual perceived another to be competing for limited resources.

Perceived interference in achieving one's goals Component of conflict in which an individual perceives another to be interfering in his/her ability to accomplish a goal.

Perceived incompatible goals Relational partners are perceived as focusing on different goals.

Relational expectations Explicit and implicit predictions for anticipated or ideal verbal and nonverbal responses. They consist of our forecasts for how someone should behave or reply in a given situation.

Relationship dissolution When one or both partners perceive the relationship as being dissatisfactory and the decision is made to terminate the connection.

Stagnating Third stage of relationship dissolution in which communication between partners is limited and the goal is simply to maintain a status quo.

Terminating Final stage of relationship dissolution when one or both partners experiences a level of dissatisfaction that motivates them to end the relationship.

Truth bias Expectation that people in close relationships will be honest with one another. Thus, deception may be ignored or overlooked due to our expectations for the truth to be told.

REFERENCES

Afifi, W. A., & Metts, S. (1998). Characteristics and consequences of expectation violation in close relationships. *Journal of Social and Personal Relationships, 15*, 365–392.

Baxter, L.A. (1988). A dialectical perspective on communication strategies in relationship development. In S. Duck (Ed.), *Handbook of personal relationships: Theory, research, and interventions* (pp. 257–273). Chichester, UK: Wiley.

Baxter, L. A., & Bridge, K. (1992). Blended relationships: Friends as work associates. *Western Journal of Communication, 56*, 200–225.

Bevan, J. L., & Samter, W. (2004). Toward a broader conceptualization of jealousy in close relationships: Two exploratory studies. *Communication Studies, 55*, 14–28.

Burgoon, J. K. (1978). A communication model of personal space violation: Explication and an initial test. *Human Communication Research, 4*, 129–142.

Canary, D. J., Stafford, L., Hause, K. S., & Wallace, L. A. (1993). An inductive analysis of relational maintenance strategies: Comparisons among lovers, relatives, friends, and other. *Communication Research Reports, 10*, 5–14.

Cayanus, J. L., & Booth-Butterfield, M. (2004). Relationship orientation, jealousy, and equity: An examination of jealousy evoking and positive communicative responses. *Communication Quarterly, 52*, 237–250.

Database Records.com – *Newsweek*. (2012). *Little white lies: The truth about why women lie*. Retrieved from www.statisticbrain.com/lying-statistics/.

Dindia, K., & Canary, D.J. (1993). Definitions and theoretical perspectives on relational maintenance. *Journal of Social and Personal Relationships, 10*, 163–173.

Duck, S. (1988). *Relating to others*. Monterey, CA: Brooks/Cole.

Graham, E. E. (2003). Dialectic contradictions in postmarital relationships. *Journal of Family Communication, 3*(4), 193–214.

Hocker, J. L., & Wilmot, W. W. (1991). *Interpersonal conflict*. Dubuque, IA: William C. Brown.

Knapp, M. L. (1978). *Social intercourse: From greeting to goodbye*. Boston: Allyn & Bacon.

Muise, A., Christofides, E., & Desmarais, S. (2009). More information than you ever wanted: Does Facebook bring out the green-eyed monster of jealousy? *CyberPsychology and Behavior, 12*(4), 441–444.

Park, H. S., Levine, T. R., McCornack, S. A., Morrison, K., & Ferrara, M. (2002). How people really detect lies. *Communication Monographs, 69*, 144–157.

Sahlstein, E. M. (2006). Making plans: Praxis strategies for negotiating uncertainty–certainty in long-distance relationships. *Western Journal of Communication, 70*, 147–165.

Serota, K. B., Levine, T. R., & Boster, F. J. (2010). The prevalence of lying in America: Three studies of self-reported lies. *Human Communication Research, 36*, 2–25.

CHAPTER 8

Understanding Groups and Communication: Let's All Work Together

Chapter Objectives

After reading this chapter, you should be able to:

- Explain what constitutes a group
- Identify multiple types of groups
- Describe how an individual's communication influences groups
- Identify the many factors that affect a group
- Explain how groups work collaboratively to make decisions

PERSONAL: Your family has decided it is time to get the house in order. You have a family meeting and discuss the division of labor. As the tasks are assigned, your siblings begin to argue with one another. Your parents quickly resolve the conflict by telling them to go to their rooms and begin working. You start cleaning your room but can hear your siblings fighting again. Each is claiming that the other is not doing the correct chore. You think it would be best if the family had a meeting where they talked about each person's roles and duties. How do you approach the subject with your family?

PROFESSIONAL: You have just graduated college and have a full-time job that you enjoy. At your job, you have been asked to be part of a new team. Being asked to join this special project at work has produced both excitement and anxiety. As a member of this special task force, you are required to work with others to generate the best possible solution to a problem in the company. You know you need to listen to the ideas of others as well as incorporate your own ideas to ensure that all members of the group contribute to the project. At your first meeting, you realize some of the members of the group don't seem to get along. They are constantly interrupting one another and negating ideas before the entire group has an opportunity to discuss them. You want to talk to the group about this so it doesn't continue. How do you start this discussion?

PUBLIC: You are excited for the school semester to start. That is, until you get to your first class and the professor announces that the class is centered on working in groups. To make matters worse, you do not get to pick the other members of your group. Instead, the professor assigns students to groups. Once you meet with your group, you decide using Facebook would make communicating easier so you "friend" each other and you begin to look at each member's profile photos. As you scan the photos on their Facebook profiles you see pictures that make you think your group members are not serious about school. In fact, some of the pictures that are posted give you the impression that these group members may depend on you to do all the work. You wonder why your group mates would post these types of photos because they create a negative impression. Though you know them from in-person interactions, their online personas do not seem to match who they appear to be in face-to-face interactions. How should you approach this situation to ensure they are willing to work hard to make the group successful?

CHAPTER OVERVIEW

You likely read the opening examples and said to yourself, "Yes, I can relate" to some of them. Working on class projects, collaborating with coworkers on tasks, and making decisions as a family are all situations that require us to interact effectively in groups. The opening scenarios illustrate the fact that we don't live in isolation and thus, we depend on others.

Poole, Hollingshead, McGrath, Moreland, and Rohrbaugh (2004) argued that individuals "live in groups" (p. 3). Throughout our daily lives a majority of what we do is performed and coordinated with other people. From the time you wake up, you depend on other people—discussing issues with roommates or family members, going to class and working on group projects, and collaborating with colleagues at your workplace—all of these situations require us to communicate with others to accomplish our common goals. It is also safe to say that these people you work with in groups probably do not behave or communicate just like you. In fact, Gastil (1993) argued that differences in individual speaking style are one of the most common problems facing groups. Additionally, Frey and SunWolf (2005) argued that communication is "the medium through which information in groups is shared and processed" (p. 173). In our professional lives, we will spend a majority of the work week working with others. In a survey of how CEOs of major corporations spent their time, of the 55 hours worked, approximately half of that time was spent working with others ("Time Crunch," 2012). In short, our lives are affected in a number of ways by groups.

GROUPS DEFINED

Group
A collection of individuals with a common purpose.

If small groups are an integral part of our lives, how then do we know if we are part of one? At the most basic level, *groups* are a collection of individuals with a common purpose. Burkhalter, Gastil, and Kelshaw (2002) indicated groups need at least three people, that the exact size of the group should be "manageable," and people in the group should be able to "see and hear one another" (p. 400). In today's world, seeing and hearing one another can be accomplished both face-to-face and virtually. In addition to having a collection of individuals, inherent to a group is the idea of mutual influence. The behaviors of one person create changes in others' behaviors. Mutual influence is like a tennis match. Both players in the match respond to the other's actions. Player A hits the ball to player B. Player B's movement is dependent upon what Player A does first. Player B's actions are in response to the previous actions by Player A. Player A then reacts to player B's actions and returns the ball.

Interdependence is like a tennis match as both players respond to the other's actions.

Related to this idea is that of interdependence. Each group member has mutual influence on others because they are dependent upon the others in the group in some way. Think of the group as being like a family. You likely depend on certain people to perform certain functions. For example, one member of the family might make dinner, another takes out the trash, another might tease everyone, yet another member is the one who always checks in on the family. A group follows this model. You expect certain people to do certain things. When one person is not present, the group (just like the family) is different and individuals may need to adjust their behaviors to assume responsibility for the missing behaviors.

Another key component of group life is that of a common purpose or goal. All group members are working together toward the completion of some task. That is, they share in the achievement of a common end state. Without this common goal or purpose, they are simply individuals interacting without an end mission in mind. It is the common purpose or goal that helps to solidify the group and bring individuals together to focus on one project.

TYPES OF GROUPS

As evidenced by the scenarios at the beginning of this chapter, there are different types of groups. These include the people you work with at school, the church groups to which you belong, the clubs and organizations in which you participate, and the people with whom you work at your jobs. As research suggests, your past group experiences will influence your future group behaviors such as commitment to the group (Forrest & Miller, 2003). That is, if you have had a terrible group experience in the past, it could impact how you work with others in the future. Based on that negative experience, you probably said to yourself, "Never again will I do this!" Thus, your past experiences influence your perception of working in groups in the future.

Do you enjoy working in groups? When asked this question, students are often divided in their response, with some indicating they like working in groups and others reporting that they despise group assignments. You will be part of a number of different types of groups throughout your life. In some instances, you will have the opportunity to choose to be part of a group while other groups will be forced upon you. While this might sound a little intimidating, understanding the different types of groups and the factors that impact group communication will enhance your effectiveness when working in a group. The following are examples of groups that you are likely to encounter in your personal, professional, and public lives (Figure 8.1). It is important to note that some of these groups are voluntary while others are involuntary. Voluntary groups are those that we self-select to be part of, whereas involuntary groups are those in which group membership is assigned.

A *peer group* is one that is "composed of members who consider one another to be equals, in terms of abilities, background, age, responsibilities, beliefs, social standing, legal status, or rights. Not all group members agree about the equality of all other members at all times, but there is overt consensus

> **Peer group**
> Members who consider one another to be equals in terms of abilities, background, age, responsibilities, beliefs, social standing, legal status, or rights.
>
> A team of athletes is considered a purposive group.

© Jamie Roach/Shutterstock.com

that members of the group are primarily equal" (SunWolf, 2008, p. xii). Reflect on the number of peer groups that you have been a member of throughout your life. Most likely, you are part of many peer groups in your own life. Examples of these include a group of friends, a troop of scouts, or a congregation of worshipers.

A *purposive group* is a group "that has a goal" (Poole et al., 2004, p. 6), that is, working toward the completion of some task. You will be a member of numerous purposive groups throughout your professional and public lives. Examples of purposive groups include work project teams, a school board committee that will give a formal presentation to the board of trustees, support groups that raise awareness of a specific cause, or groups at school that work together to complete an assigned project.

Factional groups are defined as those "in which members are representatives or delegates from social entities" (Li & Hambrick, 2005, p. 794). That is, individuals from divergent areas of expertise are brought together to work toward the completion of a common goal. Especially prevalent in your professional life, for example, are

> **Purposive group**
> A group that is attempting to achieve the completion of a goal.

> **Factional group**
> When group members are representatives or delegates from other social entities.

FIGURE 8.1

Types of groups.

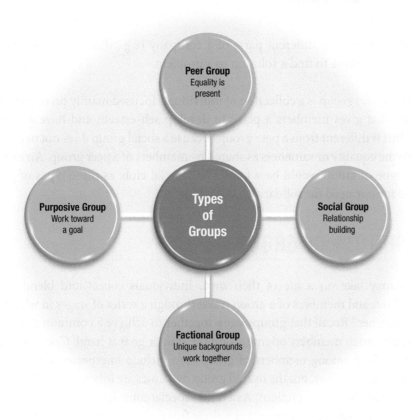

A family is a type of social group.

© szefei/Shutterstock.com

individuals from two different parts of a company (e.g., those in marketing and sales) who combine to find a solution to a problem.

 **Social group**
Collection of individuals focused mostly on relationship-building that gives members a place to develop self-esteem.

Finally, a *social group* is a collection of individuals focused mainly on relationship-building that gives members a place to develop self-esteem and have a sense of unity. This is different from a peer group because a social group does not necessarily contain the equality or sameness as shared by members of a peer group. An example of this type of group would be a family or a social club, as these types of groups provide for our need for solidarity.

THE NATURE OF GROUPS

Groups may take on a life of their own. Individuals collect and blend unique personalities and members of a group travel through a series of stages in which they "come together." Recall that groups work together to achieve a common goal. These stages help group members orient toward the task or goal at hand. Communication that takes place among members of groups can include interpersonal interactions among group members, but the overall group dynamics are inherently different from interpersonal, dyadic interactions. As a result, special consideration needs to be given to what makes group communication unique from other types of interactions.

Groups develop and "come together" in stages. One popular way to explain this process is by exploring the five stages of group development: forming, storming, norming, performing, and adjourning (Tuckman, 1965; Tuckman & Jensen, 1977). In the *forming stage*, individuals gather together and assemble the group. During this period, members of the group begin orienting to the task, search for a leader, and determine the purpose of the group. Communication tends to focus on polite interactions to ensure we don't "step on others' toes" and small talk to learn more about one another. In the *storming stage*, the group may experience conflict as a result of individuals' emotional responses to completing tasks. Members of the group may have different approaches toward accomplishing the goal, multiple people may want to fulfill the same role (e.g., be the leader), and arguments may ensue about how the group should proceed. It is not uncommon for group members to clash during this period; in fact, this is typically the stage where most of the conflict occurs. Once the group works through the conflicts, they reach the *norming stage*. Group members have calmed the rough seas of storming and determined how best to work with one another. Individuals begin to adopt roles and share ideas with others. Rules are created for interaction and performance. In the *performing stage*, the roles that were adopted in the norming stages become cemented. In essence, the "kinks" have been worked out and the group is able to address both the completion of tasks and the social demands of working with others. In essence, the group becomes a "well-oiled machine." Once the tasks are completed or the goal is accomplished, some groups cease to exist. During the *adjourning stage*, individuals have performed their duties and reached the conclusion of the group experience. During this time, emotional changes such as sadness or excitement as members leave the group may occur. During this stage, there should be critical reflection of individual and others' performance.

> **Forming stage**
> Initial stage in group development.

> **Storming stage**
> Second stage of group development, where most conflicts will occur.

> **Norming stage**
> Third stage of group development in which members create behavioral standards and punishments.

> **Performing stage**
> Fourth stage in group development in which all members are working toward completion of the group's task.

> **Adjourning stage**
> Final process of group life that signals the completion of tasks.

To effectively perform groupwork during each of these stages, Hawkins and Fillion (1999) argued that several communication skills are essential. First, they emphasize the importance of effective listening. You have already learned about the listening process in Chapter 5. Remember that listening is a skill that requires effort. Working with others provides a unique opportunity to attend to and comprehend their messages. Additionally, everyone should understand each person's role as part of the larger work group. That is, all members of the group need to know how they "fit" with the others in the group. Building from this idea, Hawkins and Fillion also indicate that all members of the group should contribute actively to the group. Each person should be sure to perform his or her roles and duties. In addition, members should ask questions, use clear and concise language, and convey nonverbal professionalism. By picking the most efficient verbal and nonverbal behaviors, we can be sure that our communicative efforts are easily understood. Efficient verbal communication could entail summarizing each person's responsibilities before concluding a meeting. Nonverbally, it is unlikely that rolling your eyes or raising your voice would be appropriate and well received by others in your group. Given the global world in which we live, it is argued that we also need to devote attention to respecting cultural differences. Simply put, our culture influences our behavior. What is considered professional in one culture might not be regarded the same in another culture. For example, a handshake is a standard greeting of introduction in the United States whereas Chinese cultures may bow or nod instead. When working with diverse individuals, care should be taken to learn about others and attempts made to understand practices.

While somewhat intuitive, these skills are not only necessary for a group to be successful, but they can also be the easiest to forget when working with individuals who are different from us or when conflict emerges. Have you ever worked with a group and someone suggested an outlandish idea? It might have been something you thought was so off the wall that you rolled your eyes or made a facial expression similar to that of disgust. Similarly, when conflict emerges, have you ever lost your temper or perhaps attacked a person and not the idea? While we carefully monitor our verbal response in these situations, we sometimes neglect to consider our nonverbal reactions. Keeping communication concepts such as effective verbal and nonverbal communication and cultural differences in mind, we now look at other factors that impact group life and our ability to be a successful group member.

Size

The size of a group is important to consider. Scholars seem to agree that the ideal group size is three to seven members to ensure effective communication. Remember, a group is a collection of individuals who influence one another.

Have you ever attended a large dinner party? Perhaps you sat at a table that was so long you could not speak to the people at the far end. We would not consider that a group because your verbal and nonverbal behaviors cannot be effectively interpreted by all of the people at the table. Ultimately, group size should manageable so all individuals in it can consider themselves a part of the group.

Task versus Social Dimensions within Groups

Task dimension
Group members focusing on solving problems, completing a task, or achieving a goal.

Once individuals begin to gather and membership in the group is established, two types of communication occur. Communication can focus on the group's task dimension or the social dimension. The *task dimension* is characterized by messages that focus on solving problems, completing a task, or achieving a goal

This study group is an example of a small group.

© Andresr/Shutterstock.com

(Fujishin, 2001), while the *social dimensions* are those conversations among group members that focus on their relationships and feelings for one another. The social dimension can dictate how individuals approach the task. For example, what if you dislike a member of your group? If that person takes over the group and becomes the leader, you now have to "report" to him and "check in." If you do not like this person, the social dimension—your negative feelings—can affect how you approach the task. You could produce lower quality work, miss deadlines, or avoid communicating with the person, if possible. Thus, both task and social dimensions must be considered when working in groups. It is important for a group to maintain effective relationships in order to accomplish its goals. This does not mean that individuals need to be best friends or even like one another. They do, however, need to establish and manage their social interactions to ensure that they don't derail the group from its purpose.

> **Social dimension** Group members' relationships and feelings for each one another.

Roles

Individuals offer unique contributions to groups through the types of roles they fulfill. One popular definition of *roles* is "that set of common expectations shared by the members about the behavior of an individual" (Bormann, 1969, p. 184). Roles are labels placed on individuals based on their function within a group. These labels have a set of expected behaviors that the individual playing that role or having that label must then perform. Roles can be formal and assigned. However, roles can

> **Roles** Labels placed on individuals based on their function within a group.

also be informal and emerge as a result of group interaction. For example, when preparing for the first group meeting, you might know that someone needs to be in charge and create an agenda for the meeting or perhaps send emails to make sure all group members are doing their work. This would be a formal role. Perhaps one group member is self-assigned the role of leader. However, during your interactions with the other group members, it becomes evident that the group needs someone to take notes during meetings because members have difficulty recalling the previous meetings' proceedings. As a result, another group member takes on the role of note-taker. This role would be an informal role because it became evident through interactions among group members that someone needed to provide the function of note-taker. The role of note-taker could be formally elected or appointed through an election process while others can evolve more informally.

Benne and Sheats (1948) proposed a typology of group roles, organizing them into three categories. In a group, your role could be task, relational, or individually focused (Table 8.1).

Task roles
Includes all roles that focus on the group's assignment.

Task roles focus on the group's assignment. A task role would include an evaluator-critic. This person focuses on setting standards and meeting goals. This individual will question the logic of others when unsure about the accuracy of a proposed idea.

Relational roles
Focus on building and maintaining connections among group members.

Individual roles
When individuals focus on self-achievement and not group efforts.

Relational roles focus on building and maintaining connections among group members. A relational role includes that of the harmonizer. This group member produces communication that strives to bring the group members together and achieve cohesiveness. *Individual roles* are those in which individuals focus on self-achievement and not the efforts of the group. An individual role would include that of recognition-seeker. This individual attempts to bring light to his personal accomplishments and will likely take on more work in an attempt to gather more praise. In Table 8.1, many of the common roles within each of the categories are presented along with examples of how these specific roles are enacted in a group setting.

The roles in Table 8.1 may be present in every group. Task and relational roles are needed and critical to successful group life. Some members of the group need to focus on achieving task completion while others take care of the individuals in the group. Individual roles, however, can prove challenging as they are typically thought of as something that detracts from the group. They focus more on individual achievement rather than the collective achievement of the group.

TABLE 8.1

Typology of Group Roles

Type of Role	Description
Task roles	**Focus on the group's goals and tasks**
Evaluator-critic	Focuses on setting standards and meeting goals. Questions others' logic when unsure about accuracy
Coordinator	Focuses communicative efforts on who in the group accomplishes what tasks and when tasks should be done
Opinion-giver	Expresses opinions and possible interpretations associated with all tasks
Information-seeker	Collects information related to tasks and completing tasks.
Relational roles	**Focus on building connections among members**
Encourager	Offers praise to others and wants to hear others' opinions and ideas
Harmonizer	Focuses communicative efforts on bringing group members together to achieve cohesiveness
Compromiser	Avoids conflict and admits any mistakes; works to incorporate all ideas presented
Gatekeeper	Ensures participation by all group members and that they are listened to and considered during group processes
Individual roles	**Focus on self-achievement**
Recognition-seeker	Likes taking on a lot of work because it means he or she will get extra attention because of it
Dominator	Focuses communicative efforts on being heard; works to control the group and their efforts
Joker	Uses light-hearted, humorous communication that is often off topic in attempts to be perceived as funny
Withdrawer	Fails to connect and interact with the group; offers few opinions and may have issues

Withdrawer
Group member who fails to connect and interact with the group, offers few opinions, and may have issues.

Evaluator-critic
Group member who sets standards and meets goals.

Coordinator
Group member that oversees who accomplishes what tasks and when tasks should be done.

Opinion-giver
Group member who expresses opinions and possible interpretations associated with all tasks.

Information-seeker Group member who collects information related to tasks and completing tasks.

Encourager
Group member who praises others and hears others' opinions and ideas.

Harmonizer
Group member who offers communication focused on achieving cohesion among group members.

Compromiser
Individual who avoids conflict and admits any mistakes in a group.

Gatekeeper
Group member who ensures participation by all group members.

Recognition-seeker Group member who takes on a lot of work for extra attention.

Dominator
Group member who likes to be heard and works to control the group.

Joker
Group member who uses light-hearted, humorous communication that is often off topic.

How are roles typically adopted in groups? Cragan and Wright (1999) suggested that groups should include "leaders" who are in charge of certain aspects of the group when assigning roles. These include a *task leader* who focuses group members on completion of assignments or a *social-emotional leader* who serves as the voice of the group members in terms of the affective orientation to the group. This idea is addressed in more depth in Chapter 9; however, it is important to note that group leaders have roles too.

One theory used to explain and predict roles that individuals perform is *Role Theory*, which concentrates on the ways in which individuals enact different social positions (i.e., roles) in their lives (Biddle, 1979). Role Theory offers five claims. First, individuals create and adopt roles based on their surrounding contexts; that is, the situation is important to consider when determining which roles are needed in the group. For example, if at a school board meeting, it is determined that all happenings should be video recorded, someone will be in charge of technology. Second, roles are commonly associated with individuals in social positions who share a common identity; that is, a role is something that individuals enact when working with others. Inherent to having a role is the idea that others must be present and you are in a group setting. Third, roles are governed by individual awareness of and expectations for each role; that is, how individuals perform a role is based on their knowledge of the role and the ideas of how the role should be enacted. For example, if you are assigned as group motivator, but are unclear of what that entails, such as motivating and reaffirming verbal communication, your ability to perform that role is diminished. Fourth, roles remain because of the consequences and functions associated with them and also due to the fact that roles are often imbedded within a larger social system; that is, groups need roles to be able to function. Roles may change over time, but the idea there is still a role to perform remains. The job duties of the note-taker may shift, but someone needs to record the happenings of the group. Finally, the fifth claim indicates that individuals must be taught the behaviors associated with each role and they must be socialized by others to properly perform a role. There is a learning curve associated with performing the role effectively. In order to play the role of family caregiver, you must first know what that role entails and the essential job functions. For example, a caregiver may be expected to clean the house, prepare meals, and pay bills.

Role Theory assumes that individuals learn the behaviors that correspond with their role. They remain in that role because that role is necessary for proper group functioning. Regardless of the type of role and how one learns the expectations associated with that role, there are some considerations to be made. As you read the list of role types, you probably thought, "I could perform a lot of these roles." If so, you experience something called *role flexibility*. This occurs when individuals have the ability to play a variety of roles and adapt according to the demands of the situation. In some instances, an individual could alternate between being the note-taker and being the emotional leader, depending on the situation. However, sometimes individuals are required to fill two or more conflicting roles simultaneously. *Role conflict* occurs when you have to perform multiple roles with seemingly contradictory behaviors. If you refer to Table 8.1, you can see by the descriptions that it would be difficult to be both a harmonizer and a dominator. A harmonizer works to bring the group together whereas the dominator is focused solely on advancing his or her position. A harmonizer tends to lighten the mood of the group, whereas a dominator may use communication that detracts from the task. Imagine working with a group of your peers on a class project. As your group works on its tasks, the harmonizer of the group would attempt to bring the group together by highlighting common interests, while the dominator of the group would try to showcase differences of other group members and pull the conversation to focus on these differences. The final consideration is called *role strain*. Have you ever been asked by others in the group to perform a role that you did not necessarily want to do? For example, if you did not want to be the leader of the group, yet the other individuals in the group encouraged you to do so, you may experience role strain. This occurs when an individual is required to assume a new role that he or she is reluctant to perform.

Collectively, there are a number of important and necessary roles that must be filled for groups to work efficiently. Because so many roles are necessary for a group to function, everyone in the group should have an active part in the group.

Rules

Do you remember when your parents told you to clean your room and they stated that if you did not do it, there would be a punishment? Throughout our personal, professional, and public lives, we encounter a number of rules associated with the roles we fulfill. *Group rules* refer to the notion that group members are expected to engage in specific behaviors, and if they do not do so, there are consequences. Rules can be both explicit and implicit. *Explicit rules* are formalized rules that are discussed and sometimes recorded in a document that all group members can access. For example, explicit or formal rules can be considered a company's bylaws or an organization's constitution. These are rules for what should happen in the group. *Implicit rules* are the unspoken expectations that everyone in the group seems to know and adhere to, although they are not formally documented. For example, members of the group understand that being on time for meetings is important.

Role flexibility
When individuals possess the ability to play a variety of roles and adapt according to the demands of the situation.

Role conflict
When you have to perform multiple roles with seemingly contradictory behaviors.

Role strain
When an individual is required to assume a new role that he or she is reluctant to perform.

Group rules
Individuals in a group are expected to do certain things, and if they do not do these things, there are consequences.

Explicit rules
Formalized rules that are discussed and often documented so that all group members are aware of them.

Implicit rules
Unspoken and unwritten expectations that everyone in the group seems to know and adhere to.

The harmonizer of the group works to bring the group together.

Norms

➤ **Norms**
Standardized behaviors individuals in the group ought to do under any circumstance.

Have you ever been part of a group where you were expected to act and behave in a certain way? These expected behaviors are called norms. *Norms* are standardized behaviors across all group members that focus on expected or anticipated behaviors. Homans (1950) argued that norms are behaviors that individuals in the group ought to perform under any circumstance. For example, if you are working in a group that has a treasurer, you would assume the treasurer would have reports of money spent and money paid and that this person could update the group on any financial happenings. These are norms. We expect certain behaviors given particular positions. In a group, your norms will largely be dictated by your group role. For example, if you volunteered to be the secretary during group meetings, you would take notes, ask others to speak loudly so you can record information accurately, and provide the group members with a written recap of the meeting. Norms for behavior can be seen in a variety of situations, and we each have expectations for how others should communicate based on certain factors. Thus, if we expect people to adhere to specific norms for behavior and they do not, it can make group life difficult. Overcoming these difficulties can be accomplished through open communication where all group members share ideas about anticipated behaviors.

Power

➤ **Power**
Ability to influence others.

Power refers to our ability to influence the behavior of others. Exercising power over others is contingent upon there being someone to control. Say you are part of a softball team. Each member of the softball team decides to skip an optional preseason workout. The only person that attends the workout is the team captain. When the team captain arrives and sees no one on the field, who will the team captain be able to influence? That is right—no one. Power typically requires the presence of an interdependent relationship among group members. Thus, individuals are dependent upon one another for the transaction of power. Members of the softball team need to be present in order for someone to enact power.

Five different power bases have been identified (Table 8.2). According to French and Raven (1960), the relationship between at least two people allows for power to be displayed.

As you can see from Table 8.2, some of these types of power are positive, whereas others are negative. You probably like receiving rewards for your behavior or completion of tasks, and it is safe to say you do not enjoy having your work criticized, especially if it occurs in front of others. Additionally, having someone in your group who has a level of expertise, knowledge, or past experience with the topic can also make for a smoother group process because that individual can offer insights others may not know.

> **Reward power**
> Ability to give out positive benefits or rewards.

> **Coercive power**
> Ability to give out punishment.

> **Referent power**
> Individuals' positive regard for and personal identification with the leader.

> **Expert power**
> Power derived from the knowledge or expertise one has.

> **Legitimate power**
> Power that is associated with a certain position. Because of his or her position in the group, an individual has a certain right to influence/oversee others' behaviors.

TABLE 8.2

Typology of Power (French & Raven, 1960)

Type of Power	Description	Example of Power
Reward power	Refers to the ability to give out positive benefits or rewards	One who ensures all tasks are completed and gives group members tangible goods once the work is done
Coercive power	Refers to the ability to give out punishments	One who scolds, reprimands, criticizes, or offers other negative outcomes
Referent power	Refers to an individual's positive regard for/personal identification with the leader. Can be manifested in perceptions of similarity or interpersonal affinity.	When others do as they are told because they find the leader likeable and socially attractive
Expert power	Refers to the knowledge or expertise one has	When individuals in a group listen to what someone says about a task because of his or her skillful mastery of a topic or expert understanding
Legitimate power	Refers to the power that is associated with a certain position. Because of his or her position in the group, an individual has a certain right to influence/oversee others' behaviors.	When a group elects a "leader" (i.e., someone to oversee the completion of tasks), this person is said to have legitimate power because social norms indicate those designated as leaders have the inherent right to exert control or influence

Compliance-gaining
Getting someone to do something you want.

When we exert power over others, we influence their behavior. In other words, we get them to do what we want. This is called *compliance-gaining*. Wheeless, Barraclough, and Stewart (1983) suggested that compliance-gaining is the implementation of power. You get others to do what you want (compliance-gaining) because you put your power to work. The authors stated, "Compliance is not only the manifestation of exercised power, it is the very reason for the existence of power" (p. 121). Marwell and Schmidt (1967b, pp. 360–361) created a typology of 16 types of compliance-gaining tactics (Table 8.3) or behaviors that can be used to get others to go along with what we want.

TABLE 8.3

Typology of Compliance-Gaining Tactics (Marwell & Schmidt, 1967b)

Type of Compliance	Description	Example
Promise	Offering a reward for compliance	"Because we all agreed to the proposed idea, we can leave the meeting early!"
Threat	Threatening with punishment	"If we do not agree to a plan, the meeting will last at least another hour."
Expertise – positive	Telling others they will comply and be rewarded because that is just how things work	"If you go along with the plan now, you will be rewarded by the company later because the company likes a team player."
Expertise – negative	Telling others that, if they do not comply, they will be punished because that is just how things work	"If you fail to agree to the proposed idea, the team will punish you in the future by not listening to your ideas."
Liking	Acting friendly and open to get the receiver in a good frame of mind	"I really like your idea and think your insights are valuable. Would you mind supporting my group's proposed plan?"
Pregiving	Offering a reward before compliance is gained	"I like your group's ideas and in the future I plan to vote in favor of any of your group's ideas. Will you consider listening to my group's work now?"
Aversive stimulation	Engaging in continuous punishment until the recipient of the message gives in	"Like I've told you before, your group's ideas will not be supported by anyone. You need to really consider alternative solutions."
Debt	Making others feel indebted; the recipient of the message has to comply because of past favors he or she has received	"Remember when my group helped your group with that large project? The one we had to work extra hours to complete? My group now needs your group's assistance to complete a task."
Moral appeal	Telling others they are immoral people if they do not comply	"It is the right thing to help my group; a good person would do it."

Self-feeling – positive	Informing the recipients that they will feel better about themselves when they comply	"My group really needs some assistance. I know you will feel better about yourselves if you all agree to help us."
Self-feeling – negative	Informing the recipients that they will feel worse about themselves for not complying	"If your group does not agree to help us, you will probably feel bad about yourselves when the group fails."
Altercasting – positive	Telling others that a "good" person would comply	"A good person, a person of quality, would help the group."
Altercasting – negative	Telling others that a "bad" person would not comply	"Only a bad person would not help the group."
Altruism	Sharing with others that you need compliance very badly and asking them to "do it for me"	"Please help the group this time. Do it for me, because of our relationship and friendship."
Esteem – positive	Informing the recipient of the message that people he or she values will think better of him or her for complying	"Your help is much needed and you will feel good about yourself knowing that you motivated and encouraged this group to achieve its task."
Esteem – negative	Informing the recipient of the message that people he or she values will think poorly of him or her for not complying	"Everyone will think poorly of you if you do not go along with what we want."

You probably read through the list in Table 8.3 and said, "Some of these would never work on me." Existing research on compliance-gaining would agree with you. Not surprisingly, individuals respond more to positive or socially rewarding techniques than negative compliance-gaining strategies (see Marwell & Schmitt, 1967a; Miller, Boster, Roloff, & Seibold, 1977; Williams & Untermeyer, 1988). How you deliver a compliance-gaining message is important as well. Individuals need to be mindful of tone, such as, for example, those who speak too softly are less likely to gain compliance (Remland & Jones, 1994). Overall, when it comes to working in groups and using power to gain compliance, it is best to approach it from a positive angle and not a negative one. The focus should be on creating a smooth road to goal completion.

Cohesiveness

Cohesiveness is defined as an individual's feeling of belonging to a given group. That is, cohesiveness is the extent to which group members feel like they are part of a group. There is a sense of "togetherness" when groups experience cohesion. In groups, cohesiveness, in general, is a positive characteristic. Generally, we want to feel like all members of the group are "in it" and that these members feel good

Cohesiveness
General sense of belonging among group members.

about being part of the group. When group members feel cohesive, they participate in group processes such as goal-setting (Brawley, Carron, & Widmeyer, 1993) and experience satisfaction with the group (Tekleab, Quigley, & Tesluk, 2009). Thus, when you experience cohesiveness with members of a group, you feel as though you are working well with others.

You can help others feel like part of the group by listening. Have you ever told someone a story and they interrupted you? Maybe even changed the subject? Have you ever offered a solution that no one took into consideration? When people listen, they do more than hear. As discussed in Chapter 5, hearing refers to having the physical ability to make sense of noise. It means you have the physical capacity necessary to perform the function. Listening goes beyond that. Not only do you hear the noise, but you also interpret and carefully consider the meaning behind the verbal and nonverbal messages. Feeling valued in the group and wanting to remain in the group often comes from being viewed as a competent source of information. This viewpoint is manifested when we listen to others.

Productivity

➤ Productivity
Ability to achieve goals in an efficient matter.

➤ Macro productivity
Achieving or finishing the group's task.

➤ Micro productivity
Smaller tasks and goals that contribute to macro productivity.

➤ Efficiency
When group members are maximizing what they do, completing the necessary tasks as correctly as possible.

➤ Effectiveness
When a group meets all of its requirements and completes all of its tasks.

When individuals work together well, they are more likely to accomplish their goals. *Productivity* refers to a group's ability to complete tasks that ultimately lead to accomplishing the group's overall mission that brought them together in the first place. Productivity in a group can be considered at both the macro and micro levels. *Macro productivity* is bigger; it is completing the task that brought the group together. *Micro productivity* refers to the smaller activities that contribute to the completion of the overall task. Consider a class project. Your teacher assigns a task—the writing of a research paper that you will submit at the end of the semester. Completing the paper and submitting a final product is macro productivity. The work that you do along the way, including the collection of research and refining ideas, is micro productivity. Micro productivity contributes to macro productivity. If a group cannot focus on what needs to be accomplished, divide work appropriately, and make thoughtful decisions, it is far less likely they will achieve group productivity.

In addition to productivity, groups must work toward efficiency and effectiveness. *Efficiency* means that group members maximize what they do to complete the necessary tasks as correctly as possible. For example, rather than all members of a group trying to tackle each part of a project or task, they might decide to divide the labor among the individuals within the group and work on tasks that fit specific individual skill sets. *Effectiveness* means that the group meets all of its requirements

Efficiency means that group members have determined how to complete tasks in an organized manner.

© MonkeyBusinessImages/Shutterstock.com

and completes all of its tasks. That is, they accomplish what was asked of or assigned to them. Productive groups work toward being efficient and effective.

Overall, productivity in groups is important and can be enhanced in a number of ways. For example, groups can use technology (McFadzean, 1997) to enhance efficiency and effectiveness. For example, if a group has weekly, brief "check-in" meetings, the group may decide to hold these meetings in an online forum, rather than in a face-to-face meeting. Group roles (Rambo & Matheson, 2003) can also be used. Consider the nature of roles. Implied in the assignment of roles is that everyone has a portion of work to do, such as the note-taker keeping record of all meetings and decisions, and the leader setting the agenda and determining when work should be completed. A final technique that can be used to create a productive, efficient, and effective group is building cohesion among group members (Podsakoff, MacKenzie, & Ahearne, 1997). For example, making sure all group members contribute to ideas, are aware of one another, and can share in the work will make the group perform better.

Conflict

Just as we experience conflict in our interpersonal relationships, we are also likely to experience conflict when working in groups. Our personalities, unique communication styles, and different approaches to accomplishing goals may cause

Conflict
Disruption or breakdown of the communication process among group members.

us to experience communication issues that need to be resolved. Keep in mind that *conflict* can be both a positive and a negative experience. Recall from our discussion in Chapter 7 that a key element of conflict is that a struggle between individuals has been expressed verbally or nonverbally. Could you experience conflict with a group member if you don't let them know that you disagree or are upset with them? While you may experience the negative emotions, if you haven't made your feelings known to the other person, conflict may not exist.

Emotional conflict
Conflict from relationships with others and can include lack of trust, feelings of dislike or animosity, and frustration.

There are two types of conflict you may experience while working with others. *Emotional conflict* refers to relational differences among group members and can include a lack of trust, feelings of dislike or animosity, and frustration (Evan, 1965). A second type of conflict is called *task conflict*, which refers to inconsistencies regarding how group members perceive the best way to complete the tasks being performed (Pelled & Adler, 1994).

Task conflict
Conflict regarding how to best complete the tasks being performed.

As the group works toward a deadline or goal, you may become frustrated, experience personality clashes with a group member, or have differing opinions on how best to complete a task. While some conflict is beneficial because it encourages the group to consider alternate viewpoints and solutions, too much conflict can tear a group apart. Consider your own response to conflict when it occurs. Do you shut down, stop working with the group, or yell at others? While you may experience one or more of these reactions, it's not likely that they will help the group accomplish its goal.

Conflict style
Our own reaction to conflict.

Each of us has our own reaction to conflict, known as one's *conflict style*. According to Kuhn and Poole (2000), "An individual's conflict style is a behavioral orientation and general expectation about one's approach to conflict" (p. 559). In Chapter 7 we discussed interpersonal conflict. While conflict in a group setting may be similar to interpersonal conflict, your style or approach to conflict may differ as you add more individuals to the interaction. Working in a group requires us to combine the personalities, opinions, and experiences of group members. Because of the multiple people you interact with in a group setting, you may respond to conflict differently than when you are simply engaging in dyadic or interpersonal communication. Your conflict style dictates the types of behaviors you display to others in the group. Three common responses that individuals apply to conflicts experienced in groups include avoidant, distributive, and integrative strategies (Sillars, Colletti, Parry, & Rogers, 1982). *Avoidant* strategies are used in an attempt to minimize or ignore the conflict. When asked if something is wrong, a group member who is avoidant will likely indicate that everything is fine. *Distributive* strategies require group members to give in to the wishes or ideas of other group members. Members of the group may adopt one solution rather than discussing all viable options. Finally, an *integrative* approach seeks to incorporate the opinions of all members of the group in order to evaluate options and arrive at the best solution.

As you can see from Table 8.4, some conflict styles lend themselves to positive conflict resolution. It is important to deal with conflict situations when they arise in groups. Allowing the conflict to go unresolved may cause relationships within the group to deteriorate and will likely deter the group from accomplishing its goal. Ignoring a conflict does not make it disappear. Identifying potential conflicts and working toward resolution can assist the group in making effective decisions by considering a variety of options or solutions proposed by group members.

TABLE 8.4

Typology of Power (French & Raven, 1960)

Conflict Style	Description	Example
Avoidant	Minimize or ignore conflict or move to another issue	When a group member brings up a topic you do not want to address, you change the subject.
Distributive	Involves one person giving in to another	A group member continuously argues for one solution until finally everyone in the group gives in and agrees to the solution.
Integrative	Individuals work together to find the best or most workable solution	Individuals in the group brainstorm, discuss, and combine ideas in order to achieve the most viable solution.

GROUP DECISION MAKING

It seems clear from our previous discussion of groups that group members must work collaboratively to make a decision. However, this collaboration might be one of those things that is easier said than done. When working in a group, have you ever felt like no one listened to your opinion, that your input was of little value to other people, or that your ideas were not taken seriously? If you answered "yes" to any of these, you may not like working in groups. It *can* be challenging to get other people to listen to you. Effective and efficient groups consider the opinions and ideas of all members.

Group decision making requires thoughtful communication and the exchange of information between members (DeSanctis & Gallupe, 1987). This open exchange

The group needs to divide the labor among all members.

© Goodluz/Shutterstock.com

of ideas that contributes to group decision making can include several steps (Kuhn & Poole, 2000):

1. *Be open to alternatives.* All members of the group have important opinions and these should be given thoughtful consideration.

2. *Answer others' objections to alternatives.* When solutions are questioned, it is important to answer any objections or questions that arise.

3. *Blend ideas and work out compromises among alternatives.* Consider integrating suggestions from a variety of group members; the best possible solutions will likely be the result of incorporating a number of ideas.

4. *Coordinate the division of labor.* To make all members of the group feel important, it is paramount to divide the labor. In other words, everyone should have a job.

This process should also consider two key components: subjective outcomes and performance outcomes. Have you ever been part of a group in which a solution was proposed and, even though you may have used proper decision-making techniques, you still did not like or feel comfortable with the decision? McGrath (1984) labeled this feeling a *subjective outcome*. It can be thought of as a feeling that is associated with the group members' level of satisfaction with the proposed plan. For example, if you are part of a group that is working on a class project and the group uses the previously identified group decision-making behaviors, but you still do not think the agreed-upon decision is the correct one and instead feel disappointed, this is

Subjective outcomes
Something that is associated with group members' level of satisfaction with a proposed plan.

a subjective outcome. In addition to feelings associated with the decision, there are also *performance outcomes*. These outcomes focus on productivity and the measurement of goal achievement. Imagine you and a group of others have been asked to improve parking on your campus. During your brainstorming sessions, your group's communication focuses on the task; communication is centered on the generation of ideas and questioning those ideas to determine the most appropriate outcome. Once a solution has been selected, it is then implemented and a plan for monitoring its success is also put into place. Through the monitoring of this solution, it is determined that the proposed solution does indeed improve parking on campus. Effective decisions take both subjective and performance outcomes into consideration. In other words, decisions that meet goals and represent something that the group feels positively toward are preferred.

> **Performance outcomes**
> Focus on productivity and measurement of goal achievement.

GROUPTHINK

A key consideration to the group decision-making process is the idea of groupthink. Have you ever been part of a group where one person suggests an idea and everyone in the group goes along with it? If no one offers other ideas or solutions and the entire group seems to "jump on the bandwagon" and agree to the proposed idea, you may have experienced *groupthink*. Groupthink occurs when all of the group members go along with an idea without engaging in thoughtful discussion or careful analysis. Janis (1972) argues that groupthink minimizes disagreement or recognition of alternative options. Your group may be experiencing groupthink if:

> **Groupthink**
> Phenomenon that occurs when group members go along with an idea without thoughtful discussion or careful analysis.

- Group members pressure others to conform to the group's ideas.
- Group members and their ideas are considered stupid or bad if they go against the group, or if members try to negotiate.
- Group members self-censor and fall silent and their silence is considered agreement.
- Group members perceive the group to be invulnerable or "untouchable," that nothing can bring them down, which can result in an overly optimistic perception of ideas.
- Group members discount others' warnings or ideas and do not reconsider their positions.

As you may be thinking, groupthink is largely characterized as a negative group experience. Groupthink has occurred a number of times in our culture. For example, consider the 1986 explosion of the space shuttle *Challenger*. While a flaw in the design of an important part of the spacecraft, an O-ring, officially caused the explosion, there were several instances of groupthink leading up to the takeoff.

For example, some engineers were concerned about the functioning of the O-ring, but these concerns were silenced and not shared with those higher in the chain of command. Other examples of groupthink in our culture include the Bay of Pigs invasion during President John F. Kennedy's tenure and the Nazi control of Germany. In all of these instances, voices of dissent were marginalized and group members failed to consider options. Groups can work to overcome this negative characteristic by working toward the best solutions, considering alternatives, not agreeing too quickly to one idea, and by asking all group members for input.

CHAPTER SUMMARY

This chapter has defined groups, discussed the nature of groups, and highlighted the communication issues with which groups deal. While you may or may not enjoy working with groups, it is important to remember that it will likely be something you have to do and it can be a better process when thoughtful attention is given to communicative behaviors. It is a process that can be enhanced with clear communication and a discussion of the roles and rules relevant to groupwork. Remaining open to the insights of others, combining these insights, dividing the labor, and maintaining positive relationships will help groups achieve goals efficiently and effectively. Throughout goal completion, it is important to note that groups can experience both task and relational strain. If left unspoken, the strain can interrupt group processes. Open communication in which all group members are able to provide input will ultimately contribute to the most successful group functioning.

Understanding what a group is, the characteristics that compose group life, and how groups work together to make decisions will enhance your success when encountering group work. While depending on others to complete tasks can prove difficult and sometimes uncomfortable, working with others is a necessary part of your professional, public, and personal lives. Once everyone in a group understands how he or she "fits" in the group, it is easier to complete tasks and manage the social aspect of group life. In the next chapter, we continue our discussion of group life and suggest ways to enhance our group communication skills.

Adjourning stage Final process of group life that signals the completion of tasks.

Coercive power Ability to give out punishment.

Cohesiveness General sense of belonging among group members.

Compliance-gaining Getting someone to do something you want.

Compromiser Individual who avoids conflict and admits any mistakes in a group.

Conflict Disruption or breakdown of the communication process among group members.

Conflict style Our own reaction to conflict.

Coordinator Group member that oversees who accomplishes what tasks and when tasks should be done.

Dominator Group member who likes to be heard and works to control the group.

Effectiveness When a group meets all of its requirements and completes all of its tasks.

Efficiency When group members are maximizing what they do, completing the necessary tasks as correctly as possible.

Emotional conflict Conflict from relationships with others and can include lack of trust, feelings of dislike or animosity, and frustration.

Encourager Group member who praises others and hears others' opinions and ideas.

Evaluator-critic Group member who sets standards and meets goals.

Expert power Power derived from the knowledge or expertise one has.

Explicit rules Formalized rules that are discussed and often documented so that all group members are aware of them.

Factional group When group members are representatives or delegates from other social entities.

Forming stage Initial stage in group development.

Gatekeeper Group member who ensures participation by all group members.

Group A collection of individuals with a common purpose.

Group rules Individuals in a group are expected to do certain things, and if they do not do these things, there are consequences.

Groupthink Phenomenon that occurs when group members go along with an idea without thoughtful discussion or careful analysis.

Harmonizer Group member who offers communication focused on achieving cohesion among group members.

Implicit rules Unspoken and unwritten expectations that everyone in the group seems to know and adhere to.

Individual roles When individuals focus on self-achievement and not group efforts.

Information-seeker Group member who collects information related to tasks and completing tasks.

Joker Group member who uses light-hearted, humorous communication that is often off topic.

Legitimate power Power that is associated with a certain position. Because of his or her position in the group, an individual has a certain right to influence/oversee others' behaviors.

Macro productivity Achieving or finishing the group's task.

Micro productivity Smaller tasks and goals that contribute to macro productivity.

Norming stage Third stage of group development in which members create behavioral standards and punishments.

Norms Standardized behaviors individuals in the group ought to do under any circumstance.

Opinion-giver Group member who expresses opinions and possible interpretations associated with all tasks.

Peer group Members who consider one another to be equals in terms of abilities, background, age, responsibilities, beliefs, social standing, legal status, or rights.

Performance outcomes Focus on productivity and measurement of goal achievement.

Performing stage Fourth stage in group development in which all members are working toward completion of the group's task.

Power Ability to influence others.

Productivity Ability to achieve goals in an efficient matter.

Purposive group A group that is attempting to achieve the completion of a goal.

Recognition-seeker Group member who takes on a lot of work for extra attention.

Referent power An individual's positive regard for and personal identification with the leader.

Relational roles Focus on building and maintaining connections among group members.

Reward power Ability to give out positive benefits or rewards.

Roles Labels placed on individuals based on their function within a group.

Role conflict When you have to perform multiple roles with seemingly contradictory behaviors.

Role flexibility When individuals possess the ability to play a variety of roles and adapt according to the demands of the situation.

Role strain When an individual is required to assume a new role that he or she is reluctant to perform.

Role Theory Ways in which individuals enact different social positions (i.e., roles) in their lives.

Social dimension Group members' relationships and feelings for each other.

Social group Collection of individuals focused mostly on relationship-building that gives members a place to develop self-esteem.

Social-emotional leader Voice of the group members in terms of the affective orientation to the group.

Storming stage Second stage of group development, where most conflicts will occur.

Subjective outcomes Something that is associated with group members' level of satisfaction with a proposed plan.

Task conflict Conflict regarding how to best complete the tasks being performed.

Task dimension Group members focusing on solving problems, completing a task, or achieving a goal.

Task leader Focuses group members on completion of assignments.

Task roles Includes all roles that focus on the group's assignment.

Withdrawer Group member who fails to connect and interact with the group, offers few opinions, and may have issues.

REFERENCES

Benne, K. D., & Sheats, P. (1948). Functional roles of group members. *Journal of Social Issues, 4*, 41–49.

Biddle, B. J. (1979). *Role theory: Expectations, identities, and behaviors.* New York: Academic Press.

Bormann, E. G. (1969). *Discussion and group methods: Theory and practice.* New York: Harper & Row.

Brawley, L. R., Carron, A. V., & Widmeyer, W. N. (1993). The influence of the group and its cohesiveness on perceptions of group goal-related variables. *Journal of Sport and Exercise Psychology, 15*, 245–260.

Burkhalter, S., Gastil, J., & Kelshaw, T. (2002). A conceptual definition and theoretical model of public deliberation in small face-to-face groups. *Communication Theory, 12*, 398–422.

Cragan, J. F., & Wright, D. W. (1999). *Communication in small groups: Theory, process, skills* (5th ed.). Belmont, CA: Wadsworth.

DeSanctis, G., & Gallupe, R. B. (1987). A foundation for the study of group decision support systems. *Management Science, 33,* 589–609.

Evan, W. (1965). Conflict and performance in R&D organizations. *Industrial Management Review, 7,* 37–46.

Forrest, K. D., & Miller, R. L. (2003). Not another group project: Why good teachers should care about bad group experiences. *Teaching of Psychology, 30,* 244–246.

French, J. R. P., & Raven, B. (1960). The bases of social power. In D. Cartwright (Ed.), *Studies in social power* (pp. 150–167). Ann Arbor: University of Michigan Press.

Frey, L. R., & SunWolf. (2005). The communication perspective on group life. In S. A. Wheelan (Ed.), *The handbook of group research and practice* (pp. 159–186). Thousand Oaks, CA: Sage.

Fujishin, R. (2001). *Creating effective groups: The art of small group communication.* San Francisco: Arcada.

Gastil, J. (1993). *Democracy in small groups: Participation, decision-making, and communication.* Philadelphia: New Society.

Hawkins, K., & Fillion, B. (1999). Perceived communication skill needs for work groups. *Communication Research Reports, 16,* 167–174.

Homans, G. C. (1950). *The human group.* New York: Harcourt Brace Jovanovich.

Janis, I. L. (1972). *Victims of groupthink.* Boston: Houghton-Mifflin.

Kuhn, T., & Poole, M. S. (2000). Do conflict management styles affect group decision making?: Evidence from a longitudinal field study. *Human Communication Research, 26,* 558–590.

Li, I., &Hambrick, D. C. (2005). Factional groups: A new vantage on demographic faultlines, conflict, and disintegration in work teams'. *Academy of Management Journal, 48,* 794–813.

Lott, A. J., & Lott, B. E. (1965). Group cohesiveness as interpersonal attraction: A review of relationships with antecedent and consequent variables. *Psychological Bulletin, 64,* 259–309.

Marwell, G., & Schmitt, D. R. (1967a). Compliance-gaining behavior: A synthesis and model. *Sociological Quarterly, 8,* 317–328.

Marwell, G., & Schmitt, D. R. (1967b). Dimensions of compliance-gaining behavior: An empirical analysis. *Sociometry, 30,* 350–364.

McFadzean, E. (1997). Improving group productivity with group support systems and creative problem solving techniques. *Creativity and Innovation Management, 6,* 218–225.

McGrath, J. E. (1984). *Groups: Interaction and performance.* Englewood Cliffs, NJ: Prentice-Hall.

Miller, G. R., Boster, F., Roloff, M. E., & Seibold, D. (1977). Compliance-gaining message strategies: A typology and some findings concerning effects of situational differences. *Communication Monographs, 41*, 37–51.

Pelled, L. H., & Adler, P. S. (1994). Antecedents of intergroup conflict in multifunctional product development teams: A conceptual model. *IEEE Transactions on Engineering Management, 41*, 21–28.

Podsakoff, P. M., MacKenzie, S. B., & Ahearne, M. (1997). Moderating effects of goal acceptance on the relationship between group cohesiveness and productivity. *Journal of Applied Psychology, 82*, 974–983.

Poole, M.S., Hollingshead, A. B., McGrath, J. E., Moreland, R. L., & Rohrbaugh, J. (2004). Interdisciplinary perspectives on small groups. *Small Group Research, 35*, 3–16.

Rambo, E., & Matheson, N. (2003). *Enhancing group-work productivity through coordinator roles.* Retrieved from http://jalt-publications.org/archive/proceedings/2003/E059.pdf.

Remland, M. S., & Jones, T. S. (1994). The influence of vocal intensity and touch on compliance gaining. *Journal of Social Psychology, 134*, 89–97.

Sillars, A. L., Colletti, S. F., Parry, D., & Rogers, M. A. (1982). Coding verbal conflict tactics: Nonverbal and verbal correlates of the "avoidance–distributive–integrative" distinction. *Human Communication Research, 9*, 83–95.

SunWolf. (2008). *Peer groups: Expanding our study of small group communication.* Thousand Oaks, CA: Sage.

Tekleab, A. G., Quigley, N. R., & Tesluk, P. E. (2009). A longitudinal study of team conflict, conflict management, cohesion, and team effectiveness. *Group and Organization Management, 34*, 170–205.

Time crunch: Breakdown of CEOs' time in a 55-hour workweek. (2012). *Wall Street Journal.* Retrieved from http://si.wsj.net/public/resources/images/MK-BS273B_CEOTI_NS_20120213203917.jpg

Tuckman, B. W. (1965). Developmental sequence in small groups. *Psychological Bulletin, 63*, 249–272.

Tuckman, B. W., & Jensen, M. A. C. (1977). Stages of small group development: Revisited. *Group and Organization Studies, 2*, 419–427.

Wheeless, L. R., Barraclough, R., & Stewart, R. (1983). Compliance-gaining and power in persuasion. *Communication Yearbook, 7*, 105–145.

Williams, M. L., & Untermeyer, N. K. (1988). Compliance-gaining strategies and communicator role: An analysis of strategy choices and persuasive efficacy. *Communication Research Reports, 5*, 10–18.

CHAPTER 9

Enhancing Groups Through Leadership and Group Processes: Who's In Charge?

Chapter Objectives

After reading this chapter, you should be able to:

- Identify different types of leadership
- Explain the approaches to leadership
- Describe how team-building activities can benefit a group
- Elaborate on why groups should avoid groupthink
- Explain the creative problem-solving process
- Identify key strategies for the improvement of group meetings

Personal: Your are planning a vacation with five of your friends. You and your friends have agreed that you want to travel during the fall and would like to visit a beach. Determining exactly what month and what beach to visit has proven more difficult. The brainstorming of ideas and dates has occurred largely via email with everyone "replying all" when offering opinions. This has proven somewhat convenient because you are able to read everyone's opinions but you are becoming overwhelmed with the amount of emails your friends are sending. No one can seem to agree on when and where to travel. You decide something should be done to take control of the situation. Where should you begin?

Professional: At your job, you have been asked to present material to a potential client about a new business solution. After agreeing to present your ideas, you discover that you will be working with four additional people to create and present a single proposal. You meet with your coworkers to discuss ideas and quickly realize that the group members are quite different. While they all have good ideas, two of the members seem to detract from the group discussion by bringing up topics that are not relevant. As the leader of the team, it is your job to refocus the discussion. How should you approach your off-topic group members?

Public: Because of your education and experience, you have been asked by the local library to be part of a project that deals with increasing literacy in the community. At the first meeting, you learn that you will be working with a collection of individuals and will present your plan to improve literacy to the local governing body. During the first several meetings, you notice most of the people in the group seem knowledgeable and share some great ideas. However, no real decisions or plans are made. Instead, at the weekly meetings, the group seems to talk about the same things without making progress. You think to yourself that something has to be done to increase the efficiency in this group. What steps should you take to do this?

CHAPTER OVERVIEW

As the opening examples illustrate, there are many instances in your life where you may have to be in charge or act as the leader of a group. Whether the situation involves planning a vacation with friends, working with others on a group project at work, or determining how to increase group productivity, working in groups often requires someone to take a leadership position and determine how to best work with others in the group. It is likely that you have either been a leader or been guided by others at some point. Understanding the leadership process and ways to enhance the group experience could make working with others easier. In

Chapter 8, we emphasized the prevalence of groups in your personal, professional, and public lives. Individuals are often required to depend on others to accomplish goals. At times, achieving these goals can prove difficult; however, understanding different communication strategies for leading others will make the process easier. In addition to understanding how to lead a group, this chapter also explores techniques groups can use to improve the group process.

LEADERSHIP DEFINED

Leadership is a concept that is often difficult to define. Numerous books have been published on the topic and there are multiple approaches to and philosophies about leadership. Communication scholars and theorists have even offered numerous views on leadership. Common definitions of leadership indicate that it includes elements of influence (Cragan & Wright, 1999) and goal accomplishment (Shaw, 1981). *Leadership* can be defined as a process by which individuals influence others' actions and behaviors in order to achieve a goal. The leadership process relies on using communication to affect and motivate group members' behaviors. Leadership is necessary to help group members work well together, motivate them, and help them accomplish the goals of the group.

> **Leadership**
> Process in which individuals influence others' actions and behaviors in order to achieve some goal.

The process of leadership or influencing others' actions is directly connected to communication. Consider being assigned to a group for a class project. As the group begins to form, several people in the group ask what specific tasks need to be accomplished. It appears as though the group members are looking for someone in the group to answer their questions and formulate a plan of action. Having an understanding of the assigned tasks, you begin to answer their questions and determine what the group needs to achieve to be successful. At the next group meeting, the group then looks to you to facilitate the meeting. To engage in leadership and influence behaviors, communication needs to be considered. In fact, various elements regarding leadership and communication have been studied and provide insight into how to enact the process of leadership.

APPROACHES TO THE STUDY OF LEADERSHIP

There are a number of ways to explore the concept of leadership. Studies can focus on the leader, the members (i.e., others in the group), or the interactions between the leaders and members. While these diverse approaches provide many

A leader guides the group to achieve its goals.

© Stuart Jenner/Shutterstock.com

perspectives for viewing leadership, they adopt inherently different orientations (see Table 9.1). Investigating leadership as something an individual possesses is called the *trait approach*. In this approach, the focus is on the common personality characteristics shared by leaders. The *situational approach* examines how leaders behave or act in a variety of situations and with different individuals. Finally, the *interaction approach* examines leadership from a relational perspective. The focus is on the communication that is exchanged between leaders and members.

TABLE 9.1

Approaches to the Study of Leadership

Approaches to Leadership	Description
Trait approach	Focuses on the characteristics of the leader
Situational approach	Focuses on the specific characteristics of the group, both the leader and followers, to achieve a given task
Interaction approach	Focuses on the communicative exchanges of leaders and members

Trait approach
One way to study leadership; focuses on the characteristics/traits of the leader.

Situational approach
One way to study leadership; focuses on the characteristics of the group members and the situation.

Interaction approach
One way to study leadership; focuses on communicative exchanges in the leadership process.

Trait Approach

The trait approach, initially developed in the early 20th century, was one of the first perspectives of leadership. Embedded in the trait approach is the idea that "a leader is born, not made." The trait approach argues that there are certain characteristics that all leaders tend to have in common. Initially, trait theories did not make assumptions about whether leadership traits were inherited or learned; rather, they stated that the qualities of leaders are simply different from nonleaders (Kirkpatrick & Locke, 1991). In other words, there are identifiable personality characteristics that leaders possess. Some traits often associated with leadership are intelligence, honesty, dependability, sociability, and communicative competence. Consider how a leader's communication behaviors reflect his or her ability to lead and motivate others. Individuals are deemed intelligent if they can offer appropriate, task-specific information. They appear confident if, while talking to others, their nonverbal cues such as facial expressions and posture appear sturdy. For example, Warren Buffet, Oprah Winfrey, and the late Steve Jobs are all leaders and viewed as competent in their respective industries; individuals who can follow through on a task; provide honest, authentic views; and are perceived as hard-working individuals that other people enjoy being around. While the trait approach is relatively easy to understand because it implies that leaders have certain qualities, there are some limitations to this view of leadership. It is fairly limiting in that it does not take into account the group members or the task; rather, it focuses only on one person and his or her inherent qualities. For example, serving as the leader for a class project you are to complete with your peers is very different than serving as the leader of a group of 6-year-olds. It is likely that your communication would be quite different with your peers versus young children.

Oprah Winfrey has evolved as a leader in the entertainment industry.

© DFree/Shutterstock.com

Situational Approach

Another approach to the study of leadership accounts for more than just the individual qualities and characteristics of the leader. The situational approach considers the combination of the leader's ability to direct tasks, the relationships between the group members, and the abilities of individual group members as these pertain to accomplishing the tasks (Hersey & Blanchard, 1993). While the leader is perceived as being "in charge," the role of group members is not ignored. Rather, in this approach, members of a group can have considerable influence on both the leader and the leadership process. It is a two-way street: The leader affects and influences the group members and the group members affect and influence the leader. For example, if members appear to be disinterested in completing group tasks, the leader needs to motivate and encourage members in order to instill a desire for the group to achieve its goal. The leader in this group situation would need to highlight additional tasks and continue to push the group members to work. The leader could compliment the work completed by the members, provide suggestions for improvement, or remind the group about progress made.

Blanchard (1985) developed the Situational Leadership II model to highlight four leadership styles based on the characteristics of the leader and the developmental level (i.e., the intelligence and skill level) of the members of the group: directive, supportive, coaching, and delegating (Figure 9.1). The leadership styles are based on two key dimensions: directive communication and supportive communication. A leader's communication can be either high or low in directive and supportive communication. Directive communication is task-focused communication whereas supportive communication focuses on relational aspects of group life. *Directive leadership* is high in directive communication and low in supportive behavior; it is focused on task completion. The leader does not spend much time trying to make others feel comfortable; rather, directions are given regarding what goals need to be accomplished and how they can best be achieved. Little to no feedback is solicited from the group members. The leader "tells" and members are expected to follow. The next style is *supportive leadership*. In this style, the leader is high in supportive communication and low in directive communication. In this style, the leader focuses primarily on relational aspects of the group. They are primarily dedicated to employing behaviors that highlight and develop the skills of the group members. A leader using this style would focus on communication that encourages others, such as complimenting their work or inquiring about how they feel about the task. Another type of leadership style focuses on coaching. The *coaching leadership* style is high in both directive and supportive communication. Leaders who use coaching focus their communication not only on achieving goals but also on meeting the emotional needs of the members. In this approach, the leader asks group members about the progress of the task and solicits their opinions or ideas on how to best fulfill the goal. Ultimately, the leader determines the proper decision for accomplishing goals. The final style of leadership is the delegating approach. The *delegating leadership* style is the opposite of coaching in that leaders

Directive leadership
Focuses on task completion.

Supportive leadership
Solicits feedback and employs behaviors that will highlight and develop the skills of group members.

Coaching leader
Type of leader who uses both highly directive behaviors and highly supportive behaviors; focuses communication on not only achieving goals but also on meeting the followers' emotional needs.

Delegating leadership
Offers little advice, input, or social support and control is handed over to the group members.

do not exhibit or provide support or direction; they are low in both supportive and directive behavior. Very little advice or input is offered from the leader. Instead, control is handed over to the group members, and little social support is offered by the leader. If a leader, for example, tells a group that a series of tasks needs to be accomplished but then allows the group to determine how to accomplish the tasks, offers little insight, and neglects the relationships among the group members, the delegating style has been used.

FIGURE 9.1

Blanchard's (1985) Situational Leadership II model.

High concern for relationship among group	SUPPORTING	COACHING
Low concern for relationship among group	DELEGATING	DIRECTING
	Low concern for task	High concern for task

Recall that the Situational Leadership II model also included a discussion of the group members in addition to the leadership styles. Called the developmental level, this focuses on the competence level of the group members (which includes ability, knowledge, and skill) and their commitment level (which includes their confidence and motivation). The group members can be classified into four levels: D1, D2, D3, and D4. They are organized by level and range from low competence to high competence. D1 group members have lower levels of task competence, while D4 group members are highly competent in the task. D1 individuals are low in competence and high in commitment. They may not know how to do something but they are excited about the challenge. For example, if you do not know much about repairing cars but your parent asks for your help and you are willing to help and continue the entire project, you would be a D1-level worker. You may not know much about fixing cars but you are willing to help and are committed to doing so.

D2 individuals are those who are competent or knowledgeable on a topic but they possess a low level of commitment. They have started learning about the job but lack the motivation to complete tasks. This could easily occur if you have been working on a task for an extended period of time or have made little progress on your task. For example, if your boss asked you to be part of a group project a year ago, but others in the group failed to meet or finish the work, you may begin to feel a decreased level of commitment.

D3 individuals have moderate to high levels of competence but are uncertain about whether they can accomplish the task themselves. That is, they have the intelligence and

D4 individuals are high in both competence and commitment when working on a task.

© Rawpixel/Shutterstock.com

skills necessary to accomplish the task but lack confidence in their ability to complete the task at hand. You may have felt like this in your personal, professional, or public life. For example, while preparing for an important group presentation at work, you may be knowledgeable about your topic, confident about the content of your speech, and proud of the work that others have done, yet you feel as though the group lacks the skills needed to give an effective group presentation. In this situation, a leader is extremely necessary as he or she needs to instill confidence in the group members.

Lastly, D4 individuals are high in both competence and commitment. These individuals truly have the necessary skills and motivation to achieve their goals. Have you ever felt prepared and excited about a task? Perhaps you are working with others who are equally knowledgeable on the topic and have a strong desire to continue the project until it is concluded. The D4 group member is knowledgeable about the topic and is determined to finish all tasks associated with the project. Ultimately, the development level or skills and commitment of the group member is an important consideration for those working in groups.

In adopting the situational approach and specifically the Situational Leadership II model, characteristics of both the leader and group member become important. Group members may enter the group experience with lower levels of competence, knowledge, and skills. To increase the group members' competence, knowledge, and skills, the leader then adjusts communication behaviors and leadership styles. As the group member gains knowledge and progresses to higher developmental levels, such as D3 and D4, the leader again reassesses and asks him- or herself what communication-based behaviors are best suited for this situation with this particular group. Situational factors influence our ability and desire to complete a task. Leaders must consider the task (e.g., the type, the size) and the people with whom they are working. Answers to these questions help the leader decide if they have D1-level group members and need to use the directive approach, or they have D2-level group members and, as a result, need to use more of a coaching style. If a mixture of levels emerge, the leader needs to assess the overall group qualities and determine what would work best to get the members to achieve group goals.

Interaction Approach

The third approach to the study of leadership is the *interaction approach*. In this approach, communicative exchanges between leaders and group members are the primary focus. Verbal and nonverbal communication behaviors of all group members are evaluated in promoting optimal group functioning. Some communication styles are better than others when working in groups. *Promotive communication* focuses on messages that contribute to the group's tasks. It includes messages that help the group stay focused. For example, while at a group meeting, if one group member reminds individuals of assigned tasks and completion dates, promotive communication has occurred since the reminder helped the group achieve its goal. On the other hand, *disruptive communication* includes messages that detract group members from accomplishing their goal. Examples of disruptive communication could include asking others about weekend plans, discussing another class, or any other conversation that strays off the topic of the group task. An efficient leader tries to increase promotive communication and minimize disruptive communication. When disruptive communication occurs, a leader needs to refocus the discussion on the team's goal. This could include inquiries about the status of projects and assigning group roles.

> **Promotive communication**
> Focuses on messages that contribute to the group's tasks.

> **Disruptive communication**
> Detracts group members from accomplishing their goals.

Communication scholars embrace the interaction approach because of its focus on the verbal and nonverbal message exchange between individuals. It takes into account that communication is the most important element of group life and that all group members affect the group's proceedings. If you reflect on your own experiences, you probably have worked with well-functioning groups as well as those groups that seemed to accomplish nothing. In these groups, did members ensure that messages were received accurately? Did group members communicate with one another to clarify assignments? Most likely, the groups that functioned the best contained members that were able to communicate about the tasks in such a way that everyone could understand and achieve the established goals.

STYLES OF LEADERSHIP

As you can see, leadership and communication work together. Your communication behaviors, verbal and nonverbal, are usually reflective of a specific type of leader. Your communication style or the way you interact when working with others mirrors the type of leader you are. For example, if your family needs to achieve a common goal, you may be more interested in learning how everyone is feeling about achieving the goal. Your communication would focus on questions such as "How does that make you feel?" or "Do you feel prepared to accomplish this goal?" However, in a professional setting, your communication behaviors could change. Rather than focusing on individuals' feelings, your message may focus on task achievement. You might ask others when they will finish certain elements of a group project or ask to schedule a meeting. You have a general style of leadership that is manifested through your verbal and nonverbal communication with others. Researchers (see, e.g., Lewin, Lippit, & White, 1939; Mumford, 2006) have identified a number of styles of leadership, including task leader, socioemotional leader, charismatic leader, laissez-faire leader, democratic leader, and authoritarian leader. Each of these is defined in Table 9.2.

TABLE 9.2

Styles of Leadership

Leader	Definition
Task leader	Focuses on the completion of the group's goals. Pays close attention to deadlines and ensures the group divides labor to achieve a common purpose.
Socioemotional leader	Concerned with the relationships among group members. Focuses on issues such as group conflict or individual experiences to ensure individuals can work well together.
Charismatic leader	Considered a dynamic individual with prosocial personality traits such as confidence, interpersonal attractiveness, and communication skills.
Laissez-faire leader	Prefers to use a nondirective approach. Typically laid-back and has little involvement in group functions.
Democratic leader	Consults group members when making decisions. Seeks inputs and listens to others to incorporate multiple ideas and opinions.
Authoritarian leader	Related to a task leader, focuses not only on task completion but communication; also addresses how tasks should be completed.

The leadership styles in Table 9.2 reflect very different approaches to managing group members. As noted above, these styles are manifested through your verbal and nonverbal communication. If, when working with others, your communication focuses on the completion of tasks, you may consider yourself to be a *task leader*. Your verbal communication is centered on specific topics including deadlines, solutions, and brainstorming. Your communication does not stray into superfluous topics; rather, you use promotive communication. As stated previously, promotive communication is centered on the completion of a task. If, when working with others, your communication has instead focused on building relationships and asking group members how they feel about the group experiences, your leadership style can be identified as a *socioemotional leader*. Rather than focus on the division of labor, your communication would center on asking the group members how they feel about their assigned tasks and if they perceive they can accomplish the tasks. It is not uncommon when working with others that both of these types of communication occur from different individuals. For example, if you were brainstorming with a group at your job, the person who summarizes potential ideas and offers additional suggestions could be referred to as the task leader while the person who asks if everyone feels like they can voice their opinions would be labeled the socioemotional leader.

Have you ever been part of a group that was led by someone you just wanted to be around, that you were naturally drawn to? They seemed to have an "it" factor. The *charismatic* leader's communication is very persuasive. Verbally, they may use storytelling as a way to draw the group to them while nonverbally, they attempt to appear confident in their posture and vocal tone. The charismatic leader often describes a bigger vision for the group experience.

Yet another type of leader style is the *laissez-faire* style. This style is hands-off. This leader typically engages in less communication with the group and instead takes a back-seat approach. This type of leader will not actively seek to be part of the group, allowing group members to "figure it out on their own." If pressured, the laissez-faire leader can step up and offer insights and motivate the group members.

A very different type of leadership is the *democratic* style. The democratic leader actively seeks out and engages with the group. The democratic leader solicits opinions and feedback, and decisions are made as a group effort. The democratic leader may need to make decisions for the group, but it is always couched with the understanding that seeking opinions from the group is top priority. Rather than simply issuing "this is how it is going to be" statements, this leader engages with the group in the decision-making process.

Task leader
Type of leader who is primarily concerned with completing the group's goals.

Socioemotional leader
Type of leader who is primarily concerned with the relationships among group members.

Charismatic leader
Type of leader who has characteristics such as confidence, interpersonal attractiveness, and effective communication skills.

Laissez-faire leader
Prefers a "hands-off" mentality to leading others.

Democratic leader
Actively consults group members before making decisions.

The task leader focuses on the completion of the group's goals.

Finally, the *authoritarian* style of leadership is similar to the task leader. This person is focused on achieving goals and tasks but this person dictates and mandates what is to be done in addition to how it is to be done. Essentially, this person "rules with an iron fist." This leader speaks and assumes that others will naturally follow along.

As you can see, the leadership styles are directly connected to your verbal and nonverbal communication. In fact, you may have to adjust your verbal and nonverbal communication in order to successfully lead a group. For example, an authoritarian leadership style may not be successful in leading a group of individuals who need motivation and coaxing to follow along. Rather, this type of leader may need to adjust behaviors and offer the group reasons or information about the benefits of a plan of action to get the group to follow it. Similarly, a democratic leadership style may not be successful if the group members are expecting to receive direct orders and assignments about tasks. Asking for others' opinions would not be beneficial. This leader may need to adjust behaviors and become more directive in communication.

To identify your own leadership type, consider the following questions:
1. When I work with others, which is more of a priority? Is it the task or the relationships among group members? If the task is more important, do

I strive to create a plan of action to achieve the goals/tasks? Task leaders focus on tasks and goals whereas socioemotional leaders focus on the relationships formed among members.

2. Do I like to pose questions and attempt to inspire new ideas by using witty banter? If so, you might find yourself to be a charismatic leader.
3. Do I like to gather insights from others and seek opinions before making decisions? If so, you could be a democratic leader.
4. Do I prefer to take a hands-off approach and allow the group to figure out how to work together, only leading if completely necessary? If so, you might find yourself using a laissez-faire style.
5. Do I like telling people exactly how to do each task? If so, you might be using an authoritarian leadership focus.

Ultimately, there is no one way to lead, and your opinion on leadership and your individual style may evolve over time. When determining how to lead, it is appropriate to consider those with whom you are working and to understand that your leadership style may need to change in order to create the best possible working environment given a particular group. The environment will be affected by the relationships among group members. When working with others, there are techniques to enhance group practices. As the leader it will become important to consider how to get the members of the group to work together. We move now into a discussion of how to create positive group experiences.

TEAM-BUILDING

▶ **Team-building**
Process that includes gathering cooperation from individuals to achieve a common goal.

In our personal, public, and professional lives, there will be many instances of groupwork. *Team-building* activities contribute to building positive relationships among group members. They are strategies that can enhance your time working with others. These techniques can create and sustain positive relationships, which in turn can enhance the quality of the tasks completed by the group. The strategies listed in Figure 9.3 and outlined here are easy to implement. When you accept a job, you sign a contract. You pledge your commitment to other people in the organization. You agree to show up, do your best work, perform tasks, and help the organization accomplish its goals. The same idea holds true for groupwork. Individuals must make a commitment to one another and the group's tasks in order to have a successful experience. Four strategies that can enhance the effectiveness of teams are establishing common goals, working together, engaging in creative problem solving, and avoiding groupthink.

FIGURE 9.3

Team-building
strategies.

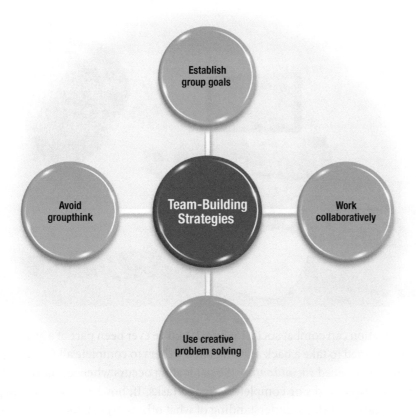

Establish Group Goals

Have you ever been part of a group that talked about performance expectations before beginning its work? Rather than immediately starting the project, the group spends time communicating about what each person anticipates will happen while in the group experience. They share ideas about how meetings should occur, discuss how the work should be distributed, and how to best approach the task. This process can be used to openly establish and clarify what each person wants and values. After all, a group is greater than the sum of its parts—each individual has ideas, experiences, and expectations about groupwork. In order to build effective teams, it is important to begin with a discussion of the individual expectations that group members bring to the group experience. Then, it is beneficial to address how each individual's ideas can be summarized and combined with the goals of the other group members in order to identify a game plan for accomplishing the task. When expectations are explicitly communicated, group members become more aware of the perceptions of others and standards of a group experience. This

A social loafer is like someone who sits around on the sofa all day watching TV.

© KPG_Payless/Shutterstock.com

communication can combat social loafing. If you've ever been part of a group where someone seemed to take a back seat and allow others to complete all the work, then you have experienced *social loafing*. Social loafing occurs when an individual fails to invest in group tasks or complete assigned tasks. If, however, all individuals in the group have a working understanding of what others expect, members are more likely to work together.

➤ **Social loafing**
Avoiding groupwork and allowing others in the group to perform tasks.

Work Collaboratively

When students are asked why they do not like working in groups, they frequently complain that all members do not equally contribute to the work of the group. When group members work collaboratively, they try to incorporate all of the people in the group and all ideas and suggestions. Ideas are combined and discussed until the best solution or idea is created. While working with others, have you ever experienced an increase in your productivity simply because others depended on you? Perhaps you even completed extra work. This is the idea behind *social facilitation*. This occurs when the presence of others, that is, working with others, increases the potential to improve our own performance. For example, when working with someone you consider to be "smart" or a "hard worker," you may strive to "keep up" with this person. You may complete tasks ahead of deadlines or volunteer to do extra work for the group due to the influence of the other person.

➤ **Social facilitation**
Presence of someone else in the group increases members' performance.

Both social facilitation and social loafing occur in groups and can hinder the collaborative experience. Social facilitators may become so eager to complete goals that they may complete tasks assigned to other individuals in the group. Social loafers may skip meetings or not contribute to the group. Should one of these instances occur, it is best for the group as a whole to discuss how to resolve the situation. Rather than ignore the situation, the group members need to communicate about the experience. Recall from Chapter 8 that one of the stages of group development, norming, was an important component of coming together as a group. It was during this time that group members "normalized" and determined how the group was going to function. Recalling and reexamining how the group decided to function can serve as a reminder for what each member should be doing.

Use Creative Problem Solving

Chances are that you will occasionally experience conflict when working in a group. After all, groups are comprised of individuals with a variety of personalities, different levels of motivation, and perhaps unique goals. No matter what situations the group faces, problem-solving techniques, when implemented, help groups work successfully. When group members work collaboratively to identify solutions, positive outcomes can occur. The following step-by-step process was created by John Dewey (1910) to help group members navigate difficulties. The steps include defining the problem, analyzing it, determining solutions, proposing solutions, evaluating solutions, and selecting a solution.

First, groups must work to define the problem. What is the specific issue the group is facing? To begin the process, it is important to clearly identify and describe the particular problem so that all group members can focus on it. For example, you might have a problem with parking on your campus. By clearly focusing on the problem you can ensure that everyone in the group is working on the same thing.

In the second step, you begin to analyze the problem. What factors contributed to the problem? Determine how long the problem has existed, what caused the problem, and what key elements contribute to the problem. In the previous example, the key problem is the inadequate number of parking spaces for all students, faculty, and staff on campus. The first step in addressing the problem would be to address all the factors that contribute to the problem. For example, your campus could have a large number of students who commute all trying to find parking spaces. There could be multiple sections of courses offered at the same time, thus making the parking lot crowded. Perhaps your campus is land-locked and has no options for expanding or building new parking lots. All of these factors contribute to the parking shortage.

In the third step, you determine guidelines for the best solutions. What are the criteria that will be used to judge all possible solutions? In solving any problem,

FIGURE 9.4

Problem solving process.

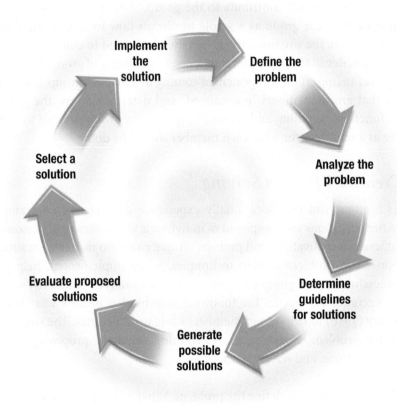

Brainstorming can be an effective way to create solutions.

© wavebreakmedia/Shutterstock.com

there are always parameters to keep in mind. For instance, if you were discussing the parking problem on your campus with individuals on the board of trustees or the president of your school, you may be told that any solution should be affordable as the school does not want to spend a substantial amount of money to fix the problem.

In the fourth step, you and your group propose solutions. What are the possible solutions? *Brainstorming* is a popular technique to help groups generate potential solutions. Although it may sound too simple to be useful, the art of free thinking (and writing it down) can actually help groups see ideas they had not previously considered. The key to successful brainstorming is not just to write some ideas down, but to write *everything* down. No idea should be deemed worthless.

Brainstorming
Technique used for generating ideas.

In the fifth step, the group evaluates the proposed solutions. You should assess the advantages and disadvantages of each proposed solution. Using the criteria identified in step three, the team should now evaluate the possible solutions. Recall that the board of trustees prefers a cost-effective solution. Other criteria your group could have considered are the potential for future growth on your campus or plans for expanding public transportation. Using the criteria your group developed, your group evaluates each proposed solution against it.

Step six requires the group to select a solution. You should pick the solution that works best or has the most merit or worth to solve the problem. Your group may decide that requiring all students to pay for parking permits will control the flow of cars and alleviate the parking issue, while also providing a low-cost solution to the problem.

Finally, your group will implement its solution. Decisions are made about how to put the solution into practice. It is important to determine a process for tracking and monitoring the effectiveness of the plan. For example, your group might decide to complete monthly monitoring of the parking, solicit student feedback, and interview administrators about their experiences with the solution after its implementation.

In addition to using Dewey's (1910) problem-solving sequence, additional suggestions that may help the group complete tasks include planning ahead, taking a break from the task or project, reassigning group roles, working toward consensus, and voting with majority rules.

Planning ahead is one of the most useful things a group can do. It is best to map out a game plan and create a schedule of tasks to be completed before the deadline. This provides the group with time to review and revise the work, if necessary, before the due date. Next, removing yourself from the project, even for a short period of time, allows you to think of different ideas to incorporate or ways to improve the problem to be solved. Have you experienced a situation in which you couldn't come up with any alternative solutions? Taking a break may enable you to clear your mind and approach the task from a fresh perspective.

Another idea is to try changing group roles. Oftentimes, individuals adopt ways of thinking that relate to their specific group role. In order to change orientations to a group problem, it can be helpful to switch things up from time to time. Breaking the routine and shifting roles can help group members experience group life in a new way and assist them in replacing habitual behaviors and tired ways of thinking.

Consensus occurs when all members of the group reach the same opinion. Every person is included; ideas are contributed, combined, and built from one another; and everyone has the opportunity to veto an idea. Consider working with a group of peers on a class assignment. The professor has asked you to complete a group assignment but the artifact you submit to the professor at the conclusion of the semester is to be selected by the members of the group. Using consensus principles, each group member is able to share ideas about what the project should be, combine ideas with others, and veto any ideas.

Finally, majority rule might be yet another technique to incorporate when working with others. This occurs when a resolution is voted on and approved by a majority of the group members. For example, if you and your group of six friends are trying to determine what movie to see and vote on which one you would prefer, a majority vote occurs when four of the six friends agree to a movie. Collectively, these tactics can be used to help groups reach thoughtful decisions that are appropriate for the task at hand. Groups should use these types of practices to avoid achieving false agreement.

Avoid Groupthink

In Chapter 8, we introduced the concept of groupthink. You'll recall that groupthink is largely considered a negative occurrence in group life. In situations where everyone in the group seems to "go along" with a proposed idea to get along in the group instead of trying to work toward the best possible solution, consider implementing strategies to steer your team away from the groupthink trap. Some suggested strategies include:

1. *Ask questions.* Sometimes, you may think it is easier to just go along with a solution rather than asking questions to ensure that you completely understand the implications of the group's decision. However, it is

important that all group members work to understand how proposed ideas or solutions fit with the group's overall goals.

2. *It is okay to be skeptical.* Related to the notion of asking questions, it is acceptable to feel skeptical or unsure. Just because everyone else in the group is going along with an idea does not make it correct. If you have doubts about a plan of action, these should be voiced. In voicing these doubts, hopefully the idea and decision can be strengthened.

3. *Openly discuss ideas.* Rather than sharing your ideas with only one or two members of the group, make sure everyone in the group has the opportunity to listen to all ideas. Sharing information with others can help new ideas surface.

It appears that finding the best possible solutions for a task while working with others requires effort and care. Everyone in the group should have a chance to voice his or her experiences and opinions. In sharing those insights, ideas and solutions are enhanced and strengthened. During your meetings with groups, several things can be done to have more efficient meetings.

ENHANCING THE MEETING PROCESS

Scheduling and coordinating group meetings can be quite difficult. An unproductive group meeting could leave group members feeling unmotivated to work and contribute to negative feelings toward working with others. There are, however, strategies to promote quality, efficient group meetings.

Manage Meeting Time

Time is valuable, and respecting the time of group members is important. The time allocated for group meetings should be carefully managed, perhaps by the leader of the group. The leader of the group could assign one person to serve in the role of timekeeper for the group to ensure that the group remains focused on accomplishing tasks within the specified time constraints. Remaining engaged and focused on group tasks can be challenging. Have you ever attended a meeting where the discussion went "off topic"? Meetings are often sidetracked due to conversations among members or discussions that are unrelated to the group's function. These unwanted discussions have an impact on the overall length of the meeting. In turn, this could affect people's commitment to the group. For example, you may think that being part of a group or a committee isn't important because "nothing gets accomplished" and so you stop attending meetings. Similarly, when members arrive late or leave early and expect time during the next meeting to be devoted to "catching them up" on what they've missed, productivity and commitment to the group diminishes.

Develop and Adhere to an Agenda

Few things are worse than a group meeting in which individuals feel negative about the group or its processes. An agenda can improve the quality of a meeting. The *agenda* is simply a list of the activities or tasks that need to be accomplished during a particular meeting. It may include what needs to be accomplished at the current meeting and also contain information about upcoming due dates or tasks. Organizing the agenda by specifying the amount of time devoted to each topic of discussion is another helpful way to ensure an effective meeting structure. *Time on task* is how much time the group will spend discussing a given topic. When writing the agenda, place items that require more time at the beginning of the agenda. By doing this, people in the group will feel productive as they move through the agenda items. It is best to tailor the agenda to fit the time allocated to the meeting. If the items that require more time are placed at the beginning of the agenda, and a meeting needs to end early, the important, necessary items have already been addressed. If you know the group will meet for only an hour, there is no need to place superfluous tasks on the agenda. Adjusting

Agenda
List of the activities or tasks that need to be accomplished at a particular meeting.

Time on task
How much time the group will spend discussing a given topic.

The meeting agenda is a list of items that need to be accomplished.

© Dusit/Shutterstock.com

the agenda to fit the group members and goals is a process that takes refinement during the initial meetings. It is also helpful to get the agenda to the group before meetings. This way, group members are able to prepare thoughts and comments and time is not wasted trying to come up with answers or suggestions. Ultimately, when an agenda contains only the tasks to be addressed, it can help the group members feel as though they actually accomplish their tasks and ultimately can accomplish the group's purpose. This, in turn, could improve the overall quality and effectiveness during the meeting.

Demonstrating Respect for Others

Consider the following example:

> Your company has noticed that people seem indifferent about coming to work. No one seems overly excited to be there; people rarely come in on time and often are quick to leave. In addition, people do not interact while at work and the overall environment seems very isolated. As a result, your company has recently created a committee to address this issue. The committee was asked to create ways to boost or increase worker morale and propose solutions for improving relationships among workers. At the first meeting, however, the person who was asked to be in charge of the committee and serve as the leader is heard saying, "I hate working with others. Who cares about relationships with other people?"

If you heard this, how would you react? Would you want to continue working on a project with someone who doesn't seem interested? You're probably thinking that the person's language is quite counterproductive to what the group is trying to accomplish. Another tool for enhancing group meetings is demonstrating respect for others. This may be done by the type of language used. Most likely, you were told as a small child to "think before you speak" or "what you say to others matters." These old adages have some utility when working with others. Be sure to use inclusive language to reinforce the collective nature of the group. Terms such as "our project" and "we can accomplish this" help create a sense of cohesiveness.

Groupwork is difficult and you and the others in the group may want to take sides when determining solutions to problems. Nonjudgmental language and questions will demonstrate respect for others and enhance the group experience. Asking questions ensures that everyone is "on the same page." Using statements such as "What I think I hear you saying is …" is one example of paraphrasing what others have said to make sure that you have understood them correctly. It's important to note that paraphrasing doesn't necessarily mean that you agree with ideas or opinions. Rather, you are attempting to understand someone else's ideas. By doing so, you will make others in the group feel valued. Ask open-ended questions. *Open-ended questions* are those that cannot be answered with a one-word statement. They often start with who, what, why, or how. By using open-ended questions, others are encouraged to share and elaborate in discussing their ideas. When everyone is given a voice, all members feel valuable. If group members feel valued, they are more likely to be committed to accomplishing the group's goal.

In situations where confrontations occur, incorporate "I" statements to explain your perception. Statements such as "I feel frustrated when I feel like nobody is listening to my ideas" show personal ownership of the experience rather than the more accusatory, "You never listen to me."

Another way to demonstrate respect for the group is by arriving on time with all previously assigned tasks completed. If, at a previous meeting, you are given a task to complete, you should be able to report on the status of that task at the next meeting. During your update of the assigned task, your communication should stay focused and not drift into superfluous or unnecessary information.

Ultimately, group meetings can be quite productive. These simple and practical steps can ensure that a meeting achieves its goals and allows everyone an opportunity to express their ideas. By managing time and respecting others' boundaries and ideas, there is a greater chance of having a positive group experience.

CHAPTER SUMMARY

There are many different approaches to leadership and leading a group. In fact, because of the different types of leaders, being an effective leader who guides group members to completing tasks can appear to be overwhelming. However, it is possible to tailor your leadership style to your particular group and task. This chapter provides tools and suggestions for determining an appropriate leadership style. These tools include considering the group's purpose, members, and potential obstacles. By doing so, you are likely to have a more positive leadership experience and a successful group. Ask yourself this series of questions:

- What is the group's purpose?
- With what type of individuals am I working?
- In what type of environment is the group working?
- What are the potential obstacles in the way of completing the task?
- Am I the best person for a leadership position?

In asking and honestly answering these questions, you have begun to understand the group's dynamics and, as a result, will communicate more efficiently and effectively. Thus, it is important to think carefully about the important components to working in a particular group and tailor your communication accordingly. This will be beneficial in your personal, professional, and public lives. It is beneficial because all members of the group can have a clear understanding of what the tasks and challenges are, everyone can share insights about the group, and you, as the leader, can create messages that guide the group to successful completion of its tasks and goals.

While working with others can be daunting, there are simple strategies that can contribute to its overall effectiveness. It is important to keep in mind that there is no one right way to lead in a group. Oftentimes, you will experience individual differences and preferences for a certain leadership style over others. You must remember that these potential differences should not interfere with the group's overall functioning. If a problem arises, engaging in careful problem solving can efficiently minimize any difficulties. Ultimately, it is best to focus the group by using simple management solutions. With these ideas in mind, you and your group can successfully achieve the group's goals.

KEY WORDS

Agenda List of the activities or tasks that need to be accomplished at the meeting.

Authoritarian leader Mandates what must be done in a group setting.

Brainstorming Technique used for generating ideas.

Charismatic leader Type of leader who has characteristics such as confidence, interpersonal attractiveness, and effective communication skills.

Coaching leader Type of leader who uses both highly directive behaviors and highly supportive behaviors; focuses communication on not only achieving goals but also on meeting the followers' emotional needs.

Delegating leadership Offers little advice, input, or social support and control is handed over to the group members.

Democratic leader Actively consults group members before making decisions.

Directive leadership Focuses on task completion.

Disruptive communication Detracts group members from accomplishing their goals.

Interaction approach One way to study leadership; focuses on communicative exchanges in the leadership process.

Laissez-faire leader Prefers a "hands-off" mentality to leading others.

Leadership Process in which individuals influence others' actions and behaviors in order to achieve some goal.

Open-ended questions Questions that cannot be answered with a one-word statement.

Promotive communication Focuses on messages that contribute to the group's tasks.

Situational approach One way to study leadership; focuses on the characteristics of the group members and the situation.

Social facilitation Presence of someone else in the group increases their performance.

Social loafing Avoiding groupwork and allowing others in the group to perform tasks.

Socioemotional leader Type of leader who is primarily concerned with the relationships among group members.

Supportive leadership Solicits feedback and employs behaviors that will highlight and develop the skills of group members.

Task leader Type of leader who is primarily concerned with completing the group's goals.

Team-building Process that includes gathering cooperation from individuals to achieve a common goal.

Time on task How much time the group will spend discussing a given topic.

Trait approach One way to study leadership; focuses on the characteristics/traits of the leader.

REFERENCES

Blanchard, K. H. (1985). *SLII: A situational approach to managing people.* Escondido, CA: Blanchard Training and Development.

Cragan, J. F., & Wright, D. W. (1999). *Communication in small groups: Theory, processes, skills* (5th ed.). Belmont, CA: Wadsworth.

Dewey, J. (1910). *How we think.* New York: Dover.

Hersey, P., & Blanchard, K. (1993). *Management of organizational behavior: Utilizing human resources* (6th ed.). Englewood Cliffs, NJ: Prentice Hall.

Kirkpatrick, S. A., & Locke, E. A. (1991). Leadership: Do traits matter? *The Executive, 5,* 48–60.

Lewin, K., Lippit, R. & White, R. K. (1939). Patterns of aggressive behavior in experimentally created social climates. *Journal of Social Psychology, 10,* 271–301.

Mumford, M. D. (2006). *To outstanding leadership: A comparative analysis of charismatic, ideological, and pragmatic leaders.* Mahwah, NJ: Erlbaum.

Shaw, M. E. (1981). *Group dynamics: The psychology of small group behavior.* New York: McGraw-Hill.

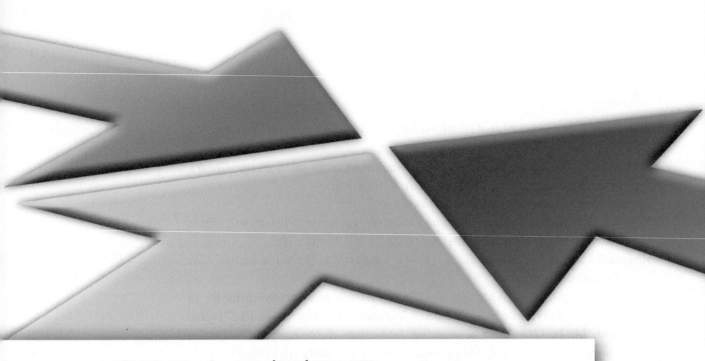

CHAPTER 10

Public Speaking in Our Lives: Beginning the Process

Chapter Objectives

After reading this chapter, you should be able to:
- Identify some of the challenges public speakers face
- Characterize the various types public speeches typically given
- Explain the purposes of each type of speech
- Provide an overview of the public speaking process

PERSONAL: You've been best friends since middle school. Throughout high school, you played on the same teams, had the same group of friends, and were in many of the same classes together. Although you went to different colleges, you stayed in contact with each other. Upon graduation, you settled in different cities and chose different career paths but still remained close friends. Now, your friend is getting married and has asked you to be in the wedding party. You are thrilled and honored, but you also realize you will be giving a toast at the reception. Although you are nervous, you want to give a toast that honors your friend. Where do you begin?

PROFESSIONAL: For the past 3 months, you've been working on a huge project at your company. Your supervisor asks you to present your findings to the board of directors at next month's meeting. You have a great deal of material to cover, but with a full agenda for the meeting you will have only 15 minutes to convey 3 months of work. Although you are accustomed to speaking to members of your own department, this speaking situation is a complete departure for you. How will you organize so much information into a 15-minute presentation?

PUBLIC: The local school district has submitted their budget for the next fiscal year and it is well over the original estimate your city council felt was appropriate. As chair of your city's parent–teacher organization, you strongly believe in the need for the additional funds requested by the school system. The city council has invited citizens to attend a special meeting to express their opinions on the issue. Although you have never been called upon to address the council before, you want to represent the needs of the students and faculty in the system as best you can. Where do you start?

CHAPTER OVERVIEW

Whether it is making a toast at your best friend's wedding, sharing the results of your work on a project, or speaking to support an issue in your community, you may be called upon to speak publicly for personal, professional, or public reasons. There are many potential scenarios in which people find themselves speaking in public. Perhaps you are an officer of a club or organization and you need to facilitate a meeting. You may be working on a project that will benefit your community and need to speak to another group to elicit their help on the project. Maybe you are presenting the results of a project to your class or representing your company and making a presentation to a potential client. Whether you are speaking to a small group of people or a large audience, there are certain elements that enable public speakers to be more effective when delivering presentations. These elements center on the preparation for and delivery of one's message. This chapter focuses on the challenges public speakers face and the common types and purposes of public speeches. In addition, we provide an overview of the public speaking process.

THE CHALLENGES OF PUBLIC SPEAKING

As you learned in Chapter 1, it is considered public speaking when one person communicates to an audience. During a public speech, typically one person speaks and the audience listens. In most public speaking situations, while the speaker is presenting, the audience responds primarily through nonverbal cues. Once the presentation is over, a question-and-answer period often allows for verbal interaction between the speaker and the audience. This process may present some challenges for many public speakers. For example, speakers may feel anxious and try to avoid public speaking altogether. Other challenges include establishing and maintaining credibility as well as being an ethical speaker. These are the challenges that we discuss in the following pages.

Anxiety

Public speakers face many challenges highlighted in Figure 10.1. One prominent challenge that speakers encounter is the anxiety they may experience. Dwyer and Davidson (2012) found speaking in public was "selected more often as a common fear than any other fear, including death" (p. 99). Communication researchers have studied communication apprehension for more than 40 years as a real phenomenon that affects some speakers (McCroskey, 1977, 2004, 2005; McCroskey, Andersen, Richmond, & Wheeless, 1981; McCroskey & Beatty, 1999, 2000). Chapter 1 defined *communication apprehension* as the fear, nervousness, or anxiety we experience when faced with real or imagined interactions. Typically, we consider there to be four forms of communication apprehension. They are trait-like communication apprehension, audience-based communication apprehension, situational communication apprehension, and context-based communication apprehension. If you have *trait-like communication apprehension*, you will experience anxiety in most speaking situations. Thus, whether you are speaking one on one, to a small group, or to a large audience, you will experience communication apprehension. *Audience-based communication apprehension* occurs when you are anxious when speaking to a particular audience or receiver. Thus, you may not experience apprehension when speaking with a group of peers in a class or with your colleagues at work, but you may become apprehensive when speaking to the board of directors of your company or in front of a group of strangers.

➤ Communication apprehension
The fear, nervousness, or anxiety we experience when faced with real or imagined interactions.

➤ Trait-like communication apprehension
Fear of public speaking (e.g., one-on-one, to a small group, or to a large audience).

➤ Audience-based communication apprehension
Fear of public speaking with a specific audience (e.g., you may not be apprehensive when you are speaking with your peers in a course but apprehensive when you are speaking to the board of directors of your company).

Most public speakers feel some level of nervousness.

© Africa Studio/Shutterstock.com

If you are normally confident meeting with your supervisor but nervous to meet with your supervisor to ask for a raise, or if you are comfortable speaking with a particular teacher but are nervous about asking this teacher for an extension on an assignment, you may be experiencing *situational communication apprehension*. This type of apprehension is based on a specific occurrence. Finally, if you are anxious about public speaking but do not have any problems communicating in small groups or in other settings, you are experiencing *context-based communication apprehension*.

Certainly, some level of communication apprehension, anxiety, or stage fright is normal for most public speakers. Some physical symptoms of communication apprehension include trembling hands, a dry "cotton" mouth, butterflies in the stomach, or a racing heart. Although you may perceive that these symptoms are obvious to the audience, typically they are not, and there are ways to mask them. For example, you may want to sip on water to alleviate the feeling of a dry mouth, place your hands down by your sides if you feel they are shaking, or take some deep breaths to relax and help you slow down a racing heart. In addition to the physical symptoms associated with communication anxiety, speakers also experience emotional or psychological symptoms. Being unable to sleep the night before a speech or having your thoughts preoccupied by the speech days before you're scheduled to present are examples of psychological manifestations of anxiety.

➤ **Situational communication apprehension** Fear of public speaking based on a specific occurrence (e.g., you are nervous about meeting with your supervisor to ask for a raise or your town's planning board to ask for a variance).

➤ **Context-based communication apprehension** Fear of speaking only in one setting (e.g., fear of speaking in public but not in other settings such as in small groups).

The good news is that for most individuals, anxiety can often be reduced through careful preparation and extensive practice. Usually, the more time you spend researching your topic, developing your speech, and practicing your delivery, the more comfortable you will be with the material. As a result, you will enhance your ability to convey your topic in an interesting and understandable manner. In addition to practice and preparation, many speakers create their own techniques to reduce anxiety. For example, some speakers use breathing exercises to calm their nerves. Breathing in slowly while counting to three and then exhaling slowly for three counts is a technique some speakers use to relax before approaching the podium. Other speakers may use positive visualization before getting up to speak in front of an audience. In this case, they visualize the audience engaged in the topic and giving positive feedback. Still other speakers use positive self-talk to reduce anxiety. These speakers internalize thoughts such as "I can do this," "I am well prepared," or "I have a lot of material that the audience will find interesting and relevant."

While speech anxiety is often considered a barrier that must be overcome, there are some benefits to this type of nervousness. Apprehension has been compared to an athlete "getting psyched" to play a game. By channeling the butterflies associated with public speaking, our anxiety may actually make us more effective speakers. When channeled appropriately, nervousness can actually lead to a more energized delivery. While we may feel we are the only ones with this type of anxiety, it is a common occurrence. Many public figures including actors have speech anxiety. For example, in 2006, when Reese Witherspoon won the Oscar for Best Actress in the movie *Walk the Line*, she said she actually hoped they would *not* call her name because "...the idea of having to give a speech in front of everyone in the world" terrified her. Likewise, Harrison Ford called public speaking "a mixed bag of terror and anxiety" (Bailey, 2008). Overall, despite the fact that many public speakers face some form of communication anxiety, usually, the more public speaking one does and the more one prepares and practices, the more comfortable one becomes.

Credibility

Credibility
Extent to which a speaker is trustworthy, knowledgeable, and well prepared.

The ability to achieve credibility is another challenge public speakers encounter. *Credibility* is the degree to which an audience believes and trusts a speaker. As speakers, we want our audience to perceive us as credible sources on our given topics. The more credible an audience perceives a speaker to be, the more likely it is that audiences will listen to and believe the speaker. Do you listen more carefully to some public speakers than others? Do you believe certain people more than others? If you answered yes to these questions, you are like most people. The truth is, we do listen to people differently and this is partially influenced by their credibility. For example, you would listen and trust the advice of a doctor versus a friend regarding how to treat a medical concern. The doctor's medical training and experience increases the doctor's credibility.

How do we achieve credibility? First, speakers can build their credibility by putting in the effort and time to carefully and competently prepare for a speaking occasion. Thus, *competence* is a key factor in credibility. If you are a competent public speaker, you are knowledgeable about your topic. You may have gained this knowledge through your education or through your professional or personal experiences. For example, a person may be perceived as a competent public speaker on the subject of French culture. This may be true because he has undergraduate and graduate degrees in French. He may also be viewed as a competent public speaker on the subject because he has taught French for several years or because he has lived and studied in France.

Another way speakers gain or lose credibility is through their perceived character. *Character* is an audience's perception of a speaker as trustworthy, sincere, and likable (Booth-Butterfield & Gutowski, 1993). Thus, if an audience likes a speaker and believes she is genuine and has the audience's best interests at heart, they are more likely to perceive the speaker as credible.

Something else to consider is that credibility can vary by speaker or by audience. You may be perceived as credible when speaking about one specific topic, but not on others. For example, your communication professor is credible when speaking about communication, but would your teacher have as much credibility if he or she spoke on electrical engineering? Likewise, credibility may vary because of the audience. One audience may view a speaker as very credible while another audience may believe the same speaker lacks credibility. For example, if you present a speech on the threat of global warming to an audience who also believes in global warming, they will be more likely to perceive you as credible. However, if the audience does not believe in global warming, they may discount whatever you say about the subject as well as your credibility. In addition, in one audience, you may be perceived as competent because you know more about the topic than your audience. With a different audience, one that perhaps has the same knowledge level as you, your competence may be perceived differently. For example, if someone is taking a introductory course in astronomy, your instructor is an expert in the subject. When your instructor goes to a convention with other professors of astronomy and scientists, the level of competence may be perceived differently.

When an audience perceives that you know your topic, your credibility increases.

For most speakers, credibility is gained over time. In your public speaking course, everyone will start with a "credibility quotient" that will either go up or down after each speech. One way to achieve credibility in a public speaking situation is through careful preparation and practice. When an audience perceives that you have devoted time researching, organizing, and practicing a speech, your quotient will go up. On the other hand, if an audience feels that you have not spent adequate time carefully preparing and practicing your speech or presentation, your quotient will decrease.

Overall, achieving credibility is a challenge for public speakers but is attainable through knowledge of the subject, careful preparation, practice, and the sincerity of the speaker.

Ethics

➤ **Ethical public speaking**
Speaking that demonstrates respect for one's audience, honesty, use of reliable and valid sources, and responsibility for everything that is said and/or done during a speech.

A final challenge that public speakers must address relates to ethics. *Ethical public speaking* involves the demonstration of respect for one's audience; honesty; use of reliable and valid sources; and accountability for the information shared during a speech. Public speakers have a number of ethical responsibilities.

First, speakers must always give credit where credit is due. It is important to cite all sources consulted for a speech. Examples of unethical practices include purchasing speeches from Internet sites or copying sections of a speech and using it without citing the original source. When using direct quotes from other sources, be sure to give credit where it's due and cite the original source. Not only is this an ethical practice, but it also demonstrates to your audience that you have thoroughly researched your topic.

Speakers also have an ethical responsibility to use appropriate and non-offensive language. Profanity or language that would insult anyone based on that person's race, ethnicity, age, gender, religion, or sexual orientation should not be used.

Third, although we are afforded freedom of speech by the First Amendment of the U.S. Constitution, speakers should not abuse this protection. It would be unethical, for example, for public speakers to give information they know is false, to slander another person, or to say something that would damage the audience's civil rights. While there are speakers who distort the truth or make offensive comments yet remain legally protected by the First Amendment, this does not necessarily mean they are ethical speakers.

Fourth, speakers should never do anything during the speech that would intentionally insult or embarrass the audience. For example, pictures or YouTube clips that would not be appropriate for public consumption should not be used in a public speech. Respect should be shown for audiences. This is ensured by maintaining honesty, avoiding plagiarism, using reliable and valid sources, and demonstrating responsibility for all that a speaker says and/or does during a speech.

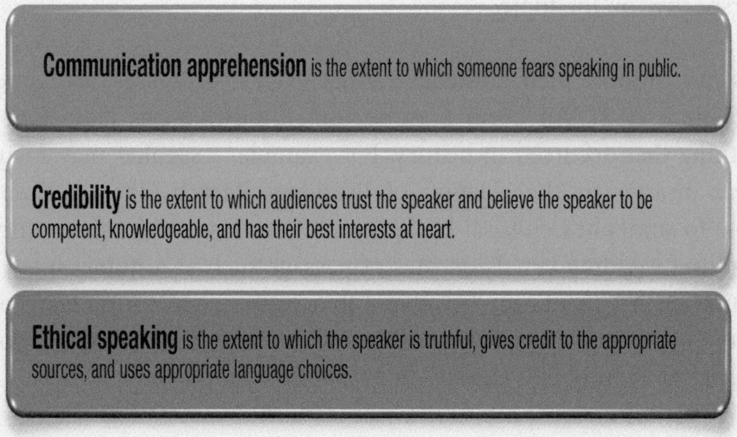

FIGURE 10.1

The challenges of public speaking.

Communication apprehension is the extent to which someone fears speaking in public.

Credibility is the extent to which audiences trust the speaker and believe the speaker to be competent, knowledgeable, and has their best interests at heart.

Ethical speaking is the extent to which the speaker is truthful, gives credit to the appropriate sources, and uses appropriate language choices.

Overall, public speakers face many challenges. Some people may be reticent to speak in public while others may be unwilling to speak in certain situations. Issues of credibility and ethics also provide challenges for some public speakers. Understanding yourself as a public speaker and the challenges you face speaking in public is the first step to becoming a competent speaker. As you go through the rest of this chapter, it is important to keep these potential challenges in mind in order to address them as you prepare the speeches you will deliver in your personal, professional, and public lives.

THREE TYPES OF PUBLIC SPEECHES

Speaking to inform, speaking to persuade, and speaking for special occasions are three common types of public speaking and are the focus of this section of the chapter. As each speech type is discussed, we examine when you would most likely use each type and some examples are provided as well.

Informative Speeches

➤ Informative speaking
Type of speech used to help an audience become aware of or better understand a topic.

Informative speaking involves the presentation of ideas and support to enhance an audience's knowledge and understanding of the topic. The primary goal is to share new information with the audience, not to change their attitudes or behaviors on the topic. Informative speeches provide the audience with insight that is unbiased and objective. Speakers increase an audience's knowledge and/or understanding of a topic by providing facts, examples, quotes by those informed about the topic, and other types of supporting material. If the audience possesses prior knowledge about the topic, then speakers may need to provide additional facts or data or provide a fresh perspective on the topic.

Speakers may inform their audiences about events, processes, ideas, people, or objects (Figure 10.2). An event may be something that has happened recently or something that occurred in history. For example, a speaker may focus on the *Challenger* disaster or the election of President Barack Obama. Events could also relate to someone's cultural background. Someone might share information about cultural wedding rituals or rites of passage such as a quinceañera or a bar or bat mitzvah. An event may be related to a professional sports team or a local celebration. For example, a speaker might inform the audience of the history of the World Series or Bunker Hill Day celebrated in Boston.

A speaker may also inform an audience about a process. Demonstration speeches are a type of informative speech where a process is explained to help an audience understand steps or procedures. Examples of demonstration speeches that explain a process may include how to bake a cake, prepare a résumé, or edit a film.

Ideas, concepts, or theories may also be topics for informative speeches. Topics in this category are generally more abstract in nature, so the challenge is to present something that is abstract in a way that the audience is able to understand. Examples may include speeches about global warming, media literacy, or stem cell transplants.

People are another common subject for informative speeches. Perhaps you have a favorite singer, author, or actor whose life you could explore. There may be an artist whose work you have always admired or someone in history who has made a difference in the world. People from sports figures to political figures to religious and cultural figures can all serve as topics for informative speeches.

Finally, informative speeches can focus on objects. These are things that have a physical existence. Hybrid cars or the latest iPhone are examples of objects that could be topics for informative speeches. In addition, places are also considered in this category. For example, famous examples of architecture such as the Eiffel Tower in France or the Prado Museum in Spain are examples of objects that could become informative speech topics.

While the topics mentioned above primarily relate to speaking within an academic setting, informative speeches are also relevant in professional contexts. In your work

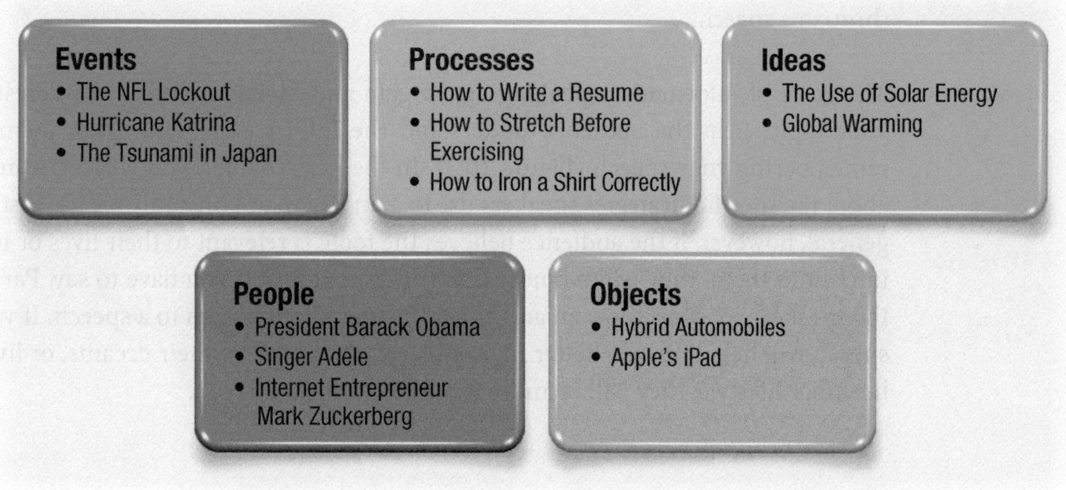

FIGURE 10.2

Topics for informative speeches.

Events
- The NFL Lockout
- Hurricane Katrina
- The Tsunami in Japan

Processes
- How to Write a Resume
- How to Stretch Before Exercising
- How to Iron a Shirt Correctly

Ideas
- The Use of Solar Energy
- Global Warming

People
- President Barack Obama
- Singer Adele
- Internet Entrepreneur Mark Zuckerberg

Objects
- Hybrid Automobiles
- Apple's iPad

In your work setting, you may be asked to present new information to colleagues.

© Monkey Business Images/Shutterstock.com

setting, you may be asked to explain a new computerized process your organization will use to track expenses, explain a new product to potential clients, or present orientation information to new employees.

Likewise, if you are part of a community group or work within your local or state government, you may be asked to speak on a variety of topics. For example, if your town is celebrating a milestone event, implementing a recycling program, or honoring a citizen, you might be asked to share information or offer an explanation through a speech.

The goals of informative speaking are to gain and maintain audience interest in your topic, help the audience understand the information, and assist them in remembering your speech (Figure 10.3). In the next chapter, you will learn more about the specific strategies speakers use to gain and maintain audience interest. In general, however, if the audience believes the topic is relevant to their lives or is of interest to them, they will be more likely to listen to what you have to say. Part of the speaker's job is to show an audience *why* they should listen to a speech. If your speech will help them do better in school, secure the job of their dreams, or live a healthier lifestyle, they will be more motivated to listen to you.

The second goal of informative speaking is to say things in such a way that your audience understands your ideas. In part, this is accomplished by using clear and descriptive language. Understanding who your audience is will help you select the language you need to use in your speech. If you are informing an audience that has little technical knowledge about how to increase the memory on their computer, it would be confusing to use terminology such as "gigabytes," "RAM," and "virtual memory." Instead, you would need to clearly define any technical words and relate these words to concepts the audience understands. Consider the fact that if a doctor tells you that you have otitis media, you might be much more upset than if the doctor says that you have an ear infection. Clarity of language makes all the difference in your audience's ability to achieve common understanding.

The third goal of informative speaking is to present your speech in such a way that your audience will remember what you said long after you have finished your speech. In addition to using clear and descriptive language, this is also accomplished by the support material you select and the manner in which you organize your speech. Various forms of support material are discussed in the next chapter. In general, if you present a variety of support materials, tailor the forms of support to the audience's knowledge and attitude toward the topic, and use support that is verbally and visually memorable, you will help your audience recall your message. In addition, presenting information in an organized fashion will help the audience recognize the main ideas of a speech. This, in turn, will help them remember the speech. Understanding the goals of informative speaking will also help you select the strategies you use to help you achieve those goals.

FIGURE 10.3

The three goals of informative speeches.

There are several strategies public speakers use to help them inform their audiences. *Strategies* are techniques speakers use to engage their audience and to keep the audience focused. Since audiences are more likely to listen to a speech if they believe your topic is relevant to them, one useful strategy is to show them how your topic will help them or is somehow meaningful to them. For example, you will be implementing a new billing system and you plan to explain it to the employees who will be using it. Your presentation will show them how it will work as well as the reasons why it will help them do their jobs more effectively. Because your presentation is relevant to them, they will be more likely to listen to you. Overall, as stated earlier, if you can show how your topic can help them do better at work or in school, get the job they want, or live a better life, they will be more likely to listen to you.

Visual aids can help to reinforce what you say in your presentation.

🔖 **Strategies**
Techniques speakers use to engage their audience and to keep the audience focused.

Another strategy informative public speakers use is to reinforce what they are saying verbally with visual support. The old adage, "A picture is worth a thousand words" is very true in public speaking. A chart, graph, diagram, picture, or any other visual means of support can help to summarize, clarify, and reinforce what you have said verbally. For example, you have summarized the growth in one of your divisions over the past 5 years and have created a chart so your audience may see this visually as you discuss it. Helping an audience "see" what you are "saying" will help increase their understanding of your material. The forms of visual support are discussed more specifically in the next chapter.

A third strategy public speakers use is to repeat their key points. Repetition helps maintain an audience's attention while helping them remember your main ideas. Thus, if a speaker says, "There are three types of …." and then explains each type and repeats the three types again, audiences are more likely to follow the speaker's points.

Another useful strategy is to provide a new or different perspective on a topic about which an audience is already knowledgeable. If an audience feels like they have "heard it all before," they are less likely to listen to the speaker. If, on the other hand, the speaker takes a different approach to a topic, the audience is more likely to engage in listening.

If an audience knows little or nothing about a topic, the focus of the informative speech might be to define the topic. For example, you might define the term *robotics* in a speech or what it means to play an "RPG" or "role-playing game." You might also define the "4 C's" of selecting a diamond (i.e., cut, clarity, carat, and color). If you are informing your audience about a process, you could use an explanation. For example, you might explain how furniture is refinished or artwork is restored. You might explain how certain events in history led up to a particular war or event.

You may also inform an audience by demonstrating your topic. By demonstrating how to salsa dance, shoot the perfect foul shot, stretch before working out, or do a favorite craft, you can inform your audience in a very visual and practical manner. Using definitions, explanations, or demonstrations in your informative speeches will help to increase an audience's understanding and knowledge of a topic.

To summarize, there are many types of informative speeches that you will encounter in your life. In general, the goals of informative speaking and the strategies you use are similar whether you are speaking in your personal, professional, or public life. If your main purpose is to help an audience become more aware of a subject or have a better understanding of it, it is considered an informative speech. If, on the other hand, you are taking a stand on an issue, trying to get an audience to believe the same way you do, or asking an audience to take action regarding something, you will be speaking to persuade.

Persuasive Speeches

Persuasive speaking is focused on three primary goals: changing an audience's existing belief, reinforcing a belief or attitude, or motivating an audience to take action or behave in a desired way (Figure 10.4). Examples of persuasive speech topics designed to change existing beliefs or attitudes may include current or controversial issues such as advocating legislation prohibiting texting while driving or the legalization of euthanasia. At times, the speaker and the audience may hold similar beliefs or attitudes. In that case, the goal of the persuasive speech may be to reinforce attitudes rather than change them. For example, while an audience may believe that exercising one's right to vote is important, many individuals may not vote on a regular basis. A persuasive speech about the importance of voting may reinforce their existing belief.

Persuasive speaking
Type of speech used to change an audience's existing belief, to reinforce their existing belief, or to get an audience to take action regarding the topic.

If the goal of the persuasive speech is to motivate the audience to action, a speaker will need to present data and arguments to influence and inspire others. For example, you might want to persuade the audience to sign up to become organ donors, volunteer for Habitat for Humanity, or exercise on a regular basis.

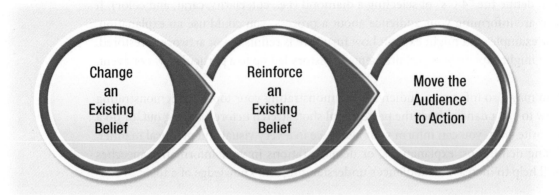

```
Change          Reinforce          Move the
an              an                 Audience
Existing        Existing           to Action
Belief          Belief
```

FIGURE 10.4

The goals of persuasive speeches.

Persuasive speaking opportunities are commonplace. You may persuade others to join a community group to which you belong, donate time to help rebuild a playground, or persuade a local school committee to accept a proposal. In a corporate setting, you may use persuasion to gain new clients, secure the endorsement of a board of directors to expand a company, or sell your company's goods or services. Likewise, you are a constant consumer of persuasion in your personal, professional, and public lives. Politicians try to gain your support, salespeople attempt to have you purchase their product, heads of companies try to secure support for a company merger and persuasion is the means by which they attempt to accomplish their goal.

While persuasion is everywhere in our personal, professional, and public lives, the roots of persuasion date back thousands of years and much of what we know about persuasion can be credited to Aristotle. Aristotle believed in using "all of the available means" to persuade an audience. These include ethos, pathos, and logos (Table 10.1). *Ethos*, as you may surmise just by looking at the word, focuses on the ethics of the speaker. If an audience is to believe what the speaker is saying and be persuaded by the speaker, they must trust the source. How does a speaker gain the audience's trust and become viewed as a credible source? As mentioned earlier in the chapter, some of this credibility is based on the source's background, experiences, and/or education, while some is based on the audience's perception that the speaker has its best interests at heart. Ethos is also influenced by a source who has thoroughly researched a topic, is organized, and who has rehearsed and is prepared to speak.

Ethos
Ethics of the speaker.

Pathos is the use of emotion to persuade. Generally speaking, we are more likely to listen to and be persuaded by speakers who are passionate about a topic. The difference between a speaker who seems not to care about the topic and one who speaks with passion about a topic will certainly influence an audience to be persuaded or not be persuaded by the speaker. Martin Luther King, Jr. spoke with passion when he delivered his famous "I Have a Dream" speech. Jim Valvano, the former head basketball coach at North Carolina State University, also spoke passionately in 1993 when he was presented with the Arthur Ashe Courage Award. His acceptance speech, titled "Don't Ever Give Up," was given roughly 8 weeks before he died of cancer. These individuals, like many others, showed the strength of their emotions and convictions about their beliefs. On the other hand, sadly, there are speakers who rely only on pathos to the exclusion of research and credibility and that can pose a danger for those listening to the speaker. As a consumer of persuasion, make certain that you listen for more than impassioned rhetoric and identify the logic and reasoning behind a speaker's arguments.

The third "means of persuasion" in Aristotle's system is *logos*, or the speaker's use of evidence and reasoning to persuade the audience. The most effective arguments are based on strong evidence and logical reasoning. Evidence includes facts, statistics, definitions, expert opinions, and examples. Reasoning draws conclusions based on the evidence. Speakers may use *inductive reasoning* and provide relevant facts and examples before drawing a conclusion based on these facts. With *deductive reasoning*, the speaker begins with a general statement called a major premise. This is followed by a specific statement called a minor premise that connects to the major premise. From this, a conclusion is drawn based on the major premise and the minor premise. In persuasive speaking, it is important to select examples that are most representative of the point you are trying to make, not the exceptions to the rule. Evidence needs to be valid and reliable and sufficient to support your ideas.

Not all speakers, however, use a logical approach when persuading others. Unfortunately, some speakers may use a tactic known as a fallacy. A *fallacy* is faulty or false reasoning and this should be avoided. There are several types of fallacies; however, only a few examples are provided here. For example, if a speaker uses only a few examples yet draws a general conclusion from those limited examples, the speaker may be relying on what is known as a *hasty generalization*. Thus, if a researcher interviews three college students and discovers none of them exercise on a regular basis, it would be incorrect to conclude that college students in general do not exercise. Another type of fallacy is what is known as the *bandwagon* or *ad populum* fallacy. With this type of faulty reasoning, one indicates that something is true because a number of people have said so—not necessarily because there is clear evidence of its truth. Advertisers have often used the claim that "everyone"

Pathos
Speaker's use of emotion to persuade an audience.

Logos
Speaker's use of sound logic and reasoning.

Inductive reasoning
Type of reasoning that provides strong and sufficient facts and examples and then draws a conclusion based on these facts.

Deductive reasoning
Type of reasoning that begins with a general statement, is supported by specific support, and then draws a conclusion.

Fallacy
Faulty or false reasoning.

Hasty generalization
Type of faulty logic when the speaker uses only a few examples yet draws a general conclusion from those limited examples.

Bandwagon fallacy
Type of faulty reasoning used when one indicates that something is true because a number of people have said it is true, not necessarily because there is clear evidence of its truth.

will benefit from their product or tell children not to be the "only one not to have" a particular toy or game. A third type of fallacy is known as *ad hominem*, which means "to the man." If a speaker attacks or criticizes a person, rather than the arguments provided or the issue itself, the *ad hominem* fallacy is being used. In political debates, candidates often try to diminish the credibility of their opponents by using this type of faulty logic. Again, these are only a few examples of fallacies or the use of faulty logic.

➤ **Ad hominem**
Type of faulty reasoning used when a speaker attacks or criticizes a person, rather than the arguments provided or the issue itself.

TABLE 10.1

Aristotle's Means of Persuasion

Appeal	Definition	Example
Ethos	The ethics of the speaker	Based on the speaker's expertise, competence, genuineness, trustworthiness, or charisma
Pathos	The use of emotion to persuade an audience	Based on the speaker's ability to evoke emotions such as fear, anger, pride, or happiness
Logos	The use of sound logic and reasoning to persuade an audience	Based on the speaker's use of examples, statistics, and other forms of reliable information as well as a well-thought-out way of organizing and presenting the evidence

➤ **Questions of fact**
Type of question or claim that may be proven true or false.

Persuasive speeches typically involve the use of claims: fact, value, and policy. *Questions of fact* are those claims that can be proven true or false. Suppose a speaker tries to prove whether the SAT is a true indicator of a student's ability to do well in college. Documented evidence and statistics examining the correlation between SAT scores and college graduation rates may provide facts to support this claim.

➤ **Questions of value**
Type of question or claim that has to do with someone's ideas of right and wrong or good or bad.

When persuasion focuses on an individual's idea of what is considered right or wrong, *questions of value* are being asked. These may be based on a person's religious or philosophical beliefs. Speeches designed to persuade an audience about airline security procedures, abortion, or sex education are rooted in individual beliefs or values. Depending on the audience's existing beliefs, you will need to organize your speech accordingly.

➤ **Questions of policy**
Type of question or claim that focuses on actions or changes that should or should not be made by governing bodies.

Questions of policy focus on formalized actions or changes that should or should not be implemented by institutions or organizations. A speech designed to persuade an audience that a single-gender institution should go co-ed involves a question of policy designed to persuade an audience to alter an existing policy on gender segregation.

Your approach to persuasion will depend on the attitude the audience has regarding your persuasive proposition. If the audience is already in favor of your proposition, or at least largely in favor of it, you will create your speech based on that knowledge. Needless to say, persuasion is easier to obtain in this scenario. Thus, if you believe in mandatory seatbelt laws and your audience does as well, you will design a speech that reinforces their and your already existing belief. You would not need to spend a great deal of time in your speech presenting the arguments in favor of mandatory seatbelt laws. Instead, you would construct your speech so the audience will take action regarding the law by voting for it or asking their legislator to vote for it.

On the other hand, if your audience is against your persuasive proposition, you will have a more challenging time persuading them to believe as you do. Although you may not persuade them in one speech, if you are able to at least get them to listen to your arguments for or against something, you will have accomplished a great deal. In this instance, you may want to provide information that will help them consider an alternative viewpoint.

There are also times when an audience has no opinion about the subject of your speech. This may happen when the audience is unaware of your persuasive topic or has little knowledge about it. They may also know about the topic but have not yet formed an opinion about it. There are also those who know about the topic and simply choose to remain neutral about it.

There are times when you will address an audience whose members have more than one perspective on your persuasive proposition. In this case, you will need to carefully word your speech so that you do not antagonize those who are against your topic, encourage those in favor to take action, and try to move those who have no opinion on the topic to your viewpoint. This is not an easy task, to say the least.

Overall, it is important to remember that audiences are more likely to listen to and be persuaded by speakers who they trust, by evidence and reasoning they view as relevant and strong, and by speakers who speak with passion and conviction. Relying on Aristotle's "available means of persuasion" will help a speaker change an existing belief, reinforce an existing belief, or move an audience to action.

Special Occasion Speeches

The third and final type of speech covered in this chapter is known as *special occasion speeches*. These types of public speech occur frequently in our lives. Special occasion speeches are used to mark distinctive events in our lives. They are given to honor someone or some occasion and to reflect on the importance of that

Special occasion speeches
Speeches that cover a broad range of settings, circumstances, and occasions and usually acknowledge, celebrate, honor, or remember someone or something.

The wedding toast's purpose is to wish the couple a long and happy life together.

© Sergey Ryzhov/Shutterstock.com

person or occasion in our lives. There are many different types of special occasion speeches. We cover 11 of these in the following pages.

One of the most popular types of public speeches that may occur in our personal, professional, or public lives is the *toast*. The chapter started by mentioning one of the most common toasts—the wedding toast. Whether the toast is given by the best man, the maid of honor, the father of the bride, or any other person close to the couple, it usually focuses on the characteristics of the people who have just gotten married and why they are perfect for each other. Often, the speaker provides brief anecdotes or humorous stories about one or both of the couple. Finally, the person giving the toast wishes the couple a long and happy life together. You may have heard a toast at a wedding or even given one. If this is the case, hopefully it was brief. In more than one case, wedding toasts have gone on and on and, like most other types of special occasion speeches we discuss, they are meant to be "short, sweet, and to the point."

Speeches of introduction are presented to highlight the accomplishments or present the credentials of a speaker before he or she begins a presentation. This type of speech helps build a rapport between the speaker and the audience and motivates the audience to listen to the speaker. If your company has invited a consultant to discuss organizational motivation or a PTO group has asked a well-known

⇒ Toast
Speech given to congratulate a person or people on an achievement or a special occasion.

⇒ Introduction speech
Brief speech given to introduce and welcome a speaker and to build a rapport between the speaker and the audience as well as motivate the audience to listen to the speaker.

educator to discuss the prevention of bullying, a representative of the group should introduce the speaker to provide the audience with the speaker's credentials and a brief overview of the topic to be discussed. A speech of introduction can be used strategically to enhance the source's credibility. If you are asked to provide a speech of introduction, your remarks should be relatively brief to avoid taking time away from the person who is delivering the presentation.

The *welcome speech* is designed to formally recognize and greet an audience to an event. Unlike the context for the speech of introduction, the welcome speech involves only the speaker presenting the welcome and is not followed by another speaker. When a convention is held in a city, the mayor or another local representative may greet attendees in a speech of welcome.

Another example of a special occasion speech is the *commencement speech*, in which a speaker is invited to represent graduates during a ceremony. Some commencement speakers are selected based on their academic achievements, while others are invited to address graduates with words of inspiration and encouragement. The essence of the commencement speech is to highlight accomplishments and provide a vision for the future.

Anniversary speeches are another type of special occasion speaking. Speeches of this type are meant to remind an audience of a person, event, or holiday that is

Welcome speech
Speech to formally recognize and greet a person or a group who is visiting, for example, a school, a convention, a special event, or a city.

Commencement speech
Type of speech often given at a graduation to review what has been accomplished and provide a vision for the future.

Anniversary speech
Type of special occasion speech used to remind an audience of a person, event, or holiday that is being commemorated.

The commencement speech offers words of inspiration and encouragement.

© bxdbzxy/Shutterstock.com

being commemorated. Speeches that celebrate our country's independence, the life of Martin Luther King, Jr., or the anniversary of the establishment of a city or town are all examples of anniversary speeches.

Dedication speeches are another type of special occasion speech. This type of speech is given when a building or a playground, for example, is being named for an individual. Colleges frequently name buildings to honor donors, past presidents, or others who have made significant contributions to the college. When the dedication is made, someone speaks on the significance of the occasion and why the building is being named for this particular person or persons.

Tribute speeches are another frequent type of special occasion speech. This type of speech is designed to praise someone. You might be asked to speak about a teacher who is being honored or a co-worker who is leaving the company or retiring. With speeches of tribute, your goal is to emphasize the accomplishments and attributes of the individual and underscore the importance of these to the audience.

Another form of tribute speech is a *eulogy*. This is a speech of praise for someone who has passed away. It is not an easy speech for someone to write or to present. It is usually given by someone close to the person who has passed away. Although it addresses the characteristics of the deceased and is usually serious in nature, some humor may be interspersed within the eulogy to demonstrate the human side of the individual being eulogized. Caution should be taken as not all in the audience will react in similar ways to humorous attempts. Some individuals may find incorporating this type of material highly inappropriate while others in the audience will find the humor a much-needed relief. Ultimately, the intent of the eulogy is to provide comfort to the mourners and help them remember the traits of the deceased that they most cherished.

Presenting an award or, if you are lucky enough, *accepting an award* are two additional types of special occasion speeches. In a school setting, you could be an officer of a student group that gives an annual award or you could be the student receiving the award. In a professional organization or a civic group, you could also be the one asked to present an award to someone or, again, you might be the recipient. No matter what the setting, presenting and/or accepting awards are common occurrences in a person's personal, professional, or public life. If you are the one presenting an award, you would first outline the purpose, history, and/or the significance of the award and the criteria used to determine the awardee. Next, you would outline the relevant achievements of the recipient and how these accomplishments satisfied the criteria employed to determine who would receive the award.

We have all heard acceptance speeches at the Academy Awards, the Country Music Awards, or one of the many other televised award shows. While we know they often differ in length (despite the best efforts of the production staff), they generally follow the same format. First, the person receiving the award recognizes the importance of the award and then expresses his or her appreciation to those who are giving the award. The awardee should also acknowledge those who helped the recipient achieve this recognition. If there were other nominees, it is also considerate to acknowledge them as well.

Speeches as you leave or enter an office are also considered types of special occasion speeches. When someone enters office, it is typical to give an *inaugural address*. Certainly, we see this type of speech when the president of the United States is sworn into office. The goals of this type of speech are to outline the key issues the newly elected officer hopes to address while in office, to look toward the future, and to thank his or her predecessor. Inaugural addresses may also be given by newly appointed presidents of colleges or universities, corporations, community organizations, and civic groups. Likewise, when someone leaves an office, it is usually a time to reflect on what has been accomplished, to thank those who helped accomplish what was done, to outline what still needs to be accomplished, and to congratulate the next individual taking office.

> **Inaugural address** Special occasion speech given when someone takes office or begins a new position that outlines the key issues to address while in that position, looks toward the future, and thanks his or her predecessor.

Informative, persuasive, and special occasion speeches are three types of speeches you will likely encounter throughout your personal, professional, and public lives. One point to remember is that these types of speeches are not mutually exclusive. For example, even though the intended objective of a speaker may be to persuade, he may also inform an audience by sharing new information. As we begin to prepare a speech, we go through several steps before actually delivering it. These steps include selecting a topic, defining your purpose, analyzing the audience, conducting research, organizing your speech, and practicing the speech. In addition, the process also includes delivering the speech and reflecting on the speech, including the audience's reaction to it. Each of these steps is discussed in the next section.

AN OVERVIEW OF THE PUBLIC SPEAKING PROCESS

Understanding the process of developing a public speech (Figure 10.5) is important as you begin to prepare any type of presentation. By adhering to the steps of this process, you will enhance your success as a public speaker.

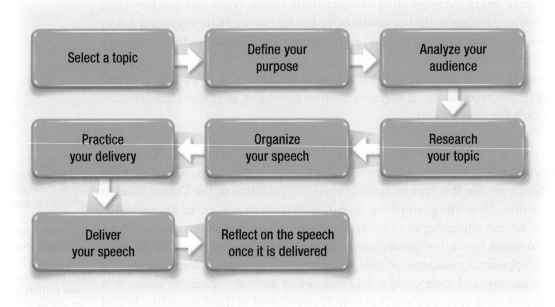

FIGURE 10.5

Select Your Topic

The first step involves selecting a speech topic. In a classroom situation, you may be provided with parameters such as the purpose of the speech (e.g., to inform or to persuade) and perhaps some suggested topics. Beyond the classroom, you may be asked to speak about something in your area of expertise or a concern. For example, in your professional career you may speak on the current financial status of your department or provide an outline of the new marketing plan for an upcoming product launch. In your public life, you may be asked to deliver a committee report that has investigated potential sustainability solutions at a city council meeting.

Regardless of the speaking context, one of the most crucial steps in the public speaking process is to select a topic. If you are allowed to choose your own topic, the first step is to brainstorm possible topic ideas. You may do this simply by thinking of and jotting down ideas for intriguing topics about which you either have current knowledge or are curious to learn more. For example, consider events, processes, ideas, people, and objects when identifying a topic for an informative speech. If you're having difficulty brainstorming ideas, read a newspaper or browse the Internet to help identify potential topics. As you begin to formulate your topic, consider how to approach the topic and how you can make it interesting and relevant to your audience.

Three key considerations should be made with topic selection: the level of interest generated, the scope of the topic, and supporting sources of information. A topic should be of interest to both you and to your audience. If you are interested in the topic, you will devote the time and effort it takes to thoroughly research the topic, select the best support material, and practice delivering it. In addition, your interest will enhance your speech delivery. The topic should also be of interest to the audience. Knowing your audience will help you select a topic that will be interesting and relevant to them.

In addition, the topic must be focused enough to meet the time limitations for your presentation. In both academic and professional settings you will be expected to adhere to time guidelines for your speech to ensure that the class or meeting stays on schedule. A topic cannot be so broad that it cannot be clearly discussed within the allotted time frame. For example, while you may be passionate about the topic of sustainability, you will need to narrow your discussion of the topic to fit the time limit you have been given for your presentation. Generally speaking, it is much better for a public speaker to cover fewer main ideas with more depth than to try to cover too many broad ideas without adequately explaining each idea.

Finally, it is also important to select a topic that can be supported through research that extends beyond the speaker. Even when you are knowledgeable about the subject, it is vital to explore what others have to say about the topic. Citing this research during your speech will potentially enhance your credibility as a speaker, since audiences want to know that speakers are well prepared and can share information that goes beyond their own opinions.

Define Your Purpose

Once you have selected a topic, the next step in the process is writing a clear and focused statement of your speech purpose. The *general purpose* indicates whether the speech goal is to inform, persuade, or present a speech for a special occasion. A *specific purpose* statement is generally one sentence that provides an overview of the speech objective or the key points of the speech. The goal of the specific purpose statement is to focus on what you want your audience to know or do by the end of your speech. For example, your specific purpose might be "to inform the audience about the types of stem cells that exist and two ways in which they are currently being used to treat diseases." Another specific purpose could be "to persuade the audience to donate blood at the upcoming blood drive at the college." Although brief, this type of statement will help guide the next steps in the speech-building process.

General purpose
Provides the broad goal for your speech (e.g., to inform, persuade, or entertain).

Specific purpose
Clear and concise statement indicating what you want your audience to know, do, or believe by the end of your speech.

A demographic analysis takes into account the audience's characteristics so you can refine your topic.

© Monkey Business Images/Shutterstock.com

≫ **Audience analysis**
Gaining knowledge about the audience such as their demographic information, their attitudes, their level of knowledge of the topic, the speech environment, and the occasion for the speech in order to best prepare the speech.

≫ **Demographic analysis**
Type of audience analysis that takes into account the characteristics of the audience including the audience's gender, age, race, ethnicity, and level of education.

≫ **Attitudinal analysis**
Type of audience analysis that considers the audience's position on a particular topic (e.g., for, against, or no opinion).

Analyze Your Audience

Once the topic is selected, and your purpose is clear, it is important to analyze the audience. There are many strategies to *audience analysis*, and the more information you have about your audience, the more effective you will be at creating a speech that they will understand and remember. One method used in the audience analysis process is called a *demographic analysis*. This type of analysis takes into account the characteristics of the audience. Look around your classroom and identify characteristics about your classmates. Demographic features include the audience's gender, age, race, ethnicity, and level of education. When you have a strong understanding of the demographics of the audience, you may find that you need to refine your choice of speech topic. For example, an audience consisting of 18- to 23-year-old college students would probably have a general understanding of what Facebook is and how it works. Instead, you might want to focus on how organizations are using this type of social media to understand marketing trends among college students. Knowing this type of information helps the speaker select appropriate support material for the speech and identify the best way to approach the topic.

Another type of analysis is an *attitudinal analysis*. Securing information about an audience's attitude toward the topic before you begin to research and write a speech is important. A speaker will need to approach a topic differently depending on whether the audience is in favor of the topic, against it, or has no opinion. For example, if a public forum is presented in a particular town and the audience is already in favor of recycling, the speaker will not need to spend time focusing on the benefits of recycling in general and can concentrate on how a recycling program can be instituted in that particular town. On the other hand, if the speaker does not know what the audience's attitude toward the subject is, the speaker should try to ascertain this information by circulating a brief survey prior to creating a speech or by speaking with the person who invited you to find out the audience's likely attitudes toward your topic.

Finally, the speaker must be aware of the occasion and the environment in which the speech will be presented. This is known as a *situational analysis*. Is the occasion formal or informal? Does it commemorate something specific or honor a person's accomplishments? Is it a solemn or light-hearted occasion? Understanding the environment will also help the speaker to construct a more effective speech. Environmental elements including the time of day at which the speech will be given, the room where it will be delivered, and the size of the audience are all important pieces of information. For example, how receptive do you think an audience would be to a formal and lengthy presentation in an organizational setting on a Friday at 4:00 P.M.? What things would you do to maintain the audience's interest? How should the room be set up for your presentation (e.g., theater or auditorium style, conference or boardroom style)?

> **Situational analysis**
> Type of audience analysis that takes into account the occasion of the speaking event as well as the time, place, and size of the audience.

Overall, gathering demographic, attitudinal, and situational information about an audience is an important step in the speech preparation process. The more information you have about an audience, the more likely you will be to construct an effective speech.

Research the Topic

Once a speaker understands the audience, the next part of the speech development process involves researching the topic. A variety of resources are available through the library and the Internet that make finding the best support material for a topic and a given audience relatively simple. Databases, websites, books, and interviews are all potential sources of support for a speech. It is the speaker's responsibility to ensure that the material selected is valid and reliable. Thus, you will want to consider factors such as who authored the article and when it was published, as well as the source of the article to determine if it is a trustworthy and useful source. In addition, you will want to cite the source of information in the speech. Most schools maintain a variety of library databases available for student use. These

Databases, websites, books, and interviews are all potential sources of support for a speech.

© Ammentorp Photography/Shutterstock.com

can be helpful for your research because they provide access to a wide range of periodicals and scholarly journal articles.

When using the Internet to search for information, exercise caution when using commercial sites (*.com*) because they may be biased since their goal is to "sell" something. Education sites (*.edu*) are usually reliable, but be careful and check who posted the material as well as the purpose for which it was posted. You may also find chapters from books and magazines as well as interviews useful as you gather information for your speech.

As a speaker, you will want to find a variety of sources as well as different forms of support. In general, facts and statistics, definitions, examples, quotes by authorities, stories, and illustrations as well as visual presentations are all types of support a speaker looks for and incorporates into a speech. These are discussed further in the next chapter. Conducting research on the topic will also help you focus your topic and help you refine the key points you want to discuss in your speech.

Organize the Speech

Once you have conducted your research and consulted a variety of sources, the next step for the speaker is to organize the material in a manner that will help the audience understand and process the topic and the information presented. It is important to note there are several ways to organize a speech and all relate to your purpose. The most common patterns include chronological, spatial, cause–effect, problem–solution, and topical order. These organizational strategies are discussed in more detail in Chapter 11.

Practice Your Delivery

Once the speech is organized, the next crucial step in the process involves practicing your presentation. While this is discussed in more depth in Chapter 12, it is important to note that the more you practice a speech, the more comfortable you will be while presenting it. Obviously, the more comfort the speaker has with the topic, how it is organized, and the support material for it, the less anxiety a speaker will experience when presenting it to the audience. Maximizing your preparation and practice is one clear way to minimize your stress when delivering your speech.

Deliver Your Speech

While this is also discussed in more depth in Chapter 12, delivering your speech is an important part of the preparation process. All of the previous steps in the process will have brought you to this moment and the more time and effort you put into those earlier steps, the more effectively you can present your speech. While you are delivering your speech, you should be aware of the audience's nonverbal feedback. This will let you know if the audience understands and is engaged in what you are saying. Knowing this information will allow you to make any adjustments while you are speaking to assist the audience to receive your message effectively.

Reflect

Once the speech is presented, a public speaker's work is not done. Just as you need to analyze your audience before and during the speech construction process, and just as you should analyze your audience while delivering the speech through the feedback you receive from them, it is just as important to reflect on the speech and how the audience responded to it after it is delivered. Thus, after every presentation or public speaking event, the speaker should reflect on the speech to determine what worked, what did not work, and how things could be improved upon for the next speech. By becoming a reflective speaker, you will learn through self-analysis and improve with each new speaking opportunity.

Overall, careful preparation and practice of any speech will provide the speaker with more confidence while delivering the speech and will increase the chance that the audience will become engaged in the speech and will remain so.

CHAPTER SUMMARY

In this chapter, we discussed the challenges of public speaking, the types of public speaking, and a brief overview of the process of public speaking. Some of the challenges a public speaker faces include communication anxiety, establishing credibility, and ethical considerations. In your personal, professional, or public lives, you will likely experience the opportunity to give a variety of speeches. To enhance your effectiveness, you must carefully consider all of the steps that are involved in the speech process.

The public speaking process entails selecting the topic, analyzing the audience, finding good support material for the topic, organizing the speech, practicing the speech, delivering the speech, and then reflecting on the strengths of the speech as well as what could have been done to improve the speech. When public speakers go through the process step by step, there is a greater chance they will be effective. As we began this chapter, we provided examples of speeches that occur in our personal, professional, and public lives. Although you may not yet be comfortable with the idea that public speaking will be a part of your life now and will continue to be a part of your life in the future, for most people, it will be. Understanding the challenges, the types of public speaking, and the process public speakers go through to help them become effective will help you as you encounter public speaking in your personal, professional, and public lives.

KEY WORDS

Accepting an award Special occasion speech by the person receiving an award that recognizes the importance of the award and expresses his or her appreciation to those who are giving the award; acknowledges those who helped the recipient achieve this recognition and, if there were other nominees, acknowledges them as well.

Ad hominem Type of faulty reasoning used when a speaker attacks or criticizes a person, rather than the arguments provided or the issue itself.

Anniversary speech Type of special occasion speech used to remind an audience of a person, event, or holiday that is being commemorated.

Attitudinal analysis Type of audience analysis that considers the audience's position on a particular topic (e.g., for, against, or no opinion).

Audience analysis Gaining knowledge about the audience such as their demographic information, their attitudes, their level of knowledge of the topic, the speech environment, and the occasion for the speech in order to best prepare the speech.

Audience-based communication apprehension Fear of public speaking with a specific audience (e.g., you may not be apprehensive when you are speaking with your peers in a course but apprehensive when you are speaking to the board of directors of your company).

Bandwagon fallacy Type of faulty reasoning used when one indicates that something is true because a number of people have said it is true, not necessarily because there is clear evidence of its truth.

Commencement speech Type of speech often given at a graduation to review what has been accomplished and provide a vision for the future.

Communication apprehension The fear, nervousness, or anxiety we experience when faced with real or imagined interactions.

Context-based communication apprehension Fear of speaking only in one setting (e.g., fear of speaking in public but not in other settings such as in small groups).

Credibility Extent to which a speaker is trustworthy, knowledgeable, and well prepared.

Dedication speech Type of special occasion speech given that speaks about the significance of an occasion (e.g., a building being named for a particular person).

Deductive reasoning Type of reasoning that begins with a general statement, is supported by specific support, and then draws a conclusion.

Demographic analysis Type of audience analysis that takes into account the characteristics of the audience including the audience's gender, age, race, ethnicity, and level of education.

Ethical public speaking Speaking that demonstrates respect for one's audience, honesty, use of reliable and valid sources, and responsibility for everything that is said and/or done during a speech.

Ethos Ethics of the speaker.

Eulogy Speech of praise for someone who has passed away.

Fallacy Faulty or false reasoning.

General purpose Provides the broad goal for your speech (e.g., to inform, persuade, or entertain).

Hasty generalization Type of faulty logic when the speaker uses only a few examples yet draws a general conclusion from those limited examples.

Inaugural address Special occasion speech given when someone takes office or begins a new position that outlines the key issues to address while in that position, looks toward the future, and thanks his or her predecessor.

Inductive reasoning Type of reasoning that provides strong and sufficient facts and examples and then draws a conclusion based on these facts.

Informative speaking Type of speech used to help an audience become aware of or better understand a topic.

Introduction speech Brief speech given to introduce and welcome a speaker and to build a rapport between the speaker and the audience as well as motivate the audience to listen to the speaker.

Logos Speaker's use of sound logic and reasoning.

Pathos Speaker's use of emotion to persuade an audience.

Persuasive speaking Type of speech used to change an audience's existing belief, to reinforce their existing belief, or to get an audience to take action regarding the topic.

Presenting an award Type of special occasion speech that outlines the purpose, history, and/or the significance of the award; the criteria used to determine the awardee; and the relevant achievements of the recipient and how these accomplishments satisfied the criteria employed to determine who would receive the award.

Questions of fact Type of question or claim that may be proven true or false.

Questions of policy Type of question or claim that focuses on actions or changes that should or should not be made by governing bodies.

Questions of value Type of question or claim that has to do with someone's ideas of right and wrong or good or bad.

Situational analysis Type of audience analysis that takes into account the occasion of the speaking event as well as the time, place, and size of the audience.

Situational communication apprehension Fear of public speaking based on a specific occurrence (e.g., you are nervous about meeting with your supervisor to ask for a raise or your town's planning board to ask for a variance).

Special occasion speeches Speeches that cover a broad range of settings, circumstances, and occasions and usually acknowledge, celebrate, honor, or remember someone or something.

Specific purpose Clear and concise statement indicating what you want your audience to know, do, or believe by the end of your speech.

Strategies Techniques speakers use to engage their audience and to keep the audience focused.

Toast Speech given to congratulate a person or people on an achievement or a special occasion.

Trait-like communication apprehension Fear of public speaking (e.g., one-on-one, to a small group, or to a large audience).

Tribute speech Special occasion speech designed to praise someone (e.g., living or in the case of a eulogy, someone who has passed away).

Welcome speech Speech to formally recognize and greet a person or a group who is visiting, for example, a school, a convention, a special event, or a city.

REFERENCES

Bailey, E. (2008). Celebrities with anxiety: Harrison Ford: Fear of public speaking, *Health Guide*. Retrieved from http://www.healthcentral.com/anxiety/c/22705/36519/celebrities- public/

Booth-Butterfield, S., & Gutowski, C. (1993). Message modality and source credibility can interact to affect argument processing. *Communication Quarterly, 41*, 77–89.

Dwyer, K. K., & Davidson, M. M. (2012). Is public speaking really more feared than death? *Communication Research Report, 29*(2), 99–107.

McCroskey, J. C. (1977). Oral communication apprehension: A review of recent theory and research. *Human Communication Research, 4*, 78–96.

McCroskey, J. C. (2004). A primer of stage fright. *Review of Communication, 4*, 86–87.

McCroskey, J. C. (2005). Motives and communibiology's texts: Whose motives? *Communication Theory, 15*, 468–474.

McCroskey, J. C., Andersen, J. F., Richmond, V. P., & Wheeless, L. R. (1981). Communication apprehension of elementary and secondary students and teachers. *Communication Education, 30*, 122–132.

McCroskey, J. C., & Beatty, M.J. (1999). Communication apprehension. In J. C. McCroskey, J. A. Daly, M. M. Martin, & M. J. Beatty (Eds.), *Communication and personality: Trait perspectives* (pp. 215–232). Cresskill, NJ: Hampton Press.

McCroskey, J. C., & Beatty, M. J. (2000). The communibiological perspective: Implications for communication in instruction. *Communication Education, 49*, 1–6.

Sellnow, D. D. (2005). *Confident public speaking* (2nd ed.). Belmont, CA: Thomson Wadsworth.

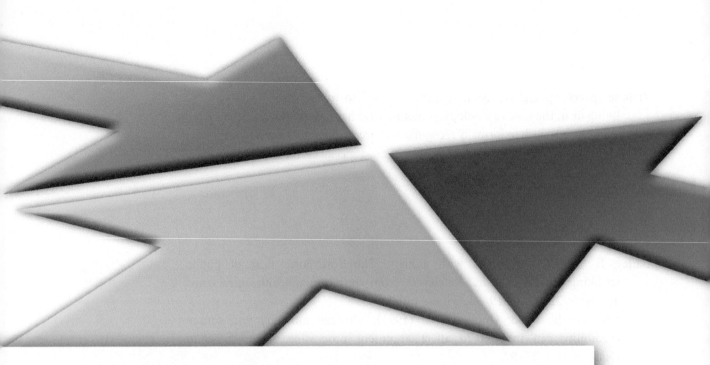

CHAPTER 11

Preparing Public Speeches: Taking the Next Steps

Chapter Objectives

After reading this chapter, you should be able to:
- Define the elements of the introduction, the body, and the conclusion
- Identify the types of organizational patterns public speakers can use
- Explain three different strategies for outlining a speech
- Prepare appropriate presentational aids for a public speech
- Identify key considerations for appropriate language use in public speeches

PERSONAL: You have been assigned an informative speech for your public speaking class. It took you a while but you have now selected a topic and you have done a considerable amount of research on it. You feel like you have narrowed the topic down enough so that it will be workable given the time limit provided by your instructor. You have a strong sense of your audience's interests since you have gotten to know many of your classmates. You feel confident that your audience will be interested in your topic. Now what?

PROFESSIONAL: You have been asked to discuss a new product with clients. Since you were involved in the development of the product, you feel very comfortable speaking about it. In addition, you have done a lot of research on comparable products in the field. In your presentation, you would like to include information about the development of the product, its advantages, and comparable product information. In addition, you also have to address any client questions. You have been given 15 minutes to accomplish all of these goals. Where do you go from here?

PUBLIC: You work for the Department of Environmental Protection. The department has sent you to a small town to present a new initiative that urges towns (and cities) to turn former landfills into solar or wind energy farms. The town has been selected as one of the sites where the state would like to see this happen. You have been asked to speak about the concept and to persuade the town to consider implementing this program. You know you will be speaking to an audience that contains residents who favor the project, those who do not favor the project, and those who have no opinion. Where do you begin?

CHAPTER OVERVIEW

No matter what type of speech you will be giving, once you know your topic, have analyzed your audience, and conducted preliminary research, the next step is to actually prepare your speech. This chapter discusses the key components found in every type of speech and how speeches are organized and prepared. In addition, the chapter focuses on various ways to outline a speech to ensure you have sufficient support for each main idea and that it is appropriately placed in your speech. Furthermore, the importance and use of presentational aids are explained and some of the techniques to ensure the appropriate use of language in public speaking are shared. Because public speaking occurs in your personal, professional, and public lives, possessing the tools to research, organize, and develop public speeches will increase the likelihood of your success when you speak in public.

THE THREE PARTS OF ANY SPEECH DEFINED

No matter how long or short, a speech always contains the same three parts: the introduction, the body, and the conclusion. Each part of a speech serves a particular purpose. In addition, connecting your material within and between main ideas are transitions that help guide the audience from one point to the next. All of these elements are discussed in the next section.

Introduction

➤ **Introduction**
Gains the audience's attention, clearly states the topic, and previews the main points to be discussed.

The first part of any speech is the introduction. The goals of the *introduction* are to gain the audience's attention, indicate the topic and purpose of the speech, and provide a preview of the intended organization. During the introduction, the speaker should also work to establish credibility and build a rapport with the audience. Gaining the audience's attention is important. If you are not able to do this within the opening moments of your speech, the audience may decide to tune you out and tune into their favorite daydream. There are several strategies that can be used to get your audience to become interested in your speech (Figure 11.1). Some speakers begin the speech with a rhetorical question. The purpose of this type of question is to entice the audience to consider your topic. Usually, it is intended to stimulate thought, and not to encourage a discussion between the speaker and the audience. Some examples of rhetorical questions include:

- How many of you have ever wondered what it would be like to experience a totally new culture where you didn't know anyone and didn't even speak the same language as everyone around you?
- What would you do if you could change the course of someone's life just by giving 3 hours of your time a week?
- Can you imagine living in a city where you are in constant fear of your life, where it is not even safe for children to play outside, or where you might lose loved one after loved one or friend after friend due to violence?
- Have you ever said something to someone at some point and wished it could be taken back?

Other speakers begin with a joke or a humorous story. Grice and Skinner (2013) stated, "The use of humor can be one of a speaker's most effective attention-getting strategies. Getting the audience to laugh with you makes them alert and relaxed" (p. 171). Not everyone is successful at using this strategy. If a speaker tells a joke, it must be a joke that would not offend anyone, and it must be relevant to the speech topic. The same may be said about a humorous story. The speaker must make certain that he or she can move from the joke or humorous story to the speech topic seamlessly and that the connection between the humorous joke or story and the topic is clear. Humor, when used appropriately and effectively, can set a light-hearted tone for the speech; however, it should be noted that what is funny to one person is not funny to all and caution should be used when crafting humorous messages.

Other speakers gain an audience's attention through the use of a direct quote that is relevant to the speech topic. Quotes can include a quote from literature, quotes by individuals from the present or past, or quotes by experts on a particular topic. Examples of literary quotes include Shakespeare's "To thine own self be true" from *Hamlet* or "It is a far far better thing I do today..." from the Dickens classic *A Tale of Two Cities*. We may also use quotes by those in the present or past to gain the attention of our audience. For example, John F. Kennedy's "Ask not what your country can do for you, ask what you can do for your country" is a memorable quote from his inauguration speech that is still relevant in today's world. Authorities are often considered experts due to their training or their education. Thus, a quote by an authority on child abuse may help gain an audience's attention, especially if the authority has studied this topic extensively. Authorities may also become experts because they have firsthand experience with a topic. For example, beginning your speech with a quote by someone who has endured child abuse would be an effective strategy to gain the audience's attention.

Statistics are one type of evidence people use to support a point.

© lightpoet/Shutterstock.com

Speakers may also use facts, figures, or statistics to gain an audience's attention. These can help provide evidence for the audience about the prevalence or importance of an issue. If an audience realizes that 8 out of 10 individuals will face a health scare before they are 30 years old or that 80% of all college-age individuals will not graduate in 4 years, it enables them to focus on the speech topic.

Similarly, many times your audience may be unaware of a particular topic. If this is the case, speakers may gain the audience's attention by beginning with a definition. Suppose your audience has never heard of Tax Form 1098-T? This is the form issued by colleges showing the amount students are "billed for qualified tuition and related expenses" that may qualify them for deductions on their tax returns. You would want to define this term before you begin to discuss it with the audience.

Examples are also used to gain an audience's attention. These include factual or hypothetical examples. Factual examples are drawn from real life. They include actual cases or incidents speakers have personally experienced, or those they have identified through research or stories shared by others. Factual examples help gain an audience's attention because they demonstrate the reality of your topic. For example, if you were persuading the audience to sign up to be organ donors, you could tell them a story about a friend who needed a heart transplant and describe the emotional details experienced as he prepared for, and then waited to receive, his heart. An example like this provides the audience with an illustration of the need to register for organ donation. Other examples may be conceivable, but not have actually occurred. These are hypothetical examples and involve asking the audience

FIGURE 11.1

Attention-getting strategies.

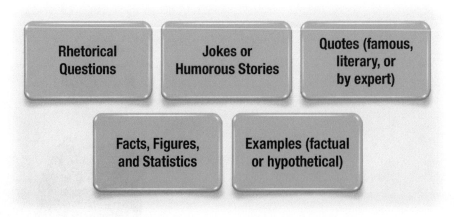

to "Picture this" or "Imagine that this happened to you." These hypothetical examples place audiences in possible, plausible scenarios and help them connect with the topic to be discussed.

Whatever attention-getting strategy is used to gain an audience's attention, it should be well thought out, help introduce the topic, and engage the audience in the speech. It should also be influenced by the purpose of the speech, the audience to whom you are presenting, and the impression you want to create.

In addition to gaining the audience's attention in the introduction, the speaker must also reveal the purpose of the speech. As mentioned in Chapter 10, three common general purposes of speeches are to inform, to persuade, or to speak on a special occasion. The specific purpose can be compared to a thesis statement. The specific purpose should clearly indicate the primary focus of the speech and should be succinct. Usually, one concise sentence indicating the goal of your speech is sufficient. Examples of speech purposes may include to inform the audience about the three primary changes to their financial aid agreements or to explain the four elements to consider when selecting a diamond ring.

Following the purpose statement, a preview of the main ideas that will be discussed is presented. This is similar to the "preview of coming attractions" one sees before the main feature begins at a movie theater. A preview gives the audience a glimpse into the highlights of the speech. It is important because it provides the audience with cues to help them listen more effectively to the speech. If an audience knows that the speaker will discuss the causes, the effects, and the treatments of a particular disease, they will be able to follow the speech more accurately.

Additional elements to be addressed in the speech introduction include connecting with one's audience and establishing yourself as a credible source on the topic. When speakers build rapport with an audience, they try to demonstrate that the topic is relevant to the audience and that they have the audience's best interests at heart. If audiences believe they will derive some personal, educational, or professional benefit from listening to a particular speech, they are more likely to pay attention. Thus, if you show your audience that they can improve their cardiovascular health, learn how to manage their time more efficiently, create a more effective résumé, or learn a more effective way to track sales, they are more likely to listen to your speech. Likewise, audiences are more likely to listen to speakers they trust. If audiences believe you are a credible source as a result of your education, experiences, and/or your careful research on a subject, they will also be more likely to attend to your speech.

FIGURE 11.2

Important elements of
the introduction.

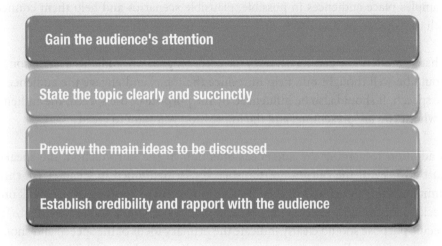

Achieving a positive first impression with the audience is a critical element in public speaking. During the introduction the speaker gains the audience's attention, states the specific purpose of the speech, previews the main ideas that will be addressed in the speech, and lets the audience know they can trust what you are saying and that you have their best interests at heart (Figure 11.2). If your introduction contains all of these elements, you will help your audience prepare effectively for the next part of your speech.

Body

➤ Body
The heart of the speech; its purpose is to state each main idea and support each idea fully.

The second part of any speech is the *body*, which constitutes the major portion of a speech. The purpose of the body is to state the main ideas and provide backing for each one. It is important to clearly articulate each main idea and then support each one with sufficient evidence. Gathering the support for your main ideas is crucial to the overall success of your speech. In today's world, it is relatively easy to gather support for speeches. Your school's library probably provides students with access to a variety of databases. Some of these databases may include:

- *Academic Search Complete* is a comprehensive scholarly, multidisciplinary, and full-text database that contains more than 8,500 full-text periodicals, including more than 7,300 peer-reviewed journals.
- *Communication & Mass Media Complete* provides research particularly related to communication and mass media. This database has coverage of more than 770 titles including full text for over 450 journals.

- *LexisNexis Academic Universe* contains full texts for about 5,000 public and commercial business, legal, newspaper, and media sources.
- *Medline* contains studies of medical issues.
- *PsycINFO*, from the American Psychological Association, is a resource for abstracts of scholarly journal articles, book chapters, books, and dissertations.

While databases are a great resource for locating support for the main points of a speech, there are a variety of other options that can also be used. Depending on the topic, you may consult newspapers, magazines, and government publications to provide the support for the ideas in your speech. Interviewing those who have expertise related to your topic or searching relevant websites may also be helpful. It is beneficial to consult a variety of sources to support your speech. However, it is important to carefully consider the credibility of the sources you select to support your points. Knowing where and how to gather evidence is important. Next, we discuss the types of information that is used to support your main ideas.

Through your research, you will find various types of information that can be used to support the main ideas of the speech. These include using facts and statistics, examples, definitions, and quotes. First, you may provide evidence by citing verifiable facts or statistics. Knowing how many people are affected by a phenomenon on a daily basis emphasizes the significance of an issue. Consider the following example:

> According to the American Automobile Association (AAA), distracted driving contributes to as many as 8,000 crashes every day. In addition, more than 1 million people have died in car crashes over the past 25 years in the United States, with 33,788 lives lost in 2010 alone. (AAA Foundation for Traffic Safety, 2010)

These facts show the extent of this issue; however, facts may also show the rarity of occurrence. Consider this example:

> According to the Progeria Research Foundation (2014), "Progeria is a rare, fatal genetic condition characterized by an appearance of accelerated aging in children. . . . It affects approximately 1 in 4–8 million newborns. There are an estimated 200–250 children living with Progeria worldwide at any one time."

Whether your support shows how extensive or rare something is, facts and statistics are useful forms of proof. When using this type of support, it is important to give credit to the source of the facts or statistics during your speech and to confirm the credibility of sources.

Examples are another type of support and are often used to help clarify something that seems abstract. Speakers use examples to explain things in real terms. Thus, if you are trying to support the idea that people who exercise can facilitate the weight loss process, providing an example of someone for whom that strategy has worked will help support that idea. You may provide statistics on the extent of homelessness; however, if you describe the experiences of someone who is homeless, it may have a greater impact on your audience since it puts a human face on the issue. When discussing techniques to gain an audience's attention, we indicated that examples may be actual or hypothetical in nature. This is also true for examples used to support an idea. If using hypothetical examples, however, they must reflect something that may not have happened but that *could* happen. Thus, when using an example, be sure that it is reasonable, relevant to the point you are trying to make, and detail-oriented to provide a clear and vivid picture in the minds of the audience.

Definitions are another form of support used by speakers. Consider a speaker who is delivering a presentation that is focused on a specific industry or specialization. Words and concepts must be clearly defined for those with no expertise or understanding of the topic in order to understand the point the speaker is making. Examples of topics that may need to be defined could include presentations discussing IPOs (initial public offerings) or the new IRS regulations for spousal liability. Providing a clear definition for difficult terminology not widely known can help the audience understand your ideas.

Quotes by authorities are another way to support the main ideas of a speech. As mentioned previously, authorities are those who are considered knowledgeable about a subject because they have studied it, have gained valuable work experience connected to it, or they have experienced it. If, for example, you are speaking to your audience about the benefits of study-abroad programs, you certainly may obtain quotes from those who have studied this topic area; however, perhaps even more compelling evidence may be the quotes of those who have participated in study-abroad programs themselves. Once you provide a quote, it is also helpful to explain the quote and make the connection to your idea. Going beyond just providing the quote will help the audience truly understand its meaning and intent.

It is important to go beyond simply stating the main ideas in a speech and take the next step to provide ample support for each of these ideas. To enhance the credibility of your ideas, go beyond simply stating what you think and provide support through facts or statistics, examples, definitions, and quotes. Keep in mind that evidence must be accurate, obtained from reliable sources, relevant, current (when that is important), and appropriately selected for the particular audience you are addressing. Researching and selecting the best evidence is a speaker's ethical obligation. In addition, it is important to vary the types of support you provide to your audience. Imagine if a speaker spouted statistic after statistic or quote after quote. After a while, the audience would most likely turn their attention elsewhere. As baseball coaches tell their pitchers, it is important to "mix your pitches." By doing so, the batter never goes on "auto pilot" and must stay alert and focused. Varying your forms of support for each idea will help an audience stay focused.

Conclusion

After providing the audience with the main ideas of your presentation, the final task is to bring the speech to a close. The purposes of the *conclusion* are to review the key points or ideas you have discussed and to leave your audience with something to remember or consider further. The conclusion may issue a challenge to your audience in order to motivate them to take action. Just as there are several techniques to gain your audience's attention in the introduction, there are several ways you may conclude your speech so they remember what you said. Provide a succinct, memorable summary of the main ideas of your speech by using short, simple statements to refocus and summarize your speech. Just as you might state in the preview section of your introduction, "Today, I will be informing you about the causes, effects, and common treatments for …" you can say, "In summary, I have discussed the causes, effects, and common treatments for …" Your summary can

Conclusion
Summarizes or reviews the main points presented in the speech and leaves the audience with a final unifying thought.

There are several ways to end your speech so that the audience remembers what you said.

© Sergey Nivens/Shutterstock.com

go one step further to briefly clarify and restate the content of your speech. Thus, instead of just noting you have discussed "causes" in your speech, you can state something like, "As I indicated in my speech, there are three main causes of ... and these occur most often in men and women between the ages of 20 and 24 ..." This will help reinforce key points in your speech.

Following the brief review of the speech's main ideas, leave your audience with something to consider or do. This can be considered the attention-getter in reverse. There are many techniques you might use to accomplish this goal. The same strategies that can be used to gain attention in the introduction can be used to reinforce an idea in the conclusion and leave a memorable impression. Use facts or statistics, rhetorical questions, quotes by authorities, or examples. Rephrase your attention-getting technique. For example, if you started your speech by asking your audience to "imagine you are sitting on a beach..." your conclusion could be "so remember, the next time you are on a beach..." The goal is to motivate the audience to continue thinking about your topic long after you have completed your speech. If they do, it is likely that they will give further consideration to your topic, accept a challenge you presented, or be motivated to take action. A strong conclusion will help guarantee the audience remembers your ideas and information.

Transitions

> **Transitions**
> Words or phrases that help listeners move smoothly from one point to the next; signal to the audience that the speaker is moving from one idea to the next or from one type of support to another.

You have likely written a paper for one of your classes that used words or phrases to connect or link ideas together. Transitions are the final element in any speech. *Transitions* help the listeners make connections and move smoothly from one point to the next. They signal that the speaker is moving from one idea to the next or from one type of support to the next. If you are moving from one major idea to the next, you may guide your audience to the new idea by stating, "Now that I have discussed the causes of ..., I will explain the effects of ..." This simple statement will alert an audience that you have completed the discussion of one main idea and are now moving on to the next main idea.

Although transitions may be used to let the audience know you are moving from one point to the next, they may also be used to indicate the next idea is similar, different, or more important than the previous one. For example, if you say, "Just like the first principle of persuasive speaking, the second principle ..." it will let the audience know that the first idea is similar to the second one. If you say, "In contrast to my first point ..." it alerts your audience to the fact that the next idea is different from the first. Finally, statements such as, "Even more important than my first two ideas is ..." lets the audience know that this idea is more significant than the preceding ones.

Transitions are also used within a discussion of a main idea. If speakers provide one form of support for an idea and are about to provide another, they may use words and phrases such as "Also," "In addition," and "Furthermore," to let the audience know more evidence is forthcoming. When speakers are completing an idea, phrases and words such as "In summary," "In conclusion," "Thus," or "Therefore" alert the audience that they are preparing to transition to the next idea.

In summary, regardless of the overall length of a speech, it always contains an introduction designed to capture the audience's attention, states the purpose of the speech, and previews the key points that will be discussed. In addition, the body of the speech clearly states the main ideas and provides support for each of them. The final part of the speech, the conclusion, provides a summary of the key points that were discussed and creates the final audience impression. Throughout each section of the speech, transitions are used to guide the audience from one idea to the next and to help them maintain their attention. As you prepare your own speeches, be sure to include each of these key elements.

ORGANIZING YOUR SPEECH

Now that you are aware of the main parts of a speech, this section emphasizes the specific ways in which speeches are organized. A well-organized speech will help

A well-organized speaker greatly helps an audience understand the concepts of the speech.

© VladKol/Shutterstock.com

an audience understand and remember your ideas. If you have ever tried to listen to a speaker but simply could not follow what they were saying, it may be due to a lack of organization on the speaker's part. Recalling the "causes, effects, and common treatments" example stated earlier, if the speaker randomly spoke about a cause, then a treatment, then another cause, then an effect, and so on, the audience would most likely have a difficult time following and remembering the ideas presented by the speaker. In this section, we present organizational patterns that are most used in public speaking. We then focus on some organizational patterns more often connected to persuasive speeches. These patterns of organization are typically used when organizing the body of the speech.

Common Organizational Patterns for Speeches

➤ Chronological order
A pattern of organization particularly useful when you are trying to describe the order in which something occurs or occurred; used to explain a process, discuss historical events, or talk about someone's life. Also known as *time order*.

One common pattern of organization used in speeches is *chronological order* or time order. This pattern is particularly useful when you are explaining a process, discussing historical events, or describing the highlights of someone's life. When the order in which something occurs is important, this is an appropriate organizational strategy to use. Imagine if you were trying to explain your life to someone and first described your life at age 5, then at age 25, before explaining age 10, and then age 20. Your audience would not get a clear sense of the order of your life experiences over the years. Likewise, if you were trying to discuss the career of a famous musician, going back and forth from that person's early career to his later career and then back to discuss his midcareer, it is likely that your audience would find it difficult to follow the career progression.

When trying to explain a process, the order in which you undertake the process will have an impact on the steps involved and the subsequent product. Suppose you are explaining how to make chocolate chip cookies. The order in which you present the instructions is important. If you instruct your audience to cream the butter and the sugar and then add the flour before telling them to add the eggs, the final product may not turn out as expected. If you state that they should bake the cookies and then add the chocolate chips, the final product would not be chocolate chip cookies as we know them. Thus, when the order of events or a process is important, chronological or time organization is an effective organizational strategy to use.

➤ Geographical order
An organizational pattern used when you want to show how the various parts relate to each other and to the whole. Also known as *spatial order*.

Another common pattern of organization is *geographical order* or spatial order. If the goal of the speech is to illustrate how various parts relate to each other or to the whole, this is an appropriate organizational pattern. There is a song that says, "The hip bone's connected to the thigh bone and the thigh bone's connected to the knee bone …" When showing the spatial relationship between the various parts, consider this organizational pattern. For example, you could use a geographical order to describe your school's campus. In this case, you would select a starting point (e.g., "When you enter the main gates of the campus …") and describe each building to the next building by describing its geographical location or proximity to the next.

A third pattern of organization is *cause–effect order*. With this pattern, events or occurrences that have resulted in a particular outcome are identified. For example, you might provide evidence for the different events that led to the closure of a business, an increase in the joblessness rate, or a decline in the economy. Public speakers may provide support for the various causes that led to a particular effect or outcome. They may also start with the effect and then trace the causes of it. When speakers want to show the connection between certain events that have caused a particular event or set of events, they often use this pattern.

> **Cause–effect order**
> Uncovering events that have resulted in a particular outcome. Speakers may also use the reverse order and begin by speaking about the effects and then go back and trace the causes.

The *topical pattern* is another strategy used in organizing a speech. This pattern takes a broad topic and breaks it down into subtopics or parts. Suppose you were asked to present a speech on the topic of pollution. Since the topic is broad, it could be organized to discuss the various types of pollution, such as noise pollution, water pollution, and air pollution. Another way to organize subtopics of pollution might include discussing the types of pollution, recent legislation that helps prevent pollution, the role of the average citizen in reducing pollution, and the future impact of pollution on our country. Thus, with the topical pattern, you organize your speech into categories and support each category with evidence.

> **Topical pattern**
> In this pattern, you divide your speech into categories and support each category with evidence.

Problem–solution is an organizational pattern also used by speakers. This pattern examines a particular problem and then offers a potential solution to the problem. Providing information on the nature, the extent, and the origins of the problem helps the audience understand the solution that you propose to solve the problem. This pattern is based on John Dewey's (1933) reflective thinking process, discussed in Chapter 9. The process employs a step-by-step process to solving a problem. The steps are (1) identifying and defining the problem, (2) analyzing the problem, (3) determining the criteria for finding a solution to the problem, (4) generating possible solutions to the problem, (5) selecting the best solution to the problem, and (6) implementing the chosen solution. The problem–solution pattern can be used in informative speaking but is also used in speeches to persuade.

> **Problem–solution**
> Pattern that examines a particular problem and then offers a potential solution to the problem; based on John Dewey's reflective thinking process.

> **Monroe's motivated sequence**
> Most often used in persuasive speaking, with this type of organizational strategy, the speaker gains the audience's attention, shows there is a need (or a need for change), provides a solution that satisfies the need, visualizes the benefits of the stated change, and moves the audience to action.

Common Organizational Patterns for Persuasive Speeches

In this section, we discuss patterns often used to organize persuasive speeches. One organizational strategy used exclusively in persuasive speeches is *Monroe's motivated sequence* (Monroe, 1935). With this pattern of organization, the goal is to guide the audience through five steps: *attention*, *need*, *satisfaction*, *visualization*, and *action*. In the first step, ensure that the audience is interested in your topic. This is similar to gaining the audience's attention in the introduction of the speech. Engage them in your speech topic. The next step involves establishing a need or explaining why they need to listen to your message, why it is somehow relevant to their lives, or why there is a need for change. The third step is the satisfaction step. In this portion of the speech, you propose a solution and explain how it will solve or help remedy the problem. Visualization is the fourth step of Monroe's motivated sequence. In this step, ask your audience to "picture this." Provide them with the benefits that will be derived if your solution is adopted. The final step in this organizational pattern is the action step. This involves clearly stating what you want your audience to do or believe and then motivating them to take action and accept your persuasive proposition. For example, if you were persuading the audience to exercise more, you might get the audience's attention by providing statistics about the general lack of fitness among college-age students; offer a rationale for why the audience needs to exercise more; specify a solution to help the audience develop an exercise program; demonstrate how it can be incorporated easily into their lives; discuss the benefits they will derive; and, finally, challenge them to begin to exercise more.

Comparative advantage pattern A speech organization often used in persuasive speaking, it demonstrates to the audience that accepting the speaker's persuasive proposition has more benefits than other possible propositions that others may be advocating.

The *comparative advantage pattern* organizes information in a way to help the audience see that accepting the persuasive proposition is more beneficial than other possible options that others may be advocating. In the business world, salespeople use this strategy when a customer is considering their product against a competitor's product. Likewise, a salesperson may explain how the product she represents will present greater benefits (e.g., cost, efficiency, ease of use) than the product the customer is currently using. For example, if your company is building a new facility and is considering two sites for the building, the project manager might compare the advantages of each site and advocate for why one of the sites would be most advantageous to the company.

Statement of reasons pattern In this pattern, each of the speaker's main points provides a reason why the proposal should (or should not) be supported.

A final organizational strategy used in persuasive speaking is known as the *statement of reasons pattern*. In this pattern, each of the speaker's main points provides a reason why a proposal should (or should not) be supported. For example, if you are speaking to persuade an audience that music education should not be eliminated in public schools, you would provide several reasons and corresponding evidence to support that proposal. Each main idea would include a reason to keep musical education in the schools. Examples of reasons might include improved learning in all subject areas, enhanced student creativity, and the development of a lifelong appreciation of music. Support for each of these reasons would take the form of statistics, quotes by authorities, and examples.

There are a variety of patterns used to organize speeches. Some are particularly useful in speeches to inform and others are better suited for persuasive speeches. Keep in mind that often, as you research, a natural organizational pattern will emerge that is appropriate for your speech's purpose. In addition, there are times when more than one organizational pattern may be integrated into a speech. For example, if you are discussing a recent trip across the country, you would most likely use the geographical or spatial pattern; however, you may also describe your journey chronologically.

Understanding the various types of organizational patterns that may be used in the body of your speech will help you focus and develop your main ideas. The next step involves organizing your ideas into an outline to help you prepare to deliver your speech.

OUTLINING YOUR SPEECH

An *outline* is a tool that speakers use to organize their main ideas and support material into a coherent speech. There are various types of outlines available to you when you write a speech. These include word, phrase, and sentence outlines. A word outline, as the name suggests, is very brief. Main ideas and support are limited to single words. The phrase outline provides slightly more detail while the sentence outline contains the most information of the three general types. The type of outline you choose depends on the nature of your speech, your familiarity with the subject and supporting material, the length of your speech, and the type and size of your audience. Each type is discussed in more detail shortly, but first let's consider the general advantages of using an outline when speaking. There are many benefits to using an outline. First, an outline helps a speaker to maintain eye contact with the audience. When you have an outline, the material is blocked out and it is easy to see the main points and subpoints for each idea. Thus, if you are on the first main idea and you have

Outline
Tool that speakers use to organize their main ideas and support material into a coherent speech.

An outline helps a speaker maintain eye contact with the audience.

© hxdbzxy/Shutterstock.com

given two forms of support for it, it is much easier to find your place (or not lose your place) if you have spoken directly to your audience. In addition, an outline is a great way to ensure that you have organized your speech effectively. At a glance, you can make sure that each subpoint belongs with the appropriate main idea. If it does not, it is easy to move each element to its appropriate location in the speech. Third, an outline is a great practice tool because it visually differentiates between main points and subpoints. Fourth, an outline helps the speaker maintain focus and avoid getting "off track" during a speech. If you are the type of speaker who tends to go off on tangents when speaking, an outline will remind you of the main ideas and the sequence in which you want to make them. Finally, an outline is useful should you need to edit a speech while you are speaking. Suppose you have three main ideas in the body of your speech and four forms of support for each idea. It is easy for you to visually see how many subpoints should accompany each main idea. For example, if you indicated in the introduction that you will discuss three main ideas, you can glance at your outline and confirm the number and order of the main ideas. If you have four subpoints for each main idea and time is limited, the outline will enable you to quickly eliminate a subpoint without losing your place or needing to eliminate one of your main points to accommodate the time limitation.

An outline is an important tool in the speech preparation process. As stated earlier, there are different types of outlines, and the one you choose is dependent on factors such as your familiarity with the topic and the supporting ideas. If you are less familiar with the topic or if you have several quotes, statistics, or other material that you need to quote directly, your outline is more likely to be prepared as a sentence outline.

Word outline
Type of outline that contains only key words to help the speaker remember the sequence in which main points should be discussed. Because of its brevity, it is most useful when the speaker is very comfortable with the speaking situation and knows the material in the speech exceptionally well.

The first type of outline is the *word outline*. This is often used by speakers when they are very familiar with the material. If you are very sure of all of the material you want to cover, you could use a word outline. This contains the least amount of information, but for speakers who know their material well and are comfortable presenting it to the audience, this type of outline serves as a way to capture the sequence of ideas the speaker wants to cover. For example, a word outline addressing the three parts of a speech might include only the following:

I.   Introduction
II.   Body
III.   Conclusion

If you look back at the material previously discussed on the three parts of a speech, you probably now realize how much may be said about each of these areas. You would need to be very familiar with your supporting material in order to use this type of outline.

You could even broaden your outline further to guide you more specifically by indicating how you want to approach each area. In that case, your word outline would look like the following:

I.   Introduction
    A.   Purposes
    B.   Techniques
II.   Body
    A.   Purposes
    B.   Techniques
III. Conclusion
    A.   Purposes
    B.   Techniques

The second type of outline is the *phrase outline*. This type of outline contains key phrases to help the speaker move from point to point. It expands on the word outline but is still relatively brief. Similar to the word outline, it helps the speaker avoid reading from the outline since most of the speech content is not on the actual outline. Thus, if you use a phrase outline, it might look like this:

I.   Introduction = first section of speech
    A.   Three purposes
        1.   Get audience's attention
        2.   State purpose/topic
        3.   Preview key points
    B.   Several techniques to gain attention
        1.   Tell a joke
        2.   Provide a definition
        3.   Ask a rhetorical question
        4.   Provide an example

Phrase outline Type of outline that contains key phrases to help the speaker move from point to point. It expands on the word outline but is still relatively brief. It does help the speaker avoid reading from the outline since most of the speech content is not on this type of outline.

Without going into each section, it is easy to see how the phrase outline gives you more information but is still brief.

When you are less familiar with the topic and its evidence, a *sentence outline*, also known as a full-content outline, is appropriate. This is a very detailed outline containing most of what the speaker will say during the speech. It is very useful for organizing a speech and for practicing it as well. Some speakers use it during their speech, while others use it only to formulate and practice the speech. Once a speaker is comfortable with the speech, the outline may be converted to a phrase outline. Changing to a phrase outline can help a speaker maintain eye contact with the audience. Using the same example as above, a sentence outline might look like the following:

Sentence outline Very detailed outline containing most of what the speaker will say during the speech. It is very useful for organizing a speech and for practicing it as well. Also called a full-content outline.

I. The first part of any speech is the introduction.
    A. There are three purposes of the introduction.
        1. The first purpose of the introduction is to gain the audience's attention.
            a. Often, the degree to which you get an audience's attention in the first 30 seconds to 1 minute is the degree to which you will maintain their attention over the course of the speech.
            b. Your goal is to captivate your audience and show them why they should listen to you.
        2. The second purpose of the introduction is to state the topic and purpose of the speech.
            a. Letting your audience know what your topic and purpose are helps them get ready to listen to you.
            b. It also lets them know if you are informing or persuading them and the perspective you will be presenting.
        3. The third purpose of the introduction is to preview the key points you will discuss in your speech.
            a. The preview helps the audience understand what your organizational strategy will be.
            b. This will help your audience listen more effectively and know when you are moving from one point to the next.

> **Presentational aids**
> Charts, bar graphs, pictures, diagrams, models, the actual object, and even the speaker him- or herself are considered to be visual aids. Audio aids include recordings of music, famous speeches, interviews, or even sounds from nature. Audio-visual aids include clips from movies, instructional DVDs, or anything that combines both sound and sight. They are all used to clarify, highlight, or summarize a speaker's ideas

Clearly, there are great differences among the three types of outlines. Again, the type you use should be based on your knowledge of a topic as well as your comfort with public speaking. The less dependent you are on an outline, the more conversational you will be while delivering your speech. The type of outline you use may also be determined by your instructor. Overall, an outline is an excellent organizational tool to help you prepare to speak in public.

DEVELOPING PRESENTATIONAL AIDS

Presentational aids are audio and/or visual types of support that help the speaker emphasize, clarify, or summarize an idea. They should never overshadow or overpower the speaker or the message. Presentational aids are simply that—aids that provide support for the speaker's points. When misused, they may actually detract from the speech, confuse the listener, or cause the audience to become distracted.

Therefore, it is important to know the types of audio and/or visual aids you may want to use in your speech as well as when to use and how to prepare them.

There are a variety of types of visual aids. Charts, bar graphs, pictures, diagrams, models or replicas; the actual object under discussion; and even the speaker him- or herself may be useful visual aids. Audio aids can include recordings of music, famous speeches, interviews, or even sounds from nature. Audio-visual aids include clips from movies, instructional DVDs, or anything that combines both sound and sight.

© Maxim Blinkov/Shutterstock.com

Visual aids should support a speaker's message.

Visual Aids

Visual aids may take many forms. For example, *charts* provide a visual display for information contained in your speech. They may help explain how things relate to each other or the sequence something goes through as it is processed. One common example is an organizational chart where each person's position in the organization and that position's relationship to the other positions in the organization are shown visually. Another common example of a chart is a *pie chart* (sometimes called a *pie graph*), which shows what amount of the total each individual "slice" of the pie contributes. Finally, *flow charts* are also commonly used by public speakers. They illustrate the sequence in which the steps of a process occur.

Bar graphs are another type of visual aid and are often used to translate statistical comparisons and relationships into visual representations. It is easier for audiences to understand the relationships among different numbers when they can see these comparisons visually. A bar graph, for example, could show enrollment trends over the last 5 years or compare how males and females scored on several different components of a standardized test.

➤ **Charts**
Visual display for information contained in a speech; help explain how things relate to each other or the sequence something goes through as it is processed.

➤ **Bar graphs**
A type of visual aid often used to translate statistical comparisons and relationships into visual representations.

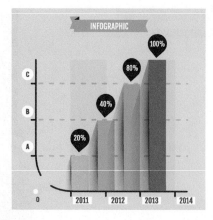

Bar graph

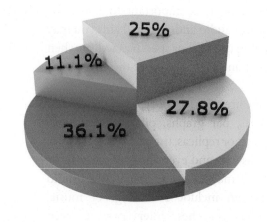

Pie chart

➤ **Pictures and diagrams**
Provide helpful visual images to augment a speaker's description of something.

Pictures and diagrams also provide helpful visual images to augment the speaker's description. For example, if you are speaking about the various sights to see while in the city of Boston, pictures of these attractions would be useful to help the audience visualize what you are discussing. Likewise, if you are trying to explain the parts of a motor and the relationships among those parts, you might use a diagram to help the listeners better understand your material.

➤ **Model**
Replica of an object used as a visual aid.

A *model* is a replica of an object and this can also be a useful visual aid. When explaining the circulatory system, it would be useful to have a scaled model or replica to show the audience while discussing the various elements of the system and its processes. In some instances, you would need a model or replica because the actual object would not be accessible or it might be too large or too small to be useful in a public speaking situation. However, there are times when the actual object may be used during a public speech. For example, science teachers have shown a healthy lung and a diseased lung to demonstrate the dangers of smoking to their students. Finally, the *speaker* may serve as a visual aid. If you are showing an audience how to stretch before or after exercising, you may describe the process and actually demonstrate it to the audience so they can actually see the stretches as you describe them. If you are explaining how to do a backhand stroke in tennis, you would become a visual aid if you were to swing a tennis racket as you describe the proper technique.

Audio and Audio-Visual Aids

Audio and/or audio-visual aids may also be helpful in public speeches. If you are speaking about a singer whose work has contributed to a particular genre of music, you may want to play a clip of that artist's work to provide an example of her style of music. If you are comparing two styles of music, you may want to give an example of each style to help the audience understand the differences between them.

Audio-visual aids in the form of clips from movies or television, for example, are also useful tools for public speaking. The Internet serves as a great resource for a wide variety of audio-visual aids. For example, if you are doing a speech on texting while driving, you may want to search YouTube for an example of a public service announcement, interview, or news report that could help you demonstrate the dangers of texting while driving.

Strategies for Using Presentational Aids

Deciding when, as well as how, to use presentational aids is an important piece of the speech preparation process. As stated earlier, presentational aids are used to emphasize, clarify, or summarize ideas. They can help you maintain the audience's attention, make the material you present more memorable, provide additional support to your ideas, make your speeches more interesting, and simplify difficult material, making it more understandable and less complex. There are several guidelines for their use. First, presentational aids of any type should not be overused and should always be relevant to the ideas you are conveying. Second, they should always be well prepared. Computer-generated presentational aids can be very professional but care should be given to the choice of fonts, colors used, and the size of the graphic so that audiences can easily see and understand each slide. Third, if you are using video or audio clips, you need to be careful about their length since they are usually incorporated into the amount of time you are given to speak. If not used carefully, they can overshadow a speech or the speaker. When using this type of presentational aid, it is best to use clips that are no longer than 30 seconds to 1 minute in length. In addition, be sure not to use clips longer than 10% of your total speaking time. Thus, if you are speaking for 10 minutes, you would not want to devote 5 minutes of your time to audio or video clips. Since most students today are knowledgeable about producing electronic presentational aids and are comfortable with the technology, and since these aids are readily available, they may help public speakers become more effective in conveying their ideas.

WORD CHOICE

When developing a speech, *word choice*, or the language you use, is important to consider. There are a variety of factors to think about when selecting the right words to express ideas in a speech. The first consideration should be your audience.

Would you use the same word choice to discuss solar energy with a group of second graders as you would use when speaking to a group of engineers attending an energy convention? It's not likely. Matching your word choice to your audience's age, education level, and experience with your topic is essential to planning an effective speech. If your audience is familiar with technical language or jargon, you can incorporate it in the presentation. However, if they know little or nothing about your topic, the use of jargon would not be appropriate. Poor word selection often results in an audience becoming distracted and not listening to the message.

A second factor to consider is the use of clear and descriptive language. Concrete language provides the audience with a clear understanding of your topic. For example, if you were to reference "my car" when presenting a speech on automobile repair, unless your audience knows what type of car you drive, they may each perceive a different make and model of car. If, on the other hand, you reference your "2002 Volvo S80 sedan," they would receive a much clearer image of your car. As you develop your speech, choose concrete and descriptive words that will help paint a clear picture for your audience.

Use of appropriate language is important for any audience.

© val lawless/Shutterstock.com

When making language choices, use words that are not ostentatious. Some speakers like to enhance perceptions of credibility by using words that are grandiose or imposing. Audiences are usually not impressed by this tactic and, in fact, may lose interest in the speech and the speaker. When speakers use this type of language, audiences often perceive them as condescending or trying to appear of higher status.

It is important to choose language that is ethical. As discussed in Chapter 10, refrain from using language that degrades or offends others based on their gender, race, cultural background, sexual orientation, or religion. Similarly, it is best to use gender-neutral language. Referring, for example, to *firefighters* and *police officers* instead of *firemen* and *policemen* will help alleviate stereotypes. Public speakers have many ethical obligations to their audiences and being conscious of the ethical use of language is very important.

Finally, public speakers should avoid using slang. Although you may be speaking in a college classroom, the use of appropriate language remains important. The use of slang may not be understood by the entire audience and it may offend some people. Keeping all of these things in mind when developing your speeches will help you be an effective public speaker.

CHAPTER SUMMARY

In this chapter, we have discussed many considerations when preparing speeches. First, regardless of the length of a speech, it always includes an introduction, body, and conclusion. The goal of the introduction is to capture the audience's attention, state the topic to be discussed, and provide a preview of the key ideas that will be presented in the speech. Transitions should be incorporated throughout the speech to guide the audience from one main idea to the next. Internal transitions are also useful signposts to indicate the direction and flow of the speech. Examples of these include phrases such as "In addition," "For example," "Furthermore," or "Finally." Ensuring that your speech contains all of these components will enhance your effectiveness as a public speaker.

In addition to ensuring that all parts of the speech are included, patterns of organization are important to consider. Organizational patterns help you divide a topic into its main ideas and this, in turn, helps you to fit your research into its appropriate and logical place within the speech. Commonly used patterns of organization include chronological, spatial or geographical, cause–effect, topical and problem–solution organization. Additional patterns of organization are frequently used in persuasive speaking include Monroe's motivated sequence, the comparative advantage pattern, and the statement of reasons pattern. Understanding and using organizational patterns will help you with the next phase of speech preparation, which involves preparing an outline of your speech.

There are three main types of outlines to assist speakers in their preparation. These include word, phrase, and full-content or sentence outlines. Choosing the type of outline depends on your familiarity with the topic and the requirements provided by your instructor if you are preparing your speech for a classroom setting. In general, full-content or sentence outlines are helpful to create because they help ensure there is enough support for each idea and that each form of support is appropriately placed under a particular main idea.

Presentation aids provide speakers with a way to emphasize, clarify, or summarize an idea. Given the technology available in today's world, presentation aids can be easily created and incorporated into public speeches. However, they should never be used just for the sake of using them. Aids should only be used when they help the speaker make a point. When overused or poorly prepared, they may actually detract from the speaker's effectiveness.

Finally, selecting words that are concrete and descriptive will help your audience understand your message. In addition, it is important to avoid using language your audience may not understand, slang, or language that would offend. Using appropriate and clear word choice will have a positive impact on the overall quality of your speech.

In conclusion, there are many things to keep in mind when preparing a public speech. The more time a public speaker dedicates to the preparation phase of the process, the more likely that the speaker will be effective and accomplish the goal of the presentation. In the next chapter, practicing and delivering public speeches are discussed.

KEY WORDS

Bar graphs A type of visual aid often used to translate statistical comparisons and relationships into visual representations.

Body The heart of the speech; its purpose is to state each main idea and support each idea fully.

Cause–effect order Uncovering events that have resulted in a particular outcome. Speakers may also use the reverse order and begin by speaking about the effects and then go back and trace the causes.

Charts Visual display for information contained in a speech; help explain how things relate to each other or the sequence something goes through as it is processed.

Chronological order A pattern of organization particularly useful when you are trying to describe the order in which something occurs or occurred; used to explain a process, discuss historical events, or talk about someone's life. Also known as *time order*.

Comparative advantage pattern A speech organization often used in persuasive speaking, it demonstrates to the audience that accepting the speaker's persuasive proposition has more benefits than other possible propositions that others may be advocating.

Conclusion Summarizes or reviews the main points presented in the speech and leaves the audience with a final unifying thought.

Geographical order An organizational pattern used when you want to show how the various parts relate to each other and to the whole. Also known as *spatial order*.

Introduction Gains the audience's attention, clearly states the topic, and previews the main points to be discussed.

Model Replica of an object used as a visual aid.

Monroe's motivated sequence Most often used in persuasive speaking, with this type of organizational strategy, the speaker gains the audience's attention, shows there is a need (or a need for change), provides a solution that satisfies the need, visualizes the benefits of the stated change, and moves the audience to action.

Outline Tool that speakers use to organize their main ideas and support material into a coherent speech.

Phrase outline Type of outline that contains key phrases to help the speaker move from point to point. It expands on the word outline but is still relatively brief. It does help the speaker avoid reading from the outline since most of the speech content is not on this type of outline.

Pictures and diagrams Provide helpful visual images to augment a speaker's description of something.

Presentational aids Charts, bar graphs, pictures, diagrams, models, the actual object, and even the speaker him- or herself are considered to be visual aids. Audio aids include recordings of music, famous speeches, interviews, or even sounds from nature. Audio-visual aids include clips from movies, instructional DVDs, or anything that combines both sound and sight. They are all used to clarify, highlight, or summarize a speaker's ideas.

Problem–solution order Pattern that examines a particular problem and then offers a potential solution to the problem; based on John Dewey's reflective thinking process.

Sentence outline Very detailed outline containing most of what the speaker will say during the speech. It is very useful for organizing a speech and for practicing it as well. Also called a *full-content outline*.

Statement of reasons pattern In this pattern, each of the speaker's main points provides a reason why the proposal should (or should not) be supported.

Topical pattern In this pattern, you divide your speech into categories and support each category with evidence.

Transitions Words or phrases that help listeners move smoothly from one point to the next; signal to the audience that the speaker is moving from one idea to the next or from one type of support to another.

Word outline Type of outline that contains only key words to help the speaker remember the sequence in which main points should be discussed. Because of its brevity, it is most useful when the speaker is very comfortable with the speaking situation and knows the material in the speech exceptionally well.

REFERENCES

AAA Foundation for Traffic Safety. (2010). *2010 Traffic Safety Culture Index.* Retrieved from www.aaafoundation.org/pdf/2010TSCIndexFinalReport.pdf.

Dewey, J. (1933). *How we think.* Boston: D. C. Heath.

Grice, G. L., & Skinner, J. F. (2013). *Mastering public speaking* (8th ed.). Boston: Pearson.

Monroe, A. H. (1935). *Principles and types of speech.* Chicago: Scott Foresman.

Progeria Research Foundation. (2014). *Progeria 101 FAQ.* Retrieved from www.progeriaresearch.org/progeria_101.html.

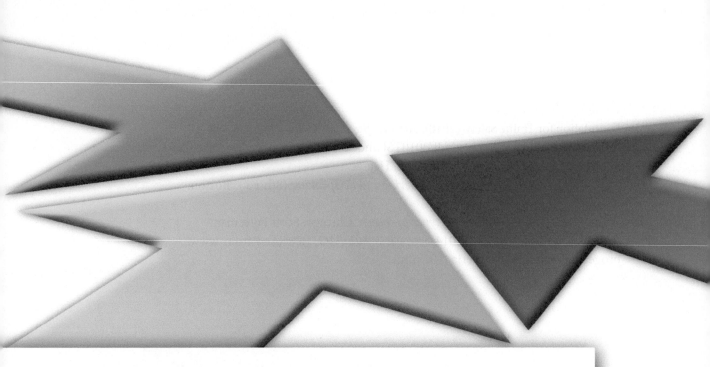

CHAPTER 12

Practicing and Delivering Public Speeches: Going Public

Chapter Objectives

After reading this chapter, you should be able to:
- Identify the various methods of speech delivery
- Recognize the importance of both verbal and nonverbal delivery in public speeches
- Effectively integrate presentational aids into your speeches
- Effectively manage question-and-answer periods
- Incorporate reflection into your public speeches

PERSONAL: You have been asked to pay tribute to your undergraduate academic advisor who is retiring at the end of the school year. Since your graduation several years ago, you have remained close. Many of the professors in the department who taught you will also be there. You have been successful in your career, and yet you are nervous about speaking at this retirement party for two reasons. First, you want to do a great job expressing what this person has meant to you and many other students like you. In addition, you find it rather daunting to speak in front of many of your former professors. As you prepare your speech, you reflect on your advisor's characteristics and how these personally helped you over the years. You identify several examples and humorous stories that support your advisor's traits; organize and outline your ideas; and spend a great deal of time practicing this relatively brief and important tribute. Despite your nervousness, you are honored to speak on your advisor's behalf. Will you be able to convey how much this person means to you?

PROFESSIONAL: As your organization's chief financial officer (CFO), it is your responsibility to address all of its members at the end of the fiscal year. Each year, you present a summary and review of the company's financials. Not only will you be speaking to those who are familiar with the financial aspects of the company, but also those who may not have a strong understanding about the financial side of a business. Since you are only one speaker on a rather large agenda, you have been allocated 15 minutes to present your summary. Over the past few weeks, hours have been devoted to creating visual aids that highlight various aspects of the company's financial picture and you have tried to put the information in terms that everyone at the meeting will be able to understand. You have reviewed everything you want to say several times over and have even practiced in front of key members of your staff. Are you ready to go public?

PUBLIC: For the last 3 years, you and a committee of seven other community members have worked tirelessly to raise funds, recruit volunteers, solicit donated materials, and rebuild a playground in your town. It has been a labor of love for you and the other members. Finally, the project has come to fruition and the formal dedication of the new space is being held. Everyone who donated money, time, or materials as well as the entire community has been invited to the dedication. An estimated 500 people will attend the event. You have been asked as chair to make the formal dedication of the playground. In your brief remarks, you plan to thank those who have helped make this dream a reality and you will speak about the importance of the new playground to the families in your town as well as how the community came together to create something significant for the town. The speech is well organized and you have practiced it countless times, but are you ready to speak in front of such a large group?

CHAPTER OVERVIEW

As you have learned in previous chapters, careful preparation and practice are essential elements of effective public speaking. Now that we have explored the various stages of speech preparation covered in Chapter 11, this chapter focuses on the concepts that will help you effectively present your speeches. There are many delivery elements that can help you when you "go public." As you will learn in the following pages, speakers present speeches using a variety of methods ranging from a full manuscript, to an outline, brief notes, or from memory. In this chapter we examine each of these delivery strategies. In addition, we discuss both verbal and nonverbal elements of delivery and how these influence the effectiveness of presentations. Finally, we identify strategies for managing question-and-answer sessions and discuss how the use of reflection before, during, and after a speech can be utilized to help you improve as a public speaker.

METHODS OF SPEECH DELIVERY

There are four basic methods of speech delivery that are frequently used in public speaking: manuscript, memorized, impromptu, and extemporaneous delivery (Table 12.1). Selection of one method over another depends on the circumstances of the speaking engagement. Factors impacting the choice of delivery method may depend on the audience, the speech purpose, and the speaker's own preferences.

Speaking from a Manuscript

Manuscript delivery
Type of delivery method where the speech is written word for word as it will be delivered; commonly used when the wording must be precise.

Manuscript delivery involves writing a speech word for word in complete-sentence and paragraph format. This allows the speaker to carefully craft what will be said and how it will be said, ensuring accuracy and predictability. Manuscript speeches are often utilized in formal speaking situations or in settings where a transcript of the speech will be placed on record. Examples of situations where a manuscript speech may be used include the inauguration of the president of the United States, or perhaps when a corporate spokesperson is asked to share their comments with the media. Speakers use this format if the wording needs to be precise or there is a concern they will be misunderstood. Thus, the advantage of this method is that it provides speakers with a script of exactly what they want to say. As long as the speaker does not go off script, the wording will be just as the speaker intended it.

Manuscript	Memorization	Impromptu	Extemporaneous
• Written word for word • Usually in complete sentence and paragraph form • Used when the wording needs to be precise or there is a concern about being misunderstood • Can cause speakers to read rather than speak to their audience • Speakers may not pick up on audience feedback as effectively	• Worded exactly as the speaker would like to present it to the audience • Speaker commits the speech to memory • May come across as "scripted" rather than conversational while speaking • If the speech is very brief and the occasion warrants it, this may be a possible method of delivery	• Preparation time is limited • Comes across as spontaneous and natural • Word choice, organization, and fluency may not be optimal • Because remarks are not written down, speakers may actually wind up saying something they hadn't intended to say	• Speakers research, organize, and practice their speeches • An outline is used • The speech isn't written word for word and speakers haven't tried to memorize it • Speakers come across as well prepared yet spontaneous in their delivery • Wording may not be as precise and may actually change during practice and delivery

TABLE 12.1

Methods of Speech Delivery

With the manuscript delivery format, the speaker can ensure accuracy.

© Matej Kastelic/Shutterstock.com

This format, however, has several disadvantages that limit its use. First, it can cause speakers to read rather than speak to their audiences. Audiences indicate a preference for speakers who are engaging and appear to be speaking to them—not reading to them. Reading a speech may also cause a lack of facial expression or inflection in the speaker's voice. Another disadvantage of this method is that it does not allow speakers to respond to the nonverbal feedback the audience may be giving them. Thus, for example, if you are using a manuscript and you notice your audience seems to be confused about something in your speech, you would be much less likely to provide a different example or explanation of that point and much more likely to simply stick to the "script" you have in front of you.

If you choose to use a manuscript, you would write the speech exactly how you would speak it. This enhances your ability to come across as more conversational and less strategic. Also, you will need to spend a great deal of time preparing, editing, and revising what you plan to say as well as practicing it so that it comes across as natural. While this method may be useful in certain situations and for certain speakers because it ensures accuracy and predictability, given the importance of building a connection with your audience through eye contact and using feedback from the audience to adjust your message while you are speaking, this method is not a preferred method in most public speaking settings.

Speaking from Memory

Memorized delivery
Type of delivery method where the speech is written word for word and the speaker commits it to memory; may be useful if the speech is brief and the occasion warrants it.

Memorized delivery is a second method of delivery. Similar to the manuscript method, speakers are able to craft the wording of the speech exactly as it will be presented to the audience. Once the speech is constructed word for word, practice sessions consist of committing the speech to memory. A wedding toast is one example of when a memorized delivery would be appropriate. This type of delivery might also be used when accepting an award since the recipient wants to appear surprised and spontaneous. Recall award shows such as the Oscars or the Grammy Awards. Nominees don't know until the moment when the winner's name is revealed that they have won. Prior to the show, many actors and musicians may find that preparing a memorized acceptance speech is more appropriate than bringing notes to the podium. If used properly, this method can come across as unplanned and natural, even if it has been very carefully planned. This can be the primary advantage to this type of delivery.

On the other hand, there are actually very few times when one would need to memorize a speech. Audiences don't mind if a speaker occasionally glances at an outline or notes as long as they feel you are speaking—not reading—to them.

As much as you might prepare for job interview questions, your responses are still impromptu.

© Monkey Business Images/Shutterstock.com

However, there are some potential disadvantages to consider with this method. First, memorizing a speech of any significant length would be difficult. Second, you may come across as "scripted" rather than conversational as you speak. Also, if you forget one piece of your speech, you may not be able to think quickly on your feet, smoothly recover, and move to the next part of your speech. Finally, at times when speakers use this method, even though they are not looking at their speech, they may still appear to be reading it. Instead of the speech being on the podium, they may visualize an imaginary speech somewhere in the space in front of them or the back wall of the room and their eyes may still give the impression of reading, lacking a direct connection with the audience.

If you do use this method, as indicated in the manuscript method, be sure to write your speech in a conversational way. Try to make it seem less formal and spontaneous. In general, if the speech is very brief and the occasion warrants it, this may be a possible method of delivery.

Impromptu Delivery

A third method of delivery is *impromptu delivery*, which involves little to no advance preparation by the speaker. Suppose you are at a school board meeting as a concerned parent and, based on the discussion, you want to share your opinion

Impromptu delivery
Type of delivery that is characterized by limited preparation time; often not as organized or carefully worded as other speech delivery types but does come across as spontaneous.

about a proposal currently being considered. You would most likely use this method of delivery. Certainly, the advantage of this type of delivery is that you come across as spontaneous and natural. On the other hand, it is more difficult to be as prepared, organized, and well thought out. You may actually wind up saying something you didn't intend to say, and this is one primary reason why public speakers state that they do not prefer to use this particular method of delivery.

If you do find yourself in this situation, quickly try to organize your thoughts so that you identify the key points you want to discuss. For example, if you are the spokesperson for a company and, at a media event, you are asked about what immediate challenges the company will face as a result of a recent merger, you would quickly think of two or three points you want to make. Once you have those in mind, indicate each challenge and provide specific examples or facts you have that support each one. Your ability to collect your thoughts and provide an appropriate and well-organized response will help you when you are called upon to speak using the impromptu method of delivery.

Extemporaneous Delivery

Extemporaneous delivery
Type of delivery where the speaker researches, organizes, and practices the speech but uses only an outline while delivering the speech to the audience.

Extemporaneous delivery is the final delivery type. With this method, speakers have advance notice of their speaking engagement and are able to research, organize, and practice their speeches. As discussed in Chapter 11, an outline of key ideas and support for those ideas is constructed. In essence, the extemporaneous speech provides you with the best of all possibilities. You have the organizational strategy mapped out, the ability to research support for your main ideas, and an outline to use when practicing your speech. The disadvantage of this method is that the precise wording of the speech may not be as carefully structured as with the manuscript or memorized methods. The wording may also change somewhat each time you practice the speech as well as during your actual presentation to the audience.

When using this method, as you prepare your outline and practice your speech, you will become more comfortable with the wording and more familiar with each of your main points and the support for each idea. The more you practice using your outline, the less you will need to depend on it. Since you don't have the speech written word for word and haven't tried to memorize it, you will come across as well prepared yet spontaneous in your delivery.

Overall, with any delivery method, it is important to consider the audience, the occasion, and the amount of time you have been given to speak. As discussed in

Chapter 10, knowledge of your audience's familiarity, attitudes, and interest level regarding your topic will help you select the supporting material and word choice to clearly develop and organize your ideas. In addition, knowing if the audience consists of colleagues, friends or family, members of the media, or the general public will help you determine what method of delivery will be appropriate. Analyzing the occasion will help you make the right choice with regard to the delivery method you will use. Is the occasion an informal gathering or will it be broadcast on live television? Are you speaking at a monthly business meeting or addressing Congress? Finally, your choice of delivery method should take into account the amount of time you have been allocated to speak. If your speech is brief, memorized delivery may be appropriate to use. On the other hand, if you have been asked to give a 10-minute speech at graduation, you may want to choose the manuscript or extemporaneous method. Knowing the advantages and disadvantages of each method as well as considering the factors mentioned above, you will be more effective in selecting the appropriate method to use in any given speaking situation.

EFFECTIVE VOCAL AND NONVERBAL DELIVERY

Regardless of the delivery method you select, attention should be given to your vocal and nonverbal delivery. In this section, we concentrate on both elements of delivery. Recall the example of the tribute speech for your former academic advisor at the start of this chapter. What if you begin your presentation at his retirement party and your nerves cause you to speak softly, avoid eye contact, and speak at a rapid pace? While you may have wonderful things to say about your advisor, will the message be as effective if the vocal or nonverbal elements of delivery are lacking? Some speakers may use appropriate volume and rate of delivery, but may lack eye contact or facial expression. There are several vocal and nonverbal considerations to help speakers deliver speeches effectively. Vocal delivery elements include the speaker's volume, rate of delivery, pitch, and vocal variety. Nonverbal elements include eye contact, facial expression, gestures, posture, and movement.

Vocal Elements of Delivery

There are several elements of your vocal delivery that can make a difference to your effectiveness as a public speaker (Figure 12.1). These include volume, speaking rate, pitch, and vocal variety.

Volume refers to the loudness or softness of your voice. You may need to adjust your vocal volume according to the environment in which you are speaking. Every member of the audience must be able to hear you without straining to do so. Just

Volume
Loudness or softness of the speaker's voice.

as you would naturally adjust your voice if you were whispering confidential information to a friend, public speakers need to adjust their volume when speaking to a large room filled with people. The goal is to identify the correct volume for the size of the room. It is difficult and annoying for an audience to listen to a speaker whose volume is too soft. In some speaking situations, a microphone may be available to assist the speaker. If a microphone is used, speakers must learn not to speak too loudly into the microphone or stand too closely to it.

Just as finding the right volume is important for public speakers, so is finding the appropriate rate of delivery. *Rate* is the speed at which someone speaks. Some speakers tend to speak very quickly. This may be the result of nerves or excitement. When speakers present their information too quickly, it doesn't allow the audience time to process the message. Speaking too slowly is not as common, but it does happen. When speakers speak too slowly, it draws out their message and audiences may become distracted and unable to focus on the message. In addition, speakers who speak slowly may be perceived as less credible. In a study examining speaking rate and perceptions of credibility (Simonds, Meyer, Quinlan, & Hunt, 2006), speakers with slower speech rates were perceived as less credible compared to those with moderate speech rates. Finding the right rate of delivery is important

Rate
Speed at which a person speaks.

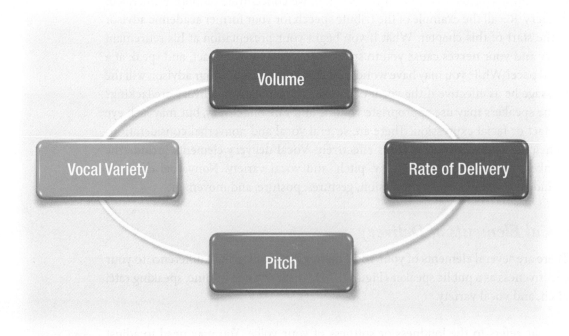

to maintain the audience's interest and help maintain the perception of credibility. If you know you tend to speak too quickly, some techniques to assist you in your delivery include visualizing yourself separating each word or writing notes such as "slow down" or "breathe" on your outline as a reminder.

Pitch is another element of vocal delivery that refers to the highness or lowness of your voice. When public speakers are nervous, their pitch may become higher than their normal speaking voice. Speakers who do not incorporate any variety in their pitch are considered to be monotone. In the movie *Ferris Bueller's Day Off*, Ben Stein's character is often described as the monotone economics teacher. This type of voice becomes very difficult for an audience to listen to for any length of time. As the movie showed, students were inattentive and had difficulty even staying awake while Stein's character spoke to the class. When speakers are tired or lack passion about their topic, they are more likely to become monotone and lose inflection in their voices. Through careful practice and perhaps sufficient sleep before you speak, speakers can add inflection to their voices.

Pitch
Highness or lowness of a person's voice.

Vocal variety refers to the changes public speakers make in their volume, rate of delivery, and pitch that help them convey their message effectively. The volume, rate, and/or pitch of your delivery may be altered to help communicate your enthusiasm, concern, or passion for your topic. Pausing or emphasizing certain words and phrases will help the audience understand the intent of your words. For example, if you are giving a presentation that contains technical jargon, it may be appropriate to pause or slow your rate of speech when defining terms. This way, your audience has an opportunity to digest what you are discussing.

Vocal variety
Changes the speaker makes in volume, rate, and/or pitch to add meaning to the speech.

In summary, your vocal delivery is critical to your success as a public speaker. Concentrating on your volume, rate of delivery, pitch, and vocal variety are essential elements of your delivery. These elements help convey your sincerity, concern, passion, confidence, and other emotional elements. Always try to listen to yourself while speaking, so that you know your audience can easily hear you, that you are speaking at a rate that allows your audience to capture what you are saying, that your voice has inflection, and that your vocal variety reinforces your message (Figure 12.2).

FIGURE 12.2

Suggestions for vocal
delivery.

Adjust your volume given the size of room, the number of people in the audience and the distance between you and the audience.

Speak at a rate that allows your audience to digest what you are sayng while maintaining your enthusiasm.

Add vocal variety to help communicate your enthusiasm, concern, or passion for your topic.

Select language that is appropriate for the audience and the occasion. Be clear, vivid, and descriptive and avoid offensive language.

Nonverbal Elements of Delivery

The elements of volume, rate of delivery, pitch, and vocal variety influence how your message is received. Another important factor in your delivery is how you communicate nonverbally. Simply put, it isn't just the words you say but also how you say them and how you communicate nonverbally that can make the difference in effective speech delivery. Consider the importance of the nonverbal delivery in the following example. As the president of the student government at her college, Tanya was asked to speak to the college's board of trustees to present student concerns about the possible elimination of some majors. When she attended the meeting, she wore a suit, walked into the room with a confident manner, and smiled at the board members. Although she had an outline of what she planned to say, she looked directly at the members of the board and her tone of voice was professional and self-assured. The board members were impressed with Tanya because she made many valid points but also because her nonverbal communication was positive and professional. Eye contact, facial expression, gestures, posture, and movement are important nonverbal elements to consider when preparing to deliver your speech (Figure 12.3).

FIGURE 12.3

Nonverbal elements of delivery.

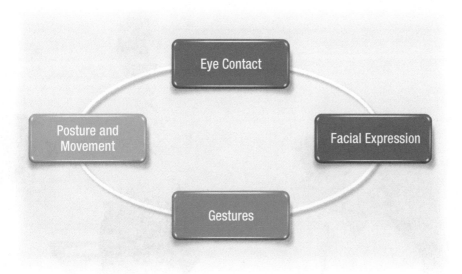

As stated earlier, audiences prefer speakers who speak to them, not those who read to them. *Eye contact* refers to the degree to which you establish and maintain a visual connection with your audience. It is the primary way public speakers connect with their audiences and engage them in the topic. Not only do speakers use eye contact to build and maintain rapport with an audience, but it also enables them to pay attention to the nonverbal feedback from the audience. When looking down at written speech notes while presenting, it is difficult to tell if an audience understands or is interested in what you are saying. Later in this chapter, we identify strategies that you can consider if an audience seems confused by what you are saying, but it is essential to maintain eye contact to remain connected to the audience and to receive feedback from them.

 Eye contact
Degree to which you establish and maintain a visual connection with your audience.

Establishing and maintaining eye contact is not an easy task for many public speakers. It takes a great deal of practice and confidence. Using the impromptu or extemporaneous method of delivery provides the best chance for public speakers to stay connected with their audiences. It stands to reason that, if you are speaking from an outline or notes, you will not try to remember the exact wording as you might if using a manuscript.

Just as eye contact is an essential tool to help public speakers connect with, engage, and maintain the audience's attention, it is also the way in which public speakers receive nonverbal feedback from their audiences that lets them know if the audience understands what is being said or if something needs to be addressed in a

Eye contact connects you with your audience.

© Andresr/Shutterstock.com

different way. For example, how would you let a speaker know if his rate of delivery was too fast? You might have a look of frustration on your face or begin to shift in your seat. This gives the speaker important nonverbal feedback that basically says, "Slow down, you are speaking too fast." Similarly, how do you respond if you didn't understand what the speaker is saying? Would you look puzzled? Again, this provides nonverbal feedback to the speaker that says, "I don't understand what you are saying." In both cases, you are communicating with the speaker and he should incorporate that feedback to adjust his message accordingly. By maintaining eye contact with your audience, you will be able to pick up on the audience's nonverbal feedback and determine if the audience is "with you" or if you need to re-explain something, provide a different example, or perhaps slow down. Although it is probably difficult for you to imagine making adjustments to your speech while you are speaking, it is often necessary.

Facial expression
Changes a speaker makes to express emotion and to reinforce what the speaker is saying.

Facial expressions provide additional nonverbal cues to enhance the message being presented. *Facial expressions* are the changes a speaker makes to express emotions and reinforce what is being said. Your facial expressions add feeling to your speech. For example, if you are selected to give a toast at your best friend's wedding, it is natural to communicate excitement through the use of a smile or extended eye contact with your friend. A wide range of emotions are communicated via facial expressions. They let the audience know if your speech is serious, sad, frightening, or perhaps humorous. As discussed in the previous section, when a speaker possesses

Gestures can help emphasize what the speaker is saying verbally.

© Monkey Business Images/Shutterstock.com

a monotone speaking voice, it is difficult to maintain the audience's attention. Similarly, a presentation that lacks facial expressiveness may result in the loss of the audience's attention. It's important to incorporate facial expressions that are appropriate for the topic and the tone of the speech. After all, you wouldn't want to grin from ear to ear when speaking about a serious subject. The facial expressions you use must reinforce what you are saying, yet they must also seem natural and unrehearsed. Practice helps most public speakers identify the appropriate facial expressions to enhance the effectiveness of their speech delivery.

Gestures are another form of nonverbal communication that can help speakers deliver their message effectively. *Gestures* are movements of the speaker's arms or hands used appropriately and purposefully to emphasize or reinforce what the speaker is saying verbally.

Gestures
Movements of the speaker's arms or hands used appropriately and purposefully to emphasize or reinforce what the speaker is saying verbally.

Gestures may also be used to visually demonstrate something to the audience. Effective gestures would include pointing to a specific area of a chart or graph, widening your hands or narrowing them to demonstrate the size of something, or holding up three fingers as you say, "There are three main areas I want to speak with you about today." As a public speaker, it is important to avoid gestures that serve no purpose in your speech. For example, fidgeting with jewelry, adjusting your hair, or wringing your hands would be distracting gestures. In fact, your audience may interpret these movements as speaking anxiety or that you failed to prepare for the presentation. These may also lessen the audience's perception of your credibility. Practicing your speech and becoming aware of the gestures you tend to use will help you eliminate ones that detract from your delivery.

Posture
How the speaker stands or the position of the speaker's body.

Posture and movements are nonverbal elements of delivery that can enhance or detract from your speech as well. *Posture* refers to how the speaker stands or the position of the speaker's body. It is the way in which you carry yourself, and it can convey confidence or reticence. Slouching over the podium or leaning against the wall conveys a negative impression. Your posture should appear natural and comfortable to convey confidence and help boost your credibility. Standing tall and strong even when you may be feeling somewhat nervous will enhance perceptions of your credibility as a speaker.

Movement
Any physical shift the speaker makes.

Movements are another aspect of nonverbal delivery to consider when presenting your speech and refer to any physical shift the speaker makes. Moving around the room or changing position while speaking is fine as long as you maintain the audience's attention and their focus is on you rather than what you are doing. Movements should be done with a purpose. They may help you transition to a new topic or communicate the importance of something you just said. Movements to avoid include actions such as swaying back and forth, crossing one leg over the other, or pacing rapidly. If you are using presentational aids, avoid turning your back toward the audience as you refer to them. Overall, your goal is to have your audience focus on listening to what you are saying rather than watching what you are doing.

Nonverbal communication is an important consideration in speech delivery. Be sure to establish and maintain eye contact; incorporate facial expressions that help convey your message; and use gestures that are purposeful and help emphasize or reinforce what you say. Also, be aware of your posture and movements (Figure 12.4). Concentrating on these elements will help you become an effective public speaker. Working on nonverbal elements of delivery will enhance your chances of being a successful public speaker whether you are in a classroom or organizational setting, at a community meeting, or giving a toast at a friend's wedding.

PRACTICING YOUR SPEECH DELIVERY

Now that you understand the various delivery options available and the vocal and nonverbal characteristics that make speech delivery effective, let's turn our attention to the importance of rehearsing or practicing your speech. Even though

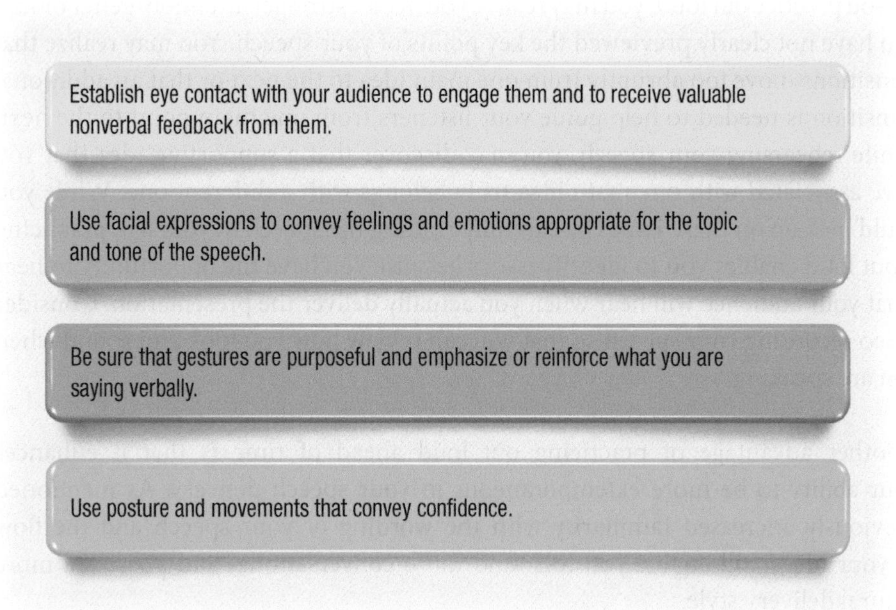

FIGURE 12.4

Nonverbal elements of
delivery.

Establish eye contact with your audience to engage them and to receive valuable
nonverbal feedback from them.

Use facial expressions to convey feelings and emotions appropriate for the topic
and tone of the speech.

Be sure that gestures are purposeful and emphasize or reinforce what you are
saying verbally.

Use posture and movements that convey confidence.

you have completed the process of researching the topic, organizing the speech, and
identifying effective methods of delivery, practicing speech delivery will further
enhance your public speaking confidence. When you practice the speech, you will
gain comfort with the sequence of ideas, word choice, and supporting material you
plan to present. Practice will also aid your nonverbal delivery.

While many of us have the tendency to procrastinate, waiting until the last minute to
prepare a speech can sabotage your ability to deliver a quality presentation. Completing
all of the steps in the speech process far in advance of when you will be delivering your
speech will enable you to devote the time you need to practice your delivery. There are
many things you can accomplish by practicing your speech ahead of time. The following
suggestions should help make your practice time more effective.

Practice Your Speech Out Loud

Be sure to practice your speech out loud. This provides several advantages.
Practicing out loud will help you simulate the real speaking situation and help you
identify any issues with your speech before you make your actual presentation. For
example, because spoken language is different than written language, speaking out
loud will allow you to actually hear the word choice and sentence structure you
plan to use and make any necessary adjustments to it before you present the speech.

As you practice out loud, you may realize you need a stronger attention-getter or that you have not clearly previewed the key points of your speech. You may realize that transitions move too abruptly from one main idea to the next or that an additional transition is needed to help guide your listeners from one main point to the next. While rehearsing your speech, you may discover that a supporting idea that you have associated with one main idea truly belongs with a different one. While you could pick up on these issues by carefully reading the speech to yourself, practicing it out loud enables you to identify issues because you have the opportunity to hear what your audience will hear when you actually deliver the presentation. Consider video recording your speech so that you can review how you look and sound when you are speaking.

Another advantage of practicing out loud ahead of time is that it enhances your ability to be more extemporaneous in your speech delivery. As mentioned previously, increased familiarity with the wording of your speech and the flow of your ideas will enable you to sound more conversational and possess a more natural delivery style.

Finally, practicing your speech out loud can potentially improve your vocal and nonverbal delivery. As you practice, you will be able to identify the tone, rate, volume, and word emphasis that should be used in order to convey your ideas effectively. In addition, practicing increases your ability to maintain eye contact

Practicing your speech out loud can improve your nonverbal delivery.

with your audience. As you rehearse, you will become more familiar with the wording and the sequence of your ideas and less reliant on the written speech. You will become more comfortable with the appropriate facial expressions and gestures that can enhance your speech, thus eliminating any nonverbal elements that may detract from your message.

Practice in Front of Others

While it might feel awkward to practice your speech in front of others, it *will* help you speak more effectively. Recruit friends or classmates to help you. Practicing in front of others will help you become aware of any issues you might not notice when you rehearse by yourself. Getting feedback from others on any areas that need to be corrected before you deliver your speech will help you strengthen the actual speech when you deliver it to the intended audience (Menzel & Carrell, 1994). Smith and Frymier (2006) also found that students who practiced their speeches in front of an audience prior to their delivery were more effective during their actual presentations. In their study, they found that students who practiced in front of an audience of four or more people scored an average of three points higher on their graded speech presentations. Over the course of the semester, practicing in front of others can have a significant impact on your grade. Overall, a volunteer audience can offer constructive feedback that will enable you to make improvements to your speech or delivery. At the very least, practicing in front of an audience should help boost your confidence.

Time Your Speech Each Time You Practice

Just about every speaker is provided with a time limit for their presentations. Your time frame will be either given to you specifically, as is the case in a classroom situation, or it will be implicit in the speaking situation because of common practice, as is the case for speakers at a commencement ceremony. Similarly, business meetings and civic organizations often use agendas to keep meetings on track. In these situations, speakers need to be mindful and respectful of the agenda and monitor the length of their presentation to meet the guidelines or parameters provided by the agenda. When speakers run too short or too long in a classroom, it can have an impact on their grade. Both inside the classroom and beyond, if you give your audience too little information, you may lose credibility. If your speech runs too long, you may lose the attention of the audience. Timing your speech several times will help ensure you meet the explicit or implicit guidelines of the speaking situation.

Give Extra Attention to Your Introduction and Conclusion

One thing you can do to help you present your speech effectively is to spend additional time practicing your introduction and conclusion. This will help you start and end your speech on a strong note. For example, if you know exactly what you want to say in your introduction, you will be able to increase your level of eye contact as you start to speak and immediately begin to develop a rapport with your audience. As speakers first begin their presentations, they often feel nervous, but become more comfortable after the first few minutes of speaking. Knowing your introduction well will help you conquer the initial nervousness you might feel. Likewise, knowing your conclusion well will allow you to end strongly. Again, this will allow you to maintain direct eye contact with your audience. Since you do not want your audience to "guess" when you are done, providing your audience with a clear sense of completion to your speech is important. Knowing both the introduction and conclusion well will help your delivery overall.

Edit Your Speech if Needed

Throughout the development and practice phases of speech preparation, it is important to continually refine your speech. Each time you practice your speech, try to evaluate what worked and what did not. Consider how you can improve both what you have written and how you deliver it. If you think a sentence is unclear or your word choice is vague, now is the time to change it. Many speakers make changes right up until the time they actually deliver their speeches. For example, on December 23, 1960, Ted Sorensen, on behalf of then President-elect John F. Kennedy, sent a telegram to several individuals including Adlai Stevenson, Dean Rusk, and John Kenneth Galbraith asking them for any suggestions they had for his inaugural address. Their suggestions and Kennedy's other revisions were given to Sorensen's secretary on January 18, 1961, who typed the final version that Kennedy delivered to the nation on January 20, 1961 (*www.jfklibrary.org*). Your own evaluation of what needs to be changed, as well as the feedback you receive when you practice in front of an audience, will help you strengthen your speech before you deliver it to the actual audience.

Practice to Increase Confidence

As alluded to previously, practicing ahead of time will increase your confidence and, hopefully, you will feel less apprehensive about speaking in front of an audience. Although some level of anxiety is normal for most speakers, as you rehearse, you will likely increase your chances of transforming potential perceptions of your nervousness into enthusiasm and excitement for your topic. This may be compared

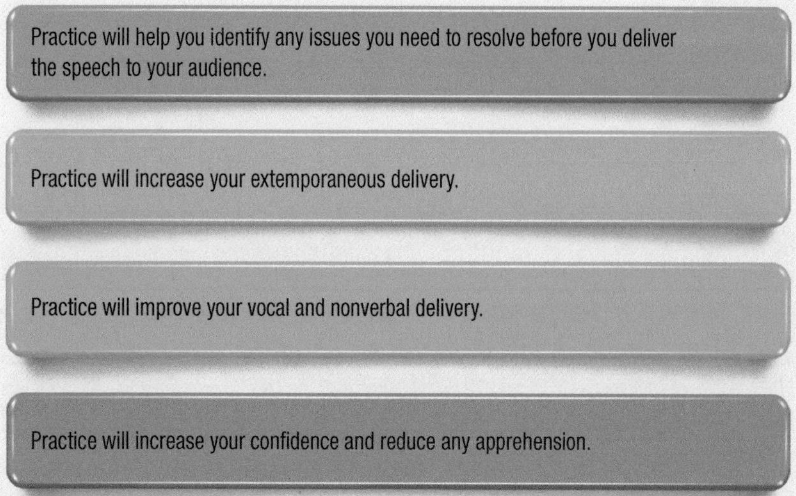

FIGURE 12.5

Practice will help you identify any issues you need to resolve before you deliver the speech to your audience.

Practice will increase your extemporaneous delivery.

Practice will improve your vocal and nonverbal delivery.

Practice will increase your confidence and reduce any apprehension.

to an athlete getting energized for a game. In addition, many speakers focus on practicing *positive visualization* when they rehearse. In other words, envision yourself succeeding in your speech delivery. As you rehearse your speech, try to imagine the audience engaged in what you are saying and envision their nonverbal reactions as they give you positive feedback. Do this during your speech as well. In the practice phase of your speech preparation, positive visualization can help replace potential negative thoughts with positive ones. Instead of telling yourself you can't do something or that you aren't good at something, this strategy will help boost your confidence level.

Positive visualization
When a speaker envisions succeeding in his or her speech delivery.

Practicing your speech has many advantages. These include your ability to recognize areas that need to be strengthened before you deliver your speech to an audience, improve the likelihood that your delivery will seem extemporaneous, increase the effectiveness of your vocal and nonverbal delivery, and increase your confidence and decrease any level of apprehension (Figure 12.5). To make the most out of your practice, prepare your speech well in advance in order to allow sufficient time to practice, rehearse out loud in front of others, and time your speech each time you practice. Be sure to devote extra attention to practicing your introduction and conclusion and edit your speech as needed. As you practice, pay attention to your eye contact, gestures, and body movements. Are there words you want to emphasize? What nonverbal gestures will help you emphasize that point?

FIGURE 12.6

Tips for practicing your speech.

> **Complete your speech early**
>
> **Practice your speech out loud**
>
> **Practice in front of others**
>
> **Time your speech each time you practice**
>
> **Give extra attention to your introduction and conclusion**
>
> **Edit your speech as needed**
>
> **Practice to increase confidence**

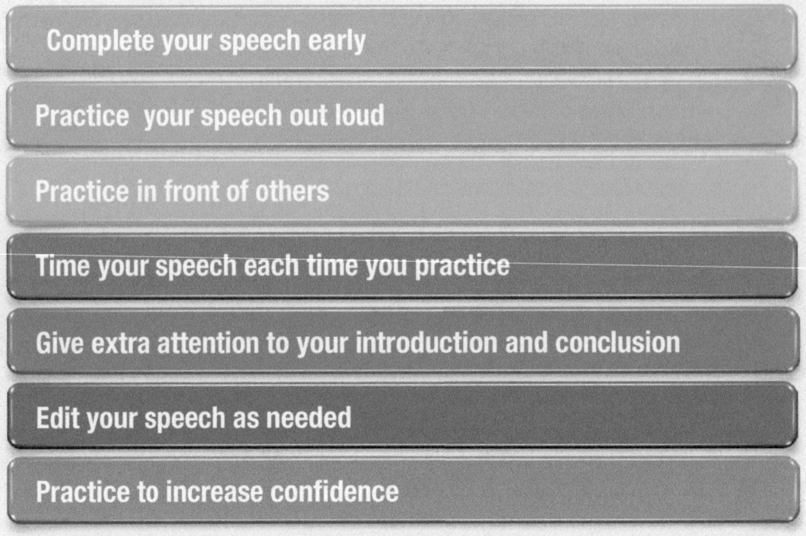

Familiarizing yourself with the nonverbal aspects of delivery during your rehearsal will help you gain the confidence you need to be perceived as an effective public speaker (Figure 12.6).

All of the suggestions above will help you deliver a more effective speech. By rehearsing your speech delivery and focusing on what you want to convey to your audience, the time devoted to preparing and practicing your speech will be well worth it. In the next sections, we discuss two other dimensions of public speaking that can help you enhance your effectiveness. These include managing the question-and-answer period and the ability to reflect before, during, and after you speak to an audience.

THE QUESTION-AND-ANSWER PERIOD

A question-and-answer (Q&A) period often occurs after a speech is presented. While it is not always easy to know what an audience may ask, it is important to consider how to approach the question-and-answer period and what potential topics may be brought up. Your audience may ask questions to solicit more information on a specific area, to get your opinion on a particular aspect of your presentation, or to clear up a point of confusion they may have about something you said. Usually, the questions asked are presented in a positive manner and provide an opportunity for the speaker to interact with the audience. Public speakers also need to be prepared, however, for an audience member who asks a confrontational question. There are some common strategies that will help you successfully manage a Q&A.

One of the best suggestions for responding to a question is to *repeat* the question the audience member has asked as part of your answer. This is beneficial for many reasons. First, this will help ensure the entire audience has heard the question. If you are in a large room and the person asking the question happens to be sitting toward the front, you may hear the question because of your proximity. It can be very frustrating for people if they are sitting behind the person asking the question, can't hear the question, or only hear the speaker's response. Second, repeating the question helps speakers know that the question the audience member asked is the one that has been received. This will allow for any clarification that needs to occur before the question is answered. Finally, repeating the question gives speakers that extra moment to consider how to respond and to organize their response.

It's beneficial to repeat a question in your response to it.

When you respond to questions, *be brief* and to the point. Lengthy answers may become confusing to the audience and if there are time constraints, they may also prevent other members of the audience from asking questions. Needless to say, some questions may naturally be answered briefly. For example, an audience member may ask a simple question such as "Can you repeat what you said the project will cost to complete?" Some questions, however, may take more time to respond, such as a question that asks, "Can you explain the major challenges of completing the project successfully and the cost of not meeting those challenges?" When speakers feel it would take too long to respond to the question, they may provide a brief response, thank the audience member for asking the question, and indicate their willingness to speak with the audience member at more length after the presentation or to correspond with them in some way.

© Karramba Production/Shutterstock.com

When asked a question, it is important to *be honest*. If you do not know the answer to a question, admit it. Audiences don't expect speakers to know everything about a subject. In the long run, providing the audience with a false or misleading response will damage a speaker's credibility and is considered unethical. If you do not know the answer to a question, respond with a statement such as, "I don't know the answer to that but I would be happy to research that and let you know."

Speakers should *be careful* about what they say and how they say it. Many politicians and public figures have said something they wished they had never said. When responding to questions, it is best to take a moment and consider what you should say and how the message may be perceived. For example, the mayor of Boston publicly stated that if he lived in Detroit he would "blow up the place and start all over." Needless to say, this statement insulted many people. While his intent was to convey that Detroit should reevaluate some of its policies and consider reforms, his poor choice of words communicated another meaning. Because public speaking is public, speakers must always be mindful of what they plan to say and how they plan to say it, especially during a question-and-answer period.

The last suggestion is to *check* to make sure that the question asked by the audience member was answered successfully. Speakers can simply ask, "Have I answered your question?" If the audience member indicates you have, you may move on to the next question. If not, the audience member may need to ask a second question or request clarification. While this is important, avoid focusing only on one audience member's question since this eliminates the opportunity for other audience members to ask their questions. If this occurs, you can ask the audience member to meet briefly after the Q&A session is complete and move on to other questions.

The question-and-answer period is an important part of public speaking and can help clarify any questions audience members have and enhance what the speaker has said. To be successful during this time, speakers need to remember to restate each question, try to answer questions briefly and honestly, and carefully consider what they say and how they say it. Just as you might try to anticipate questions an interviewer might ask you on a job interview, it is also important to consider what potential questions an audience may ask. In doing so, you will be more prepared to respond effectively.

THE IMPORTANCE OF REFLECTION

Thus far, we have spoken about the methods of delivery public speakers use, the vocal and nonverbal elements of speech delivery, the importance of practicing

FIGURE 12.7

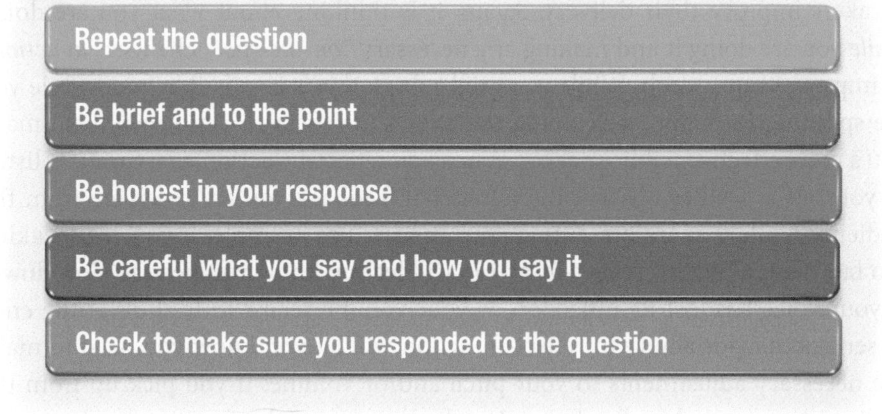

Repeat the question

Be brief and to the point

Be honest in your response

Be careful what you say and how you say it

Check to make sure you responded to the question

your speech, and the question-and-answer period that typically follows public speeches. Your ability to speak effectively may also be enhanced through reflection. *Reflection* means giving something serious thought or consideration. This should occur before you speak, while you are delivering your speech, and once you have completed your speech.

Reflection
Giving serious thought or consideration to something.

Before you speak, reflection should guide your speech preparation. First, you should analyze your audience. Having a deeper understanding about the audience to whom you will be speaking is a reflective activity that will help you research and organize your speech effectively, select the best methods of support for your ideas, and even choose the best way to word your ideas and support. Reflecting on the type of audience, the occasion at which you will be speaking, and even the time of day the speech will be given will assist you in preparing an effective speech and this, in turn, will help you deliver your speech successfully.

Reflecting during your presentation will also help you deliver a more effective speech. Schön (1983, 1987) highlighted the need for reflection-in-action as a way to improve one's level of performance. According to Schön, when individuals use *reflection-in-action*, they isolate and name a problem that needs attention; frame the problem to help organize and clarify how they will solve it; and reframe the problem in such a way that it provides a new understanding of it and possible alternative ways of acting to resolve it. Schön underscored the need for reflection-in-action, which he believed helps people consider what and how they are doing while they are doing it. In turn, this can be used to improve their performance. He notes that musicians and athletes, for example, do this constantly and often make needed changes in a split second to improve their performance.

Reflection-in-action
Thinking about what you are doing while you are doing it and making any necessary adjustments immediately.

What does all of this mean for public speakers? Reflection-in-action can help public speakers improve their delivery. Again, it is thinking about what you are doing *while* you are doing it and making any necessary "*on-the-spot*" changes "*in action*" to improve your speech. While you might think this is impossible to do while you are speaking in public, developing the ability to reflect-in-action will help make you a more effective public speaker. When you reflect-in-action, you carefully listen to yourself as well as observe the nonverbal feedback you are receiving from the audience while you are presenting your speech. For example, if you are speaking too fast, your ability to reflect-in-action will let you know you need to slow down. If your voice has lost its inflection or your volume seems to trail off at the ends of sentences, your ability to reflect-in-action will let you know you need to make the necessary adjustments to your pitch and/or volume. If you pick up from the audience's nonverbal feedback that they don't understand something you have said, again, if you are reflecting-in-action, you know you need to adjust your message to make your ideas clear to your listeners.

Similarly, having the ability to reflect-in-action will allow you to edit your speech while speaking if necessary. Perhaps because you repeated something or provided a different example of something, you are almost out of the time you have been given to speak. Through your ability to reflect-in-action, you could give two forms of support for an idea rather than three or paraphrase a quote rather than providing the entire quote for the audience. If you can train yourself to reflect-in-action, you can improve your speech delivery and make those types of "on-the-spot" adjustments that musicians and athletes make in order to improve.

Reflection-on-action
Thinking about what you did and how well you did it and what you would do differently the next time.

The last type of reflection comes after your speech has concluded. Schön (1983, 1987) called this *reflection-on-action*. Once you have delivered your speech, analyze your strengths, what areas need improvement, and any elements you would change if you were to deliver that same speech again. By reflecting on what you did and how you could do it better, you will help yourself be more effective during your next presentation. In a classroom situation, you may be evaluated by your instructor and perhaps even your classmates. While this feedback is intended to provide the constructive steps you need to take to improve for the next time, what happens after the course is complete and you are not receiving their feedback? If you can learn to reflect on what things worked well and what things needed to be improved each time you deliver a speech, you will continue to improve as a speaker long after the course ends. If you can learn to self-reflect each time you speak in public, you will analyze what you could have done to make your speech even better.

Overall, learning how to reflect before you speak, while you are speaking, and after you have spoken will help you become a more effective public speaker. Reflection before you speak will help you construct an effective presentation, which, in turn, will help your delivery. Reflecting while you are speaking will also help your delivery because you will make any necessary adjustments to help you improve during your presentation. Finally, reflecting on your speech and on its delivery after you have presented it will help you analyze what strengths you brought to the public speaking situation and what areas should be strengthened for the next time.

CHAPTER SUMMARY

In this chapter, we discussed the four types of delivery methods commonly used by public speakers and the advantages and disadvantages of each type. Public speakers need to determine which type of delivery method is best given a particular speaking situation. This chapter also focused on the vocal and nonverbal elements of your delivery. The vocal elements of volume, rate, pitch, and vocal variety as well as the nonverbal elements of eye contact, facial expression, gestures, posture, and movement are critical components of a public speaker's delivery. Furthermore, this chapter focused on the various reasons why practice is important, and some things to keep in mind when practicing your speech. Managing a question-and-answer period was also discussed as part of a speaker's delivery. Finally, the chapter examined the use of reflection to help you improve as a public speaker before, during, and after you speak. Keeping all of this in mind as you research, organize, prepare, practice, and deliver any type of speech is important to becoming an effective public speaker.

KEY WORDS

Extemporaneous delivery Type of delivery where the speaker researches, organizes, and practices the speech but uses only an outline while delivering the speech to the audience.

Eye contact Degree to which you establish and maintain a visual connection with your audience.

Facial expression Changes a speaker makes to express emotion and to reinforce what the speaker is saying.

Gestures Movements of the speaker's arms or hands used appropriately and purposefully to emphasize or reinforce what the speaker is saying verbally.

Impromptu delivery Type of delivery that is characterized by limited preparation time; often not as organized or carefully worded as other speech delivery types but does come across as spontaneous.

Manuscript delivery Type of delivery method where the speech is written word for word as it will be delivered; commonly used when the wording must be precise.

Memorized delivery Type of delivery method where the speech is written word for word and the speaker commits it to memory; may be useful if the speech is brief and the occasion warrants it.

Movement Any physical shifts the speaker makes.

Pitch Highness or lowness of a person's voice.

Positive visualization When a speaker envisions succeeding in his or her speech delivery.

Posture How the speaker stands or the position of the speaker's body.

Rate Speed at which a person speaks.

Reflection Giving serious thought or consideration to something.

Reflection-in-action Thinking about what you are doing while you are doing it and making any necessary adjustments immediately.

Reflection-on-action Thinking about what you did and how well you did it and what you would do differently the next time.

Vocal variety Changes the speaker makes in volume, rate, and/or pitch to add meaning to the speech.

Volume Loudness or softness of the speaker's voice.

Word choice Carefully selecting words to convey your message clearly, vividly, and ethically.

REFERENCES

Menzel, K. E., & Carrell, L. J. (1994). The relationship between preparation and performance in public speaking. *Communication Education, 43*(1), 17–26.

Schön, D. A. (1983). *The reflective practitioner: How professionals think in action.* New York: Basic Books.

Schön, D. A. (1987). *Educating the reflective practitioner: Toward a new design for teaching and learning in the professions.* San Francisco: Jossey-Bass.

Simonds, B. K., Meyer, K. R., Quinlan, M. M., & Hunt, S. K. (2006). Effects of instructor speech rate on student affective learning, recall, and perceptions of nonverbal immediacy, credibility, and clarity. *Communication Research Reports, 23*(3), 187–197.

Smith, T. E., & Frymier, A. B. (2006). Get "real": Does practicing speeches before an audience improve performance? *Communication Quarterly, 54*(1), 111–125.

CHAPTER 13

Understanding What We Do Not Know: Communicating with Diverse Others

Chapter Objectives

After reading this chapter, you should be able to:
- Define the concepts of culture and diversity
- Identify reasons for studying cultural differences and their impact on communication
- Explain three primary characteristics of culture
- Identify co-cultures in the United States
- Examine the impact of beliefs, needs, attitudes, and values on our communication with diverse others
- Explain the importance of cultural values for understanding different approaches to communication

PERSONAL: On the first day of class, your professor announces that students will be assigned to work in groups on a project that will count for 40% of the final course grade. She has randomly assigned students to groups, and you notice that a student from another country has been assigned to your group. You've heard his responses during class discussions and immediately assume that it will be up to you to complete the bulk of the work on the project since his English skills are very weak. Will it be easier to do the work yourself than to try to understand him?

PROFESSIONAL: In your role as project manager at Beebout Enterprises, you are part of a management team that is faced with the task of promoting a promising employee. The primary criterion for this promotion is exceptional technical skills. The team decides to offer the position to a Generation X employee (38 years of age) who has been with the organization for 2 years over a Baby Boomer (approximately 57 years of age) who has more than 14 years of experience with the company. You consider the Baby Boomer to be a good friend. What should you say or do to maintain your relationship with your friend who did not receive the promotion?

PUBLIC: While attending a Chamber of Commerce forum in which candidates for the upcoming city election are being introduced, you overhear two men seated in the row behind you whispering and chuckling as they exchange racist and sexist jokes targeted toward two of the candidates. As the meeting progresses to the question-and-answer session, one of the gentlemen stands up and introduces himself as the director of the community youth athletic programs and asks a question of the candidates. Knowing what you just overheard, how do you address the situation?

CHAPTER OVERVIEW

As you look around campus on the first day of class, you notice the diversity that exists among students at your school. On the surface, you seem so different. But after a while the distinctions seem to blur. Sound idealistic? Probably. After all, one only needs to glance at the daily news headlines for stories of the challenges faced when cultures clash. Our goal in addressing the topic of culture as it relates to communication is simple—if by the end of this chapter you have an increased understanding for *how* cultures differ and *why* these differences influence our interactions, we will have accomplished our objective. Have you ever heard yourself describe another culture's behaviors or norms as "weird," "strange," or "gross"? How would you respond to the question, "On which side of the road do the British drive?" If you said, "The wrong side of the road!" this demonstrates our tendency to judge cultures based on our own cultural practices. Rather than label differences as "wrong," our goal is for you to view them as merely "different."

You may have noticed the diversity on campus your first day of school.

© Joy Brown/Shutterstock.com

The chapter title "Understanding What We Do Not Know" was used for a reason. While we might think that we know how our cultural differences influence our own communication style and how we interpret the messages sent by others, the reality is that we do not. If we become comfortable with the knowledge that it is not possible to understand the nuances of every culture, we may reduce our frustration with miscommunication and become more effective in our personal, professional, and public communication. In this chapter, we explore the many facets of culture and diversity and their relationship to communication. In addition, we discuss various reactions to diversity in an attempt to enhance our interactions with others.

DIVERSITY AND CULTURE DEFINED

Diversity
Distinctions among individuals or groups.

Diversity can be defined as that which is different. While this definition is simple, it serves as the conceptual foundation that influences our interactions with others. Consider the diversity encountered on a daily basis as you travel from home to school and work. If you were to create a list of the differences you see, items included might identify racial, ethnic, and gender differences. However, diversity runs much deeper than what we are able to see on the surface. In fact, the most important aspects of culture are often those that we never talk about in our interactions with others. If we took the time to communicate and truly get to know the other person, we would uncover an excess of differences that would be mind-boggling. Additional

Consider the ways in which we are similar to others rather than focusing on our differences.

© Monkey Business Images/Shutterstock.com

characteristics such as religious beliefs, value of education, and attitudes toward work would likely be revealed as you begin to interact with others. In Chapter 2, the concepts of perception, self, and identity were discussed. We typically draw conclusions about how similar we are to others by focusing our attention on specific characteristics we decide to use when evaluating the ways in which we are alike or different. For example, we might choose to focus on age or political affiliation to assess how similar we are to someone while ignoring other characteristics such as gender or religious beliefs. In order to understand the most influential aspects of our differences, we need to add culture to the equation. *Culture* is a term that refers to the common characteristics and shared perceptions that unify a group of people and shape their communication expectations. These commonalities create a sense of unity and identity for a group. Anthropologists have broadly defined culture as being comprised of perceptions, behaviors, and evaluations. Others have adopted a more descriptive approach to explaining culture. These definitions include components such as knowledge, morals, beliefs, values, customs, art, music, and laws.

➤ **Culture**
Shared perceptions that shape the communication patterns and expectations of a group of people.

Scholars have examined the creation of cultures in a variety of contexts ranging from organizational culture to family culture to fan culture. From Disney employees who adopt a common language of words such as "guests" instead of "tourists" and "cast members" instead of "employees" to the Japanese students who are committed to doing what is best for their project team and who avoid eye contact with their instructor as a sign of respect, we are bombarded with cultural differences on a daily basis.

Most cultures take pride in accentuating their distinctions from others. The more distinct we are, the more defined our culture becomes. While we take pride in our differences from other cultures, we expect the members of our own culture to conform. Values, beliefs, and attitudes serve as core principles, and members of an organization often reward those members who adhere to the cultural norms and form negative perceptions of those who do not.

Have you ever researched the Internet for information about another country before traveling abroad or downloaded an iPhone app to provide you with insights on a city that you are visiting on vacation? A lot of time is devoted to researching and understanding the customs and highlights of a new city or country when we are traveling, but we often fail to devote the same amount of time to considering the cultural differences that we might encounter in our daily interactions with others.

THE RELATIONSHIP BETWEEN CULTURE AND COMMUNICATION

Explaining the relationship between culture and communication is simple. Communication and culture are inseparable. Communication is the primary means for teaching the core characteristics of a culture. We share stories about our heroes and legends in an attempt to instill commonly held values. However, our culture also teaches us "how" to communicate. We begin learning the preferred language of our culture at a very young age. Family members teach us appropriate words and gestures for expressing ourselves, and they reprimand us for deviations that are considered to be unacceptable. This learning continues as we attend school.

As you pursue your personal and professional goals in the 21st century, you will encounter a society and workforce that are much more diverse than in previous decades. Chapter 3 addressed the challenges created by differences in verbal communication, and the distinctions in nonverbal behaviors were discussed in Chapter 4. This chapter builds on that foundation by exploring theories and concepts relevant to enhancing your understanding of and appreciation for diversity and its impact on communication.

THE REASONS FOR STUDYING INTERCULTURAL COMMUNICATION

The phrase "shrinking world" has been used to describe the increased potential for interactions between diverse people. With the introduction of Facebook and other new media, students now can interact and build relationships with others from cultures that would never have been possible before the Internet. We no longer depend on letters or library research to inform us of cultural nuances. Instead, if we have a desire to build relationships with diverse others we can simply "friend" them and begin exchanging messages. In the following section, three specific reasons for the importance of exploring culture and communication are discussed.

Understanding the Self

Perhaps the most fundamental reason for studying culture and communication is the opportunity it provides us for understanding our own cultural background and identity. Recall our discussion of the self in Chapter 2. Have you ever stopped to consider *why* you communicate the way you do? While language and history classes provide insight into the "big picture" of cultural influences that have shaped our identity, a closer look at distinctions that shape our perceptions and responses is invaluable. One of the authors was raised in a rural community with a population of approximately 350 people that could best be described as extremely homogeneous. The entire community was Caucasian, with most having a connection to the occupations of farming or coal mining. Imagine the challenges encountered when she moved from a small town to a large metropolitan city following high school graduation. Initial descriptions of her encounters with others focused on their "strange" behaviors and "odd" styles of dress. New words and phrases such as "market" in reference to the "grocery store" and "gum bands" instead of "rubber bands" were confusing. Enrolling in an intercultural communication class proved to be "eye-opening." Learning the unique words, phrases, and gestures was simple. On the other hand, examining core components of the culture of origin provided insight into *why* she reacted the way she did to the deviations from expected behaviors. Our culture becomes part of our core identity and we become comfortable being around those who are like us. When we step out of this comfort zone, we may experience culture shock. There is truth in the phrase, "In order to truly understand others, you must first understand yourself."

Technological Responsibility

When Marshall McLuhan first coined the term "global village" in the 1960s, many thought his predictions were so far into the future that we would never be affected by the changes he proposed. Little did we know then that when Atari introduced its first game console in 1972 that only 30 years later Xbox would launch a technology that would enable game play with people from around the world. McLuhan was a visionary who anticipated widespread opportunities for people to interact and travel with ease. Coworkers utilize Skype to communicate with colleagues from halfway around the world, and travelers can encounter new cultures firsthand through enhanced modes of transportation. Technology has exponentially increased our opportunities for intercultural contact. Elementary schools collaborate with other schools to create international email "pen pal" programs to enhance students' cultural awareness and language skills, while colleges encourage students to broaden their cultural horizons through study-abroad programs. Because of these increased opportunities for interactions, understanding the factors that influence culture and communication is essential to appreciating these learning opportunities.

Demographic Influence

The demographic composition of the United States has changed dramatically over the past two decades. Predictions for the 2020 census highlight the significant demographic shifts that will continue to occur in the workplace as a result of immigration and changes in educational achievement (Figure 13.1). With these changing demographics come increased opportunities for confusion and misunderstanding. No longer will we be interacting solely with those who "look like us." Instead, we will encounter a workforce that is more diverse in terms of age, sex, and racial and ethnic composition.

Opportunities to expand our linguistic, political, and social knowledge about the world abound. However, changing demographics present many challenges as well. Uncertainty about one another has given rise to tension among some groups. News stories such as those describing the challenges associated with Alabama HB 56 (see box) are becoming more frequent. Fear and lack of knowledge contribute to the apprehension and anxiety associated with these cultural encounters. Enhancing your understanding of intercultural encounters will prove to be beneficial as you begin to navigate your professional career.

> Alabama HB 56, otherwise known as the Hammon-Beason Alabama Taxpayer and Citizen Protection Act, is the nation's strictest anti-illegal immigration law. Signed into law in June 2011, the impact of the law was witnessed in schools and industries across the state. Numerous Hispanic children attending Alabama public schools stopped attending out of fear, despite the fact that the law did not include provisions to exclude immigrant children from pursuing their educations. Farmers reported a shortage in available labor to assist with the harvesting of crops.

FIGURE 13.1

Estimated demographic composition of the U.S. labor force in 2020. Source: Workforce 2020, Hudson Institute, www. diversitycentral.com/business/diversity_statistics.html#labor_force.

CHARACTERISTICS OF CULTURE

Culture Is Learned

As indicated earlier in the chapter, we begin learning about our culture as children. Language learning begins at a young age and continues through college. Standardized exams such as state achievement tests, the SAT, and the ACT ensure that we are correctly using the words and phrases preferred by our culture. Foods are connected to a culture's identity, and radio stations promote the musical styles that are representative of a culture's preferences in music. Everywhere we turn, messages are being conveyed that inform us of the norms of behavior in order to be viewed as a member of our culture.

How do we learn about culture? Learning occurs at two levels. *Explicit learning* involves more formalized instruction. In the United States, schools teach students about the history of our country in U.S. history courses, and many states promote their identities through classes such as "Ohio History" or "West Virginia History." As we prepare for our professional careers, business dining etiquette classes provide instruction on which fork should be used to eat salad and how to determine which

Explicit learning
Direct or formalized instruction about a culture's expectations.

Standardized exams are designed to evaluate our use of the words preferred by the majority in a culture.

⌦ Implicit learning
Indirectly acquiring information about a culture, usually via observation.

bread plate is yours. We may ask friends and family members for insight or information about cultural differences we encounter. Programs such as Rosetta Stone and Berlitz promise rapid learning of a second language; however, this explicit instruction of language provides us with only a small portion of information about a culture.

In order to truly understand a culture, implicit learning must take place. Colleges recognize this when they provide students with experiences for language immersion. *Implicit learning,* or acquiring information by observing, often provides valuable insight into what is considered acceptable and unacceptable by a culture. One implicitly learns what a culture values, how its members view various communicative behaviors, and its approach to forming relationships by using this information. Reading about cultural differences provides us with only a snapshot of a culture. Spending time with diverse others gives us the opportunity to experience the details of cultural distinctions from differences in styles of humor to varied perceptions of gender roles. For example, someone from the United States may use self-deprecating humor to "break the ice" at the start of a business meeting only to discover that other cultures view this as diminishing one's credibility. Both explicit and implicit learning can enhance our understanding of cultural differences.

Culture Is Dynamic

While cultures take great pride in their history, most are unable to resist the pressure to change. Events occur, innovations are revealed, and members learn about "new" ways of doing and being. Sometimes change is forced upon a culture in order to adapt to its social and physical environment, or cultures may choose to adjust their norms and expectations. Consider the change that has occurred as a result of the widespread introduction of the Internet in the mid-1990s. Many organizations have forced employees to adopt this technology in order to gain access to company information. Paper memos and even faxes are things of the past. Now documents are shared electronically, and rather than wait for a signature to be delivered via the U.S. mail we simply scan a document into PDF format and send it. What cultural changes have you witnessed during the past five years? Changes in clothing styles, the introduction of new words and gestures, and an evolution in the

The introduction of new technologies has increased our ability to interact with those from other cultures.

© iodrakon/Shutterstock.com

view of women's roles in the workplace are only a few of the cultural adjustments that we have encountered in the United States.

Later in this chapter we discuss uncertainty avoidance as a factor that distinguishes cultures from one another. Some cultures are eager to introduce change, and thus can be described as embracing uncertainty. Others are more comfortable in promoting tradition and history, and often view change with hesitation or suspicion. How do you know if your culture is one that promotes uncertainty and embraces change? Create a list of the changes you have noticed. However, labeling a culture as "innovative" or "traditional" may not be as easy as simply looking at one aspect of change. Japan is known for its technological innovation, yet it is a culture that encourages its members to value tradition. For example, elders are viewed as the wisest members of society and are often consulted on important decisions.

FIGURE 13.2

Characteristics of culture.

| Culture is Learned | Culture is Dynamic | Culture is Pervasive |

Japanese culture views its elders as the wisest members of society.

© imtmphoto/Shutterstock.com

Klopf (1995) identifies two primary factors that influence a culture's approach to innovation and change. *Cultural borrowing* occurs when one culture sees the benefits of aspects of other cultures. In the United States, comparisons are made to the business practices and educational systems of other cultures in order to ensure that we maintain our corporate and academic competitive edge. *Disasters and crises* often force cultures to change. The 2011 earthquake and tsunami in Japan have prompted proposed changes in architectural styles and building codes to ensure the safety of its residents. Post-9/11, the United States adapted its attitudes toward safety and security and new procedures for screening guests to our country were implemented. While some members of a culture may be resistant, our interactions with others often result in inevitable change.

➤ **Cultural borrowing**
Process through which a culture identifies benefits of other cultures and decides to adopt similar practices.

➤ **Disasters and crises**
Factors that may force cultures to change.

Culture Is Pervasive

Take a look around you and identify anything that is representative of your culture. From the Apple icon on your computer or cell phone to your classmates' style of clothing, examples of cultural influences are visible everywhere we turn. However, it is important to note that culture also influences us in invisible ways. Artifacts may be used to communicate outwardly what a culture values. Culture is represented not only in our material possessions, but also in the values, beliefs, and attitudes that comprise our personal orientation system. It shapes virtually every aspect of our lives and influences our thoughts and actions.

CO-CULTURES WITHIN THE UNITED STATES

Within the broader cultural context, multiple co-cultures exist. *Co-culture* refers to the smaller cultures that comprise the larger culture. These smaller cultures may create names or labels to refer to themselves in order to establish their identity within the larger culture. The term "co" is used to refer to these smaller cultures because they must coexist through interactions with other smaller cultures within the communication environment of the larger culture. Membership is not restricted to only one or even a few co-cultures. Rather, an individual may associate or identify with multiple co-cultures. It is important to understand how these groups have shaped your identity to begin to appreciate the impact that these co-cultures have on our communication. Create a list of the co-cultures of which you are a member. Did you include political or religious affiliations, college or university, gender, hobbies and interests, or ethnic heritage on your list? A student whose list includes teenage, male, Caucasian, Texas, Methodist, athlete, and Republican readily claims membership in at least seven co-cultures. Negotiating the differing expectations by multiple co-cultures can prove to be challenging. At election time, we may question our political affiliation when candidates express beliefs and attitudes that differ from our own. Combining the conflicting elements of various co-cultures highlights the complexity faced in our personal, professional, and public lives. In this chapter, we examine three of the many co-cultures that have been identified as contributing to our distinct preferences for communication (Figure 13.3). The three co-cultures we examine here are race, age, and gender.

Co-culture
Smaller cultures that comprise a larger culture.

Diversity in the United States

| Gender | Sexual Orientation | Race | Religion | Age | Ethnicity |

FIGURE 13.3

Examples of U.S. co-cultures.

What is the difference between race and ethnicity?

⇒ Race
Inherited biological characteristics such as hair texture and color, eye shape, skin color, and facial structure.

⇒ Ethnicity
Common heritage or background shared by a group of people.

Race

Race is a term often used to refer to inherited biological characteristics such as hair texture and color, eye shape, skin color, and facial structure. Categories used to describe these racial differences include Caucasian, African American, and Asian. Similar categorizations occur in other cultures around the world although the names assigned to racial groups may be different. While the terms race and ethnicity have often been used synonymously, these two categories are distinct from one another. *Ethnicity* refers to the common heritage, nationality, ancestry, or background shared by a group of people. Categories may be established to identify the culture from which one's ancestors came. These include Irish American, Polish American, or Mexican American. While there has been some debate over the connotations associated with the labeling of some of these groups, the intention of naming is simply for identification purposes.

Earlier in this chapter we addressed the changing demographics in the United States. Some demographic shifts are the result of increases in the number of interracial marriages. In 1997, the U.S. Census adopted new categories to lessen the restrictions associated with classifying one's racial identity. Previously, citizens were forced to choose a single race with which they identified. In 1997, instructions on the census were revised to permit the selection of one or more races in describing one's racial identification.

Age

Chances are that you have probably heard your parents reference the generation gap that presents us with unique communication challenges. Many colleges and universities are experiencing a growth in their nontraditional-age student population (e.g., 23+ years of age), and the diverse age span of the employees within a single organization highlights the importance of understanding the impact of age as a factor that contributes to cultural misunderstandings. From musical preferences to political views, members from different generations sometimes clash in the differences among their values and beliefs. Websites such as "When Parents Text" (*www.whenparentstext.com*) highlights the challenges faced by the older generation as it attempts to adapt to the preferred communication channels of today's younger generations. Samples of texts exchanged between parents and their children showcase the humorous misunderstandings or annoyances that occur when different generations try to interact via innovative modes of communication. Consider the following example:

MOM: Your great aunt just passed away. LOL
ME: Why is that funny?
MOM: It's not funny, David! What do you mean?
ME: Mom. LOL means laughing out loud!
MOM: Oh my goodness!! I sent that to everyone. I thought it meant lots of love. I have to call everyone back!

Not only do generational differences result in misunderstandings when it comes to technology use, but this age diversity also influences our interactions in the workplace. Economic, social, and personal reasons have resulted in some employees deferring retirement to later in life. At one point we equated the age of 65 with that ideal milestone that employees dreamed of achieving. Today, according to Social Security Online (*http://ssa.gov/pubs/ageincrease.htm*), the "full retirement age" of 65 has increased to 67 for those individuals born in 1938 or later. What does this mean for our workplace interactions? The increasing diversity in generational differences results in unique preferences for leadership approaches, work ethic, philosophies of work–life balance, and attitudes and preferences for the workplace environment. Figure 13.4 highlights a few of these differences that you may encounter as you begin your professional career and work with colleagues of different ages.

FIGURE 13.4

Distinctions among generations in the workplace. Source: www.generationsat-work.com.

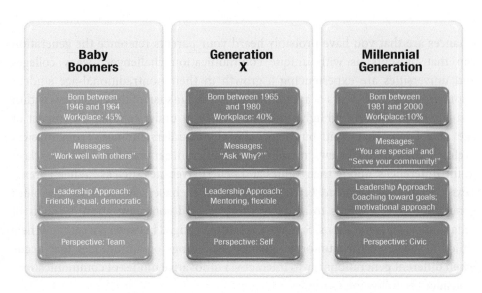

Baby Boomers	Generation X	Millennial Generation
Born between 1946 and 1964 Workplace: 45%	Born between 1965 and 1980 Workplace: 40%	Born between 1981 and 2000 Workplace:10%
Messages: "Work well with others"	Messages: "Ask 'Why?'"	Messages: "You are special" and "Serve your community!"
Leadership Approach: Friendly, equal, democratic	Leadership Approach: Mentoring, flexible	Leadership Approach: Coaching toward goals; motivational approach
Perspective: Team	Perspective: Self	Perspective: Civic

While categorizing the general preferences for each generation in the workplace is important, we need to be cautious about assuming that employees of similar ages are the same. Stereotyping all Millennials as having an "attitude of entitlement" can be inaccurate and unfair. Rather than using the labels and descriptors to stereotype employees, organizations should use this information to promote effective workplace relationships and enhance the promotion of products and services to a more diverse audience. For example, knowledge that a Millennial would rely on the feedback and reviews posted by strangers on product websites is important. This information could be invaluable in shaping how messages about the product are distributed. Equally important is the knowledge that Baby Boomers place more value on the recommendations of friends and family members in making purchasing decisions.

PERSONAL ORIENTATION SYSTEM AND COMMUNICATION

➤ Personal orientation system Composed of our needs, values, attitudes, and beliefs that guide our behaviors and responses.

At the core of any culture is the personal orientation system that guides the communication of its members. Our *personal orientation system* is composed of our needs, values, attitudes, and beliefs that guide our behaviors and responses toward others. In Chapter 2, we discussed our identity and how it influences our interactions with others. Recall that our identity is composed of needs, beliefs, values, and attitudes. These predispositions are often instilled through our interactions with others in our culture. These same components also guide our decisions when communicating with others.

Our personal orientation system reinforces our sense of self. As we increase our self-awareness, we better understand the choices we make in our reactions to and interactions with others. Consider the fact that each of us has a unique set of experiences that shapes our perceptions of events, people, and cultural differences. Sometimes these experiences are the result of your own encounters, and other times they stem from the experiences of others. What are your initial thoughts about being assigned to work with a student from Germany on a class project? How easy will it be to work together? If you have never encountered someone from Germany, you may rely on the portrayal of Germans in news stories and other media to provide you with a foundation for understanding your classmate. If you draw upon stories about Hitler from your world history classes, negative perceptions may occupy your thoughts. Alternatively, perhaps you recall a story that was shared by a work colleague who described a business trip to Germany and recounted how much fun she had during Oktoberfest. Even if you lack any direct experience with individuals from Germany, you create impressions about them based on the information shared by others.

In Chapters 3 and 4, we addressed cultural distinctions in verbal and nonverbal communication. At the core of both verbal and nonverbal behaviors are the rules and norms that guide their use. In addition to the words being spoken, our personal orientation system guides us in understanding the amount of verbal expressiveness preferred by a culture or the guidelines for communication based on the roles of the interactants. For example, some cultures encourage younger members to speak up, whereas others promote silence by listening and learning from elders. Reactions to differences in clothing and hairstyles may result in overt nonverbal responses that may lead to verbal conflict. Each culture's time consciousness creates misunderstandings in our interactions. Cultures that are very *monochronic* view time as a commodity that must be carefully scheduled and not wasted. The United States is an example of a monochronic culture. *Polychronic* cultures approach time as flexible and secondary in importance to the relationships. Many Latin American cultures are considered to be polychronic, and rather than interrupt lunch with a friend to head back to a business meeting, their focus is on the relationship, which they view as being most important. They believe business can wait for a few minutes.

Monochronic
Time as a commodity that must be carefully scheduled; do one thing at a time.

Polychronic
When time is flexible and not viewed as important as relationships.

Every individual has a set of predispositions that serves as a guide for our thoughts, actions, and behaviors. These predispositions are composed of one's needs, beliefs, values, and attitudes. Communication plans are developed and organized by these characteristics. Many of these components of the personal orientation system are learned within the cultural context. When faced with decisions regarding the proper way to respond in situations, our needs, beliefs, values, and attitudes assist us in guiding our perception of the situation.

Needs

Most of us recall studying Maslow's Hierarchy of Needs (Figure 13.5) at some point in our academic careers. The needs can be categorized as ranging from basic physiological needs such as food, clothing, and shelter to the higher-level need of self-actualization, which encompasses elements such as our morality and reaching our full potential. Our needs prompt us to experience desires that in turn motivate us to communicate with others in an attempt to fulfill these wants. A community member who perceives cultural diversity as a threat to his need for safety may communicate in negative ways in public settings. Employees who perceive their self-actualization needs as being threatened may express prejudice against affirmative action hiring practices. A student whose desire is to fulfill social needs may seek out opportunities to interact with other students.

Some cultures are limited in their ability to provide the resources necessary to meet some of even the most basic needs of their members. Communication is the key to understanding individual needs and in comprehending the value placed on need fulfillment.

Beliefs

A second component of our personal orientation system is the beliefs that guide our thoughts and behaviors. Beliefs play a key role in shaping our decisions to approach

FIGURE 13.5

Maslow's
Hierarchy of Needs.

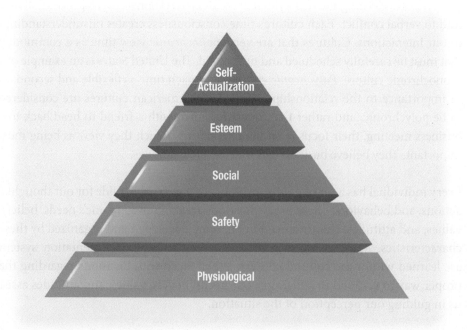

relationships with others or to avoid communication. They guide the words that we use to let others know what we believe to be true. *Beliefs* are defined as personal convictions regarding truth or existence. Miscommunication may be attributed to our inability to take into consideration the role that our differing beliefs plays in shaping our impressions of others. Consider the beliefs that you possess as a student in the United States. Based on information you receive from the *U.S. News and World Report* or the Princeton Review, you may believe that some colleges provide a better education than others, and perhaps these beliefs include judgments about the best "value" for your tuition dollar, best social climate, and best faculty. These beliefs shape our messages. During a job interview, you may find yourself saying, "I probably don't have a chance because there were Harvard graduates who applied." Each culture's method of reasoning influences the development of beliefs in its members, and it is important to consider how these judgments influence our interactions. Beliefs about religion, morality, and even superstitions may cause us to view others as irrational. However, it is important to respect differences of beliefs. Simply appreciating that these different beliefs exist may be the first step in understanding how difficult it is to change someone's beliefs. Respecting these differences may help us avoid confrontations or offensive interactions.

> **Beliefs**
> Personal convictions regarding truth or existence.

Values

Values refer to our personal philosophy that guides our actions or our behaviors. They assist us in evaluating what we should and should not do in an ethical situation. Kluckhohn and Strodbeck (1961) describe values as being either explicitly or implicitly expressed. This definition highlights the relationship between values and communication. Most of our communicative behaviors reflect the values that are firmly established in our personal orientation system.

> **Values**
> One's personal philosophy that guides actions and behaviors; assist us in evaluating ethical situations.
>
> What are the meanings associated with gift-giving across cultures?

Cultures explicitly communicate those values they deem as being important through the use of proverbs. Statements such as "A bird in the hand is worth two in the bush" indicate our culture's emphasis on practicality, while the Japanese proverb of "The nail that sticks out gets hammered down" emphasizes the cultural values of conformity and group harmony. Organizations communicate their values through mission statements to identify the principles that guide their approach to doing business. Wendy's mission statement includes

© PhotoProIndonesia/Shutterstock.com

the phrase "Quality is our recipe." This communicates the value of providing customers with the best product possible. Understanding the values that are being communicated explicitly and implicitly is essential to avoiding misunderstandings. Consider the communicative messages associated with the practice of gift-giving in many Asian cultures. It is common practice in Asian cultures for students to give their college teachers a small gift or token of appreciation to indicate the value of the knowledge shared and the lessons learned. To many in the United States, this custom would be viewed as a form of bribery that conflicts with the U.S. values of ensuring equality and fairness in education. Understanding the values held by a culture's members as well as the ways in which values are communicated might assist us in avoiding misunderstandings.

CULTURAL VALUE ORIENTATIONS

In order to understand the values shared by a culture's members, many scholars have developed models for studying these value orientations (e.g., Figure 13.6). Scholars such as Hall (1976) and Hofstede (1980) proposed models of cultural values that assist us in identifying and understanding the differences that often result in frustration and miscommunication. Differences are characterized along a continuum representing the broad range of communicative responses that reflect what a culture views as being important.

Low context
Cultural orientation that emphasizes the spoken word and direct verbal expression.

High context
Cultural orientation that emphasizes indirect communication, typically focusing on nonverbal cues or unspoken messages.

Cues that provide the context for our interactions are used to describe the value that a culture places on the spoken word versus nonverbal cues. Cultures classified as *low context* value the spoken word and encourage members to be direct in their verbal expressiveness. A philosophy of "say what you mean" is embraced. The United States is considered to be a low-context culture. *High-context* cultures prefer a more indirect style of communication in which cues about the messages intended by others are inferred through nonverbal channels. Silence is highly valued in a high-context culture, and a greater variety of meaning is attributed to what we do not say as opposed to what we do say. Many Asian cultures are considered to be high context. Meanings are perceived through unspoken, nonverbal behaviors. For example, someone from a high-context culture may be able to accurately perceive that you were having a bad day by paying attention to nonverbal cues, such as your late arrival to lunch, lack of facial expressiveness, or negative posture. However, consider the communication challenges encountered when a person from a low-context culture conducts business with a colleague from a high-context culture. Low-context cultures expect direct messages in response to inquiries about the feasibility of suggestions for organizational improvement, while high-context

FIGURE 13.6

Cultural values.

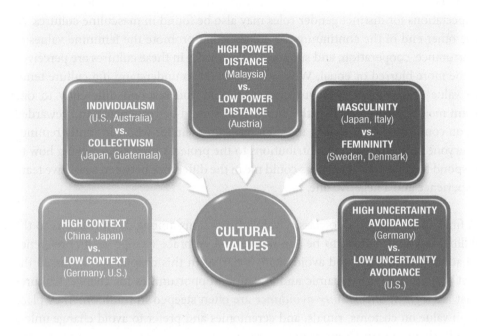

➤ **Individualism**
The self is viewed as most important; valued for independence and self-reliance.

➤ **Collectivism**
Group viewed as most important; valued for dependence and shared responsibility among group members.

➤ **Low power distance**
Emphasizes equality among members. Mutual respect and shared responsibility are valued.

➤ **High power distance**
Rank and status are valued; hierarchies of power and structure influence interactions.

➤ **Masculinity**
Cultural value for assertiveness, ambition, and achievement.

➤ **Femininity**
Cultural value for nurturance, cooperation, and support among members.

cultures will remain silent and assume their silence is interpreted as disapproval as opposed to directly communicating their lack of agreement.

Individualism and *collectivism* are used to depict the relative value of an individual versus the value of a group's members. In general, U.S. culture promotes and values individualism. Group members are encouraged to compete against one another and to assert their individual needs and goals, which is reflected in messages such as "You need to take care of yourself first!" Collectivism is the primary value held by many Asian cultures. Group harmony and support are paramount and take precedence over individual needs.

Cultures have also been classified in reference to the value they place upon power, status, and distance. Power distance refers to the distribution of power in personal relationships as well as within organizations. *Low power-distance* cultures value equality among members. Tendencies to communicate favoritism based on characteristics such as age, status, or gender are minimized. *High power-distance* cultures value status and emphasize power differentials in their communication.

Masculinity and *femininity* are also categories that can be used to classify and understand distinctions among cultural values. Masculine cultures demonstrate a preference for assertiveness, ambition, and achievement. While not always true, expectations for distinct gender roles may also be found in masculine cultures. At the other end of the continuum are cultures that promote the feminine values of nurturance, cooperation, and support. Gender roles in these cultures are perceived to be more blurred or equal. Why is it important to understand if a culture tends to value achievement over nurturance? Would you respond differently to one team member who feels that the entire team should be recognized and rewarded upon completion of a project and another team member who constantly reminds everyone of his individual contributions to the project's success? Knowing how to respond to these team members could mean the difference between a positive team experience and a negative one.

A final dimension used to classify value distinctions among cultures refers to the willingness of a culture to be innovative and embrace change or its preference to adhere to tradition and avoid change. Earlier in this chapter we discussed the fact that cultures are dynamic and encounter opportunities for change. Cultures that are *high in uncertainty avoidance* are often steeped in tradition. They place high value on customs, rituals, and ceremonies and prefer to avoid change unless absolutely necessary. Cultures that score *low in uncertainty avoidance* are excited and intrigued by innovation and are eager to take risks and alter their routines.

High uncertainty avoidance
Lack of tolerance for risk, ambiguity, and change; cultural emphasis on traditions, rules, and laws.

Low uncertainty avoidance
Cultural tolerance for novelty and innovation; risk and change are encouraged.

Understanding these dimensions provides valuable insight into the values promoted within a culture. By equipping ourselves with this information, we will be more effective in determining the appropriate methods to approach our interactions with others. In addition, an increased awareness of our culture's values provides insight into our own approach to communication.

Attitudes

Attitudes are learned predispositions that result from our decision to respond in a favorable or unfavorable way toward a particular object or person. At the beginning of this chapter, we stated that our primary goal is to help you identify your tendency to respond in positive and negative ways to cultural differences. Understanding our own attitudes and how our culture has influenced their formation is an essential component of effective interactions in our personal, professional, and public lives. Consider the attitudes described in the following story that have influenced a student's college experience.

Attitudes
Learned predispositions to respond favorably or unfavorably toward another person, group, or object.

Stereotyping

Stereotyping refers to our tendency to view individuals as possessing the characteristics we have assigned to a group to which they belong. Rather than exploring unique aspects of an individual, we rush to make generalizations in order to make decisions about "how" to communicate. Three steps are involved in the process of stereotyping. The first involves categorizing a group of people based on observable characteristics they have in common. Next, we associate observable characteristics as being typical across a group of people. Finally, we apply those characteristics to any person who is a member of that group. A teacher who stereotypes student-athletes as lazy and not focused on their academic goals is one example of how these conclusions impact our interactions.

> **Stereotyping**
> Tendency to make generalizations about groups and assume that all members of that group possess the same characteristics and engage in similar behaviors.

Prejudice

Prejudice is one type of attitude. It refers to the outward and visible expression of our negative reactions based on inflexible assumptions. Examples of how these attitudes and preconceptions have created problems for interactions among members of co-cultures within the United States can be seen in the expression of racism, ageism, and sexism in our society. Assumptions that senior citizens are incapable of making rational decisions or valuable contributions to society are promoted and reinforced through media portrayals. Sexist attitudes have traditionally been directed toward

> **Prejudice**
> Type of attitude in which we directly express negative reactions toward another individual or group.

females in the United States, and females have experienced discrimination in the workplace and other walks of life.

Scholars have identified two primary forms of prejudice. *Verbal abuse* refers to the process of engaging in verbal comments, name-calling, or jokes that are insulting or demeaning to members of a culture or co-culture. Recently, ESPN reprimanded two of its employees for racist comments made in reference to New York Knicks player Jeremy Lin. Just making others aware of the negative impact of these comments may sometimes be a deterrent, as this awareness often leads to embarrassment about this type of behavior.

Discrimination refers to the practice of denying others their equal rights. Perhaps this attitude is rationalized by the belief that if the group experiences frustration as a result of the denied access, they will go away and we can avoid communication. Title VII of the 1964 Civil Rights Act bans organizations from discriminating against employees on the basis of sex, race, religion, color, and national origin. Affirmative action laws are designed to protect members from inequitable treatment. In 2014, the U.S. Supreme Court reviewed a case filed by a Muslim woman who asserted that she was discriminated against by Abercrombie & Fitch due to her religious beliefs. During her job interview with the retailer, she wore a head scarf and received an acceptable evaluation for her fashion style from the hiring manager. However, she was later informed that she was not hired for the job.

ESPN TERMINATES EMPLOYEE FOR RACIST COMMENT

ESPN fired one employee and suspended another in 2012 for using the same racist word in reference to New York Knicks guard Jeremy Lin. The fired employee used the word in an ESPN Mobile headline — "Chink in the Armor" — after the Knicks lost to the New Orleans Hornets. An ESPN commentator was suspended for 30 days for using the reference during a broadcast.

ESPN issued the following apology on their website (www.espn.com) on February 21, 2012: "We again apologize, especially to Mr. Lin," ESPN wrote. "His accomplishments are a source of great pride to the Asian-American community, including the Asian-American employees at ESPN. Through self-examination, improved editorial practices and controls, and response to constructive criticism, we will be better in the future."

Source: Mandell and Deutsch (2012).

In addition to the forms that prejudice takes, there are also several functions that are fulfilled by communicating prejudice to others (Figure 13.7). The *acceptance function* is reflected when we make prejudiced statements about a group that we do not actually believe in an attempt to gain the approval or acceptance of others. An example of this function is when a fraternity member expresses his hatred for a rival fraternity's members. Upon closer examination, he admits that he does not really know "why" he makes such strong statements, other than to fit in with his own fraternity members.

Sometimes we express prejudices against others in an attempt to protect our ego. This *ego-defensive function* provides us with a scapegoat to blame others for our misfortunes. Not receiving a job offer may result in comments such as, "I was the best candidate for the position. I'm sure they hired a woman or a minority because of the affirmative action laws." This outward expression of prejudice enables us to save face by hinting at unfair treatment.

The *information function* of prejudice is simply to provide us with information to use in guiding our communication with others. Humans are uncomfortable with uncertainty. Unfortunately, we use prejudice as a way to build a knowledge base

> **Acceptance function**
> Expression of prejudice against another in an attempt to gain acceptance.

> **Ego-defensive function**
> Expression of prejudice in an attempt to place the blame or make excuses for our misfortunes on another.

> **Information function**
> Expression of prejudiced attitudes in an attempt to create a foundation for expectations of behavior.

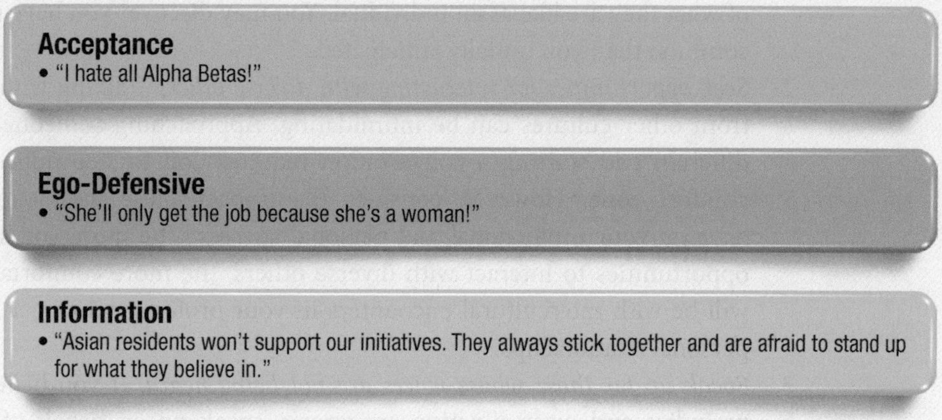

Acceptance
- "I hate all Alpha Betas!"

Ego-Defensive
- "She'll only get the job because she's a woman!"

Information
- "Asian residents won't support our initiatives. They always stick together and are afraid to stand up for what they believe in."

FIGURE 13.7

Functions of prejudice.

about diverse people with whom we have had little or no previous interaction. We jump to conclusions and assume we understand the other person's values and beliefs without ever getting to know him or her. Often the source of information is the media's portrayals of diverse groups.

EFFECTIVE COMMUNICATION WITH DIVERSE OTHERS

Since we know that our attitudes can impact our ability to communicate effectively across cultural differences, how do we manage our tendencies to respond and react? Fortunately, you are already engaging in the first step to enhancing your interactions with diverse others. Examining and understanding the impact of your culture's value system will help us explain the different approaches to communication. While it is sometimes easy to simply believe news stories or media portrayals about diverse groups, avoid the tendency to assume that you have accurate knowledge about a culture and its members based solely on secondhand information. Three strategies that you can incorporate into your communication plan to enhance interactions with diverse others include:

1. *Be open-minded.* While stereotyping is a typical behavior that enables us to form expectations for our interacting with others, be flexible and willing to alter your preconceived notions. Talk to others to gain a full understanding of what they are like as an individual. You may discover you have more in common than you initially anticipated.

2. *Seek opportunities for interacting with diverse others.* Talking with people from other cultures can be intimidating. Approaching someone who is different and starting a conversation requires you to step outside your comfort zone. However, consider the impact these interactions can have on your professional and personal success. The more you seek out opportunities to interact with diverse others, the more comfortable you will be with intercultural encounters in your professional career or your personal relationships.

3. *Speak up for those whose voices are not being heard.* If you believe that prejudice and discrimination are wrong, speak up on behalf of others. This often requires careful thought and consideration, but the benefits of speaking up are important to ensure that others are treated with respect.

CHAPTER SUMMARY

Throughout this chapter, we have discussed the impact of cultural differences on our interactions with others. Rather than focus on viewing our diversity as "strange," our goal is to promote an approach that views differences as only that—differences. Understanding the ways in which our culture has shaped our personal orientation system is essential to managing our responses to differences. While our initial instinct may be to identify diversity based solely on observable characteristics such as race, ethnicity, or sex, the core elements that are most influential in our interactions with and reactions to others are our needs, beliefs, values, and attitudes. Understanding yourself and the cultural influences on your perceptions and communication style is an important first step in enhancing your interactions in your personal, professional, and public lives.

KEY WORDS

Acceptance function Expression of prejudice against another in an attempt to gain acceptance.

Attitudes Learned predispositions to respond favorably or unfavorably toward another person, group, or object.

Beliefs Personal convictions regarding truth or existence.

Co-culture Smaller cultures that comprise a larger culture.

Collectivism Group viewed as most important; valued for dependence and shared responsibility among group members.

Cultural borrowing Process through which a culture identifies benefits of other cultures and decides to adopt similar practices.

Culture Shared perceptions that shape the communication patterns and expectations of a group of people.

Disasters and crises Factors that may force cultures to change.

Discrimination Form of prejudice that involves the practice of denying others their equal rights.

Diversity Distinctions among individuals or groups.

Ego-defensive function Expression of prejudice in an attempt to place the blame or make excuses for our misfortunes on another.

Ethnicity Common heritage or background shared by a group of people.

Explicit learning Direct or formalized instruction about a culture's expectations.

Femininity Cultural value for nurturance, cooperation, and support among members.

High context Cultural orientation that emphasizes indirect communication, typically focusing on nonverbal cues or unspoken messages.

High power distance Rank and status are valued; hierarchies of power and structure influence interactions.

High uncertainty avoidance Lack of tolerance for risk, ambiguity, and change; cultural emphasis on traditions, rules, and laws.

Implicit learning Indirectly acquiring information about a culture, usually via observation.

Individualism The self is viewed as most important; valued for independence and self-reliance.

Information function Expression of prejudiced attitudes in an attempt to create a foundation for expectations of behavior.

Low context Cultural orientation that emphasizes the spoken word and direct verbal expression.

Low power distance Emphasizes equality among members. Mutual respect and shared responsibility are valued.

Low uncertainty avoidance Cultural tolerance for novelty and innovation; risk and change are encouraged.

Masculinity Cultural value for assertiveness, ambition, and achievement.

Monochronic Time as a commodity that must be carefully scheduled; do one thing at a time.

Personal orientation system Composed of our needs, values, attitudes, and beliefs that guide our behaviors and responses.

Polychronic When time is flexible and not viewed as important as relationships.

Prejudice Type of attitude in which we directly express negative reactions toward another individual or group.

Race Inherited biological characteristics such as hair texture and color, eye shape, skin color, and facial structure.

Stereotyping Tendency to make generalizations about groups and assume that all members of that group possess the same characteristics and engage in similar behaviors.

Values One's personal philosophy that guides actions and behaviors; assist us in evaluating ethical situations.

Verbal abuse Process of exchanging negative verbal comments that are intended to be insulting or demeaning.

REFERENCES

Hall, E. T. (1976). *Beyond culture.* Garden City, NY: Anchor.

Hofstede, G. (1980, Summer). Motivation, leadership, and organizations: Do American theories apply abroad? *Organizational Dynamics*, pp. 42–63.

Klopf, D. (1995). *Intercultural encounters: The fundamentals of intercultural communication.* Englewood, CO: Morton Publishing.

Kluckhohn, C., & Strodbeck, F. (1961). *Variations in value orientations.* Evanston, IL: Row, Peterson.

Li, A. (2012, February 12). Self-segregation alive and well on the OU campus. *Athens News.* Retrieved April 6, 2014, from www.athensnews.com/ohio/article-36073-self-segregation-alive-and-well-on-the-ou-campus.html.

Mandell, N., & Deutsch, K. (2012, February 21). Racist headline about Jeremy Lin and the Knicks prompts quick apology from ESPN. *New York Daily News.* Retrieved from www.nydailynews.com.

CHAPTER 14

Mediated Communication:
The Channel Matters

Chapter Objectives

After reading this chapter, you should be able to:
- Define mediated communication
- Distinguish between mass and social media
- Identify strategies for effective communication via mediated channels
- Describe reasons for using mass media and social media
- Discuss the impact of media on relationships
- Identify strategies for improving media use

PERSONAL: Your friend tells you about a conflict he recently had with his romantic partner. The conflict is the result of a text message. Your friend told his partner that he wanted to go to the movies this weekend. His partner replied, "Yeah, right, that will totally happen." Your friend was confused and hurt when after the weekend was over, he and his partner never went to the movies. He defends his actions to you and indicates that he was very explicit in what he wanted to happen and felt unclear about why his partner would agree to a movie then never take him. How did the text message cause confusion on the part of both individuals?

PROFESSIONAL: At work, you have been asked to be part of a team that includes members from your home office and people from an office overseas. Because of clear geographical differences, in order to have face-to-face communication, the team decides to use Skype for meetings. All meetings are scheduled via email and you need to prepare for the meeting scheduled for next week. During your preparations, what should you consider when using an online system for communication?

PUBLIC: You have recently graduated from college and during your transition to adult life, you begin to review your social media profiles on Facebook, Twitter, and Instagram. You realize that some of the information on your profile might not be appropriate for an employer to see. After all, you want to project a professional image. What kinds of information should you delete from your profile?

CHAPTER OVERVIEW

As the opening examples illustrate, you spend a large portion of your day surrounded by or using mediated communication. It can be useful to accomplish daily tasks and maintain your social life. In fact, this form of communication might be something you rely on so heavily that you cannot imagine living without it. In this chapter, you learn about the various mediated sources we use and consume daily. Specifically, we address the many forms of mediated channels of communication that are available to us, and why we choose to use mediated forms of communication. We also highlight the unique challenges of mediated communication and identify tips to improve and enhance your usage.

MEDIATED COMMUNICATION DEFINED

You wake up in the morning to your favorite song, which you downloaded from the Internet. As your day begins, you catch up on the news on television then listen to sports talk radio in the car as you drive to work. During the day, you watch

Americans' daily media consumption, 2013 versus 2012, in hours. Source: Copyright © by Marketing Charts. Reprinted by permission.

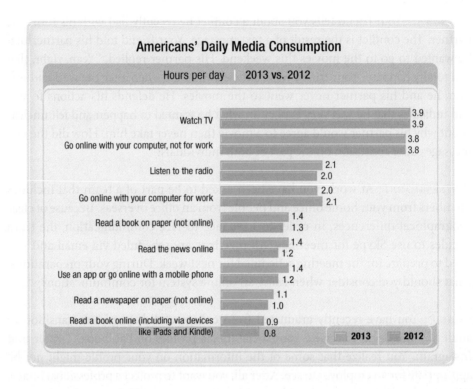

Americans' Daily Media Consumption

| Hours per day | 2013 vs. 2012 |

	2013	2012
Watch TV	3.9	3.9
Go online with your computer, not for work	3.8	3.8
Listen to the radio	2.1	2.0
Go online with your computer for work	2.0	2.1
Read a book on paper (not online)	1.4	1.3
Read the news online	1.4	1.2
Use an app or go online with a mobile phone	1.4	1.2
Read a newspaper on paper (not online)	1.1	1.0
Read a book online (including via devices like iPads and Kindle)	0.9	0.8

YouTube videos, read magazines, and research recipes for dinner. In the evening, you send emails to your family, catch up with a long-distance romantic partner via FaceTime, and spend a few moments reviewing your favorite blog. As a society, we are inundated with mediated forms of communication. Throughout the day, we encounter a wide variety of media. As the chart in Figure 14.1 shows, in 2013 Americans spent over half their day engaged with some form of media.

Not only are you bombarded with mediated forms of communication, but the messages communicated via these channels impact you in a variety of ways. Worsnop (1989) identifies several ways in which media impacts our lives. Specifically, media:

1. Helps us understand the workings of our immediate world. It gives us information about current events, locally, nationally, and internationally.
2. Serves as a source of stories. Media outlets serve as the authors of the stories we consume.
3. Requires us to learn and use critical thinking skills. When turning to the media for information, we should be examining what we consume for accuracy.
4. Defines how we communicate. Media can shape our communication with others by influencing the channels we use for communication and the topics of our conversations.

How much time do you spend online each day?

© Spectral-Design/Shutterstock.com

5. Helps us (mis)understand ourselves and others. It serves as a tool for helping us learn more about who we are and who we are not.

6. Explains how things work. Media can provide us with useful insights about the processes of events and gather explanations of how happenings occur.

7. Brings us pleasure. We can turn to media to view videos and articles that bring us joy or help us escape from the mundane routine of life.

Considering the amount of time we spend with media and the multiple types of information and impact it can have on us, it seems crucial to understand the role it plays in our lives. The scope of media and the constant consumption of mediated messages can affect nearly every aspect of our lives.

Mediated communication involves individuals utilizing technology as a channel of delivery for a message. Mediated forms of communication include cell phone calls, texts, and emails. Recall from Chapter 1 that mediated communication includes both *mass media* and *social media*. When you watch television and listen to commercials, you are a receiver of mass media communication. "Mass" refers to the large audience that receives the message, and "media" refers to the technological channels used to communicate the message. *Mass media* utilizes technology to send messages to a large number of people. *Social media* are websites used to create an online identity and may include sites such as Facebook or Instagram that build communities of people.

Mediated communication
Utilizing technology as the channel of delivery.

Mass media
Utilizing technology to send messages to masses of people with the intent to influence behaviors.

Social media
Websites that allow for individuals to create a profile to build communities.

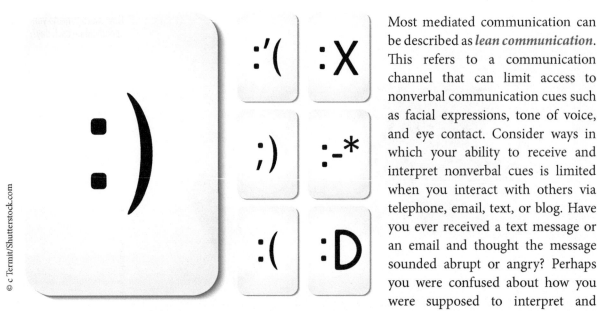

Do you use emoticons in your text messages?

➤ **Lean communication** Communication channels that reduce access to nonverbal communication, such as facial expressions, touch, and eye contact.

Most mediated communication can be described as *lean communication*. This refers to a communication channel that can limit access to nonverbal communication cues such as facial expressions, tone of voice, and eye contact. Consider ways in which your ability to receive and interpret nonverbal cues is limited when you interact with others via telephone, email, text, or blog. Have you ever received a text message or an email and thought the message sounded abrupt or angry? Perhaps you were confused about how you were supposed to interpret and respond to the message. Nonverbal communication cues are valuable tools that assist us in understanding the intended meaning behind the message. We depend on both nonverbal and verbal communication in order to understand the intended meaning behind the message, as both dimensions of communication provide insight into how the message is interpreted. Some mediated channels of communication—for example, email or text messaging—reduce access to this nonverbal information. You may use emoticons (such as a smiley face) or acronyms (such as LOL) to help the receiver of the message understand the ways in which the message should be interpreted; however, it can still be difficult to interpret the message accurately.

DISTINGUISHING TYPES OF MEDIATED COMMUNICATION

At its most basic level, mediated communication involves the use of technology, such as a computer to send an email or a cell phone to call or text someone. However, these are not the only mediated forms of communication. Radio, television, magazines, billboards, and websites all provide us with channels to share messages with others. Communication scholars focus on specific types of mediated communication: mass media and social media. Mass media utilizes technology to send messages to a large number of people. In Table 14.1 you can see there are many types of mass media. Mass media can be useful in terms of shaping ideas, sharing culture, and influencing behaviors. For example, do you remember television shows such as *Friends* and *Jersey Shore*? Each of these shows was popular at one point in time, and both created social impact. For example, Rachel, a character on *Friends*, had a very popular hairstyle that influenced a number of women to ask their hairstylists for "The Rachel." Characters on *Jersey Shore* had a distinct verbal style and vocabulary. They wore glittery t-shirts designed by Ed Hardy and described not-so-attractive women as "grenades." These t-shirts soon became embraced by our society and their description of unfortunate women became a popular phrase.

TABLE 14.1

Types of Mediated Communication

Channel	Examples
Mediated communication	Email, cell phone calls, and texts
Mass media communication	Radio, newspaper, billboards, television, news magazines, Internet
Social media communication	Collaborative projects (e.g., Wikipedia), blogs, content communities (e.g., YouTube), social networking sites (e.g., Facebook), virtual game worlds (e.g., World of Warcraft), and virtual social worlds (e.g., Second Life)

Boyd and Ellison (2008) describe ***social media*** as websites that individuals use to create or portray profiles to a list of users with whom they interact. According to Kaplan and Haenlein (2010) there are a number of types of social media, and examples of these are included in Table 14.1. Each of these social media has a unique focus. ***Collaborative projects*** focus on co-creating information with other individuals. These would include websites such as Wikipedia where individuals can add or delete information. ***Blogs*** are often more personal in nature and can be considered an online journal. They are typically written from a one-person perspective and shed light on any number of topics. Websites that aim to build both personal and professional connections with others are called ***social networking***. Examples of social networking sites include Facebook, Instagram, and LinkedIn. ***Virtual game worlds*** and

> **Collaborative projects**
> Focus on co-creating information with other individuals.

> **Social networking**
> Sites that aim to build both personal and professional connections with other individuals.

> **Virtual game worlds**
> Online games that include a created reality and encourage the following of rules to play a game.

> Virtual game worlds create fictional lives for players.

© Barone Firenze/Shutterstock.com

Virtual social worlds Provide a space for individuals to create another life and interact with others and include games such as Second Life.

virtual social worlds create fictional lives. Game worlds focus on players following the rules of a game and include games such as *World of Warcraft*. Social worlds provide a space for individuals to create another life and interact with others and include games such as *Second Life*. While participating in virtual game worlds, people wear headsets that allow for verbal interaction with their opponents. Virtual social worlds allow for interaction in the game as characters can interact.

Mediated forms of communication—be it using a phone, playing a game online, or watching your favorite television show—are prevalent in our daily lives. Each form of mediated communication has unique qualities. We first explore mass media communication and then turn our attention to social media. Included in our social media discussion is an examination of texting, calling, and emailing. While distinct from social media, texting, calling, and emailing do aid in relationship initiation, maintenance, and termination. As a result, these channels of communication share many of the same properties as social media.

MASS MEDIA IN OUR LIVES

Mass media is noteworthy because you have choices and decide what you listen to and watch. It can be used as a tool to influence our interactions with others. A popular television show from 1998 until 2003 was *Dawson's Creek*. Actors on the show included James Van Der Beek and Katie Holmes, and the plot focused on their lives as teenagers. It was a favorite show of one of the authors, and she often watched it with her friends. The next day at school she and her friends would discuss the current week's episode. When other friends would join the group, they were often told the topic and asked to wait until they were finished discussing the show before starting a new topic of conversation. In this way, the television impacted the flow of interaction. It informed the topic of conversation (the topic was the current episode) and who could participate in the discussion (only those who had watched the episode).

Many times we have a choice about what media we consume (e.g., listening to the television at your home or the radio in your car); however, not all mass media consumption is by choice. The billboards you pass while driving are considered mass media, and the content shared on these signs is beyond your control. However, recall the perception process. You do not take in and comprehend every message to which you are exposed; rather, we make careful decisions about what we will be able to recall based on certain criteria. The same can be said of the decision-making process behind mass media consumption. You make careful decisions about the media you put into your life.

Selecting Media Sources

Suppose you have a favorite television show you never miss. You and your friends may discuss the characters or storyline. Perhaps you find yourselves "taking sides" and having emotional reactions to the characters' experiences (called *parasocial interactions*, an idea that is discussed later in the chapter). Additionally, you may have websites that you frequently visit. For example, for the latest news, you may only check *www.cnn.com*. Your decision to select specific media is often based on the utility of the information, the relevance of the message, or how similar the message is to your existing attitudes, beliefs, and values. Thus, you focus on mass media messages that hold value for you. Once you believe that the message is either helpful or has the potential to be of benefit in the future, you are likely to select it.

One theoretical lens used to understand how individuals use media is the *Uses and Gratifications Theory*. The uses and gratifications approach argues that media are strategically selected in order to meet our personal needs. This theory seeks to understand the relationship individuals have with the media. While it might seem odd to think of yourself as in a relationship with media, you use the media to fulfill personal needs and, in doing so, you are gratified or get something out of it. When selecting media, we may use it before we have a need for information, persuasion, education, or entertainment. Media can also be selected to meet cognitive needs, affective needs, personal integrative needs, social integrative needs, and/or entertainment needs (Katz, Blumler, & Gurevitch, 1974). Each of these needs is described in Table 14.2. Suppose you have had a bad day at work, then you remember that your favorite television show airs that night. Once at home, you eagerly sit in front of the television as your show starts. For the next hour it is as if nothing else matters. You selected a favorite show and are now using it to get away from the bad day you had.

Uses and Gratifications Theory focuses on the audience—that is, it seeks to comprehend why individuals use media in an effort to explain the media choices individuals make and the consequences experienced. The Gratifications Sought and Obtained Scale highlighted in Figure 14.2 (Palmgreen, Weener, & Rayburn, 1980) helps to explain further why people use media and what needs the media fulfills for them.

> **Parasocial interaction**
> Your perceptions of connections to individuals in the media.

> **Uses and Gratifications Theory**
> Theoretical lens through which relationships individuals have with media is understood.

TABLE 14.2

Needs Satisfied by the Media (Hamilton, 1998)

Need	Description	Example
Cognitive	Seeks information or knowledge	View the nightly news on television to gather information about the world in which you live
Affective	Seeks emotional reassurance, positive feelings	Watch sitcoms such as *How I Met Your Mother* because the show contains feel-good messages
Personal integrative	Seeks self-esteem support	Read a book about popular interviewing techniques and ways to prepare for an upcoming interview
Social integrative	Seeks interaction with others	Log on to your favorite gaming website because it allows you to connect with others
Entertainment	Seeks fun and excitement	Meet with friends on a weekly basis to watch *Real Housewives of New Jersey* because you perceive the television show to be full of drama

FIGURE 14.2

The Gratifications Sought and Obtained Scale.
Source: Philip Palmgreen, Lawrence A. Wenner, J.D. Rayburn, *Communication Research, Volume 7, Issue 2,* April 1980, pp 161-192, Copyright © 1980 by SAGE Publications. Reprinted by permission of SAGE Publications.

This scale has been used to understand why people watch TV news. Below are 15 reasons people have given. As you read each one, please indicate how much it applies to you. If the reason <u>very definitely applies to you, give it a 5</u>; if it <u>does not apply at all, give it a 1</u>. If it applies somewhere in between, give it a 2, 3, or 4 depending on how much.

1. I watch TV news to keep up with current issues and events. _____
2. I watch TV news so I won't be surprised by higher prices and things like that. _____
3. I watch TV news because you can trust the information they give you. _____
4. I watch TV news to find out what kind of job our government officials are doing. _____
5. I watch TV news to help me make up my mind about the important issues of the day. _____
6. I watch TV news to find out about issues affecting people like myself. _____
7. I watch TV news because it's often entertaining. _____
8. I watch TV news because it's often dramatic. _____
9. I watch TV news because it's often exciting. _____
10. I watch TV news to support my own viewpoints to other people. _____
11. I watch TV news so I can pass the information on to other people. _____
12. I watch TV news to give me interesting things to talk about. _____
13. I watch TV news because the newscasters give a human quality to the news. _____
14. I watch TV news to compare my own ideas to what the commentators say. _____
15. I watch TV news because the reporters are like people I know. _____

Philip Palmgreen, Lawrence A. Wenner, J.D. Rayburn, *Communication Research, Volume 7, Issue 2,* April 1980, pp 161-192, Copyright © 1980 by SAGE Publications. Reprinted by permission of SAGE Publications.

The Gratifications Sought and Obtained Scale assesses several key ideas. The first three questions pertain to general *information-seeking* or the extent to which you attempt to gather information about happenings in the world. Questions 4–6 seek to address your *decisional utility*, or the extent to which media are used to gain information and make informed decisions. Questions 7, 8, and 9 focus on *entertainment* or the extent to which you find media to be a source of pleasurable distraction. Questions 10–12 seek to understand your *interpersonal utility*. That is, do you perceive media to be a source of useful information that can be used in your relationships with other people? The final questions address **parasocial interaction**. These questions assess your perceived interpersonal or relational connections with individuals in the media. Have you ever heard a news report that details someone stalking a celebrity? For the person doing the stalking, in his or her mind a relationship is present with the famous person; the two individuals are connected. This instrument serves as one way to address the various functions media fulfills. By using media, we gather information to discuss with others. This information can assist us in building relationships or serving as a starting place for potentially difficult conversations.

Retention of Media Info

Given that we are inundated with messages, recalling everything that we've been exposed to on a daily basis would be a daunting task. It would be nearly impossible to remember every message. Humans are limited-capacity processors. This refers to the fact that we can only retain so much information. When studying for a test, for example, have you ever thought there is no possible way you will be able to take in any additional information? It is almost as if your brain is "full." To retain or recall information, we need to perceive the information to have utility. If the information is viewed as being helpful, we can recall it. We also remember information if it is novel or new. When we say to ourselves, "Wow, that is interesting" or "Hmmm, I had no idea," it is likely information that we will be able to recall later. In our interactions with others, you have likely expressed statements such as "Guess what I heard today on television…?" Media informs our discussions and gives us new topics of conversation. This information is helpful for our personal, professional, and public lives. If, for example, you have ever been on a job interview and created a list of topics to discuss as you prepared for the meeting, you may have used something that you heard from mass media.

FUNCTIONS OF MASS MEDIA

The media fulfills a variety of functions. We look to mass media as a source of information, in addition to fulfilling the needs previously discussed. Katz et al. (1974) argues that we use media "to match one's wits against others, to get information and

Information-seeking
Extent to which you attempt to gather information about happenings in the world.

Decisional utility
Extent media is used to gain information and make an informed decision.

Entertainment
Extent to which you find media to be a source of pleasurable distraction.

Interpersonal utility
Extent to which media is perceived to be a source of useful information that can be used in your relationship.

advice for daily living, to provide a framework for one's day, to prepare oneself culturally for the demands of upward mobility, or to be reassured about the dignity and usefulness of one's role" (p. 20). Mass media provides insight on a variety of topics. From gathering information about current events to understanding how families communicate, we often use mass media to gather information about the world in which we live that we then use to help us form ideas.

Information Gathering and Idea Formation

Consider the following example. Your friend encourages you to purchase a new car. You are open to suggestions, and your friend is eager to offer advice. She encourages you to buy a Ford. Since you have never driven a Ford, you have no previous knowledge about the company or its vehicles. You begin researching the Ford your friend wants you to purchase. Information is gathered from commercials, the Internet, radio, and television, and you notice that with every mass media message you take in, each has a different opinion of the product. From all of these messages, you begin to form an opinion about the product.

Mass-mediated messages can be a valuable resource for gathering information about the world in which we live. Turning on the television or surfing the Internet for insights about current events is easy. In fact, the media are often the primary source of information when we are gathering information, deciding on purchases, researching information on lawmakers and policies, and seeking entertainment. However, during this consumption, there are some key ideas to consider. According to the Center for Media Literacy (n.d.), all media have five core concepts that individuals should consider that center around authorship, format, audience, content, and purpose (Figure 14.3). First, authorship refers to the idea that all media messages are constructed, created, or produced by someone or some entity. It is important to note who created it as those individuals likely have a vested interest in it. Each person and the company he or she represents have allegiances, alliances, and values that impact what messages are conveyed. Additionally, all messages are created in a particular format, such as advertisements in a magazine, billboards on the highway, or banners that appear on a Web page. These messages are produced for an intended audience. A company, for example, may produce an advertisement for a magazine and the targeted audience is the consumer of the magazine. It is important to note that different people experience the same message differently. As discussed in Chapter 2, our perception may cause each of us to react differently to the same message. Thus, even if we are exposed to the same media, each of us may interpret the messages in very distinct ways. You and your friend could be exposed to the same commercial yet create different impressions of the same content. The content used in the media is influenced by the audience who is being targeted and

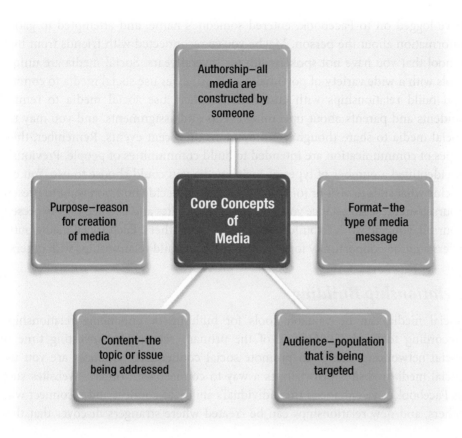

FIGURE 14.3

Core concepts of media.

Authorship–all media are constructed by someone

Purpose–reason for creation of media

Core Concepts of Media

Format–the type of media message

Content–the topic or issue being addressed

Audience–population that is being targeted

includes particular language or visuals that are used to grab the viewer's attention and it is important to pay attention to these cues. Finally, purpose refers to the idea that much of mass media is produced for the purposes of gaining attention, power, or profit. These motivations impact how a message is created. It is important to be a thoughtful consumer of mass media and check facts with multiple sources.

Hopefully by now you realize that mass media serves a significant purpose in our lives. It has a noteworthy impact on our beliefs, it informs our language system, and it ultimately impacts our interactions with others. Other forms of media impact and influence our knowledge and interactions too. We now turn our attention to social media.

SOCIAL MEDIA

Chances are either you or someone you know has used social media to either collect information about someone else or to connect with others. Perhaps you have logged on to Facebook, entered someone's name, and attempted to gather information about the person. Maybe you've reconnected with friends from high school that you have not spoken with for several years. Social media are unique tools with a wide variety of potential uses. Businesses use social media to connect and build relationships with customers, teachers use social media to remind students and parents about upcoming events and assignments, and you may use social media to share thoughts and opinions on recent events. Remember, these types of communication are intended to build communities of people. Previously, we identified a number of types of social media you could choose to use. You can decide what sites to visit or join, and you can also decide how you want to present yourself on these sites. Once you have joined these sites and decided how to present yourself, you will work to build relationships with others. Each social media outlet offers a unique opportunity for us to connect and build relationships with others.

Relationship Building

Social media can be valuable tools for building or enhancing relationships. According to boyd (2006), one of the primary reasons for investing time in social networking sites is to promote social connections. Chances are you use social media websites primarily as a way to connect with others. Websites such as Facebook have enhanced the individual's ability to connect and reconnect with others, and new relationships can be created where strangers discover that they

Websites such as Facebook have helped people (re)connect with others.

© Twin Design/Shutterstock.com

share a common interest or activity. Quan-Haase and Young (2010) utilized Uses and Gratifications Theory to understand the gratifications individuals experienced when using Facebook versus instant messaging. They found that individuals perceived using Facebook as fun and a shared social activity. That is, if a friend suggested using Facebook, participants in the study were likely to listen to their friends and join the social networking site. Additionally, they found that college students view Facebook as an entertaining networking opportunity. Thus, your social networks play an important role in the types of social media you choose to use, and, because of their influence on your choices, you could gain a larger social network because you may connect with individuals you had not previously connected. While the study above addressed Facebook, there are many different types of social networking sites individuals can choose from when interacting with others. Sites such as Instagram, LinkedIn, and Pinterest are also social networking sites individuals can use to connect with others. According to boyd (2008), there are benefits in using social networking sites. These benefits include:

1. Outlets or opportunities for involvement with the community;
2. Enhancement and growth of individual creativity through sharing of art or music;
3. Growing or developing ideas from the creation of blogs, podcasts, or videos;
4. Expansion of one's online connections; and
5. Fostering of one's individual identity and unique social skills.

While social media can promote the creation of relationships, it too can diminish the quality of a relationship. Consider the following example posted on the website *www.thinkbeforeyousend.com*:

> "My wife was forwarding an e-mail from her father. She had made sarcastic comments about a friend in her email, and prior to forwarding the email, forgot to delete the sarcastic comments. That friend was one of the people who received the forwarded message. This situation seriously strained the friendship."

This example illustrates the concept addressed in Chapter 1: communication cannot be reversed. While this concept is true of all communication, this idea becomes particularly salient to mediated communication because the message is written and recorded. Often the time and date of the message accompany it for later reference. Emails, text messages, or social media posts can be revisited and reread and used as evidence in conversations. Thus, it proves more difficult to deny or change communication and it could, as a result, hurt relationships.

Networking and Social Movement

Two particularly interesting aspects of social media are its networking and social movement abilities. First, online communities such as LinkedIn and Facebook provide opportunities to network with others. Organizations and companies may turn to social media sites such as LinkedIn when recruiting new employees. People can search sites and locate reputable talent to assist them in projects. Companies can promote their services and build their identities. These online relationships can supplement face-to-face relationships or serve as the primary medium of connection.

Additionally, social media sites can be used as a way to create a social movement. Unze (2010) describes how a 17-year-old boy used Facebook as a way to gather support for a skate park proposal. The plan needed to be approved by the city council. The teen created a Facebook profile describing the cause so users could follow and "like" the information. As a result of the Facebook support generated, the teen had evidence of the impact of the project and funding was eventually allotted for the park. Due to the widespread popularity of social media sites, many celebrities and political candidates have turned to Facebook, Twitter, and Instagram to share their opinions and messages. Consider, for example, President Barack Obama's use of social networking websites during the 2008 election. He tried to connect with voters by turning to websites such as Facebook and Myspace. Previous to this election, this strategy had been less utilized.

Social media sites can be used as a way to create social movement.

© PiXXart/Shutterstock.com

Social media efforts connect individuals and companies alike. Moreover, they can be used strategically as a means of persuasive communication and to gather support for incentives. These powerful tools should be used with caution, however. Social media users should be mindful of what types of information they are disclosing. In fact, websites are dedicated to cautioning people about the uses of social media. For example, Microsoft cautions users to be careful when clicking on links, mindful of whom you allow to be your friend, and selective in deciding what social media websites you use.

ONLINE IDENTITIES

It is important to keep in mind that when we use social media, we often first create an online identity or person—a public image of ourselves that we share with others. One key concern for communication scholars investigating mediated forms of communication is that of identity or *impression formation*. Scholars refer to the sense-making of others' actions and disposition as impression formation. Typically, through our interactions with others, we form a general impression or idea about the other person's character or qualities and personality (Hancock & Dunham, 2001). For example, after meeting and interacting with someone for the first time, you may think to yourself, "He seemed polite," "I really liked her clothing," or "They seemed a little uncomfortable." All of these are possible impressions that we form of others and that others form of us. Impression formation is a two-way street with us forming impressions of others and others forming impressions of us. If everything you do sends a message, it is important to consider the impressions created by words and photos that are posted online.

Impression formation
Sense-making of others' actions and disposition.

Social media profiles enable us to share a variety of information. All of this information is "up for interpretation" by the reader. Impressions are formed based on the information you choose to share. Perhaps you post the lyrics from a country music song and a coworker then invites you to attend a country music concert with her. In reality, you do not enjoy country music, you just appreciated the message behind the lyrics. In this example, we see then that the way you meant to send information, liking a song for meaning, can be interpreted differently, that you actually enjoy country music.

Hancock and Dunham (2001) found that after viewing a person's profile with whom you have no relational history, judgments made are more intense than if the people had met and communicated face-to-face. That is, interacting with a person's online persona (via their profile information) left viewers with stronger attributions and perceptions of the individual. Online representations often fail to incorporate a person's complete or true identity. Because of this, individuals who view your profile can make exaggerated explanations about your personal qualities. They may, for example, stereotype you based on some aspect of your persona. If you disclose online that you enjoy country music, a reader may assume that you are a conservative person too. Thus, individuals should use caution in online forums and work to manage the impressions they can elicit in others.

Self-Presentation and Decision Making

Perhaps one of the most interesting aspects of social media is the fact that you are in control of the information that you share with others. You decide what material you disclose to others and what information you choose to keep private. Individuals often make careful decisions about what they post for others to see or read. These decisions are called *self-presentation* strategies. As mentioned in Chapter 2, Goffman (1959) describes self-presentation as impression management. Self-presentation strategies are the choices about content (e.g., photos, quotes, or other demographic information) that we make when sharing with others. These choices guide the creation of the online personal profile. Individuals make a conscious effort to control how their audience perceives them. This effort becomes especially heightened in online mediums. In an online format, images are often carefully selected and perhaps even edited to convey physically attractive qualities. Quotes and phrases are chosen to reflect a person's attitudes, and friendships are created and maintained by sharing information about interests and hobbies.

Self-presentation Choices about content (photos, quotes, information, etc.) that individuals make when crafting an online profile.

© Michael Tureski/Icon SMI/Corbis

Unfortunately, the anonymity of our online presence results in some instances of deception and dishonesty. The MTV television show *Catfish* follows individuals that have built relationships online. People meet and interact online without physically meeting one another, then television crews share their stories as they meet for the first time. The most notable aspect of the show is that oftentimes the individuals have been talking to a fake persona. Consider, for example, former University of Notre Dame linebacker Manti Te'o. Te'o, who was drafted to play in the National Football League in 2013, was duped into believing a woman he was communicating with and dating online was a real person. The person he thought he was communicating with, however, didn't exist. In fact, an acquaintance of Te'o's admitted to creating the fake profile. When using mediated forms of interaction and building online relationships, it is possible to experience deception, that the creator of the profile may have strategically altered information or photos.

What do you have on your Facebook page?

© dolphfyn/Shutterstock.com

While the source or creator of a profile can control the content posted on social media sites, when it is viewed by others, the responses they may acquire cannot be controlled. While you may be able to post a specific photo, you are not able to control how people will perceive that post and respond to it. In fact, individuals can perceive, react, and respond to the same post in a variety of ways. Determining how to respond to others' social media presence is an important component in the decision-making process. Remember that using social media is not just about creating responsible profiles, but it is also deciding how to respond to others' profiles. Shea (1995) crafted rules of etiquette for the Internet to provide guidelines for appropriate online interactions. Her book *Netiquette* summarizes some best practices for Internet use:

Rule 1: Remember that there is a human component. There is a real person on the other side of the social network site. Use caution and treat others as you would prefer to be treated.

Rule 2: Adhere to the same standards of behavior online that you follow in real life. Most people tend to follow laws and rules. Use an ethical compass to guide your behaviors.

Rule 3: Know where you are in cyberspace. Much like the public speaking process, which calls for audience analysis, you too should analyze a website before you begin posting. Standards of conduct vary from website to website.

Rule 4: Respect other people's time. Your message is important, but so too is the reader's time. Make sure to create efficient and effective communication.

Rule 5: Make yourself look good online. The content and quality of your message will be judged. Take care in the tone, spelling, and grammar of your message.

Rule 6: Share your expertise. If you know the answer to another's question, offer your insights.

Rule 7: Help keep flame wars under control. Flaming occurs online when individuals attack one another or offer insults. When individuals "flame," they are freely sharing emotions and not "pulling any punches." While flame wars can be entertaining initially, they can lose value quickly.

Rule 8: Respect others' privacy. It seems likely that you would not invade someone else's space by examining the contents of a man's wallet or a woman's purse. The same should be true of someone's email.

Rule 9: Do not abuse your power. If you have access to another's private information, respect the person and do not read materials.

Rule 10: Forgive others' mistakes. All users start somewhere. A lack of experience on websites or blogs could contribute to errors. Give others a break.

Because mediated communication appears to be only increasing in popularity, individuals need to use caution when determining how to convey themselves in online settings. Remember, because you cannot control the reader's perceptions, you should take care to create a thoughtful profile. Esterline (2009) offers guidelines to create positive personal, professional, and public social media identities. These tips can be used when creating your online identity, specifically when creating a profile online and subsequently updating the profile information.

Tip 1: Status updates. Do not update your status with information an employer may not want to know.

Tip 2: Photos. Post photos with caution. Avoid posting photos that compromise your image.

Tip 3: Groups and applications. Avoid joining groups, fan pages, and applications that are not relevant to your field.

As you can see from the above list, a number of considerations should be taken when creating an online profile. Online personas should reflect carefully thought-out and planned communication. In many instances the positive connections you form online can "spill over" or be continued in face-to-face relationships. For example, you may post a status or an article that other people enjoy reading and can discuss in face-to-face interactions.

THE IMPACT OF SOCIAL MEDIA ON FACE-TO-FACE RELATIONSHIPS

Given the nature and prevalence of social media, it makes sense that it would impact your face-to-face relationships. You can probably recall a time when social media helped you learn information about someone that caused you to feel emotionally close to the person. Perhaps you discovered new information that you had not known previously. Just as social media may be useful in forming relationships, it may also be helpful in maintaining existing relationships and promoting feelings of closeness and relational satisfaction. However, some also indicate that social media can be used as a replacement for face-to-face interactions and contribute negatively to relationships.

Lickerman (2010) argues that the overuse of social media may serve to isolate a person. Data suggests that we spend approximately 16 minutes out of every hour engaged in online social media sites (Finn, 2013). This isolation takes time away from face-to-face interactions and may diminish the quality of a relationship. The author argues for using a balance of mediated and face-to-face communication. Thus, not all interactions should occur on social media channels. Face-to-face communication does allow for important elements of nonverbal communication, such as the use of touch, that social media does not allow. Consider, for example, asking your relationship partner to marry you. You may determine that face-to-

What elements of nonverbal communication do you get from face-to-face interaction that social media does not allow?

© Rob Marmion/Shutterstock.com

face communication is better for this communicative exchange because it allows you to hear your partner's response.

Kearsley (1998) recommends the following rules for communicating via mediated channels. These recommendations will likely be useful when communicating professionally, personally, and publicly. These tips are useful when sending email communications, building websites, or using chat functions, all of which are part of the relationship-building function of social media sites. First, being brief is likely best. All messages, files, and photos should have focus. For example, do you have a friend that updates his or her Facebook status multiple times a day? What impression does that create in your mind? Over-posting could be perceived negatively. It could make someone think that you do not have anything better to do with your time or that you are scattered and cannot decide on one status you like. Also, remember these are public domains. Think carefully about what you write. If, for example, in an email you indicated to a coworker that you do not like a policy that your boss is enforcing and your coworker forwards the message to your boss, this communicative act cannot be undone. Always assume that anything you post could be made public. Additionally, remember to be kind. There is no need to make social network sites a negative place where people attack one another. Presenting different opinions and discussing issues is very different from attacking someone's character and competence. Finally, you should provide structure in your messages. When you send an email, for example, take a moment to create a subject line or description that your receiver will not only understand but that will help orient him or her to the purpose/context of the information.

Hopefully, throughout this chapter, you have been thinking about your own social media use. Social media can be a helpful tool in building relationships and it provides us with a unique method of communication with its own strengths and weaknesses. Much like mass media, we get to make decisions regarding our social media use. Because we are in control of the content, it is important to select content that is representative of us as individuals and creates a positive impression on our receivers.

CHAPTER SUMMARY

Mass media and social media provide us with opportunities for including information-gathering, entertainment, and relationship creation and maintenance. There are many strategies for successfully using mass and social media in your personal, professional, and public lives such as using caution with photos and posts. Ultimately, you need to make careful decisions about the types of media you consume. Each mass media outlet comes with its own biases and viewpoints. It is important to consider these when determining how to use the messages you receive. Social media, in all its forms, can contribute to relationships. It allows us to initiate contact to build relationships, maintain the status of those relationships, and diminish relationships and quality. Ultimately, we need to remember to be cautious in our online personas, as communication in this format can leave a lasting record. Remember, once something is posted, it cannot be undone.

KEY WORDS

Blog Online journal.

Collaborative projects Focus on co-creating information with other individuals.

Decisional utility Extent media is used to gain information and make an informed decision.

Entertainment Extent to which you find media to be a source of pleasurable distraction.

Impression formation Sense-making of others' actions and disposition.

Information-seeking Extent to which you attempt to gather information about happenings in the world.

Interpersonal utility Extent to which media is perceived to be a source of useful information that can be used in your relationship.

Lean communication Communication channels that reduce access to nonverbal communication, such as facial expressions, touch, and eye contact.

Mass media Utilizing technology to send messages to masses of people with the intent to influence behaviors.

Mediated communication Utilizing technology as the channel of delivery.

Parasocial interaction Your perceptions of connections to individuals in the media.

Self-presentation Choices about content (photos, quotes, information, etc.) that individuals make when crafting an online profile.

Social media Websites that allow for individuals to create a profile to build communities.

Social networking Sites that aim to build both personal and professional connections with other individuals.

Uses and Gratifications Theory Theoretical lens through which relationships individuals have with media is understood.

Virtual game worlds Online games that include a created reality and encourage the following of rules to play a game.

Virtual social worlds Provide a space for individuals to create another life and interact with others and include games such as Second Life.

REFERENCES

boyd, d. m. (2006, December). Friends, Friendsters, and MySpace top 8: Writing community into being on social network sites. *First Monday*. Retrieved from http://131.193.153.231/www/issues/issue11_12/boyd/index.html.

boyd, d. m. (2008). *Taken out of context: American teen sociality in networked publics.* Retrieved from www.danah.org/papers/TakenOutOfContext.pdf.

boyd, d. m., & Ellison, N. B. (2008). Social network sites: Definition, history, and scholarship. *Journal of Computer-Mediated Communication, 13*, 210–230.

Center for Media Literacy. (n.d.). *CML's five key questions and core concepts of media literacy for deconstruction.* Retrieved from www.medialit.org.

Esterline, R. M. (2009). *8 tips to building and maintaining a professional online image.* Retrieved from http://bizzywomen.com/2009/8-tips-to-building-and-maintaining-a-professional-online-image/.

Finn, G. (2013, April). *Study: 27% of time online in the U.S. is spent on social networking.* Retrieved from http://marketingland.com/study-27-of-time-online-in-the-us-is-spent-on-social-networking-40269.

Goffman, E. (1959). *The presentation of self in everyday life.* New York: Doubleday.

Hamilton, N. T. (1998). Uses and gratifications. *Theories of Persuasive Communication and Consumer Decision Making.* Retrieved from http://www.ciadvertising.org/studies/student/98_fall/theory/hamilton/leckenby/theory/elements.htm.

Hancock, J., & Dunham, P. (2001). Impression formation in computer-mediated communication revisited: An analysis of the breadth and intensity of impressions. *Communication Research, 28*, 325–347.

Kaplan, A. M., & Haenlein, M. (2010). Users of the world unite!: The challenges and opportunities of social media. *Business Horizons, 53*, 59–58.

Katz, E., Blumler, J., & Gurevitch, M. (1974). Utilization of mass communication by the individual. In J. Blumler & E. Katz (Eds.), *The uses of mass communication: Current perspectives on gratifications research* (pp. 19–34). Beverly Hills, CA: Sage.

Kearsley, G. (1998). *A guide to online education.* Retrieved from http://home.sprynet.com/~gkearsley/online.htm#rules.

Lickerman, A. (2010). The effect of technology on relationships. *Psychology Today.* Retrieved from www.psychologytoday.com/blog/happiness-in-world/201006/the-effect-technology-relationships.

Palmgreen, P., Weener, L. A., & Rayburn, J. D. II. (1980). Relations between gratifications sought and obtained: A study of television news. *Communication Research, 7*, 161–192.

Quan-Haase, A., & Young, A. (2010). Uses and gratifications of social media: A comparison of Facebook and instant messaging. *Bulletin of Science, Technology and Society, 30,* 350–361.

Shea, V. (1995). *Netiquette.* San Francisco: Albion.

Temkin Group. (April, 2013). *American's daily media consumption, 2012 vs. 2013.* Retrieved from http://trends.e-strategyblog.com/2013/04/04/americans-daily-media-consumption/10074.

Unze, D. (2010, March). Facebook helps spark movements. *USA Today.* Retrieved from www.usatoday.com/news/nation/2010-03-25-facebook_N.htm.

Worsnop, C. M. (1989). *Media literacy through critical thinking: Teacher materials.* Retrieved from http://depts.washington.edu/nwmedia/sections/nw_center/curriculum_docs/teach_combine.pdf.

CHAPTER 15

Communication in Contexts:
Applications for Life

Chapter Objectives

After reading this chapter, you should be able to:

- Explain how employees communicate dissatisfaction or dissent in the workplace
- Describe types of parenting communication styles
- Identify types of work–life balance messages shared in families
- Explain communication responses to stress encountered in health situations
- Describe specific skills acquired by communication studies majors
- Identify potential career options for communication studies graduates

PERSONAL: Everything is going wrong. Your 15-year-old sister has not spoken to you in the past week, and your parents have decided to file for divorce. To make matters worse, your grandfather recently suffered a stroke, and your mother has taken on primary responsibility for deciding how to provide the best care for him. Everyone in your family is always on edge and avoids talking about issues. You are sad because the family is quickly drifting apart. How can you initiate a conversation with your mother, sister, and father to begin addressing these issues?

PROFESSIONAL: Your supervisor has been assigning you more duties and responsibilities. Each new task is accompanied with the reinforcing phrase, "You are one of the best we have here at Imperial Communication! I don't know what we ever did before you joined the company." You feel dedicated to the organization and, because of your work ethic, you always reply with a reassuring response, "No problem! I'll make it happen!" While flattered by the compliments, you are growing increasingly frustrated by the neverending list of tasks you have to accomplish each day. What started as your dream job is quickly transforming into job burnout. How could the career you always dreamed of turn into something you dread so quickly? You want to have a conversation with your boss, but where do you begin?

PUBLIC: At your company's annual employee retreat, your supervisor asks you to create a presentation to explain the new changes that employees will encounter as a result of the organization's new healthcare provider. There will be a question-and-answer session at the conclusion of your presentation. You anticipate several employees will ask questions about how President Obama's healthcare reform will impact their benefits and provider options. How do you prepare to present and discuss these health issues with this audience?

CHAPTER OVERVIEW

Up to this point, the primary focus of this textbook has been to explain concepts and to build a foundation for understanding our communication with others. We've explored the role of verbal communication and language, nonverbal communication, and how communication functions in interpersonal relationships, online conversations, and group or team settings. Providing a foundation of human communication is essential to understanding how these elements function in our daily lives. In the opening examples, it is evident that each relationship and situation we encounter requires us to consider specific communication strategies to ensure that we accomplish our goals. Each of the categories (personal, professional, and public) is potentially encountered in a variety of communication contexts. In this chapter, we provide a glimpse into how communication is studied in organizational, family, instructional, and health contexts. At the conclusion of the chapter, we turn our discussion to focus on career options available for communication studies majors and offer some suggestions for applying what you've learned in this course to your job search.

ORGANIZATIONAL COMMUNICATION DEFINED

By now you've noticed that one of the primary areas we have chosen to focus on in the scenarios at the beginning of each chapter is the professional dimension. Chances are that you have decided to pursue a college degree as the next step in your journey toward your professional career. While classes required in your major field of study typically focus on content specific to your chosen profession, the knowledge and skills directly related to communication effectiveness with your superiors, coworkers, and clients will be valuable in virtually any career. For example, if you've completed an accounting or biology class it is unlikely that much attention was devoted to the communication expectations in careers focusing on these fields. Once you complete your academic studies and pursue your professional career, knowledge about how to effectively interact with your supervisor, your colleagues, and your clients will be important in your daily workplace interactions.

Organizational communication
Subfield of human communication that focuses on the messages exchanged between members of an organization.

Organizational communication is a subfield of human communication that focuses on the messages exchanged between members of an organization. Richmond and McCroskey (2009) define organizational communication as "the process by which individuals stimulate meaning in the minds of other individuals by means of verbal or nonverbal messages in the context of a formal organization" (p. 20). To provide you with an overview of the variety of topics studied by scholars, Figure 15.1 lists sample areas of focus in organizational research.

Organizational dissent
Method of reducing uncertainty that involves directly soliciting information about another person.

Upward dissent
Directly communicating one's dissatisfaction or frustration with an organization's upper management or administration.

Scholars in the field continue to explore issues encountered in organizations. Reflect on the opening scenario in which you were uncertain how to effectively communicate your frustration with your supervisor. Kassing (1997) has studied *organizational dissent* to better understand how employees express dissatisfaction with their supervisors or their jobs. Kassing helped organizational members recognize "how" members communicate their dissatisfaction and with "whom" they share these messages of discontent as they express their frustration. He identified three primary strategies that employees use to express their dissatisfaction. *Upward dissent* is one tactic in which employees directly communicate their frustrations with their supervisors. If you have a good relationship with your boss, you may be more comfortable going to him or her directly and confronting situations that

Romantic Relationships/ Friendships at Work	Management Communication Style/Leadership	Bullying in Organizations
Organizational Culture and Identity	Communicating Change in Organizations	Crisis Communication
Conflict Management in Organizations	Fairness and Justice in Organizations	Employee Satisfaction/Burnout

FIGURE 15.1

Sample areas of focus in organizational communication research.

Lateral dissent Expression of dissatisfaction or frustration to coworkers.

Displaced dissent Communication strategy in which organizational members share dissatisfaction or frustration with family members and non-workplace friends.

Upward dissent is one tactic in which employees directly communicate their frustrations with their supervisors.

frustrate you as opposed to avoiding or ignoring them. When employees vent their dissatisfaction to their coworkers, *lateral dissent* occurs. Caution and trust need to be given careful consideration when expressing dissent to coworkers. Information that you think is confidential may end up shared with others. Consider the opening scene in a professional context. If you vent frustration to a coworker, what could happen if he or she is interested in a job opportunity that you are also interested in pursuing? It is possible that the coworker could strategically disclose the things you shared in order to gain an advantage in the interview process. Since expressing one's dissatisfaction in the workplace can be risky at times, some members choose the communication strategy of *displaced dissent*. Displaced dissent occurs when frustrations are shared with nonworkplace friends and family members. While this approach may seem the safest of the three, it does little to help resolve the issue at hand. Why is research on employee dissent relevant ? The answer is quite simple: It can help organizational leaders, human

© GG Pro Photo/Shutterstock.com

resources managers, and even employees recognize when dissatisfaction is being communicated and enable them to address the issue directly, thereby maximizing organizational efficiency. Otherwise, venting about issues as opposed to seeking solutions may waste too much time.

Another area that has generated significant attention in organizational communication is research that focuses on power and how it is communicated in the workplace. French and Raven (1968) initially conceptualized five core power bases that impact our professional interactions. Understanding how organizational members influence one another to accomplish goals is essential to one's professional success. In Chapter 8, we introduced the concept of French and Raven's five power bases. Figure 15.2 provides a review of these concepts. In our professional lives, we need to be aware of the influence of these power bases on our interactions with our supervisors and our colleagues. Understanding why we give power to others is an important step to becoming more effective in our professional and personal interactions in the workplace.

FIGURE 15.2

French and Raven's
(1968) five bases of
power.

Other scholars have built on the work of French and Raven and explored how communication in the workplace influences employee motivation (e.g., Adams, Schlueter, & Barge, 1988) and how organizational leaders use power and strategies to gain employee liking and support to increase employee satisfaction (Richmond, McCroskey, & Davis, 1986). Studies like these continue to generate new information to help organizations understand how perceived power is communicated and the resulting impact on employee motivation and satisfaction.

In the 21st century, new issues in the work context have expanded the scope of relationships studied in organizations. If you work full time, chances are that you will spend nearly one-third of your waking hours with your coworkers. Because we spend so much time with our colleagues at work, it should come as no surprise that many friendships and romantic relationships are formed here. Current studies of organizational communication focus on how we negotiate the balance between these personal and professional relationships. Sias and her colleagues explored workplace friendships and our communication with coworkers. Most recently, Sias, Pedersen, Gallagher, and Kopaneva (2012) found that as more people telecommute or work from home, the value or importance placed on being physically close to our friends at work decreases since we can rely on texting, cell phones, and email to stay connected even when we're not in the office.

A 2013 study by the Society for Human Resource Management found that 24 percent of employees report that they have had a romantic relationship with a coworker.

Legitimate power
Assign power to another based on their position or title within the organization.

Referent power
Assign power to another person because of your personal relationship with them.

More than 24 percent of employees say they've had a romantic relationship with a coworker.

© Zurijeta/Shutterstock.com

Horan and Chory (2009) explored perceptions of coworkers as they studied the messages communicated by workplace romances. They found that coworkers feel less comfortable sharing information with colleagues who are involved in a romantic relationship with a supervisor. When a coworker is dating someone of higher status in the organization, friends at work are less likely to trust him or her and are more likely to manipulate information. They may even avoid disclosing or sharing information for fear the coworker will "tell the boss."

Other studies have addressed some of the negative communication that interferes with productivity in the workplace. Cowan's (2011) research on workplace bullying has helped managers and employees better understand how verbal and nonverbal messages can cause distress in the workplace and her studies have helped human resources managers effectively deal with these issues. From superior–subordinate relationships to coworker or peer relationships, knowing how to communicate effectively may ultimately contribute to your success in your professional endeavors. The ability to interact with our clients or customers, to work effectively with our colleagues, and to exchange necessary information with our supervisors in order to accomplish the organization's goals and objectives is essential to our career success.

FAMILY COMMUNICATION

Consider the meanings that you attribute to family rituals. How have your family's customs for celebrating holidays and birthdays influenced your expectations for these rituals? Can you recall the last time you became discouraged when attempting to communicate with a family member? Have you ever become frustrated by sibling rivalry and competition? It's ironic how, when interacting with parents and siblings, we know one another's communication patterns so well that we can often complete one another's sentences, yet at other times it seems as if we struggle to be understood. Family communication is an area in which every student has a lifetime of experience. However, that does not mean that we are always successful in our interactions. Siblings can laugh together and share secrets one minute, and engage in bitter conflict the next. Parents can become frustrated if their teen is embarrassed when they post a "Happy Birthday" message on their Facebook page. Why is it sometimes so difficult to communicate effectively with those whom we love and know the best? These are just some of the questions that family communication scholars address in their research.

By examining patterns of communication in our family of origin, we may gain valuable insight into why we communicate the way we do. Many of the theories we use to explain and describe communication in interpersonal relationships can be directly applied to understanding our interactions with family members. Recall our discussion of dialectical tensions discussed in Chapter 7. Now consider the ways in which the same dialectical tensions function in the context of family relationships. Parents and children often identify with the dialectical tension of autonomy and connectedness. From a young age, children are taught to be independent. Parents begin encouraging toddlers to dress and feed themselves. As they grow older, they gradually take on additional responsibilities such as completing homework and chores. Children are expected to become more self-sufficient, thus fulfilling the desire to teach them autonomy and independence. As they approach the teenage years, however, teenagers start to identify more closely with their friends, start driving, and rely less on their family relationships. Parents' desire for connectedness may result in challenging conversations, particularly when social media is involved.

Family communication can be defined as the process of creating and sharing meaning through the exchange of verbal and nonverbal messages with those whom we consider to be family. A key element in this definition is your perception of *who* you consider to be a part of your family and *how* you define what it means to be a family. Increasing diversity in family composition has been a topic that communication researchers have turned their attention to in recent studies. Stereotypical perceptions of what it means to be a "family" have changed since the days of the traditional nuclear family portrayed by the Cleavers from *Leave It to Beaver* or Mike and Carol's blended family from *The Brady Bunch*. Various family types, such as single-parent families, foster care families, gay and lesbian families, sibling families, and interracial families, have redirected the focus beyond the

> ⟫ **Family communication**
> Process of creating and sharing meaning through the exchange of verbal and nonverbal messages with those whom we consider to be family.

WHAT HAPPENS WHEN PARENTS AND CHILDREN COMMUNICATE VIA SOCIAL MEDIA?

Is it considered "uncool" to add mom or dad as a Facebook friend? Are parents who follow their children's Tweets spying on them? Family communication via social media might be more beneficial than you think. A 2013 study at Brigham Young University found that children and parents who connect with one another via Facebook, Twitter, and other social media sites report feeling closer in their relationships. Data collected from 491 families found that teens who "friend" their parents on Facebook or "follow" them on Twitter were less likely to experience depression or to engage in aggressive or delinquent behavior. Connecting online appears to increase feelings of connectedness in real life.

Source: Coyne, Padilla-Walker, Day, Harper, and Stockdale (2014).

The way members of a family interact has changed dramatically over the past few years.

© Rocketclips, Inc./Shutterstock.com

traditional concepts of what it means to be a family. In addition, many people often describe close friends not related by blood or legal ties to be "like family" and form relationships that are closer than those formed with biological relatives. Television shows such as *Friends*, *The Big Bang Theory*, and *How I Met Your Mother* depict the closeness of these voluntary relationships in which friendships function in much the same way that family relationships do. Family communication scholars examine the dynamics of family relationships. Figure 15.3 highlights some of the current family communication studies presented at the 2013 National Communication Association convention.

FIGURE 15.3

Examples of family communication studies presented in 2013.

- Identity Privacy Management among Adult Children with Lesbian and Gay Parents
- "In This Day and Age, You Just Don't Know": An Examination of How People in Romantic Relationships Use Communication to Manage Financial Uncertainty
- "I Just Can't Clean the Bathroom as Well as You Can!": Communicating Domestic Labor Task Resistance and Equity among Married Individuals
- "He Became Like My Other Son": Discursively Constructing Voluntary Kin Relationships
- "I'm the Parent and the Grandparent": Constructing the Grandfamily
- Memorable Familial Messages about Sex
- Family Interactions and Disordered Eating Attitudes
- My Sister's Keeper: Sibling Social Support and Chronic Illness
- Mothers' Memorable Messages about Popularity: Mothers' Socialization of Children's Popularity Orientations

One may gain valuable insight into the way their preferences for communicating evolved by examining the parenting styles experienced in families. Scholars have identified four different parenting styles. While the original research on parenting styles focused on how communication is used in the disciplining of children, later studies have applied these styles to understand the parent–child relationship better. Baumrind identified the first three categories of parenting styles in 1967, and a fourth style was added later. Figure 15.4 summarizes each of these.

Authoritarian parents adopt the philosophy that children should be "seen and not heard." It is expected that children will simply adhere to rules without asking questions. "Because I am the parent and I said so!" is a typical response to a child's inquiry or request for explanations. Very little responsiveness or clarification is provided, with the parent clearly in high control. At the opposite end of the spectrum are *permissive parents*. These parents are best described as being extremely supportive and nurturing to ensure that their child is happy and satisfied while exerting very little control or discipline. Children of permissive parents often report that there are few or no rules in the family, and the parents are often more focused on being the child's best friend than being an authority figure. *Authoritative parents* take a more democratic approach in their communication with their children. High levels of control accompany high levels of supportiveness. Parents make it a priority to listen to children, to encourage them to ask questions, and to offer explanations as to why rules are being enforced. Maccoby (1992) found that children of authoritative parents indicated that they were happier and

➤ Authoritarian parents
Parenting style in which low levels of support and high levels of control are exhibited. Children are expected to follow rules without questioning them.

➤ Permissive parents
Parenting style in which high levels of support and low levels of control are demonstrated. Parents often try to be their child's "friend" with few rules and little discipline.

➤ Authoritative parents
Parenting style in which high levels of support and high levels of control are exhibited. Parents listen to their children and offer explanations for rules.

Different family types pose unique communication challenges for their members.

© Andresr/Shutterstock.com

FIGURE 15.4

Parenting styles.

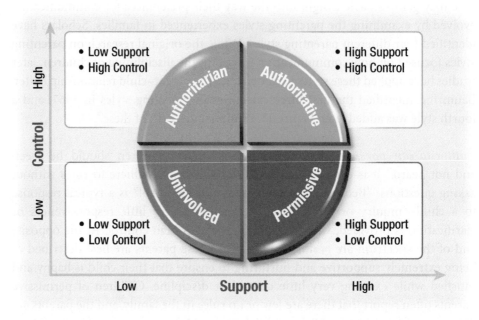

- Low Support
- High Control

Authoritarian

- High Support
- High Control

Authoritative

- Low Support
- Low Control

Uninvolved

- High Support
- Low Control

Permissive

High / Low — Control

Low / High — Support

ultimately more successful. As more dual-career families evolved, it was discovered that the demands of work sometimes interfered with one's ability to take an active role in parenting. In addition, some single parents struggle to provide for the basic needs of their children and often work multiple jobs while depending on siblings or other family members for assistance. As a result, a fourth parenting style was added to account for families in which parents offer little support or nurturing in their communication with their children and enforce little or no control in discipline. *Uninvolved parents* rarely engage in communication with their children. While these parents often make sure the child's basic needs are met, they devote little to no effort communicating or spending time together. An example of this may be seen in a family where a nanny is primarily responsible for disciplining or nurturing children due to a parent's busy work schedule. As a result of the low level of involvement, children may experience feelings of frustration and exhibit low levels of self-esteem and self-control.

Uninvolved parents
Parenting style in which low levels of support and low levels of control are exhibited. Parents are often described as being "too busy" to be involved in the child's life.

Over the past 30 years, a growing number of women have pursued full-time careers to contribute to the family income. Taking on new roles in the workplace while caring for children and maintaining a household have resulted in additional stress. Television shows and movies portray the dilemmas faced by both working mothers and fathers who depend on effective communication with one another to coordinate childcare and family responsibilities.

Can you recall messages that your parents have shared with you regarding how they managed to balance work and family demands? A 2006 survey of 312 college students asked them to recall messages that their parents shared with them regarding how to effectively balance work and family life (Medved, Brogan, McClanahan, Morris, & Shepherd, 2006). The goal of these *balance messages* is to emphasize the importance of managing the demands associated with having both a career and a family. Students recalled four types of balance messages that their parents directly or indirectly shared with them as they offered insight into effectively managing a career and a family. *Work choice messages* discuss the various career options that enable parents to pursue a career while enjoying their children. Max's mother is an elementary school teacher, and as he contemplates what he should major in at college, she shares, "You've always been so good at math and you enjoy working with children, so you should think about majoring in education. Teaching is a great career because your schedule will be similar to your children's. You will be able to coach their sports teams and spend your summers and holidays with them." When parents emphasize the importance of prioritizing and organizing the personal versus the professional aspects of one's life, *life-planning messages* are being shared. Eliza's father encouraged her first to complete her medical internship and residency before adding children to her family. He pointed out that by doing so, she would be established in her career and later would be better able to devote attention to her children. *Combining messages* emphasize that both work and family can be enjoyed at the same time. Parents make comments such as "Don't let people tell you that you have to choose between a career and a family. You can have both!

➤ **Balance messages**
Communicate the importance of and strategies to assist in managing the demands of both career and family.

➤ **Work choice messages**
Discuss the various career options that enable parents to pursue a career while enjoying their children.

➤ **Life-planning messages**
Emphasize the value in prioritizing and segmenting one's personal and professional lives into two distinct areas.

➤ **Combining messages**
Communicate that it is possible to balance the responsibilities of both work and family simultaneously.

Combining messages emphasize that both work and family can be enjoyed at the same time.

© Monkey Business Images/Shutterstock.com

Prioritizing
messages
Statements that focus on
the need to place family
first and career second.
Does not necessarily
imply that one must
take the place of the
other; simply emphasizes
that family should take
priority.

It may be stressful at times, but you'll figure it out." *Prioritizing messages* focus on the importance of placing family first and work second. When her daughter, a successful pharmaceutical sales representative, struggled with frequent traveling during the week, Jane advised her to "Consider your children. After all, they grow up so quickly. Career opportunities in the medical sales field will continue to grow. You should ask your boss if you can take some assignments closer to home while the children are young." By sharing this message, Jane emphasized the importance of placing family first while still maintaining a career.

In response to the changing composition of families in the 21st century, scholars are also attempting to help families effectively communicate about a number of issues that present new challenges. Today, parents not only need to be aware of the television shows that their children watch and have conversations with them about their viewing, but they also need to have discussions with their children about Internet safety and portrayal of the self on sites such as Facebook, Snapchat, and Instagram. In addition, subjects such as drugs and alcohol abuse, safe sex, school violence, and bullying require parents to talk with their children and reassure them about their safety. Researchers have examined a variety of contemporary issues facing families, ranging from how couples communicate with friends and family

MILITARY WIVES' DISCLOSURES OF STRESS TO THEIR DEPLOYED HUSBANDS

A survey conducted by Joseph and Afifi (2010) of 105 military families with at least one child examined how wives talked about stressful situations that they were experiencing while their husbands were deployed. Situations identified by wives as stressful included:

- Risk of spouse's injury or death (28%)
- Parenting alone during deployment (24%)
- Loneliness (11%)
- Worrying about child's well-being (6%)
- Husband missing milestones in children's lives (5%)
- More responsibilities during deployment (5%)
- Talking with children about deployment (2%)

Wives indicated that they most often disclose about their stress by talking with their husbands, with friends in their military community, or through conversations with their own parents. By engaging in open conversations about their fears and stresses, women reported being more satisfied in their marriages.

members about infertility issues (Bute & Vik, 2010) to how military wives choose to disclose and discuss stressful issues with their husbands who are deployed overseas (Joseph & Afifi, 2010; see box).

Studies in family communication not only provide us with an opportunity to explore and explain our family's style of interaction, but they may also help us better understand our own communication preferences.

HEALTH COMMUNICATION

Recall your last visit to your primary care doctor. Did you feel comfortable sharing your health concerns? Did your doctor exhibit nonverbal indicators of listening as you explained your symptoms? Did you ask follow-up questions as your doctor provided instructions for enhancing your health? If your doctor prescribed medication or explained a treatment option, did you understand the information being shared? If you answered "no" to any of these questions, you are not alone. Many patients indicate that they are afraid to ask questions or share concerns when visiting their physician. The *Journal of the American Medical Association* refers to this fear as "white coat silence," and it often results from perceived barriers in interactions between physicians and patients. Such obstacles may include the status differential or doctor's authority, not wanting to be perceived as a "difficult"

Many patients don't feel comfortable talking with their physician.

© Alexander Raths/Shutterstock.com

patient, and the perception of a doctor's time as being very limited. Thus, patients feel rushed during a visit.

The focus on health communication as an area of study gained momentum in the mid-1970s (Rogers, 1996) and the interest and demand in the field continues to grow. Communication scholars examine a variety of health-related topics including patient–doctor interactions, social support and caregiving, and health campaigns and initiatives. In 2013, the World Health Organization shared new data that indicates the average lifespan of humans has increased from 64 years in 1990 to 70 years in 2011. Advances in medical care options have contributed to this extended lifespan. With the aging population, children are often involved in communication about healthcare issues for elderly parents. Now more than ever, individuals and doctors realize the important role that communication plays in promoting and providing quality healthcare. This focus on health spans a variety of communication contexts as we exchange messages about health-related issues. From political advocacy for health issues, such as legalization of medical marijuana and one's right to make decisions about his or her own health, to studying effective communication across the healthcare team of doctors, nurses, pharmacists, and insurance providers, the impact of messages and achieving shared meaning is undeniable. Watch one episode of *Grey's Anatomy* and you will come to realize the value of effective communication among the healthcare team that provides patient care.

It is estimated that U.S. citizens spent more than $2.3 trillion in 2008, or an average of $7,680 per person, focusing on health-related visits and resources (CBS News, 2010). While that estimate may seem high, consider the ways in which you focus on ensuring your own health. Visits to dentists and physicians, purchase of medications and vitamins, eating healthy and working out—these costs add up quickly. Patients no longer rely solely on their healthcare provider for information about diagnosis and treatment of ailments. Online sites, such as WebMD, and support forums for topics ranging from diabetes management to bereavement to what to expect during pregnancy provide a wealth of information that often leads to self-diagnosis.

Earlier we discussed the anxiety that patients encounter during medical visits. Recall our earlier discussions of communication apprehension. While these chapters focused primarily on apprehension in the public-speaking context, communication scholars have found that our apprehension also impacts our desire to share information in the health context. Communication apprehension is a potential barrier to effective communication between healthcare providers and their patients, and the lack of sharing information may result in additional problems. Consider the patient that is afraid to disclose that he has been experiencing severe indigestion because he is afraid that his doctor will require him to undergo tests for heart issues. Perhaps an individual fails to disclose her recent dental surgery with her personal trainer at the gym because she perceives that it is "not that big of a deal." This reluctance to share information can interfere with effective diagnosis and medical advice. What are some of the possible behaviors of patients who have a high level of communication apprehension? They may simply listen to the doctor's orders without asking questions, refrain from seeking second opinions because of their anxiety over further communication with new doctors, or even avoid visiting and communicating with healthcare providers altogether (Booth-Butterfield, Chory, & Benynon, 1997). It should come as no surprise that patients who have a high level of communication apprehension report lower levels of satisfaction with both their healthcare provider and their treatment (Richmond, Smith, Heisel, & McCroskey, 2001). Health communication scholars continue to examine the impact of this apprehension and to recommend strategies to encourage effective patient–physician interactions.

Another area that has gained the attention of researchers is how stress influences our interactions with others. Health-related issues, such as the diagnosis of a terminal disease or decisions regarding healthcare options, often produce stress and understanding how people communicate while coping with these situations may enable us to provide support. Three types of coping strategies identified by Kohn (1996) may assist healthcare providers and caregivers in recognizing the verbal and nonverbal signs of stress. *Emotional-focused coping* is exhibited when individuals openly express their frustrations, are sensitive to messages from others, or are very emotional when faced with stressful situations. Consider the different coping styles portrayed in the following scenario. Alonzo and Kourtney's son was diagnosed with leukemia at the age of 5. Each parent reacted to this news in very distinct ways. Kourtney exhibited signs of emotional-focused coping when they first heard the news. She spent hours blaming herself as she cried to her sister and her friends. Alonzo's reaction to the news was very different. He began actively researching the Internet to educate himself about the disease, and he coordinated a team of coworkers and friends to participate in the Light the Night Walk to raise funds for leukemia research. Alonzo used *problem-focused coping* strategies to gain information and research opportunities to assist the family in adjusting to the stressful news. Alonso's parents chose to use *avoidance-focused coping* in response to the news of their grandson's illness. They mentally and physically disengaged in situations where their grandson's health issues were discussed. Often they would quickly change the subject or leave the room to refrain from talking about his illness. Increasing our awareness of how people differ in their

Emotional-focused coping
Coping strategy in which individuals respond emotionally to stressful news.

Problem-focused coping
Coping strategy in which individuals actively research and seek solutions to assist in the management of stressful situations.

Avoidance-focused coping
Coping strategy in which individuals mentally or physically avoid conversations about stressful situations.

responses to stressful situations can shed insight into how to discuss these difficult topics and assist them in the coping process.

As college students, you encounter a variety of situations in which you act as both a source and receiver of health-related messages. For example, you may find yourself in situations where you're required to talk to a friend or roommate about alcohol use. Lederman and her colleagues (2007) developed the LTAI (Let's Talk About It) simulation to encourage students to consider the types of messages that should be communicated about decisions related to drinking. In studies where the LTAI was used, college students reported that they would use a variety of communication strategies to help protect a friend who was intoxicated. These strategies ranged from "tricking" the friend to avoid potentially embarrassing or dangerous situations (e.g., telling them that they were leaving a party and going to someplace more fun) to communicating for their friend when it became evident that they were too impaired to speak for themselves (e.g., informing others that the friend was intoxicated and unable to make good decisions).

Chances are that, after college graduation, you will continue to encounter a variety of health-related messages. Organizations promote health awareness among their employees in an effort to decrease insurance claims, and the media constantly bombards us with messages about the latest diet, vitamin supplements, or exercise phenomenon that is guaranteed to give us the results we desire. The ability to process messages about health-related issues that are sometimes the subject of debate—such as President Barack Obama's healthcare plan, the Affordable Care Act—will better prepare you to engage in conversations and express your opinions about health legislation. Health-related messages are everywhere, and identifying strategies for sharing and seeking information as well as communicating our decisions to others is an essential element in ensuring healthy living.

Communication occurs in a variety of contexts. Chances are you have already experienced interactions in the organizational, family, and health contexts. Understanding how we adjust our messages across communication settings is critical to ensure your success as a competent communicator in the personal, professional, and public aspects of your life.

WHAT CAN YOU DO WITH A COMMUNICATION STUDIES DEGREE?: CAREER OPPORTUNITIES

As you conclude your exploration of human communication, there is one final question that students often ask: What can I do with a communication studies degree? Those who have already declared communication as their major field of study often encounter the question, "So do you want to be the next Anderson Cooper or Barbara Walters?" While careers as news broadcasters certainly depend on effective human communication skills in order to effectively interview guests or share valuable information with a public audience, the field of communication provides many more opportunities for graduates.

Figure 15.5 highlights some well-known individuals who have focused on the study of human communication as part of their undergraduate careers. As you review the list, consider the role that communication has played in their success in forming relationships, sharing information, and exchanging messages. Chances are these former communication students would indicate that language, nonverbal behaviors,

FIGURE 15.5

Famous students of
communication studies

John Quincy Adams
- Former president of the United States
- Taught rhetoric at Harvard University

Robert Iger
- CEO of Disney
- Communication Studies - Ithaca College

James Gandolfini
- Actor
- Communication Studies - Rutgers University

Earvin "Magic" Johnson
- NBA athlete
- Communication Studies - Michigan State University

Brian Lamb
- Retired CEO of C-SPAN
- Speech Communication - Purdue University

Oprah Winfrey
- Television Host/Actress/CEO/Author
- Speech and Drama - Tennessee State University

Nancy Cartwright
- Voice talent, "Bart Simpson"
- Communication Studies - Ohio University

Dave St. Peter
- President of Minnesota Twins
- Communication Studies - University of North Dakota

public speaking and interpersonal skills, effective group communication, and social media skills have all played a valuable role in their success. That is what makes the field of communication studies a viable and valuable degree option; it touches every aspect of virtually any career you choose to pursue. Critical thinking, problem solving, decision making, teamwork, effective listening, conflict resolution, writing, and research are just a sample of the skills acquired in the major that are valued by employers across a variety of fields. Even if your interests have guided you to disciplines such as business, education, health, and political science, communication skills are valuable in your field and may be useful as an academic minor.

How can a communication studies major or minor help you achieve your professional goals? After all, you've been communicating your entire life, so why should you select it as your focus of study? As stated throughout this text, communication touches every aspect of your life: personal, professional, and public. Consider our discussion of interpersonal relationships and, more specifically, the messages exchanged with family members. Knowledge of effective communication skills is crucial not only to your success in classes, but also in improved relationships with family and friends. The benefits of communication skills reach far beyond your personal satisfaction and contribute to your professional success. Fortune 500 executives list oral and written communication skills among the top three skills sought in new employees, and speaking skills are rated second only to one's knowledge about the job as essential in career success. As a member of a democratic society, you depend on communication to be part of an active and informed public. Gaining knowledge about issues, debating topics, and sharing information and opinions with others is a part of your civic rights. See Table 15.1 for a sampling of careers for communication studies majors.

TABLE 15.1

Overview of 2014 Sample Career Opportunities for Communication Studies Majors

Title	What Do They Do?	Important Skills	Pay (2010 Median Wage)
Training and Development Manager	• Evaluates employee needs for training • Creates training manuals, online training modules, or other educational materials • Evaluates the effectiveness of training programs	• Critical thinking • Decision making • Interpersonal • Managerial • Public speaking	$89,170
Human Resources Manager	• Coordinates administrative functions in organizations • Recruits, interviews, and hires employees • Assists top management in strategic planning • Serves as a liaison between organizational managers and employees	• Decision making • Interpersonal • Managerial • Organizational • Public speaking	$99, 180
Health Educator	• Provides education about health and wellness behaviors • Designs and delivers programs to encourage healthy decisions • Evaluates the effectiveness of health programs and material • Advocates for enhanced health resources and policies • Serves as a liaison or advocate for patients and their families • Assists organizations in promoting healthy behaviors among employees/members • Develops employee incentive programs for adopting healthy behaviors	• Analytical • Instructional • Interpersonal • Problem solving • Writing	$45,830
Sports Information Director	• Prepares/edits media guides for sports teams • Serves as a liaison between media and team • Coordinates and schedules interviews • Compiles statistics and information on athletes • Updates information on website and other publications	• Decision making • Interpersonal • Managerial • Organizational • Public speaking • Persuasion	$89,800

Source: United States Department of Labor (Bureau of Labor Statistics). Occupational Outlook Handbook. Retrieved from www.bls.gov/ooh/home.htm.

CHAPTER SUMMARY

Throughout this chapter we have answered some of the questions about how the study of communication applies to a variety of contexts and how research in areas such as family, organizational, and health communication enables us to improve our knowledge and skills so we can enhance our effectiveness. Understanding the value that human communication plays in your personal, professional, and public lives is important as you identify your field of study and continue working toward your career goals. While the field of communication may at first appear to be broad and sometimes vague, the value and influence of the skills gained by studying human communication is far-reaching and infinite.

KEY WORDS

Authoritarian parents Parenting style in which low levels of support and high levels of control are exhibited. Children are expected to follow rules without questioning them.

Authoritative parents Parenting style in which high levels of support and high levels of control are exhibited. Parents listen to their children and offer explanations for rules.

Avoidance-focused coping Coping strategy in which individuals mentally or physically avoid conversations about stressful situations.

Balance messages Communicate the importance of and strategies to assist in managing the demands of both career and family.

Coercive power Assign authority to another person based on their perceived ability to punish or deliver negative consequences for noncompliance.

Combining messages Communicate that it is possible to balance the responsibilities of both work and family simultaneously.

Displaced dissent Communication strategy in which organizational members share dissatisfaction or frustration with family members and non-workplace friends.

Emotional-focused coping Coping strategy in which individuals respond emotionally to stressful news.

Expert power Assign power to another based on their knowledge or expertise.

Family communication Process of creating and sharing meaning through the exchange of verbal and nonverbal messages with those whom we consider to be family.

Lateral dissent Expression of dissatisfaction or frustration to coworkers.

Legitimate power Assign power to another based on their position or title within the organization.

Life-planning messages Emphasize the value in prioritizing and segmenting one's personal and professional lives into two distinct areas.

Organizational communication Subfield of human communication that focuses on the messages exchanged between members of an organization.

Organizational dissent Method of reducing uncertainty that involves directly soliciting information about another person.

Permissive parents Parenting style in which high levels of support and low levels of control are demonstrated. Parents often try to be their child's "friend" with few rules and little discipline.

Prioritizing messages Statements that focus on the need to place family first and career second. Does not necessarily imply that one must take the place of the other; simply emphasizes that family should take priority.

Problem-focused coping Coping strategy in which individuals actively research and seek solutions to assist in the management of stressful situations.

Referent power Assign power to another person because of your personal relationship with them.

Reward power Assign power to another person based on their perceived ability to deliver benefits or incentives as a result of compliance with their requests.

Uninvolved parents Parenting style in which low levels of support and low levels of control are exhibited. Parents are often described as being "too busy" to be involved in the child's life.

Upward dissent Directly communicating one's dissatisfaction or frustration with an organization's upper management or administration.

Work choice messages Discuss the various career options that enable parents to pursue a career while enjoying their children.

REFERENCES

Adams, C. H., Schlueter, D. W., & Barge, J. K. (1988). Communication and motivation within the superior–subordinate dyad: Testing the conventional wisdom of volunteer management. *Journal of Applied Communication Research, 156*, 69–81.

Baumrind, D. (1967). Child-care practices anteceding three patterns of preschool behavior. *Genetic Psychology Monographs, 75*, 43–88.

Booth-Butterfield, S., Chory, R., & Beynon, W. (1997). Communication apprehension and health communication behaviors. *Communication Quarterly, 45*, 235–250.

Bute, J. J., & Vik, T. A. (2010). Privacy management as unfinished business: Shifting boundaries in the context of infertility. *Communication Studies, 61*, 1–20.

CBS News. (2010, January 5). *$2.3 trillion spent on health care in 2008*. Retrieved from www.cbsnews.com/2100-250_162-6057429.html.

Cowan, R. L. (2011). "Yes, we have an anti-bullying policy, but...": HR professionals' understandings and experiences with workplace bullying policy. *Communication Studies, 62*(3), 307–327.

Coyne, S. M., Padilla-Walker, L. M., Day, R. D., Harper, J., & Stockdale, L. (2014). A friend request from dear old dad: Associations between parent–child social networking and adolescent outcomes. *Cyberpsychology, Behavior and Social Networking, 17*(1), 8–13.

French, J. R. P., & Raven, B. (1968). The bases for social power. In D. Cartwright (Ed.), *Studies in social power* (pp. 150–167). Ann Arbor: University of Michigan Press.

Gerencher, K. (2013, June 30). When should you fire your doctor? *Wall Street Journal.* Retrieved from http://online.wsj.com/news/articles/SB10001424127 8873243282045785716402159952804

Horan, S. M., & Chory, R. M. (2009). When work and love mix: Perceptions of peers in workplace romances. *Western Journal of Communication, 73*(4), 349–369.

Joseph, A. L., & Afifi, T. D. (2010). Military wives' stressful disclosures to their deployed husbands: The role of protective buffering. *Journal of Applied Communication Research, 38,* 412–434.

Kassing, J. W. (1997). Articulating, antagonizing, and displacing: A model of employee dissent. *Communication Studies, 48,* 311–332.

Kohn, P. M. (1996). On coping adaptively with daily hassles. In M. Zeidner & N. S. Endler (Eds.), *Handbook of coping* (pp. 181–201). New York, NY: Wiley.

Lederman, L. C., Stewart, L. O., Bates, C., Greenberg, J., LeGreco, M., & Schuwerk, T. J. (2007). *Let's talk about it.* New Brunswick, NJ: Center for Communication and Health Issues, Rutgers University.

Maccoby, E. E. (1992). The role of parents in the socialization of children: An historical overview. *Developmental Psychology, 28,* 1006–1017.

Medved, C. B., Brogan, S. M., McClanahan, A. M., Morris, J. R., & Shepherd, G. J. (2006). Family and work socializing communication: Messages, gender and ideological implications. *Journal of Family Communication, 6,* 161–180.

Richmond, V. P., & McCroskey, J. C. (2009). *Organizational communication for survival: Making work, work* (4th ed.). Boston, MA: Allyn & Bacon/Pearson.

Richmond, V. P., McCroskey, J. C., & Davis, L. M. (1986). The relationship of supervisor use of power and affinity-seeking strategies with subordinate satisfaction. *Communication Quarterly, 34,* 178–193.

Richmond, V. P., Smith, R. S., Heisel, A. D., & McCroskey, J. C. (2001). Nonverbal immediacy in the physician/patient relationship. *Communication Research Reports, 18,* 211–216.

Rogers, E. M. (1996). The field of health communication today: An up-to-date report. *Journal of Health Communication, 1,* 15–23.

Sias, P. M., Pedersen, H., Gallagher, E. B., & Kopaneva, I. (2012). Workplace friendship in the electronically connected organization. *Human Communication Research, 38*(3), 253–279.

Workplace Romance. (2013). Retrieved from http://www.shrm.org/research/surveyfindings/articles/pages/shrm-workplace-romance-findings.aspx

GLOSSARY

Ability language Language that focuses on the shortcomings of a person rather than emphasizing the person as a human.

Accent Way in which we pronounce words.

Acceptance function Expression of prejudice against another in an attempt to gain acceptance.

Accepting an award Special occasion speech by the person receiving an award that recognizes the importance of the award and expresses his or her appreciation to those who are giving the award; acknowledges those who helped the recipient achieve this recognition and, if there were other nominees, acknowledges them as well.

Accommodation Conflict management strategy that recognizes the presence of a conflict, but one party concedes or gives in to the other in an attempt to resolve the issue.

Active strategies A method of reducing uncertainty that involves directly soliciting information about another person.

Ad hominem Type of faulty reasoning used when a speaker attacks or criticizes a person, rather than the arguments provided or the issue itself.

Adaptors Nonverbal gestures that are often performed without intent; may be used to indicate the emotional state or feelings associated with the verbal message.

Adjourning stage Final process of group life that signals the completion of tasks.

Agenda List of the activities or tasks that need to be accomplished at the day's meeting.

Anniversary speech Type of special occasion speech used to remind an audience of a person, event, or holiday that is being commemorated.

Appreciative listening Listening for enjoyment.

Association Making a connection between one thing and another; a strategy used to aid memory.

Attitudes Learned predispositions to respond favorably or unfavorably toward another person, group, or object.

Attitudinal analysis Type of audience analysis that considers the audience's position on a particular topic (e.g., for, against, or no opinion).

Audience analysis Gaining knowledge about the audience such as their demographic information, their attitudes, their level of knowledge of the topic, the speech environment, and the occasion for the speech in order to best prepare the speech.

Audience-based communication apprehension Fear of public speaking with a specific audience (e.g., you may not be apprehensive when you are speaking with your peers in a course but apprehensive when you are speaking to the board of directors of your company).

Auditory discrimination The ability to distinguish sounds.

Authoritarian leader Mandates what must be done in a group setting.

Authoritarian parents Parenting style in which low levels of support and high levels of control are exhibited. Children are expected to follow rules without questioning them.

Authoritative parents Parenting style in which high levels of support and high levels of control are exhibited. Parents listen to their children and offer explanations for rules.

Autonomy versus connectedness Dialectical tension that focuses on one's desire to be close to another while maintaining independence.

Avoidance Conflict resolution strategy that involves denying the presence of a conflict.

Avoidance-focused coping Coping strategy in which individuals mentally or physically avoid conversations about stressful situations.

Avoiding Third stage in the relationship dissolution process in which partners make an effort to avoid being in the physical presence of one another.

Balance messages Communicate the importance of and strategies to assist in managing the demands of both career and family.

Bandwagon fallacy Type of faulty reasoning used when one indicates that something is true because a number of people have said it is true, not necessarily because there is clear evidence of its truth.

Bar graphs A type of visual aid often used to translate statistical comparisons and relationships into visual representations.

Behavioral familiarity Strategy to assist in identifying deception. The level of familiarity with typical patterns of behaviors enables us to easily identify uncharacteristic behaviors that may signal deception.

Beliefs Personal convictions regarding truth or existence.

Bias Language that conveys stereotypes, insensitivity, or negativity toward a group of people or about a topic.

Blog Online journal.

Body The heart of the speech; its purpose is to state each main idea and support each idea fully.

Bonding Final stage of coming together in the relationship development model. Formalized or legalized declarations of commitment mark this phase as couples publicly acknowledge their dedication to one another.

Brainstorming Technique used for generating ideas.

Breadth Variety of topics that we are willing to disclose about yourself in discussions with others.

Categorization The process of classifying information or placing information into logical categories; a strategy used to enhance memory.

Cause–effect order Uncovering events that have resulted in a particular outcome. Speakers may also use the reverse order and begin by speaking about the effects and then go back and trace the causes.

Channel Medium through which message is sent.

Charismatic leader Type of leader who has characteristics such as confidence, interpersonal attractiveness, and effective communication skills.

Charts Visual display for information contained in a speech; help explain how things relate to each other or the sequence something goes through as it is processed.

Chronemics Study of the messages we associate with how others manage and use time.

Chronological order A pattern of organization particularly useful when you are trying to describe the order in which something occurs or occurred; used to explain a process, discuss an historical event, or talk about someone's life. Also known as *time order*.

Chunking A strategy that helps maintain information in short-term memory by remembering information in sections or pieces ("chunks").

Circumscribing Second stage in the process of relationship dissolution in which communication is limited to safe, superficial topics. Both the quality and quantity of conversations between partners is limited.

Co-culture Smaller cultures that comprise a larger culture.

Coaching leader Type of leader who uses both highly directive behaviors and highly supportive behaviors; focuses communication on not only achieving goals but also on meeting the followers' emotional needs.

Coercive power Assign authority to another person based on their perceived ability to punish or deliver negative consequences for noncompliance.

Cognitive function Using language to gather information, to reason, and to make sense of the world.

Cohesiveness General sense of belonging among group members.

Collaboration Most effective conflict resolution strategy that requires both parties to communicate their concerns while proposing solutions that would be acceptable.

Collaborative projects Focus on co-creating information with other individuals.

Collectivism Group viewed as most important; valued for dependence and shared responsibility among group members.

Combining messages Communicate that it is possible to balance the responsibilities of both work and family simultaneously.

Commencement speech Type of speech often given at a graduation to review what has been accomplished and provide a vision for the future.

Communication Accommodation Theory Theory that argues we change our verbal communication during the course of an interaction based on our perceptions of the interaction and with whom we are speaking.

Communication apprehension Fear, nervousness, or anxiety we experience when faced with real or imagined interactions.

Communication competence Ability to produce messages that are perceived as appropriate and effective.

Communication Process of sending and receiving verbal and nonverbal messages to achieve shared meaning.

Comparative advantage pattern A speech organization often used in persuasive speaking, it demonstrates to the audience that accepting the speaker's persuasive proposition has more benefits than other possible propositions that others may be advocating.

Competition Approach to conflict management in which individuals struggle or compete for power or control.

Compliance-gaining Getting someone to do something you want.

Compromiser Individual who avoids conflict and admits any mistakes in a group.

Concealment Form of deception that involves withholding important or relevant information.

Conclusion Summarizes or reviews the main points presented in the speech and leaves the audience with a final unifying thought.

Conflict Expressed struggle between two or more interdependent parties who perceive incompatibility, scarce resources, and interference from others as obstacles in accomplishing their goals.

Conflict style Our own reaction to conflict.

Connotative meaning Individualized meaning that reflects unique personal views of the user of the language.

Content information Verbal communication or the actual words being said.

Content meaning Actual information that is being exchanged in a message.

Context Situation or where the communication occurs.

Context-based communication apprehension Fear of speaking only in one setting (e.g., fear of speaking in public but not in other settings such as in small groups).

Converge When individuals become more similar in their verbal choices.

Conversational narcissism Extreme self-focus in a conversation in which an individual does not allow the other person in the interaction an opportunity to speak.

Coordinator Group member that oversees who accomplishes what tasks and when tasks should be done.

Credibility Extent to which a speaker is trustworthy, knowledgeable, and well prepared.

Critical listening Listening to make a judgment.

Cultural borrowing Process through which a culture identifies benefits of other cultures and decides to adopt similar practices.

Culture Shared perceptions that shape the communication patterns and expectations of a group of people.

Decisional utility Extent media is used to gain information and make an informed decision.

Decoding Process where individuals attempt to make sense or interpret the encoded message.

Dedication speech Type of special occasion speech given that speaks about the significance of an occasion (e.g., a building being named for a particular person).

Deductive reasoning Type of reasoning that begins with a general statement, is supported by specific support, and then draws a conclusion.

Defensive listening When a listener perceives what is said as a personal attack.

Defensive message Message that is produced in response to some kind of threat.

Deintensification Subduing or controlling the intensity of emotion that is expressed.

Delegating leadership Offers little advice, input, or social support and control is handed over to the group members.

Democratic leader Actively consults group members before making decisions.

Demographic analysis Type of audience analysis that takes into account the characteristics of the audience including the audience's gender, age, race, ethnicity, and level of education.

Denotative meaning Dictionary definition of a word or the literal meaning of a word.

Depth Level of intimacy or amount of detail that is disclosed about a particular topic.

Dialectical tensions Contradictory pulls between opposing goals or desires in a relationship.

Differentiating First stage in the process of relationship dissolution in which partners focus on their differences as opposed to their commonalities.

Directive leadership Focuses on task completion.

Disasters and crises Factors that may force cultures to change.

Discrimination Form of prejudice that involves the practice of denying others their equal rights.

Displaced dissent Communication strategy in which organizational members share dissatisfaction or frustration with family members and non-workplace friends.

Disruptive communication Distracts group members from accomplishing their goals.

Diverge When individuals become increasingly different in their verbal choices.

Diversity Distinctions among individuals or groups.

Dominator Group member who likes to be heard and works to control the group.

Effectiveness When a group meets all of its requirements and completes all of its tasks.

Efficiency When group members are maximizing what they do, completing the necessary tasks as correctly as possible.

Ego-defensive function Expression of prejudice in an attempt to place the blame or make excuses for our misfortunes on another.

Emblems Nonverbal gestures that have a direct verbal translation. A common meaning for a gesture exists among members of the same culture.

Emotional closeness Perception or feeling of trust or solidarity with another individual.

Emotional conflict Conflict from relationships with others and can include lack of trust, feelings of dislike or animosity, and frustration.

Emotional-focused coping Coping strategy in which individuals respond emotionally to stressful news.

Empathic listening Listening from the other person's perspective to support or help that person.

Empathy The ability to understand how someone else is feeling or thinking.

Emphasizing Directing attention to a particular aspect of the verbal message by using nonverbal cues to accentuate the message.

Encoding Process of translating thoughts, feelings, experiences, or ideas into words and/or gestures.

Encourager Group member who praises others and hears others' opinions and ideas.

Entertainment Extent to which you find media to be a source of pleasurable distraction.

Entry stage First stage of relationship development that relies on expectations for behavioral norms to guide communication. Characterized by small talk and exchange of demographic information.

Equivocation Deception strategy in which one uses vague or ambiguous language in an attempt to avoid speaking the truth. Often used in situations where we attempt to spare someone's feelings.

Ethical communication Individual's ability to be honest and use a set of standards to guide appropriate or positive behaviors.

Ethical public speaking Speaking that demonstrates respect for one's audience, honesty, use of reliable and valid sources, and responsibility for everything that is said and/or done during a speech.

Ethics Standards, values, beliefs, and principles we use to help us determine what is right or wrong.

Ethnicity Common heritage or background shared by a group of people.

Ethos Ethics of the speaker.

Eulogy Speech of praise for someone who has passed away.

Evaluating Considering the message and the credibility of the speaker and separating fact from opinion to judge the meaning of the message.

Evaluator-critic Group member who sets standards and meets goals.

Exaggeration Form of deception that involves stretching the truth, adding details or information to enhance a story, or repeating oneself in an attempt to be convincing.

Exit stage Final stage of relationship development that involves making the decision to terminate or end the pursuit of the relationship; characterized by liking or similarity.

Expectancy Violation Theory Examines the role of communication when our anticipations are not met. Violations may be perceived as positive or negative.

Experimenting Second stage of relationship development that involves the exchange of multiple questions and answers as we attempt to gain more information about the other person and to identify areas of commonality.

Expert power Assign power to another based on their knowledge or expertise.

Explicit learning Occurs when we are told what to do and when it should be done.

Explicit rules Formalized rules that are discussed and often documented so that all group members are aware of them.

Expressed struggle Conflict is openly expressed and each partner is made aware of the presence of issues in the relationship.

Extemporaneous delivery Type of delivery where the speaker researches, organizes, and practices the speech but uses only an outline while delivering the speech to the audience.

Eye contact Degree to which you establish and maintain a visual connection with your audience.

Facial expression Changes a speaker makes to express emotion and to reinforce what the speaker is saying.

Factional group When group members are representatives or delegates from other social entities.

Fallacy Faulty or false reasoning.

Family communication Process of creating and sharing meaning through the exchange of verbal and nonverbal messages with those whom we consider to be family.

Feedback Cues that the receiver provides while listening to the sender.

Femininity Cultural value for nurturance, cooperation, and support among members.

Forming stage Initial stage in group development.

Friendship-warmth touch Touch used to communicate messages of affection and caring.

Functional-professional touch Touch typically initiated by professionals in order to accomplish a task associated with their occupation.

Gatekeeper Group member who ensures participation by all group members.

General purpose Provides the broad goal for your speech (e.g., to inform, persuade, or entertain).

Geographical order An organizational pattern used when you want to show how the various parts relate to each other and to the whole. Also known as *spatial order*.

Gestures Movements of the speaker's arms or hands used appropriately and purposefully to emphasize or reinforce what the speaker is saying verbally.

Group A collection of individuals with a common purpose.

Group identity function Using language as a signal of membership in a group or a sign of solidarity with a collection of individuals. Often, individuals outside the group do not understand the meaning in the verbal communication.

Group rules Individuals in a group are expected to do certain things, and if they do not do these things, there are consequences.

Groupthink Phenomenon that occurs when group members go along with an idea without thoughtful discussion or careful analysis.

Haptics Study of how touch is used to communicate meaning.

Harmonizer Group member who ensures participation by all group members.

Hasty generalization Type of faulty logic when the speaker uses only a few examples yet draws a general conclusion from those limited examples.

Hearing The physiological act of taking in sounds.

High context Cultural orientation that emphasizes indirect communication, typically focusing on nonverbal cues or unspoken messages.

High power-distance Rank and status are valued; hierarchies of power and structure influence interactions.

High uncertainty avoidance Lack of tolerance for risk, ambiguity, and change; cultural emphasis on traditions, rules, and laws.

Illustrators Gestures used to clarify or add emphasis to a verbal message.

Immediate memory Attending to something that is later discarded or placed in short- or long-term memory.

Implicit learning Observational learning of communication behaviors.

Implicit rules Unspoken and unwritten expectations that everyone in the group seems to know and adhere to.

Impression formation Sense-making of others' actions and disposition.

Impromptu delivery Type of delivery that is characterized by limited preparation time; often not as organized or carefully worded as other speech delivery types but does come across as spontaneous.

Inaugural address Special occasion speech given when someone takes office or begins a new position that outlines the key issues to address while in that position, looks toward the future, and thanks his or her predecessor.

Individual roles When individuals focus on self-achievement and not group efforts.

Individualism The self is viewed as most important; valued for independence and self-reliance.

Inductive reasoning Type of reasoning that provides strong and sufficient facts and examples and then draws a conclusion based on these facts.

Information function Expression of prejudiced attitudes in an attempt to create a foundation for expectations of behavior.

Information-seeker Group member who collects information related to tasks and completing tasks.

Information-seeking Extent to which you attempt to gather information or happenings in the world.

Informational listening Listening to understand or comprehend.

Informative speaking Type of speech used to help an audience become aware of or better understand a topic.

Initiating First stage of coming together in the relationship development model. Focuses on the initial communication that occurs when we first meet someone.

Insensitive listening When listeners pay attention only to a speaker's words but fail to interpret other nonverbal cues that would enhance understanding of the speaker's intent.

Integrating Fourth stage of coming together in relationship development in which the lives of partners begin to merge and their status as a couple is acknowledged both personally and publicly.

Intensification Exaggeration or overemphasis of a felt emotion via facial expressions.

Intensifying Third stage relationship development that is characterized by more intimate expressions of commitment and by testing the impressions that others may have formed about the relationship.

Interaction approach One way to study leadership; focuses on communicative exchanges in the leadership process.

Interactive strategies Using direct communication to reduce uncertainty in the initial stages of a relationship.

Interdependence Contributing factor to conflict that results as a result of relational partners depending on one another.

Interpersonal communication Interactions that take place between at least two people who simultaneously take on the roles of both sender and receiver.

Interpersonal utility Extent to which media is perceived to be a source of useful information that can be used in your relationship.

Interpretation The third phase of the perception process where we attach meaning to what we have selected and organized.

Interpreting Going beyond just the actual words that are said; focusing on the verbal, nonverbal, and relational components of the message.

Intrapersonal communication Most basic type of communication; occurs within an individual.

Introduction Gains the audience's attention, clearly states the topic, and previews the main points to be discussed.

Introduction speech Brief speech given to introduce and welcome a speaker and to build a rapport between the speaker and the audience as well as motivate the audience to listen to the speaker.

Jealousy Negative or potentially destructive communicative response to a perceived threat to a relationship.

Joker Group member who uses light-hearted, humorous communication that is often off topic.

Kinesics Study of the messages communicated by the use of body movements and gestures.

Knowledge Understanding of the appropriate messages or behaviors used in a given situation or with a particular person.

Laissez-faire leader Prefers a "hands-off" mentality to leading others.

Lateral dissent Expression of dissatisfaction or frustration to coworkers.

Leadership Process in which individuals influence others' actions and behaviors in order to achieve some goal.

Lean communication Communication channels that reduce access to nonverbal communication, such as facial expressions, touch, and eye contact.

Legitimate power Power that is associated with a certain position. Because of his or her position in the group, an individual has a certain right to influence/oversee others' behaviors.

Lies Form of deception that involves the fabrication or falsification of information.

Life-planning messages Emphasize the value in prioritizing and segmenting one's personal and professional lives into two distinct areas.

Listening A psychological process where you take in the sounds and process them in order to understand, interpret, and respond to what you have heard.

Logos Speaker's use of sound logic and reasoning.

Long-term memory The brain's filing system, which has a limitless capacity to store information that you may have heard months or even years ago.

Love-intimacy touch Touch reserved for close family members and intimate partners; used to communicate intense emotions and caring.

Low context Cultural orientation that emphasizes the spoken word and direct verbal expression.

Low power-distance Emphasizes equality among members. Mutual respect and shared responsibility are valued.

Low uncertainty avoidance Cultural tolerance for novelty and innovation; risk and change are encouraged.

Macro productivity Achieving or finishing the group's task.

Manuscript delivery Type of delivery method where the speech is written word for word as it will be delivered; commonly used when the wording must be precise.

Masculinity Cultural value for assertiveness, ambition, and achievement.

Masking Replacing the actual emotion that is experienced with a more appropriate and socially desirable facial expression.

Mass media communication Large-scale communication that includes a large audience and a channel other than face-to-face.

Mediated communication Communication that relies on a media channel to communicate.

Memorized delivery Type of delivery method where the speech is written word for word and the speaker commits it to memory; may be useful if the speech is brief and the occasion warrants it.

Message formation Way in which a message is put together.

Message Words that are said or sent.

Micro productivity Smaller tasks and goals that contribute to macro productivity.

Minimizations Form of deception when we downplay the truth.

Mnemonic devices Techniques that help you retain information in a more effective way than in its original form (i.e., lists, acronyms).

Models Replica of an object used as a visual aid.

Monochronic Time as a commodity that must be carefully scheduled; do one thing at a time.

Monroe's motivated sequence Most often used in persuasive speaking, with this type of organizational strategy, the speaker gains the audience's attention, shows there is a need (or a need for change), provides a solution that satisfies the need, visualizes the benefits of the stated change, and moves the audience to action.

Motivation Desire to obtain results or accomplish a goal. We have to want to be competent communicators.

Movement Any physical shifts the speaker makes.

Neutralization Refraining from exhibiting any type of emotion via facial expressions.

Noise Anything that interferes with our ability to interact or listen to others.

Nonverbal communication Exchange of meaning without the use of words.

Nonverbal immediacy Use of nonverbal behaviors to enhance the perceptions of physical or psychological closeness with others.

Nonverbal sensitivity Ability to accurately decode the nonverbal cues that signal the mood or emotions of others.

Norming stage Third stage of group development in which members create behavioral standards and punishments.

Norms Standardized behaviors individuals in the group ought to do under any circumstance.

Novelty versus predictability Dialectical tension that addresses our need for routine and consistency and our conflicting desire to experience things that are unique.

Oculesics Study of how eye behavior is used to communicate meaning.

Open-ended questions Questions that cannot be answered with a one-word statement.

Openness versus closedness Dialectical tension that reflects our need to share information with others while keeping some aspects private.

Opinion-giver Group member who expresses opinions and possible interpretations associated with all tasks.

Organization The second phase of the perception process, which involves categorizing what we have received.

Organizational communication Subfield of human communication that focuses on the messages exchanged between members of an organization.

Organizational dissent Method of reducing uncertainty that involves directly soliciting information about another person.

Outline Tool that speakers use to organize their main ideas and support material into a coherent speech.

Parasocial interaction Your perceptions of connections to individuals in the media.

Passive strategies Method of reducing uncertainty that involves indirect or unintended methods of gathering information when initiating a relationship.

Pathos Speaker's use of emotion to persuade an audience.

Peer group Members who consider one another to be equals in terms of abilities, background, age, responsibilities, beliefs, social standing, legal status, or rights.

Perceived incompatible goals Key component of conflict. Discrepancies in goals between two relational partners.

Perceived interference in achieving one's goals Component of conflict in which an individual perceives another to be interfering in their ability to accomplish a goal.

Perception checking The process whereby we validate the accuracy of our perceptions.

Perception process A three-step process that includes selection, where we focus our attention on something and ignore other elements in the environment; organization, where we form what we have received into meaningful patterns; and interpretation, where we attach meaning to what we have selected and organized.

Perception The process by which our senses receive something and it is then filtered and interpreted.

Performance outcomes Focus on productivity and measurement of goal achievement.

Performing stage Fourth stage in group development in which all members are working toward completion of the group's task.

Permissive parents Parenting style in which high levels of support and low levels of control are demonstrated. Parents often try to be their child's "friend" with few rules and little discipline.

Personal orientation system Comprised of our needs, values, attitudes, and beliefs that guide our behaviors and responses.

Personal stage Second stage of relationship development that is characterized by the exchange of more personal or emotional information such as one's attitudes, beliefs, and values.

Persuasive speaking Type of speech used to change an audience's existing belief, to reinforce their existing belief, or to get an audience to take action regarding the topic.

Phrase outline Type of outline that contains key phrases to help the speaker move from point to point. It expands on the word outline but is still relatively brief. It does help the speaker avoid reading from the outline since most of the speech content is not on this type of outline.

Physical attraction One of three types of attraction; refers to characteristics that cause us to be physically or sexually drawn toward another.

Physical noise Any type of audible interference that is present in the communication environment.

Pictures and diagrams Provide helpful visual images to augment a speaker's description of something.

Pitch Highness or lowness of a person's voice.

Polychronic When time is flexible and not viewed as important as relationships.

Positive visualization When a speaker envisions succeeding in his or her speech delivery.

Posture How the speaker stands or the position of the speaker's body.

Power Ability to influence others.

Prejudice Type of attitude in which we directly express negative reactions toward another individual or group.

Presentational aids Charts, bar graphs, pictures, diagrams, models, the actual object, and even the speaker him- or herself are considered to be visual aids. Audio aids include recordings of music, famous speeches, interviews, or even sounds from nature. Audio-visual aids include clips from movies, instructional DVDs, or anything that combines both sound and sight. They are all used to clarify, highlight, or summarize a speaker's ideas

Presenting an award Type of special occasion speech that outlines the purpose, history, and/or the significance of the award; the criteria used to determine the awardee; and the relevant achievements of the recipient and how these accomplishments satisfied the criteria employed to determine who would receive the award.

Prioritizing messages Statements that focus on the need to place family first and career second. Does not necessarily imply that one must take the place of the other; simply emphasizes that family should take priority.

Problem-focused coping Coping strategy in which individuals actively research and seek solutions to assist in the management of stressful situations.

Problem–solution order Pattern that examines a particular problem and then offers a potential solution to the problem; based on John Dewey's reflective thinking process.

Productivity Ability to achieve goals in an efficient matter.

Promotive communication Focuses on messages that contribute to the group's tasks.

Proxemics Study of messages communicated through our use of personal space and territoriality.

Pseudo-listening Pretending to listen to others while thinking about something else.

Psychological noise Internal interference that impedes our accurate reception of a message.

Public communication Occurs when a source communicates information to a relatively large audience.

Purposive group A group that is attempting to achieve the completion of a goal.

Questions of fact Type of question or claim that may be proven true or false.

Questions of policy Type of question or claim that focuses on actions or changes that should or should not be made by governing bodies.

Questions of value Type of question or claim that has to do with someone's ideas of right and wrong or good or bad.

Race Inherited biological characteristics such as hair texture and color, eye shape, skin color, and facial structure.

Racist language Insensitive and derogatory language about a group of people.

Rate Speed at which a person speaks.

Receiver Individual receiving the message.

Reciprocal self-disclosure Similar exchange of the type of information shared and the amount of information disclosed when communicating with others.

Recognition-seeker Group member who takes on a lot of work for extra attention.

Referent power Individual's positive regard for and personal identification with the leader.

Reflected appraisal The concept that we develop of who we believe we are by the way in which others view us; in other words, our perception of how we imagine others view or see us.

Reflection Giving serious thought or consideration to something.

Reflection-in-action Thinking about what you are doing while you are doing it and making any necessary adjustments immediately.

Reflection-on-action Thinking about what you did and how well you did it and what you would do differently the next time.

Regulators Nonverbal gestures that are used to control the flow of communication.

Relational expectations Explicit and implicit predictions for anticipated or ideal verbal and nonverbal responses.

Relational information Nonverbal messages that accompany spoken words.

Relational meaning Emotional response associated with a message.

Relational roles Focus on building and maintain connections among group members.

Relational satisfaction Feeling positive and content in our relationships.

Relationship dissolution When one or both partners perceive the relationship as being dissatisfactory and the decision is made to terminate the connection.

Remembering The act of retaining something in your memory.

Repeating Replicating the verbal message by following it up with a corresponding nonverbal message.

Repetition A strategy to help improve your short-term memory by restating to yourself over and over again what you need to remember.

Responding Selecting the appropriate message to send back to the speaker.

Reward power Assign power to another person based on their perceived ability to deliver benefits or incentives as a result of compliance with their requests.

Role conflict When you have to perform multiple roles with seemingly contradictory behaviors.

Role flexibility When individuals possess the ability to play a variety of roles and adapt according to the demands of the situation.

Role strain When an individual is required to assume a new role that he or she is reluctant to perform.

Role Theory Ways in which individuals enact different social positions (i.e., roles) in their lives.

Roles Labels placed on individuals based on their function within a group.

Scopic listeners Listeners who develop an open interest in many topics.

Selection The first part of the perception process where we focus our attention on something within our environment.

Selective listening Listening to only portions of an entire message.

Self-concept A set of perceptions we have about ourselves.

Self-disclosure Sharing of personal information with others in an attempt to build or maintain a relationship

Self-esteem How we feel about ourselves or the value we place on our abilities and behaviors.

Self-fulfilling prophecy The idea that when we believe something is true, it may become true. In other words, when we expect a particular outcome, either positive or negative, it is more likely that outcome will occur.

Self-presentation Presenting yourself to another as you would like to be perceived.

Self-serving bias The tendency for us to interpret the things we do in the most positive way or deny personal responsibility for the negative things that happen to us.

Sender Individual creating the message.

Sentence outline Very detailed outline containing most of what the speaker will say during the speech. It is very useful for organizing a speech and for practicing it as well. Also called a *full-content outline*.

Sexist language Language that does not account for both male and female experiences and instead communicates about ideas as inherently male or female.

Shared meaning Result of communication that is accurately sent and received.

Short-term memory Memory with a limited capacity that is stored for a brief time unless it is important enough to be moved into long-term memory.

Situational analysis Type of audience analysis that takes into account the occasion of the speaking event as well as the time, place, and size of the audience.

Situational approach One way to study leadership; focuses on the characteristics of the group members and the situation.

Situational communication apprehension Fear of public speaking based on a specific occurrence (e.g., you are nervous about meeting with your supervisor to ask for a raise or your town's planning board to ask for a variance).

Skill Ability to produce or utilize the appropriate behaviors.

Small group communication When a collection of at least three people communicate and collaborate with one another.

Social attraction Characteristics that we seek in forming relationships with those whom we enjoy spending time with and socializing.

Social dimension Group members' relationships and feelings for each other.

Social facilitation Presence of someone else in the group increases their performance.

Social group Collection of individuals focused mostly on relationship-building that gives members a place to develop self-esteem.

Social loafing Avoiding groupwork and allowing others in the group to perform tasks.

Social media communication Websites that work to build communities of people.

Social networking Sites that aim to build both personal and professional connections with other individuals.

Social Penetration Theory How individuals share information with one another as the relationship progresses from one stage to another.

Social reality function Using language to create our reality of the world around us. Language changes and responds to the world in which we live.

Social-polite touch Touch used as a form of greeting or acknowledgment.

Socioemotional leader Type of leader who is primarily concerned with the relationships among group members.

Special occasion speeches Speeches that cover a broad range of settings, circumstances, and occasions and usually acknowledge, celebrate, honor, or remember someone or something.

Specific purpose Clear and concise statement indicating what you want your audience to know, do, or believe by the end of your speech.

Stage hogging Turning the conversation toward oneself rather than listening fully to the other person.

Stagnating Fourth stage of relationship dissolution in which communication between partners is limited and the goal is simply to maintain a status quo.

Statement of reasons pattern In this pattern, each of the speaker's main points provides a reason why the proposal should (or should not) be supported.

Stereotypes Generalizations we hold about a group or a category of people.

Stereotyping Tendency to make generalizations about groups and assume that all members of that group possess the same characteristics and engage in similar behaviors.

Storming stage Second stage of group development, where most conflicts will occur.

Strategies Techniques speakers use to engage their audience and to keep the audience focused.

Subjective outcomes Something that is associated with group members' level of satisfaction with a proposed plan.

Substituting Using a nonverbal message in place of a verbal message.

Superficial information Basic demographic information shared with others during the initial stages of a relationship.

Supportive communication Type of communication that occurs when an individual feels as though he or she has little reason to have anxiety or concern about the communication being received.

Supportive leadership Solicits feedback and employs behaviors that will highlight and develop the skills of group members.

Symbols Abstract ideas or concepts that represent something and can be both verbal and nonverbal.

Task attraction Characteristics that are identified as being important when forming working relationships where we depend on others to accomplish a task or goal.

Task conflict Conflict regarding how to best complete the tasks being performed.

Task dimension Group members focusing on solving problems, completing a task, or achieving a goal.

Task leader Type of leader who is primarily concerned with completing the group's goals.

Task roles Includes all roles that focus on the group's assignment.

Team-building Process that includes gathering cooperation from individuals to achieve a common goal.

Terminating Final stage of relationship dissolution when one or both partners experiences a level of dissatisfaction that motivates them to end the relationship.

Thought–speech differential Difference between what human beings can understand per minute (roughly 400–500 words) and the rate at which the average person speaks (roughly 120–180 words per minute).

Time on task How much time the group will spend discussing a given topic.

Toast Speech given to congratulate a person or people on an achievement or a special occasion.

Topical pattern In this pattern, you divide your speech into categories and support each category with evidence.

Touch apprehension Fear or anxiety associated with touch that often results in withdrawing from or avoiding situations in which touch is used.

Trait approach One way to study leadership; focuses on the characteristics/traits of the leader.

Trait-like communication apprehension Fear of public speaking (e.g., one-on-one, to a small group, or to a large audience).

Transitions Words or phrases that help listeners move smoothly from one point to the next; signal to the audience that the speaker is moving from one idea to the next or from one type of support to another.

Tribute speech Special occasion speech designed to praise someone (e.g., living or in the case of a eulogy, someone who has passed away).

Truth bias Expectation that people in close relationships will be honest with one another. Thus, deception may be ignored or overlooked due to our expectations for the truth to be told.

Uncertainty Reduction Theory Explains how we engage in conversations during the initial stages of a relationship to decrease our uncertainty about others.

Understanding Making sense of the message you heard.

Uninvolved parents Parenting style in which low levels of support and low levels of control are exhibited. Parents are often described as being "too busy" to be involved in the child's life.

Upward dissent Directly communicating one's dissatisfaction or frustration with an organization's upper management or administration.

Uses and Gratifications Theory Theoretical lens through which relationships individuals have with media is understood.

Values One's personal philosophy that guides actions and behaviors; assist us in evaluating ethical situations.

Verbal abuse Process of exchanging negative verbal comments that are intended to be insulting or demeaning.

Verbal communication Exchange of meaning with the use of words.

Verbal modeling Listening to how others speak, and then consciously using the same words or phrases they use.

Virtual game worlds Online games that include a created reality and encourages the following of rules to play a game.

Virtual social worlds Provide a space for individuals to create another life and interact with others and include games such as Second Life.

Vocal variety Changes the speaker makes in volume, rate, and/or pitch to add meaning to the speech.

Vocalics Study of meanings associated with the various ways in which we use our voice when communicating a message; focuses on vocal aspects such as pitch, rate, and volume.

Volume Loudness or softness of the speaker's voice.

Welcome speech Speech to formally recognize and greet a person or a group who is visiting, for example, a school, a convention, a special event, or a city.

Withdrawer Group member who fails to connect and interact with the group, offers few opinions, and may have issues.

Word choice Carefully selecting words to convey your message clearly, vividly, and ethically.

Word outline Type of outline that contains only key words to help the speaker remember the sequence in which main points should be discussed. Because of its brevity, it is most useful when the speaker is very comfortable with the speaking situation and knows the material in the speech exceptionally well.

Work choice messages Discuss the various career options that enable parents to pursue a career while enjoying their children.

INDEX

NOTE: Page references in *italics* refer to figures and tables.

power and, 198–201, *199, 200–201*
productivity, 202–203
roles and, 193–197, *195*
rules of, 197
small group communication, 14
task *versus* social dimensions within groups,
192–193
group identity function, 60

H

Hall, Edward T., 93
haptics, 87–90, *88*
harmonizer, 195, *195*
hasty generalization, 255
health communication, 393–397
hearing, 104
Hierarchy of Needs, 344, *344*
high context cultures, 346
high power distance, 347, *347*
high uncertainty avoidance, 348
humor, 274–275
HURIER model, *104,* 105

I

idea formation, 366–367
identity, online, 371–374
illustrators, 87
immediacy, nonverbal, 97
immediate memory, 108–109
implicit learning, 9, 336
implicit rules, 197
impression formation, 49–50, 371
impromptu delivery, 302, *303,* 305–306
inaugural address, 261
individualism, 347, *347*
individual roles, 194, *195*
inductive reasoning, 255
informational listening, 112
information function, *351,* 351–352
information gathering, 366–367
information-seeker, as group role, 195, *195*

information-seeking, mass media and, 365
informative speaking, 248–253, *249, 251*
initiating stage, of relationship development model,
147, 148
insensitive listening, 123–124
integrating stage, of relationship development model,
147, 150–151
intensification, nonverbal communication and, 90
intensifying stage, of relationship development model,
147, 149–150
interaction approach, to leadership, 217, *217,* 222
interactive strategies, of Uncertainty Reduction
Theory, 139
intercultural communication, study of, 332–335. *see
also* cultural communication
interdependence, 177
interpersonal communication, 128–155. *see also*
relationships
attraction theory, 134–137, *135*
defined, 13, 130
overview, 129–130
relationship development model, *147,* 147–151
self-disclosure, 140–144
social penetration theory, 144–147, *145*
stages of interpersonal relationships, 132–134
types of interpersonal relationships, 130–132
Uncertainty Reduction Theory, 137–139, *139*
interpersonal relationships. *see* relationships
interpersonal utility, 365
interpretation, perception and, 32
interpreting, listening and, 110–111
intimacy jealousy, 174
intrapersonal communication, 12
introduction of speeches, 274–278, *276, 278,* 318
introduction speech (speech type), 258–259
isolation, social media and, 375

J

jealousy, 173–175
jobs, in communication, 397–400, *399*
joker, 195, *195*
Journal of the American Medical Association, 393

N

networking, social movement and, 370–371
Neupauer, Nicholas, 142
neutralization, 90–91
noise, 7
nonverbal communication, 78–101
    characteristics of, 80–84
    defined, 80
    elements of speech delivery, 310–314, *311, 315*
    monitoring, 13
    nonverbal immediacy and, 97, *97*
    nonverbal sensitivity, 98
    online communication and, 96, *96*
    overview, 79–80
    perception and, 48
    relationship between verbal communication and, *84,* 84–85
    types of, 85–96, *89, 93*
norming stage, of groups, 191, 229
norms, in group communication, 198
novelty *versus* predictability, 162

O

observation, for perception checking, 39
oculesics, 91–92
"onion" model, of Social Penetration Theory, *145*
online communication
    health communication via, 394
    jealousy and, 175
    maintenance of relationships and, 164
    nonverbal communication and, 96, *96*
    online identity, 371–374
    self-disclosure and, 141–143
    social media as mediated communication, 367–371
    social media impact on face-to-face relationships, 375–376
open-ended questions, 236
openness *versus* closedness, 162
opinion-giver, 195, *195*
organization
    perception and, 31–32
    for public speaking, *262,* 266–267

of speech elements, 283–287
organizational communication, 382–386, *383, 384*
organizational dissent, 382
organizational settings, listening and, 119
outline, for speeches, 287–290

P

parasocial interaction, 363, 365
parenting styles, 389–392, *390. see also* families
passive strategies, of Uncertainty Reduction Theory, 138–139
pathos, 255, *256*
peer groups, 188–189, *189*
perception, 28–53
    defined, 30
    influence on, 32–36, *33*
    of others, 48–50
    overview, 30
    perceived competition for scarce resources, 177–178
    perceived incompatible goals, 177
    perceived interference in achieving one's goals, 178
    perception checking, *37,* 37–40
    process, 31–32
    of self, 40–48
performance outcomes, 207
performing stage, of groups, 191
permissive parents, 389–390, *390*
personal communication examples
    communication context, 381
    communication overview, 3, 21–22
    cultural communication, 329
    group communication, 185
    interpersonal communication, 129
    leadership, 215
    listening, 103
    nonverbal communication, 79
    perception, 29
    public speaking, 241
    public speech delivery, 301
    public speech organization, 273
    relationship, 157
    verbal communication, 55